Computer Technology and Social Issues

G. David Garson
North Carolina State University

IGP

IDEA GROUP PUBLISHING
Harrisburg, USA • London, UK

Senior Editor: Mehdi Khosrowpour
Managing Editor: Jan Travers
Printed at: Rose Printing

Published in the United States of America by
Idea Group Publishing
1331 E. Chocolate Avenue
Hershey, PA 17033, USA
Tel: 717-533-8845
Fax: 717-533-8661
E-mail: jtravers@idea-group.com
URL: http://www.idea-group.com

and in the United Kingdom by
Idea Group Publishing
3 Henrietta Street
Covent Garden
London WC2E 8LU
Tel: 071-240 0856
Fax: 071-379 0609

Library of Congress Catalog Card No. 94-78932

British Cataloguing in Publication Data
A Cataloguing in Publication record for this book is available from the British Library.

Printed in the United States of America

ISBN 1-878289-28-4

Preface

Computer-related books are usually read by computerists for whom the blessings of information technology are a given. At the other end of the spectrum are critical theorists and other humanists who may attack computerization with both airy generalizations and concrete anecdotal evidence. Between these extremes, it seems to me, there is a much-needed role for objective social science, which is what I hope I have provided here, drawing on the relatively small but growing body of empirical research on just what information technology is doing to our society, our organizations, and even to us as individuals.

In obtaining pre-publication reactions to this work from a wide variety of sources, I was struck by the fact that what seems common sense to one group may be quite different in another group. In fact, common ideas in one group may seem almost subversive to another's credo. For instance, I found it was not uncommon for commentators from computer science to view discussions of alienation and dehumanization as "radical" or at least as "irrelevant" minor issues. I found commentators from business schools could see discussions of productivity and computing to be wrongly focused when the spotlight was on "if" —rather this group often assumed computerization yielded competitive advantage and only wanted instruction on "how". As an emerging social phenomenon of immense proportions, the subject is still the elephant waiting to be perceived part by part by the proverbial blind men.

If there is a theme to this book, claiming to peek through the blindfolds, it is that technology has to do with power— personal, organizational, societal. Information technology is perhaps even more inherently political than other technologies because of the intimate way in which it becomes bound up with structuring data for decision-making. Some have gone so far as to suggest that if the sociology of knowledge centered at the dawn of this century on relationships to the means of production, so now near the start of the next the sociology of knowledge must center on relationships to the means of information and specifically to control over information technology. In this work, however, I have tried to steer a course between the dangers of technological determinist reasoning, apocalyptic Luddite critiques, and computer consulting firm happy-talk systems analysis.

In teaching this subject, I have found students react well to the acknowledgment that computing involves social issues and political choices. A great many can relate personal examples illustrating themes contained in the following chapters from their own work experiences. As other instructors emphasize the social issues of information technology more and more, this field of study is sure to expand greatly in the coming decade.

I wish to thank Melanie Paul for her talented assistance in the preparation of this manuscript. I would also like to thank its numerous peer reviewers, often anonymous, for the valuable suggestions which they made in the course of revising this work. Finally, I am appreciative of the help received in this and all my academic endeavors by my department and our college's excellent program of research support.

David Garson
August 20, 1994

Computer Technology and Social Issues

Table of Contents

CHAPTER I

The Potential of Computing to Threaten Democratic Values

Computing lends itself to images of authority and domination. Themes of technology-based power and control sometimes can appear in pathological form, as in fears of an Orwellian *1984* dictatorship made possible by omniscient and omnipresent computers. Some have even argued that the vast amount of information which can be mobilized by computer technology and thrown before the public has a stupefying effect, heightening boredom and decreasing sensitivity so that it becomes the contemporary equivalent of Marx's 'opiate of the people' (Klapp, 1986). This subjective aspect of computing as a threat to democratic values could, some think, induce a sense of fatalism and loss of what psychologists call "internal locus of control" (Rotter, 1966: Muir, 1987, 1988a, 1988b). That is, belief in the omnipotence of computer technology may encourage an "external locus of control" — a mindset characterized by the belief that events are determined by factors outside one's own control.

Weizenbaum (1976, 1983) studied the pathologies and mindsets associated with computing. These range from the microworld of the "hacker" to the global fantasies of the military computer gamer in the Pentagon. To some, computing seems to be an all-beneficent "deus ex machina" solving human problems at every turn (Kraemer and King, 1986: 494). However, to others it is quite the opposite. Of all the visions, fears, and fantasies associated with computing, perhaps none is so recurring and important as that associated with the issue of whether computing is a force for the centralization of political and organizational power.

Thus it seems appropriate to start this book with an examination of computing as a threat to democratic values. First, I assess the empirical basis for fears of an emerging "technocratic elite." I then look at related fears that computing will produce alienation, dehumanization, deskilling, and disemployment. While it is theoretically possible for a democratic society to exist with an alienated, dehumanized, deskilled, and unemployed population, most consider these to be forces which undermine democracy's need for an informed citizenry motivated to work and vote for that which they think is best for the country as a whole. Coverage of these topics leads into a general discussion of computing as a "tool for those at the top". The final section concludes on what is the theme of this book: the essentially political nature of computing and how it is embedded in systems of interest group conflict.

The Vision of a Technocratic Elite

Although many argue that computer technology may have broad democratizing effects (this is discussed in Chapter 2), the reality is that computers tend to be owned by upwardly mobile, relatively well-to-do professionals with little interest in using new technology to create a democratic revolution. In fact, serious computing power is the province of large organizations and those who control them. In this context numerous writers have raised fears of computerization leading to pervasive invasion of privacy by all-seeing bureaucrats, perhaps reminiscent of George Orwell's *1984* (Bovard and Bouvard, 1975; Wicklein, 1979; Donner, 1981; Reinecke, 1984).

This anti-technocratic imagery was reflected in the slogan of 1960s radicals, "Do not fold, spindle, or mutilate", a term found on then-common IBM cards. This slogan carried the implicit belief that computerization was an impersonalizing autocratic force to be resisted. Scholars were more tempered in their warnings but nonetheless, often hypothesized that computerization would lead to technical experts gaining power at the expense of elected officials or corporate CEO's simply because such experts had control over the means of information (Downs, 1967). In extreme form, the vision of a technocratic elite is the fear we are moving toward a system of technological apartheid. For instance, David Burnham (1983) painted a picture of a high-tech city of the future in which a privileged class ruled through computerized business, education, entertainment, and security, while a poverty-stricken underclass was unable to even enter the high-tech world without computer-enforced work passes.

Are Technocratic Workers a Social Class?

There is considerable evidence from studies of developing nations that technology can be associated with the rise of technocratic elites. For instance, a Harvard study of satellite telecommunications in Algeria and educational television in El Salvador concluded that the introduction of new technology led to a greater concentration of power, increased centralization, and a growing technocratic elite. Neither technology seemed to contribute to the solution of problems of undereducation, underproduction, or national strife (Clippinger, 1976).

In this country some studies show that computing produces what some might call an "information elite" who benefit from increased power as a result of their position in information systems (IS) (see Kraemer and Danziger, 1984; Danziger and Kraemer, 1987). However, while technocratic power is not solely an issue for the developing world, the more technologically advanced the society, the more power is dispersed among functional organizations and specialized interest groups rather than being concentrated in a single social class - technocratic, military, bureaucratic, or otherwise (Ferkiss, 1970).

Marxists defined the term "social class" in terms of categories of workers who shared a common relationship to the means of production. This was thought to give them (and their families) common interests which eventually translate into common ideology and political action. While information workers may be an "elite" if that term is defined by possession of special knowledge, skills, and roles, they are not a social class. Those who use computers may be owners or workers, line managers or support staff, vendors or clients, officials or citizens—there is no common relationship to the means of production. More to the point, information workers do not share common interests allowing their mobilization as a class. They are notoriously independent and disinterested in unionization, for instance. They are not a unified voting bloc nor are their professional associations significant political forces outside the information industry itself.

Although IS professionals are not a social class, this is not to say they don't represent a constellation of interests within an organization. Like other professional groups, they tend to have distinctive standards, orientations, and peer reference groups. In a study of IS professionals in over 500 local government units, Danziger (1979) found this group tended to define their role according to standards of their professional associations, not according to the standards of either their supervisors or their clients. Danziger also found that one of these professional standards was expansionism: the evangelical belief that information systems (IS) are good and that it is the role of IS professionals to bring the gospel of IS to the unenlightened operating departments.

The context for concern over technocratic power in America is not so much about technocrats as a social class but about their role in organizations. The concern is that database management is part of a larger process of collecting, processing, manipulating, exchanging, and utilizing information within and among commercial and governmental units (King and Kraemer, 1984). By performing these functions, information workers define the categories by which the organization perceives everything from the behavior of its staff, to its external environment. Like the historians of Orwell's *1984*, there is the potential for recreating the history and memory of an organization or even society along lines which conform to guidelines set by information technocrats (Weizenbaum, 1976: 238). Even more important, information system design may institutionalize certain evaluative standards and long-term organizational goals.

Why Technocratic Decisions are Political

The influence of information systems is often cast in terms of its preference for easily quantified measures rather than diffuse but important qualitative factors. As Field (1970: 32-33) noted long ago, computers can bias organizations "in the direction of repressing vital information that does not fit the pipes in the channel." Weizenbaum likewise noted the tendency of electronic information systems to enshrine as "the truth" those selected data which are easily entered into computers. While it is true that information systems are more apt to track, for instance, the dollars spent by consumers than to track consumer opinions, the political importance of technocratic decisions goes far beyond this commonly-cited quantitative bias.

Behind seemingly neutral data categories such as the unemployment index or the consumer price index lie intense worlds of political struggle and controversy (de Neufville, 1975). The unemployment index, for instance, can be defined in many ways. Is a person who has given up looking for a job unemployed or not? Is an English literature Ph.D. working at McDonald's fully employed? Is someone holding a part-time job who wants full-time work employed? How unemployment is defined will determine what the numbers work out to be and how unemployment benefits will be distributed. These politics of data apply to virtually anything the organization may choose to put into its database system in the way of performance or productivity indicators. The categories used to track data concretize the meanings by which the organization understands the world. These assumptions have as much to do with the nature of decision-making within an organization as any other set of factors.

To provide an example of how this works, consider the familiar example of the university as an organization. The top management of a university may choose to require use of student course evaluations and incorporate them into faculty tenure and promotion processes. This may elevate the teaching goals of the institution vis-a-vis the research goals. Courses may be evaluated very differently depending on the selection of teaching indicators: student evaluations, research publication lists, course enrollments, course learning objectives, student performance on standardized tests, peer evaluations by visiting faculty teams, etc. The selection of performance indicators is both a strong reflection and a strong determinant of the nature of the organization and its objectives.

To take a second example of the impact of performance indicator decisions, consider a public employment agency which decides to keep data on job placements by its counselors as part of an information system. Tracking by this indicator (number of job placements) may motivate counselors to place applicants on jobs even if such placement predictably will not work out—simply to increase the measured rate of placement for that counselor. Unmeasured job functions such as actual counselling may be neglected by employees as well. What data are kept almost invariably has the strongest sort of impact on organizational behavior and employee relations. Data management requires defining what is to be measured, recorded, and analyzed. This defining of the situation involves the exercise of power.

Ironically, it is not uncommon for top management to fail to understand the importance of this power to determine what performances are to be measured within the organization. When this happens, power is abdicated and falls into the hands of information managers or even data technicians. These control issues were discussed in a *Government Computer News* article which examined the rise of a new class of administrators responsible for office computers. "The responsible person," Herbert Reines wrote in this article, "is called the 'systems administrator,' and may become the best loved or the most hated individual in the office. It is not a position to assign to short term or temporary employees or the 'low person on the totem pole' " (Reines, 1985). Much like the budget officer in traditional government bureaucracies, the agency's information management officer can come to play a premiere role in the management of the organization.

Technocrats and Power: Encroachment or Delegation?

Early on in the computer era, writers such as Field (1970) predicted that computerization might eventually mean that top management would become "programmed" by technocrats at lower levels, "stripping the power of the mighty". Management decisions could become perfunctory as technocrats structured computer data and analysis, predetermining the alternatives presented and making "obvious" the choices to be made. In fact, it was predicted that top management might even shrink in size as its functions became less necessary. Thus far these predictions have proved mostly incorrect but scholars like Drucker (1988) argue that in the future, as information technology lets managers interact quickly and directly with lower subordinates, the span of control will increase and organizations will require fewer levels of management. Whether or not computing eliminates managerial jobs, such predictions remind us that power and control issues are central to computerized information systems.

The microcomputer revolution of the 1980s buttressed the delegation of power to technical support staff. Departmental minicomputers, distributed processing by satellite computers, and distributed special-purpose minicomputers and microcomputers gave lower echelons of the bureaucracy unprecedented information access and the potential for influence that derives therefrom. King and Kraemer, for instance,

Figure 1: The Omni Study: Do Managers Delegate Too Much?

There is some evidence that managers are all too willing to turn computing over to technocratic professionals.

A survey of over 3,000 managers by The Omni Group documented widespread boredom with computing among top managers. Management is seen as a generalist function, whereas, computing is seen as applied and as such something to be delegated to lower levels.

In this survey a minority (36%) of managers, still a very large number, even held the belief that computers could do little to help them manage (Ambrosio, 1985). This prevailing information culture is conducive to going beyond mere delegation of technical matters to abdication of policy control embedded in technical decisions.

The Omni study showed almost two-thirds of managers had begun to delegate database management and other computer tasks to lower support staff. The Omni data also showed some two-thirds of managers in the largest firms stated they were rewriting job descriptions for support staff to incorporate IS skills, often with new job titles.

Thus, delegation leads directly to the creation of a technocratic class of employees. Whether they are servants of management or a power unto themselves, or both, depends upon complex organizational and external factors.

concluded, "Like the centralized technology that went before it, the new decentralized technology of mini and microcomputers will require new arrangements for control within individual government agencies, and new kinds of group dynamics and information exchange among agencies" (King and Kraemer, 1983).

Although computerization often increases managerial control (e.g., Rule and Attewell, 1989: 237-239) and does affect the control structure of organizations in complex ways, the fears of the rise of an outright "technocratic elite" seem little justified. In fact, studies of computer programmers and their managers have found little interest in unionization or other forms of organization to assert interests as a class (Kraft, 1977; Fidel and Garner, 1987). This is in line with the Marxist view that IS professionals, like intellectual workers generally, are tools of 'those at the top' (Siegel, 1986; for a non-Marxist view rejecting theories of the emergence of a technocratic elite, see Vig, 1988). At the same time, information management has become required curriculum at accredited business and public administration programs in the 1990s, diminishing the likelihood of top management abdication of power through ignorance of the nature of computer systems.

Do Computers Generate Alienation and Dehumanization?

The charge that computerization is dehumanizing reflects fears that human interactions will be stripped of their interpersonal component if they are mediated or even assisted by computers. Where such interactions are particularly central, as in social services, dehumanization has become a major issue. Note that we are not talking here about the fact that artificial intelligence is in its infancy and that few computer programs adequately substitute for professional human services. For instance, on-line bibliographic services do not substitute for having the services of librarians (Azubuike, 1988). Rather, the dehumanization argument focuses on the inherent limitations of computerized services even when software meets all empirical objectives. It is the argument that something important is irretrievably lost when machine interaction is substituted for human interaction.

Fears of Alienation and Dehumanization

Employees, particularly service professionals, often fear that computerization will mean "people-processing" in a demeaning and depersonalized manner. For example, some have sharply condemned the dehumanizing nature of computer-assisted psychotherapy, diverting people into "fraudulent" computer-human interactions (Weizenbaum, 1976). Similarly, library patrons may perceive depersonalization because they may be expected to interact with computer terminals rather than human librarians (Raitt, 1986). Hospital patients may feel they are treated in a dehumanizing manner if the are monitored by computer rather than by nurses directly (Lynch, 1985). Likewise, critics of bank-by-phone systems believe banks will alienate customers if they force them to converse with electronic rather than human intermediaries (Crockett, 1990). One of the most serious charges of this sort is that computerization may abstract human problems to a depersonalized level so that social workers become insensitive to client needs, doctors to patient needs, and so on. In the military arena, Beusmans and Wieckert (1989: 946) write "computer simulations of warfare distance users from the consequences of their actions", leading NATO "to adopt an unacceptable first-use strategy that, if ever called upon, would at the very least destroy Europe."

As one would expect, some of the loudest protests about dehumanization come from humans who might be displaced by computerization. Thus in 1992, the Communications and Electrical Workers of Canada launched a campaign to convince Canadians to request a

Figure 2: Turing's Man

The British mathematical genius, Alan Mathison Turing, served during World War II as part of the team which created the Colossus encoder, which was designed to decipher codes from German Enigma encrypting machines. The Colossus was the first operational electronic computer and Turing went on to lead other efforts in the construction of early computers. Visits to America led to talks with Norbert Wiener, the founder of cybernetics, and subsequently Turing's work focused on the question of whether machines can "think". In his classic article, "Can a Machine Think?", Turing answered his own question in the affirmative. He proved that machines can perform deductive analysis and make logical decisions by creating a computer that simulated the human thinking involved in the game of chess. Turing was found dead at the age of 42, poisoned by potassium cyanide which was held at the inquest to have been self-administered.

In 1984, J. David Bolter's *Turing's Man* appeared, defining the popular conception of dehumanization through computers. "Electronic man," Bolter wrote, "creates convenient hierarchies of action by dividing tasks into subtasks, routines into subroutines. The end is reached when the 'subproblems' become trivial manipulations of data that are clear at a glance. In this way, all complexity is drained from a problem, and mystery and depth vanish, defined out of existence by the programmer's operational cast of thought" (Bolter, 1984: 222). Turing's conception of man, Bolton argued, is the embodiment of the bureaucratic ideal type at its most rigid--total rationality devoid of the capacity for understanding personal truths.

human response when dealing with telephone companies. This campaign was directed against introduction of Automated Billing Services (ABS) and Voice Response (voice synthesis) technologies. The union asserted that such technologies dehumanized the operator's job and left customers to be serviced by synthesized voice messages (Harrison, 1992).

Some find dehumanization in electronic mail as well. Crawford (1982) studied e-mail at the Digital Equipment Corporation and found that while managers liked e-mail, many found it to be formal, sterile, and terse. The reduction in face-to-face contact was perceived as a loss, depersonalizing the work environment. As Kiesler (1986) noted, electronic mail removes the dynamic personal content of messages which many consider central to human communication. Information about reactions, attitudes, status, appearance, race, gender, personality and other human attributes is lost, making the term dehumanization quite descriptive. Gardner and Schermerhorn (1988) believe that as organizations rely more and more on telecommunications for messages, the symbols and sentiments which form the glue which holds organizations together will be diluted, undermining the organization's self-identity.

Summary: Dehumanization as Both Subjective and Objective

The political dimension of the dehumanization argument holds that clients are not only dehumanized but are also exploited by control centralized through computing. This argument is expressed by Cnaan (1989) when he speaks of the need to develop practice-relevant software to protect and empower those who might be victimized by information technology in the domain of social work (see also Phillips, 1993). Kolleck (1993: 458) likewise argues that "inequalities in power and influence between organizations are enlarged by computers". Studies such as these focus on the potential centralizing effects of computing, on their use for purposes of mystification of clients, and on their potential use in objectifying problems which otherwise would have to be dealt with in human confrontations. In response to fears of technololocratic exploitation of the disadvantaged there have arisen a number of groups whose purpose is to place computer power in the hands of "have-not" groups, much as Cnaan advocates (Cassell, Fitter,Fryer, and Smith, 1988; Downing, 1989).

There appears, however, to be no study providing empirical evidence that policy outputs attributable to computing systematically disadvantage certain classes or social groups. On the contrary, it is very difficult to demonstrate any correlation of computerization with substantive policy change. Computing is only one of many variables affecting organizational outcomes (Thompson, Sarbaugh-McCall, and Norris, 1989). Moreover, computerization has the potential to force administrators to clarify goals as part of the process of determining indicators to be tracked in an information system. For instance, computer models used for tax policy analysis require making explicit such factors as progressivity of the tax, coverage, and timing, and also allows instant analysis of who benefits and who loses from proposed tax reforms. Such goal clarification is thought to improve policy debate and increase democratic accountability.

The goal clarification process implicit in information systems implementation depends on situational human rather than technological factors. Specifically, the policy impacts arising from greater use of computing is largely determined by existing power relationships, not by anything intrinsic to information processing technology. Thus, if a generalization is to be made about power and computing, it is that computing functions to amplify existing tendencies within an organization as goals become clarified and better achieved through new information systems (Robey, 1977, 1981; Caporael and Thorngate, 1984: 11; Olson and Primps, 1984; Kraemer and King, 1986; Marx and Sherizen, 1986; Jackson, 1987; Calhoun and Copp, 1988).

If we rule out the Marxist view of computer investment, that exploitation accompanies alienation and dehumanization. What of the widespread perceptions that dehumanization does, in fact, occur? The subjective nature of these perceptions is evident. If you feel dehumanized when you use an ATM machine rather than the services of a human bank teller, for instance, then it is difficult for someone else to tell you that you aren't. Computer scientists and chief information officers in corporations and government may take the view that people shouldn't feel this way and that "they will get used to it"— but this does not change the fact that some people do feel dehumanized by computerization and thinking so is tantamount to being so.

On the one hand, organizations ignore perceptions that computing is dehumanizing at their peril. Subjective factors are still real forces within organizations and many large-scale computer efforts have failed as a result of human resistance. On the other hand, initial resistance to computer services often does yield to acceptance later on as the technology becomes familiar. Proper implementation can go a long way toward gaining this acceptance. Even in sensitive areas like psychotherapeutic human services, for instance, it is not necessary for computer software to anthropomorphically role-play doctors if that is perceived as "defrauding" patients, and in any event the overwhelming majority of users do not find use of such programs to be impersonal (Erdmann and Foster, 1988: 77-78). Moreover, computer services may be less dehumanizing than the intimidation sometimes associated with interaction with a high-paid, high-status human professional. For instance, Wark et al. (1991) compared computer-assisted therapy with pen-and-paper and with personal approaches. They found that the computer approach was marked by equal user satisfaction and self-concept gain, involved users in greater individual effort, and was probably more thorough.

Although the dehumanization argument is often posed in terms of displacement of human interactions by machines, in fact the function of computer-based services is often to supplement rather than to replace human professionals. People often like this supplemental assistance. Thus in a study of counseling services for college students, Arbona and Perrone (1989) concluded that students found human counseling more satisfying and helpful than interacting with a computer counsellor. It is noteworthy, however, that mixed computer/human counseling was found to be just as satisfactory as all-human counseling while still improving efficiency in service delivery. The IT literature now frequently emphasizes conscious efforts to "humanize" work through information systems which afford employees the opportunity for self-actualization (cf. Kaltnekar, 1991).

In summary, alienation from computers and perceptions of dehumanization because of computing is common. That such perceptions by employees and the public are subjective and might not be made by computer professionals does not make them less real. Organization development efforts, participatory approaches to implementation, and honesty-in-advertising can make or break organizational attempts to benefit from new information technology. While fears of dehumanization need to be taken seriously, however, employee and public attitudes toward computer services are based primarily on such factors as whether computerization has improved access, convenience, service, and value. The telephone did undermine the human art of correspondence and something "human" may be lost in computerization as well, but humans are remarkably resilient and seem to find new ways of establishing authentic interpersonal relationships regardless of the state of technology.

The Threat that Computer Technology May Create a De-Skilled Underclass

Early industrial sociologists such as Blauner (1964) predicted that computing would dictate a more skilled rather than a de-skilled labor force. Likewise, Bell (1980) predicted that the computer age would spawn a large, egalitarian "knowledge elite". However, other scholars believed that computerization would mean that employees would lose discretion over their jobs and would become regulated by machines. Fear of becoming a de-skilled servant of intelligent machines in the workplace has long been recognized as being an important obstacle to the implementation of information technology projects (Berkwitt, 1966). Conomikes (1967) even predicted that computing would crush esprit de corps in organizations, creating an underclass of dispirited workers devoid of dedication to the organization.

Whereas alienation and dehumanization are subjective concepts which exist only in the minds of those involved, de-skilling is an objective concept based on observable skill levels. The de-skilling issue has to do with the fear that for every creative job as a programmer, information technology creates a hundred low-paid jobs where the main skill is exemplified by the ability to recognize a hamburger icon so as to press the right key in automated fast food establishments. Although often mentioned in the same breath, de-skilling and dehumanization are different dimensions for those affected by computerization.

One can experience de-skilling without feeling de-humanized, and one can feel de-humanized where no de-skilling is involved. For instance, electronic scanner technology in supermarkets has a definite de-skilling effect, sharply reducing requirements for such skills as ability to read, to do simple math, and to make change. However, a doctoral study by Tolich (1992) of grocery clerks found, contrary to

Marxist theory, that clerks themselves did not define de-skilling as alienating or dehumanizing. Rather they were more apt to find alienating the checkstand encasing the scanner. Anything in a situation can be potentially alienating and, as Tolich points out, employees can be very creative in defining just what that is.

Does Computing De-skill the Work Force?

Donald Tepas, a founder of the Psychonomic Society and an early enthusiast for computing (Tepas, 1972), is among those scholars who have come to believe that computer technology poses a threat to the workplace structure of American society. In the last two decades, his optimism turned to pessimism. He now believes, "The innovations of the industrial revolution often led to dull jobs that were mindless, boring, monotonous, and/or fatiguing" and now again in our own times "the misapplication of computer systems in the current technological revolution is also leading us to dull jobs" (Tepas, 1991: 101). Tepas observed that negative workplace attitudes are becoming more common in computer-driven jobs, "owing to the underutilization of workers, monotonous duties, fear of job loss, and/or frequent shortages of trained technical staff" (p. 103). Although thousands of psychologists work in the computer industry and in spite of the existence of the Human Factors Society (4,500 members, half psychologists), human factors issues such as de-skilling rarely receive the emphasis they deserve (Tumage, 1990).

The pessimistic view is most strongly articulated by Marxist and critical scholarship. Harry Braverman's analysis, *Labor and Monopoly Capital* (1974) launched a small industry of industrial sociological studies of the de-skilling issue (cf. Greenbaum, 1979; Goldthorpe, 1982; Thompson, 1983). Wright and Singleman (1982) argued, for instance, that computerization was linked to de-skilling, the proletarianization of work, and a changing class structure in the United States. Likewise, Salaman (1982) linked computerization with social control and class structure, and Abercrombie and Urry (1983) believed computerization would devalue white collar work, an objective they saw to be in the interests of capital. Others have seen de-skilling not so much as a matter of exploitation of workers in general so much as oppression of women workers in particular (see Figure 3).

Figure 3: De-Skilling as a Woman's Issue

Some writers such as Servan-Schreiber (1985) reasoned that computing would advantage women on the ground that computerization emphasizes mental over physical labor and therefore would mean greater work equality for women.

While it is true that computerization tends to affect disproportionately positions usually held by women (Gutek, 1983; Form and McMillen, 1983; Gutek and Bikson, 1985; Mowshowitz, 1986; Gattiker, Gutek, and Berger, 1988), some investigators have viewed this negatively, arguing that computerization reduces women workers to semi-skilled levels, degrading their status (Downing, 1980; Morgall, 1983).

Computerization of jobs such as typing does reduce skill levels needed (e.g., because of increased ease of correction, automatic spell-checking) and may increase specialization (the word processor, unlike the typist, for example, may never even see the printed product, which may be sent via a network to a desktop publishing station elsewhere).

Moreover, in a study of Fortune 500 companies, Gattiker, Gutek, and Berger (1988) found the computer's perceived contribution to the quality of work life was lower for women than for men. Another study (Machung, 1988) found that word processing increased bosses' work turn-around expectations, sometimes to unrealistic levels, so that productivity advantages of computing did not benefit secretaries, who were found to lose interest in word processing after about six months and to decline in productivity.

Empirical studies sometimes do support the belief that computerization involves de-skilling. Mowshowitz (1986), for instance, is among those who found that computerization of clerical work set the stage for the industrialization of professional work as well. This is a common theme in radical criticisms of automation and has also surfaced in conventional research, as in studies of the over-control of rank-and-file employees such as social workers (Karger and Kreuger, 1988: 115; Kraut, 1987b; Garson, 1988). Barbara Garson, for instance, traced how MacDonalds has sought to replace human decision making by computerized mechanisms. She also pointed to how American Airlines instituted standardized computer-prompted reservation scripts to eliminate employee discretion in telephone transactions, eliminating the need to know connecting routes. Iacono and Kling (1984) have also traced de-skilling in the airline and telephone industries. Perrolle (1986) surveyed a variety of empirical studies showing the de-skilling effect (Downing, 1980; Gottfried, 1982; Ayres and Miller, 1983; Straw and Foged; 1983 Shaiken, 1984). Based on experiences in clerical and other sectors, Perrolle concluded that due to computerization, in the future mental labor would be devalued through such IS thrusts as expert systems. As this happened, she predicted, mental laborers would emphasize cultural symbols (e.g., suits, briefcases, job titles) rather than actual skills and decision-making power.

Empirical research has shown computerization can reduce the autonomy of middle managers (Bjorn-Anderson, Eason, and Robey, 1986) and may involve the sort of close control over professionals previously associated only with lower-skilled occupations (Aydin, 1989). Although top management usually associates computerized monitoring of work with increased productivity, employees often feel increased stress, lower satisfaction, and decreased quality in relationships with peers and management as a result (Irving, Higgins, and Safayeni, 1986). At least in some professions like design, computerization has meant greater specification of job duties and more reliance on standardized operating procedures rather than individual professional judgment (Majchrzak et al., 1987).

Numerous other studies support the de-skilling hypothesis. Buchanan and Boddy (1983) found that in a bakery setting computerization was associated with de-skilling from status as bakers to that of machine operators. Kraut, Dumais and Koch (1989: 236) found a computerized record system in a utility company "de-skilled the jobs, both by making them less complex, interesting and challenging, and by making service representatives' previous skills and training less relevant" and led to 'decreased workers' satisfaction and involvement with their work colleagues." Even efforts to make computing more "user-friendly" can have the effect of de-skilling workers.

Other studies such as that by Harvard Business School professor Shoshana Zuboff (1982) have shown that even some managers may feel a loss of a sense of control when computerization is introduced, sometimes to the point of inducing frustration and anger. Zuboff (1988a) quoted a worker as saying, "In the old way you had control over the job. The computer now tells you what to do. There is more responsibility but less control." Another worker says, "It's like driving down the highway with your lights out and someone else pushing the accelerator." Zuboff believes information systems may well become instruments of comprehensive control over subordinates, at the same time eliminating the human element of face-to-face engagement. There are many instances in which computerization is used to automate certain human skills, creating work processes in which jobs are fragmented into domains with narrower skill requirements (Glenn and Feldberg, 1977; Gregory and Nussbaum, 1982; Murphree, 1984).

Figure 4: Is User-Friendliness De-Skilling?

Computer hardware and software designers are motivated by market forces, one of which is that buyers are often new users or supervisors of new users who don't want to incur high training-time costs.

However, the drive to reduce complexity by increasing system defaults and reducing operations to all-encompassing "black boxes" can go too far.

Reducing complexity is reducing choices and this can prevent users from creating new value because of the software system's constraints. That is, extreme "user-friendly" software systems can assume substantial analytical and decision-making authority formerly held by skilled professionals.

With this de-skilling, the organization can lose critical employee capabilities and may find employee motivation declines (*Personal Workstation*, 1991).

Linstrum (1991) discusses how many workers have been demoted to operate computer systems modeled on the skills they used to employ themselves prior to computerization. He urges system designers to provide these employees with empowering options which allow them to do more than press buttons.

The fear of reduction of performance appraisals to computerized formulas or even a reduction of professional tasks to computer-checked piece-work quota systems is a particularly important specific focal point both in academic debates over computing as a force for workplace alienation (e.g., on faculty merit reviews by computer, see Hudson, 1989) and in real-world union negotiations with employers. In a study of social workers, Mandell (1989: 40) found "considerably lower levels of acceptance [of computer technology] when related to the organization's power to monitor and evaluate the worker's performance" and "a substantial number of respondents were threatened by this power". Among social workers' fears was the possibly valid view that computer performance records might be a poor indicator of actual performance (p. 37).

Marx and Sherizen (1986) have published anecdotal evidence that workers may feel exploited when computer monitoring of performance is introduced. Chamot (1987) has found that such monitoring increases job stress. Gardner and Schermerhorn (1988) have found workers fear telecommunications connectivity because it allows "silent supervision" of their performance and in fact networks are often used for this purpose at such companies as AT&T and American Express (Beardsley, 1987). This was noted as a major stumbling block to the acceptance of computer-assisted collaborative software ("groupware") (Geake, 1990). The Department of Labor has reported that two-thirds of employees who work at terminals are monitored. Computerized monitoring raises serious labor law issues in the United States (Lund, 1991). In Europe, the Commission of the European Community has been alarmed enough by the practice to recommend its abolition (Scherrer, 1991: 137).

Studies supporting the de-skilling viewpoint make it clear that in many circumstances, de-skilling can occur as part of the computerization process. De-skilling appears to be more likely for lower-status workers, the corollary of which is disproportionate effects on women and minorities. Technology does have the ability to reduce the amount of skill needed for many jobs. This has led in Europe to labor unions seeking "New Technology Agreements" for bargaining with management over the introduction of new technology. Nearer to home, Canadian unionists have been found to be more favorable toward computerization than non-union counterparts in the same job because unionists were more involved in the processes leading to technological change (Duffy, Flenday, and Pupo, 1992). The potential for de-skilling has, in Baldry's view, destabilized labor relations in some of the stablest European countries (Baldry, 1989: ch. 5). While this has not been the case in the United States, where the labor movement is in widespread defeat and restricts its attention largely to wages and benefits, many of the same underlying factors are present.

Factors Mitigating the Threat of De-Skilling

In spite of substantial evidence for de-skilling as a threat to the

American job structure, the preponderance of evidence is that office automation is appreciated by employees and is seen either neutrally or as empowering, not de-skilling, even for women employees. Judith Perrolle cited studies finding, for instance, that secretaries report feeling their jobs enriched and more fun as a result of word processing (Cassedy and Nussbaum, 1983: 91). Iacono and Kling (1984) found word processing gave an appreciated career path for women clerical workers, in spite of the drawbacks of closer work monitoring, eye strain, and less flexibility in work scheduling. Narayanan (1989) found women clerical workers perceived computers to have a positive effect on job satisfaction, job skills, marketability of their skills, job security, and pay.

It can be argued that computerization is actually up-skilling. Servan-Schreiber (1985), for instance, contended that computerization can lead to more interesting, challenging, humane, and rewarding work, allowing employees unprecedented access to information and greater control over their lives. Thus in a study of inventory management, Kling and Iacono (1984a) found computerization increased interdependence, which in turn increased peer involvement in work - a factor normally associated with self-actualization, not de-skilling. Likewise, a recent review concluded that "Some of modern automation 'de-skills' the work place, but on balance it calls for a higher level of literacy, reasoning, and mathematical thinking" (Wolman, 1990: 16).

Librarians now search on-line databases and are freed from typing endless catalog cards (Saffo, 1991). Similarly, bank teller jobs (largely held by women) have been enlarged to include more functions and problem-solving (Bosch-Font, 1985). In general, other research shows office equipment is rarely associated with women's dissatisfaction with work (Form and McMillen, 1983). Frequently but not invariably, computerization may lead to work expansion: data entry personnel may become involved with spreadsheet analyses and typists may learn desktop publishing, leading to increased worker satisfaction (Piturro, 1989a: 144). Kraft (1987) found that although there was some evidence that introduction of microcomputers retarded the growth of clerical worker positions, microcomputing was associated with increases in employment for women in spite of the fact that it is traditionally male-dominated occupational groups such as management that grow. Likewise, Kling and Iacono (1989) found many social and technological contingencies in desktop computerization which lead to complex ramifications rather than uniform effects in the direction of work degradation.

From the beginning, more researchers than not have found that computerization tends to increase rather than decrease overall skill levels in an organization (Mann and Williams, 1960; Anshen, 1960; Shaul, 1964; Delehanty, 1966). As a consequence, computerization often makes work more fulfilling (Giuliano, 1982; Spinrad, 1982; Norris, 1992). For instance, Attewell (1987b) found that in the insurance industry in 1966-1980, a period of rapid computerization, skills were upgraded, contrary to the de-skilling hypothesis. Insurance examiners no longer had to calculate deductibles or check duplicate payments, allowing them to spend more time on examining dubious claims. Yankelovich and Immerwahr (1983), based on opinion polls, found that information technology was helping increase the amount of discretionary effort in job content, increasing control over one's work. Bjorn-Anderson, Eason, and Robey (1986) found workers believed computers helped them develop a more enriched view of their task, although they did fear increased task monitoring.

Many other studies dispute the de-skilling hypothesis. A study of 2,400 government workers by Danziger and Kraemer (1986) showed that for three-quarters, computing increased their sense of accomplishment, contradicting predictions that computing would be "de-skilling" and would lead to alienating jobs. Apart from data handling professionals, computing seemed to be associated with decreases in time pressure and therefore with a better working environment. Majchrzak et al. (1987) found computer-assisted design (CAD) increased overall skill levels, particularly skills in communication, coordination, and creativity. Millman and Hartwick (1987) found computerization of information workers' jobs increased skill levels, making their jobs more demanding.

A survey of studies on information workers likewise found most studies conclude the impact of computerization on the quality of the work environment is minimal and/or positive rather than negative, although some studies associate computing with time pressure and stress (Kraemer and Danziger, 1990: 607). A study of the electronics industry by Salzman (1987) also found little evidence of a de-skilling effect. Bratton (1991) found microprocessor-based technology increased managerial control in manufacturing. Even among social workers, among the most vociferous in voicing fears of computerization, an empirical study by Gandy and Tepperman (1989) found that in practice social work staff affected by computerization voiced little concern after the initial implementation period. A majority of staff in people-changing organizations did not find computerization a threat to their discretion, autonomy, or relations with clients (Gandy and Tepperman, 1990: 177). A substantial minority actually felt computerization increased their levels of discretion. Moreover, others have shown how human services can use computing strategies to enhance outreach, community action, and client participation—outcomes opposite to critics' fears (Bynum, 1991).

Conclusion: Technological Up-Skilling and De-Skilling

Although the preponderance of evidence fails to support the deskilling theory, this does not mean it can be dismissed. Often both deskilling and upgrading can be occurring at the same time (Attewell and Rule, 1984). Dealing with such fears is a critical element in development of an information culture supportive of IS initiatives, whether or not such fears are well-founded. Since de-skilling is an objective rather than subjective phenomenon, one might think it would be easy to "get the facts" and come to a conclusion. However, nearly all studies of de-skilling have studied particular job classifications in isolation. Some were de-skilled, others were upskilled. But there are few objective studies of changes in overall skill levels in society, on top of which skill research is marked by a lack of rigor (Vallas, 1990).

Among the few studies of overall effects of computerization on community skill levels is research on six British cities. In this study, Gallie (1991) found that evidence failed to support either the deskilling hypothesis or the belief of Wolman and others that computerization is up-skilling. Instead, the trend was toward polarization of skill levels, with more clustering of jobs at *either* the high skill *or* the low skill levels. Perrolle (1991b), likewise, has found that computerized expert systems threaten middle skill level jobs, incorporating their skills into computer systems used by high-skilled staff. The jobs of the middle skill level support staff are de-skilled after introduction of expert systems, at least in the cases Perrolle studied.

It should be noted that many of the studies of de-skilling are based on employee perceptions, not actual skill levels measured objectively. In this context, it is important to understand that organizations try to match employees to the technology in place. For instance, at the Mrs. Fields cookie firm, the company selects for enthusiasm, commitment, and people skills, not for education, job experience, or analytic skills.

Figure 5: The UTOPIA Project: Planning for Up-Skilling

The UTOPIA project, implemented in a newspaper company setting, was planned by an information systems team composed of union representatives and typesetters. Their explicit goal was to enhance the typesetting craft. Company management was excluded from the design team.

The result was development of computer capabilities which allowed typesetters to scale, fine tune the contrast of, and otherwise enhance layouts beyond what had been possible previously.

Organizational changes were made so that reporters would not enter typesetting codes into their articles, reserving layout decisions for the typesetters.

Moreover, design participation enabled typesetters to "buy in" to IS implementation (Ehn, Kyng, and Sundblad, 1983; Howard, 1985; Hirschheim and Klein, 1989: 1200).

Thus in an industry where other studies have associated computerization with de-skilling, in the UTOPIA project the opposite occurred, showing de-skilling can be avoided when this is an organizational goal.

That is, the company does not seek to maximize job skills as a goal in itself but rather matches recruits to appropriate technology in place (Walton, 1989). As the ongoing recruitment process continues, the employees available for survey at any given time may not have an objective perspective on de-skilling in relation to the jobs they hold. That is, as Tolich (1990) points out, incumbent workers may view jobs as de-skilled which new workers may not perceive as such.

An obvious fact, often ignored in studies of de-skilling, is that whether computerization is skill-enhancing or skill-debasing has a lot to do with implementation. It is true that IS implementation is often a top-down affair emphasizing technical and economic factors and ignoring human factors. A study of knowledge engineers implementing expert systems, for instance, showed that not a single systems engineer interviewed acknowledged job de-skilling as a valid issue

(LaFrance, 1990: 22). However, this is not intrinsic to computing. Mumford (1981) is among those who have argued that unless the quality of working life is explicitly addressed during the design process, business pressures will force its degradation. A few experimental companies have shown that up-skilling can be implemented effectively when it is an explicit organizational objective as part of computerization (see Figure 1-4).

The importance of institutional culture in determining de-skilling/ up-skilling outcomes in computerization was also studied by Zetka (1991). Basing analysis on contrasting case studies of General Electric and British Telecom plants, Zetka found that what determined the type of outcome was the extent to which the corporation enhanced a de-skilling/managerial control philosophy. Other examples of the importance of taking social factors into account in technical design are given by Eason (1988: 45), whose text is one of several which shows IS designers how to create systems that people like to use and which makes the case that de-skilling is not technologically fated.

Finally, it should be noted that a related problem eclipsing de-skilling itself is the lack of skills training among American workers. In the 1986-91 period, the number of workers who had to use computers on their jobs grew 48%, and in some industries like finance, insurance, and real estate, over 70% of workers must now use computers (Currid, 1991a: 62). The Hudson Institute predicted in 1989 that by the year 2000, 40% of the workforce may need to read or write technical or scientific articles, whereas only 7% then had this ability. Some 59% are projected to need to know how to read computer and technology-related manuals and to write business communications, capacities held in 1989 by only an estimated 16%. As a consequence, organizations are being forced to increase the level of education and training in the workplace (Wolman, 1990). Several major national commissions and works such as that by Marshall and Tucker (1992) cogently argue that the American workforce must be educated and trained in a more effective manner than in the past.

The Disemployment Issue

The fourth horseman of apocalyptic theories of computing, along with despotism, dehumanization, and deskilling, is the fear of disemployment though automation. Examples may be found which give weight to these fears. Computerization correlates with job elimination among clerical workers in industries like banking and insurance, for instance (Reinecke, 1982: 142; BIFU, 1982; FIET, 1980). Technological disemployment has also impacted traders and other workers in the securities industry (Krass and Caldwell, 1991). To take just one software package as an illustration, IBM's *INFOREM* inventory management software automates the reordering of inventories, eliminating jobs traditionally done by professional buyers (Linstrum, 1991). Likewise, the automation of printing presses has put printers out of work. Because of impacts like these, some analysts argue that as computer investment becomes widespread, there needs to be an accompanying national program of work creation (Laver, 1989: Ch. 5).

In the 1960s, when computerization was being widely implemented in industry, there were fears that automation would lead to high unemployment. Simon (1960a), for example, reasoned that computerization would mean smaller human employment relative to the total workforce due to the comparative advantage of automated machines. However, many of these fears have proved groundless when broad job categories are considered. Clerical workers were once predicted to take the brunt of computerization, decimating their ranks (Simon, 1960). Later predictions merely speculated that the growth of the clerical class was slowed, not reversed, by computerization (Lee, 1967). Still later, empirical researchers could find no impact of IS on clerical employment (Hunt and Hunt, 1986; Swart and Baldwin, 1971). Menkus (1987: 49) reported, "the numbers of clerks who often worked in what amounted to a factory setting are gone. They have been replaced by throngs of knowledge workers, analysts, planners, programmers, researchers."

Information technology is seen by many managers as a means to achieve greater productivity through labor savings. Parsons' (1990) dissertation on the Canadian banking industry documented how computerization in the form of on-line branch teller terminals represented the substitution of technology for other inputs, particularly labor. However, the general tendency of computing investment is to lead to quantitative and qualitative changes in output but not to absolute labor savings. While IS investment in automated tellers and the like does substitute technology for human jobs, other jobs are created to manufacture, distribute, and service ATM machines as well as banking jobs to process the higher volume of transactions associated with this technology. Defenders of information technology assert that as many jobs are created as are lost (Uris, 1963; Hill, 1966; Kraemer and King, 1986; Weil, 1988: 86). There appear to be no empirical studies contradicting this unproved assertion.

Ken Eason (1988) surveyed research done by the HUSAT (Human Sciences and Advanced Technology) project he helped found at the Loughborough University of Technology. Eason found three major reasons why big job losses predicted in the 1970s failed to materialize in the 1980s. First, many jobs predicted to disappear proved to be less routine and amenable to automation than thought.[1] Second, as some jobs were lost to automation others were created in computer support. Third and most important, managers and employees resisted organizational changes such as centralization which would have been required to make significant job cuts. Not only did major job cuts fail to occur, but the issue was often deemed unimportant by the organizations themselves. Eason found that in most cases no one bothered to document whether more or fewer jobs existed after IS implementation.

Because the causes of employment are so complex, making firm research-based conclusions nearly impossible, it is difficult to contradict the contention that in the long run computing creates as many jobs as it displaces (Weber, 1988). Nonetheless, computerization is associated with problems of worker displacement and retraining in particular organizations even if it does not affect overall unemployment levels (Lund and Hansen, 1986; Baldry, 1988: ch. 2). In some cases, often involving blue collar workers, dislocations can be major and costs of retraining high. Justified or not, fear that the computer will replace humans is a major factor in resistance of employees to new information technology.[2]

That fear is fed by the fact that in the 1990s, the United States and other developed nations face historically high levels of unemployment. In 1993, the Organization for Economic Cooperation and Development predicted that unemployment in its 24 member nations would average 8.5% and would go higher in 1994 (Levinson, Burger, and Powell, 1993: 46). While a fraction of this unemployment might be attributed to computerization of existing jobs, the overarching factor is the rise of global competition. Low-productivity jobs in labor-intensive industries like shoes and apparel are lost to imports. Information sector jobs can be performed abroad by lower-paid and sometimes better-trained workers, instantly transmitting their work back to industrial countries through worldwide telecommunications. Firms engaged in global competition come under intense pressure to eliminate every organizational element—managers, departments, services—which does not directly add value. The connection of computing to unemployment may be less through the direct route than its indirect effect in enabling an intense, fast-paced global competition which induces companies "to do more with fewer people and to ship less-skilled parts of the job abroad" (Levinson, Burger, and Powell, 1993: 47).

Computing as a Tool for 'Those at the Top'

Once one gets past the arguments about information technology bringing on an age of despotism, dehumanization, de-skilling, and disemployment, there are still arguments that computing undermines American democratic values because it is a tool which reinforces the power of "those at the top". IS professional journals themselves frequently emphasize the theme of how the status of their IS readers may be increased by seeking to support top management more closely so that IS chiefs can become as much a part of the inner circle at the top as are budget directors now. What is painted is a picture of technocratic workers as upwardly mobile individuals jockeying for status, not a picture of an emergent elite class bent on radical interests of their own.

To the extent that one is content with the productivity of American enterprise and the accountability of American governmental agencies, one is apt to disagree with the premise that serving as a tool for "those at the top" is detrimental to democratic values in the first place. In fact, a more balanced view of IS literature would also note that it places great emphasis on serving the needs of end users throughout the organization, not just top management, and for support for distributed processing which lets even low-level staff access organizational information resources. Nonetheless, it is worthwhile to consider whether information technology tends to augment the power of chief executives at the expense of other interest groups within and without

Figure 6: Critics of Computer Power

Critics of public and private management often also tend to see computing as a tool for those at the top, but they attach a negative evaluation to this (Kling and Iacono, 1988).

* Civil libertarians see computing as a danger to the rights to privacy and a temptation to the abuse of power.

* Unionists object to threats to occupational health arising from constant proximity to computer monitors.

* Peace activists see software unreliability as creating the threat of accidental war.

* A particular focus of criticism has been military influence. Military contracts have favored elite schools and have influenced the relative numbers of scientists being trained in particular fields and the subjects on which research was done (Winograd, 1984). In some fields, such as electrical engineering, a majority of graduates go into military-related work, creating what some call a "military-industrial-academic" complex (Barus, 1987).

the organization.

Computing in the Service of Executive Power

The image of computing as a "tool of those at the top" is reinforced by assumptions embedded in many, if not most texts and commentaries, on how to go about information systems planning. For instance, early on, W. R. King (1978) argued that IS managers should start their work by identifying the policies top managers held to be their priorities. Information executives were to take these management-set organizational strategies (e.g., reducing internal investments), then gear the information systems to present data on these strategies (e.g., data on alternative means for such reductions) so that top managers could make better decisions. That is, information managers were not to set strategies or even select alternatives. They were not even to participate in debates over strategies and alternatives but rather simply provide relevant data to the powers that be. Many contemporary texts such as Frenzel (1992: 80) explicitly follow this model.

Much of the research on decision-making in major computer-related projects emphasizes the subordination of technical considerations to political priorities of top managers and their overseers. For instance, Kraemer, Dickhoven, Tierney, and King (1987: 29) conclude, using federal computer modeling as examples, that "our findings emphasize the importance of political over technical considerations" in determining the extent to which computer systems are adopted. These authors found successful efforts are those which marketed themselves to top decision-makers and catered to their needs in development, packaging, and other forms of support —not those where technocrats pursued their own professional goals (as would be implied by "technocratic elite" theory). Other studies also confirm that in most important situations, it is managers, not officials in the IS unit, who make the ultimate decisions (Saunders and Scamell, 1986; Kraft, 1987).

Computers by themselves typically have only marginal impact on the nature of professional work relations. However, lower-level employees are more likely to fear and resist computerization. In many settings computerization may require redesign of jobs, disproportionately jobs of rank-and-file employees. Thus in social work, for instance, computerization for street-level human services workers "will require more reporting, data collection, broader professional exposure, a lower level of individual recording, and more detailed explanations of professional activities—tasks that most social workers dislike and will do their best to avoid" (Cnaan, 1989: 6).

For their part, top managers recognize the importance of control and seek to defend the prerogatives of their power. In the computerization of hospitals, for instance, doctors have sometimes felt that their autonomy was eroded, setting off political struggles over control of medical decision-making (Shuman, 1988). Computer-based information systems can centralize information quickly in the hands of top management. The scope of the manager's span of control can be extended greatly. In fact, some studies show that the desire to use computing and information technologies to increase managerial control is one of the main reasons for their application (Buchanan and Boddy et al., 1983).

There is even some evidence from the public sector that officials tend to invest in computer software that enhances executive control compared to that which provides direct services (Kraemer and Kling, 1985). Attewell (1987a), in a study of a medical insurance firm, similarly found electronic surveillance software does not consistently improve productivity. In fact, it frequently backfires. If computerized surveillance increases stress[3] yet does not increase productivity, one must infer that its widespread use has more to do with manager's seeking to preserve or enhance their power and control rather than with technical or economic considerations.

Computerization can have a centralizing effect and in the process serve as a tool for top management. Studies have found that upper management decisions determine how information technology is to be employed and dictate the organizational outcomes which flow from its implementation (Walton and Vittori, 1983; Zuboff, 1985a). Zuboff (1988b) notes that the capacity of information systems to "informate" (give all organizational levels information about entire processes) as well as automate can lead to greater hierarchical surveillance and policing. The "democratizing" of information need not lead to democratization of power.

Figure 7: Computing as a Two-Edged Sword

While computing undoubtedly does serve as a tool for executive power, it is a two-edged sword. This is illustrated by a survey of computing in the social work profession by Dick Schoech (1982). On the one hand, these forces increased executive power:

1. The power of top management increased due to better and faster information flow.
2. Improved data allowed decisions to become centralized higher in the organization.
3. Decision-making became less flexible as it relied more on quantitative indicators and programmed reports.

On the other hand, Schoech also came to three other conclusions which point to effects not limited to enhancing the power of top management:

1. Those who understand and use the information management system increased in power. They may or may not be part of top management.
2. Power shifted to those in boundary-spanning roles linking the IS process to organizational planning and budgeting.
3. Interdependence among organizational units increased through mutual reliance on a common database.

Other research on computers in the human services also points to (1) the rising importance of a technical staff (which some might label a technocratic elite) and (2) their increasing inclusion in advisory processes serving top management decision-making (Caputo, 1989: 224-6). Many of these conclusions apply to other work domains as well.

Summary: Limits to Computing as a Tool for Power

There is some evidence that how you look at computing as a "tool for power" depends on where you are in the organization hierarchy (Panko, 1984). Conclusions from the study of municipal employees, for instance, shows that greater employee influence over others in the workplace is attributed to the computer as the employee's rank in the agency hierarchy increases. That is, the closer one is to top management, the more one is likely to believe that computers increase one's power over others. However, this finding should not be exaggerated since at all levels most perceive the computer as *not* changing influence relationships (Kraemer and Danziger, 1984). Computing is perceived as a "tool for those at the top" but also as a "tool for everybody". Computing is only one among a great many factors affecting the power structure of the organization. Indeed, some studies find hierarchical level in the organization is not correlated with differences in perception of office technologies at all (Gattiker, Tutek, and Berger. 1988).

Trading control for other objectives is the principal motive behind decentralization (see Hammer, Lyons, and Strain, 1984; Hammer et al., 1985; Baker and Platman, 1985). To illustrate with an example, the establishment of a hospital database system, decentralization was chosen for a variety of reasons other than increasing control (Lyons, Hammer, and White, 1987). Although a centralized mainframe was available, programming it to provide the reports needed by decentralized units would have cost a quarter million dollars—a prohibitive amount. Modifications to mainframe procedures had a long history of delay and backlog, often one to four years (Konsynski, 1984: 7), and the centralized computing service was subject to intense competition and organizational politics. In this environment, decentralized databases administered by local units but containing common link fields to the mainframe database was the attractive way to go and was supported by top management.

Numerous similar examples could be cited to show that top administrators do not always favor computer centralization. When "downsizing" became popular in the late 1980s and early 1990s, motivated by cost-cutting in an economic recession, such examples of decentralization of computer resources and power became more the rule than the exception. Although primacy is sometimes given to control, the goal structure of top management is not homogenous, single-mindedly focusing on power for its own sake. Other goals may be dominant besides control alone. In particular, managers may be willing to trade the control which comes from centralization for other values such as rapid access to information.

Conclusion: Political Conflict as a Way of Life for Information Systems

Many observers have worried that the rise of information technology may have adverse implications for America's constitutional system of separation of powers and of checks and balances among the branches of government (Kraemer and King, 1987; Miewald and Mueller, 1987). Computerization holds the potential to afford an advantage to one branch of government over another. These Constitutional issues come into focus most clearly in the area of computer surveillance and threats to privacy, popularized in such books as *The Naked Society* (Packard, 1964) and *Dossier Society* (Laudon, 1986). More broadly, there is a widespread belief that information technology provides competitive advantages for technology-rich agencies (e.g., Ives and Learmonth, 1984) or, in the words of a *Washington Post* reporter, "the agency with the most computer and information firepower wins" (Schrage, 1985: B-1). By extension, it is predicted, the branch of government with the most "information firepower" is the executive branch, which as a result may come to overshadow the other branches and undermine the well-balanced framework of American democracy.

Information Technology in the Constitutional System

Kraemer and King (1987) were able to give only a few empirical examples of erosion of federal checks and balances. They concluded that the threat was "at the margins" (p. 93), a danger for the future. On the one hand it is true that the executive branch is routinely better prepared than Congress in handling budget requests, for example, and this is due in part to greater computerization. On the other hand, congressional agencies such as the Congressional Budget Office (CBO), the General Accounting Office (GAO), and the Office of

Technology Assessment (OTA) are themselves power players in the information systems field.

Moreover, Congressional staffs have increasingly included individuals with IS expertise. This has been encouraged by programs such as the Congressional fellowship program of the AAAS (American Association for the Advancement of Science), started in 1973. By one estimate, about half the technical staff of members of Congress are former AAAS fellows (Grimm, 1988a: 25). Representatives can also take advantage of the Member Budget Information System (MBIS) which is part of the House Information System (HIS), giving on-line information on current and previous year expenditure data. The Comparative Statement of Budgetary Authority (CSBA) computer program, to take another example, gives data on the President's budget at any given point in the budget process (Frantzich, 1984).

Figure 8: Congressional Resources for Information Technology

Congress has numerous computer resources at its disposal to counterbalance those under presidential control. These information resources have come about largely in the last 20 years:

* The Legislative Reorganization Act of 1970 reconstituted and expanded the Congressional Research Service (CRS).

* The Technology Assessment Act of 1972 created the Office of Technology Assessment (OTA).

* The Budget Impoundment Act of 1974 established the Congressional Budget Office (CBO).

Telecommunications gives direct information access for members of Congress through the CBO, OTA, and CRS and its Science Policy Research Division in the Library of Congress.

Congressional committees and offices utilize computers to give real teeth to the Freedom of Information Act (FOIA) provisions by which Congress may request executive agency data.

Congressional committees and individual senators and representatives call on the General Accounting Office (GAO) frequently to conduct audits and analyses of existing and proposed information technology projects. These GAO reports are often highly critical of the agencies involved and are perceived as providing an important element of legislative oversight of the information bureaucracy.

Congressional oversight of information technology was summarized by Representative Dan Glickman (D-Kan), sponsor of the Computer Security Act (HR 145). "I think there's plenty of good technical support out there, but I think the real issue is whether Congressional members will take the time to avail themselves of that support" (Grimm, 1988a: 25). IS is frequently only one of dozens of issues facing Congressional members and it is usually relatively low on the priority list. That is, nothing intrinsic to information technology predetermines that Congress (or the judiciary) must be undermined by superior "information firepower" rooted in the executive branch. In fact, Congress has impressive computing resources (see Figure 1-8). Having the resources and having the motivation to use them, as Glickman points out, are two different things.

Though the judicial branch as the third division of the check-and-balances system is relatively computer-poor, it can require agencies and private organizations to supply computer data regardless of cost. In a 1979 anti-trust case against IBM, for instance, the courts refused to allow into evidence a large portion of IBM's 60 million pages of documents but required IBM to produce an additional five billion documents at an estimated cost of $1 billion (Wessell, 1980: 16). IBM prevailed in the case but it did illustrate the court's ability to disallow or require computer-generated information as it sees fit.

The situation at the state level appears not to be much different, although both executive and legislative branch information systems are less well developed. Klay and Yu (1988: 196) found that at least in Florida, IS has been carefully designed to maintain traditional constitutional relationships among the branches of government. The central computing facility is under the governor's office but it is jointly directed by a gubernatorial appointee and by staff directors of the House and Senate Appropriations Committees. As with Congress's creation of the CBO and OTA, this sort of organizational arrangement illustrates the diverse forms of response by which the legislative branch may counterbalance the greater computing power housed in the executive.

Information Technology and Interest Group Politics

IS policy-making is a political process. Almost any study of computer system implementation notes the involvement of many competing interest groups. For instance, a study of electronic funds transfer (EFT) in banking found it served elite interests of the Federal Reserve Board and of banking management, not populist or civil liberties interests, which it threatened (Kling, 1983). Reviewing a number of such studies, Kling (1980) concluded, that a common theme was institutional segmentation.

That is, the conflict of segments of an organization is a political process which arises from the fact that the introduction of new computer technology disrupts existing power alignments and organizational roles. Kling noted that conflict in which computing was used as an instrument to aggrandize power was endemic to organizational life and was not necessarily eufunctional. Even in a highly technical area, such as the development of computerized missile guidance systems, historians have shown that outcomes arise from a complex process involving politics and marketing by corporation and laboratories, not a simple technological imperative. Thus Soviet and American missile guidance systems both achieved high accuracy but through rather different technological choices associated with their different organizational and political cultures (MacKenzie, 1990).

A study of NASA's Johnson Space Center (JSC) by Overman and Simanton (1986) found information policy processes could be described in terms of "iron triangles" (users, managers, and designers) and "issue networks" (broader coalitions of computer-literate participants), just as in other policy areas. Initially, IS policy decisions may be determined by the conjunction of interests among users needing services, managers seeking productivity and growth, and designers seeking advanced technology and applications (the "iron triangle").

The "iron triangle" concept is sometimes presented in more sweeping terms. This more critical viewpoint sees the politics of technology as a function of the interests of what President Eisenhower called the "military-industrial complex". Authors like Molina (1991) call this the capital-government-military-science "social constituency" associated with the politics of microelectronics. Molina's research on national trends in technological development showed on a grand scale the importance of military priorities, the needs of large corporations to compete globally, government policies, and priorities of "big science" lobbies.

In larger and more mature IS policy systems like JSC, however, the process is more complex and fluid than the term "iron triangle" might suggest. Overman and Simanton (1986) suggested that the term "issue network" might be more appropriate. In environments like the JSC there is strong potential for conflict among groups of end users. This conflict may be accentuated by vendors of competing technology systems. Issues of centralization and decentralization become more important. At JSC, for example, more than 20 principal contractors, a host of subcontractors, and numerous consultants were among the participants in the IS interest group process. Some wished to centralize databases, others to keep data locally; some wanted one type of communications system, others another. "Smart public managers," Overman and Simanton (1986: 588) write, "will build an issue network around their desired policy outcome" (Overman and Simanton, 1986). The importance of forming such issue coalitions is frequently recognized explicitly by information resource managers (e.g., Cynthia Rand, IRM director for the U.S. Department of Transportation,

Figure 1-9: Mini-Case: The FTS 2000 Issue Network

FTS 2000 is the federal government's $25 billion project to reconstitute federal telecommunications.

The General Services Administration official charged with contracting authority for FTS 2000 was supported by an Independent Advisory Committee (IAC), presided by the chair of the prestigious National Academy of Public Administration.

The IAC, in turn, was supported by the Source Selection Evaluation Board, which had its own complex network of committees.

The FTS 2000 Steering Committee represented no less than 16 agencies. In addition, a Telecommunications Interagency Management Council was mandated by Congress and presided by an official of the Justice Department.

Anticipating the need for oversight, stipulations in the 1988 contracts further called for the contracting firm to establish a Service Oversight Center for each of the two major networks in FTS 2000 (Miles, 1988b: 89).

FTS 2000 and its welter of committees illustrates how information technology projects exist within "issue networks" of public and private interests, reflected in the headline, "Intricate Network of Advisers Supports FTS 2000" (Hosinski, 1988).

Government Computer News, 1991a: 46).

Involving all stakeholders in an issue network has become a "law" of good information systems implementation. All those with a stake in IS proposals, particularly end users, should have incentives to play their intended roles. Designing such incentives is sometimes called "stakeholder analysis". For example, in implementing a computerized land development system, IS planners in Austin, Texas, consciously targeted certain interest constuencies, making sure the information system to be implemented met some deeply-felt group needs even though meeting those needs was not the technologically optimum thing to do.[4]

Information systems issues are embedded in a political process. Governmental advisory committees on information technology, for instance, are often dominated by IS interests from the private sector. Such advisory committees can constitute a "structure of access" allowing private interests to overturn governmental policies. This happened, for instance, when the computer communications lobby successfully applied pressure against the Department of State to assure that its policy would be the official U.S. policy in international negotiations about transborder data flows (Roche, 1987).

It should be noted, however, that not all private sector interest groups have as their goal protecting the profit margins of business. Private interest groups also include public-oriented organizations such as the Electronic Frontier Foundation and Computer Professionals for Social Responsibility, both of which have led in the fight for privacy rights. Marc Rotenberg, Washington liaison for Computer Professionals for Social Responsibility, for instance, organized a mass letter-writing campaign which mobilized 30,000 individuals to protest successfully an experimental product (Marketplace Households, from Lotus Development Corporation and Equifax) which would have facilitated mass "junk mail" operations by anyone with a PC, a CD-ROM, and a printer (Barlow, 1991: 23).

In spite of the existence of public interest groups, by far the largest organized interest group in the IS area is the Information Industry Association (IIA), formed in the late 1960s as a lobbying group representing over 800 IS firms. Primary goals of the IIA are to protect their members' property rights (as through copyright legislation) and to minimize governmental provision of information services which might compete with the private sector. Although relatively small, it is disproportionately effective because it represents a high-growth economic sector which most political leaders want to see prosper.

During the Reagan and Bush administrations the IIA successfully supported policies which restricted government dissemination of data online. IIA supporters held that the public benefits when the private sector is given the incentive to develop information resources by being assured they won't be undercut by subsidized government services. Opponents argue that the IIA is seeking windfall profits for its members, who make some $1.5 billion annually by reselling government information and that the public is better served by low-cost governmental online access services such as the Toxic Release Inventory of the Environmental Protection Agency, which alerts the public about chemical emissions (Margulius, 1989: 79). Whether one agrees or disagrees with the IIA on these issues, it is clear that information system policy cannot be treated as matters with purely technical solutions which can be "solved" by experts. Instead, political controversy among competing interest groups is a way of life in the information technology arena.

Summary: Information Technology and Democratic Processes

Computing seems to generate both utopian and dystopian visions. Vannevar Bush, science advisor to Franklin Delano Roosevelt, was one of the utopians. His 1945 *Atlantic Monthly* article, "As We May Think", envisioned a desk-sized "memex" which would give access to vast archives of books. Douglas Engelbart headed Stanford University's project "to augment the human intellect" in the 1960s, studying how time-shared computers could be linked to enhance analysis and decision-making. By 1980, when Alvin Toffler wrote *The Third Wave* about how telecommunications was creating an "infosphere", the utopian vision of computing as a mind-expanding, empowering force was well established. At the same time a dystopian literature developed (Dunlop and Kling, 1991). Joseph Weizenbaum's *Computer Power and Human Reason* (1976) and Ian Reinecke's *Electronic Illusions* (1984) were parts of this tradition of skepticism toward computing and what it might do for - or to - humankind. Social scientists have found that the impacts of computing on society cannot be represented as either utopian or dystopian in nature.

It is difficult to generalize about the politics of computing and information technology. Where Overman and Simanton found "iron triangles" yielding to "issue networks", another study of IS politics came to different conclusions about interest groups and politics. Isherwood and Blacklock (1988) studied implementation of IS in a local school board setting, focusing on the interactions of elected school board leaders, school administrators, computer staff, planners, and vendors as interest groups. Like Overman and Simanton they found a highly political process. However, rather than finding a consensual "iron triangle" yielding to an administrator-led "issue network", Isherwood and Blacklock found a much less consensual pattern.

In the school board study, politics centered on tension over planning processes. The school board sanctioned "strategic planning" by a director of planning, with the involvement of innovative principals and top administrators. However, the director of computer services for the schools sought to restrict users to dumb terminals, to stonewall the school board support group, to make procurement decisions not consistent with goals of others in the process, and generally to go against the stated goals of the school system as embodied in planning processes.

Isherwood and Blacklock found that over three years the director was relatively successful in influencing high-level school administrators away from plans of a Steering Committee and toward his own goals. This resulted in a two million dollar investment (closely supported by vendor interests) in central facilities which left little for investment in the decentralized processing desired by others. In addition to illustrating the power of those who controls the budget, Isherwood and Blacklock concluded that their study cast doubt on the view of organizations as rational goal-attainers and instead revealed the importance of political conflict. They found goals often to be attached to roles and even personalities. Rather than characterize the process as emergence of a coherent "issue network", these authors found their study supported Mintzberg and McHugh's (1985) imagery of organizations as forums for competing, often incompatible interests.

In summary, this chapter looked at the hypothesized threat to American democracy from computing as a force for despotism, dehumanization, de-skilling, and disemployment. While each of these charges contains elements of truth deserving serious treatment, the apocalyptic view of information technology is not supported by empirical evidence. Although computing may be considered as a "tool of those at the top", there is much more research supporting the belief that information technology serves to reinforce existing power structures. However, this should not be associated with a monolithic view of power. Chief executives seek to maximize a mix of many values, not just power, with the result that they may be quite willing to trade control for achievement of other objectives. The operative word here is "trade": information technology issues are enmeshed in an ecology of interest group trade-offs, conflict, competition, and compromise. In this respect, the politics of information does not undermine or overthrow American democracy, but rather reflects its essential nature.

ENDNOTES

[1] For instance, knowledge workers are more mobile, less supervised, and more prone to use voice communications, all of which mitigates against automation of their functions (Menkus, 1987).

[2] For instance, employee resistance to computing in social work due to fears of disemployment is discussed by Smith and Bolitho, 1989.

[3] The U.S. Office of Technology Assessment has found that electronic and computer surveillance, which affects some six million Americans directly, tends to increase worker stress (U.S. Office of Technology Assessment, 1987).

[4] Specifically, the IS team targeted tedious manual reports for replacement with computer-generated reports, implementing the printed computer output replacements early in the implementation process even though the eventual purpose was to replace all paper reports with online access. "By identifying strategic manual tasks that required time-consuming and tedious clerical effort and then replacing them with computerized reports", the IS planners wrote, "clerical resistance to the new system gradually dissolved. What seemed at first as redundant work received their allegiance only after it began to produce tangible benefits" (Arbeit, Heald, and Szkotak, 1987: 175).

CHAPTER II

The Potential of Computers to Democratize American Life

Chester Barnard, the noted corporate executive and organizational theorist, wrote "The structure, extensiveness, and scope of organizations are almost entirely determined by communication" (Barnard, 1938:8). Today some believe computers and telecommunications are leading to a far more democratic structuring of organizations. Moreover, at a societal level, some also think that we are moving or at least should move toward a system of teledemocracy in which decisions are made by citizens in computer-assisted referenda. Congress's main duty then would be to oversee this electronic decision process and the President's primary responsibility would be only to find superior candidates to fill top government jobs (Rubens, 1983). These beliefs are not without some foundation. Many studies have found that computing can change politics (e.g., Cunningham, 1985) as well as human relationships within organizations (e.g., Shallis, 1984). Will telecommunications prove to be "the great equalizer" (Rheingold, 1991b) ushering in a revitalization of American democracy? Or will computerized telecommunications be an incremental improvement, not a revolution, much as cable television extended commercial broadcasting but failed to live up to early promises of interactive wired cities once predicted to transform American democracy (Smith, 1972; for critique, see Laudon, 1977, 1987)?

The Vision of a Democratic Information Society

In principle, information systems could lead to a new epoch of decentralization and democratization. The concept of a "democratic information society" or "electronic democracy" has been set forth for two decades by a number of writers (Sackman and Nie, eds., 1970; Hiltz and Turoff, 1978; Becker and Scarce, 1984; see also Caporael, 1984; McCullough, 1991; for a European view, see Frosini, 1987). All of these writers believe technological change may have potentially profound social and political impacts which, in theory, could democratize decision-making at organization, city, and even national levels. Some even envision computers making possible the replacement of representative democracy with a direct democracy in which citizens using computers would vote directly on government issues and laws instead of electing representatives (Cohen, 1984). As found in a survey by Kling and Iacono (1988), views on this subject can be quite ideological and varied but the common underlying belief is that as computerization increases, more and more opportunities arise by which the social world will be remade, largely in a spontaneous, decentralized manner benefitting everyone.

The concept of electronic democracy was given a major impetus in the 1992 Presidential election campaign when it was endorsed by independent candidate Ross Perot. Perot, who had become wealthy selling computer services to the health industry, advocated a system under which he would hold periodic electronic referenda on issues like new taxes. Hundreds of private electronic bulletin boards figured heavily in the Perot campaign and for the first time a major Democratic candidate (Jerry Brown) campaigned on electronic BBS services like CompuServe instead of just on television, radio, and the press (Higgins, 1992).

Interest in electronic democracy has come primarily from futurist authors and political activists. Political scientists have done little to study the democratic implications of computers and telecommunications (Dutton, 1992). However, electronic democracy reflects an important division among political theorists. On one side are advocates of using "teledemocracy" to revitalize democratic processes such as through electronic referenda or who simply see in new technology a force for democratization (e.g., Cleveland, 1985). On the other side are those who fear that such efforts would be a step toward "managed democracy" (Laudon, 1977). That is, government by plebiscite has traditionally been associated with Mussolini fascism and demagogues. It is seen as a strategy of a strong-man leader who wants to sidestep normal democratic processes by appealing to "the people", whose opinions the leader plays a strong role in shaping in the first place. Thus James Fishkin, chair of University of Texas's Department of Government, said of the Perot proposal, "Electronic town meetings are just a device to step outside established political mechanisms—to abandon traditional forms of representation and elections—in order to acquire a mantle of higher legitimacy. And in the very worst case, it could be invoked toward extra-constitutional ends" (*Time*, May 25, 1992: 28).

Computers and Political Activism

The vision of electronic democracy originated during the free-wheeling early days of microcomputing in the 1970s and early 1980s. Tom Stonier, whose *The Wealth of Information* appeared in 1983, wrote of this vision:

> In late communicative society, we will stop worrying about material resources. And just as the industrial economy eliminated slavery, famine, and pestilence, so will the post-industrial economy eliminate authoritarianism, war, and strife. For the first time in history, the rate at which we will solve problems will exceed the rate at which they appear (Stonier, 1983: 214).

A concrete embodiment of hopes for electronic democracy was the Community Memory experiment, a Berkeley, California, project to provide a public access bulletin board and message system. Organized by former peace activist Lee Felsenstein, later designer of the Osborne computer, Community Memory was intended as a high tech but grass-roots instrument for social change. As one commentator summarized, radical efforts like Community Memory "point to the potential for political participation and organization through networks of computers connected by phone lines; the ability of individuals and small groups to gain access to and manipulate data, do typesetting, and perform other tasks which previously required large and costly machines; and, perhaps most important, the demystification of computers themselves" (Siegel, 1986: 116).

A more prominent example of activist computing is HandsNet, a national telecommunications network providing support for grass-roots activists in health, poverty, housing, and other areas, as well as a gateway to other activist networks. Other on-line networks for activists include EcoNet, PeaceNet, ConflictNet, and the Institute for Global Communications Network (Vance, 1991).[1] Use of computers in community organizing and social change is detailed by Mizrahi, Downing, Fasano et al. (1991).

Activist and community computing organizations (see Figure 1) serve only a minuscule fraction of the number who could be involved. Although the notion of "empowering the powerless" is very much part of the community computing movement, the emphasis is often on empowerment in the personal growth and job training sense. For instance, after condemning the bureaucracy-enhancing effects of

Figure 1: Examples of Activist Computing

*** Big Sky Telegraph**
A project of Western Montana College which has published an extensive guidebook to community computing (Odasz, 1990). It provides a network linking Montana women's centers, while at the same time it seeks to "empower" rural one-room schools, encourage "grassroots" economic initiatives, promote public health issues, and offer college courses on-line.

*** New York Computer Activists**
An political activist computer support group (see Downing et al., 1991: 3). Activities of such groups include organizing workshops to share computer knowledge among activists, applying computing to activities like voter registration or tenant organizing, or networking in support of causes such as refugees, peace, and the environment (McCullough, 1991).

*** Computing for women's groups**
For a listing of women's computer groups, see Eastman, 1991: 50-53). A particular focus is working through small grass-roots community organizations which would otherwise lack access (Levy, 1989; Cordero, 1991).

*** Public Data Access, Inc.**
An organization which has played an important role in disseminating on-line information about toxic waste dumps (see Goldman, 1991).

*** Jesse Jackson campaign, 1988**
Various groups provided computer and telecommunications access for minority presidential candidate Jesse Jackson in 1988 (see Bernstein, 1991).

* Playing to Win (New York City) and Computers And You (San Francisco)
Community computing organizations.

computing in social services, Kolleck (1993: 463) argues that "the powers which are in new techniques have to be given back to the people to help them stand on their own and act responsibly."

However, the specific empowering reforms Kolleck advocates are simply introducing computer courses in youth centers, providing more computer education to the disadvantaged, and decentralizing information and counseling through computer telecommunications. Worthy as these objectives are, they are not of the type likely to alter the nature of American democracy or change empowerment levels in society. Even when directed at strengthening activist political groups, effects are minor compared to the simultaneous IS advances by organizations with which such groups contend. All of this is not well calculated to have any significant impact on American political or economic structures.

Computers and Civic Democracy

As McCullough notes, information in and of itself is not power, nor need it be an activist threat to power (McCullough, 1991: 12). Information and telecommunications technologies such as voice mail, computers, interactive cable television, touch-screen kiosks in malls, and electronic bulletin boards have been used by local governments in Kansas City, MO; Mercer Island, WA; Pasadena, CA; and by the New York Municipal Management Association (*Public Management*, 1989). This sort of role sees IS as a "tool of governance", not a vehicle of revolutionary upheaval. IS reinforces participatory involvement in local government in relatively minor ways having minor impacts. Civic computing of this type seems to be more representative of the realistic potential of IS rather than the more radical impacts envisioned by some of early 'electronic democracy' advocates.

Many computer-based information services now exist to enhance civic affairs without any pretense of affecting politics. The California General Assembly's "Capitol Connection" electronic bulletin board was an early experiment in providing access to legislative issues and a forum for discussion of policy issues with legislative staff and with other citizens (Fredell, 1987).[2]

In the 1980s, the City of New Orleans experimented with a human services-oriented public data access system operating in conjunction with that city's cable television system (Ruberg, 1989). The People's

Electronic Exchange of Somerville, N.J., provides a medium for on-line classified ads and community announcements (Balas, 1990). Others include Hawaii FYI, National Capital Freenet, Cupertino (CA) City Net, and the Community Computer Network in Wellington, New Zealand (Cisler, 1993). Similarly, libraries around the country have begun offering on-line access to their card catalogs as well as adult-education listings, city and school board meeting calendars and minutes, and other civic information (Mallory, 1991).

The civic democracy orientation toward computing is also reflected in groups such as Computer Professionals for Social Responsibility, the Center for Informatics Law at the John Marshall Law School, and the Electronic Frontier Foundation. Themes at the 1991 Electronic Democracy Conference[3] made use of government electronic data by the media, making such data available to public and educational interests, forming "an electronic Bill of Rights", creating "twenty four hour city halls" through telecommunications, influencing government information policy for public interest ends, and other freedom of information concerns. Some of this has found its way into everyday practice. For instance, Public Technology, Inc., and IBM have supported 24-hour city hall projects placing electronic kiosks in over a dozen municipalities.

A survey by Dutton (1992) found that "electronic democracy" initiatives of local governments fall into the five general categories of broadcasting (e.g., touch-screen multimedia PCs used to disseminate civic information), transaction processing (e.g., use of magnetic 'smart cards' in the New York City food stamp program), public records access (e.g., dial-up electronic bulletin boards in the Pasadena, CA, PARIS/PALS program), interpersonal communication (e.g., computer conferencing in Santa Monica's PEN system: see Figure 2-2 [4]), and surveying/monitoring (e.g., electronic surveillance as in Caltrans experiments with toll collections). While individually worthwhile, none of the five promise radically democratizing effects.

Electronic civic democracy is necessarily limited by the very propensity of on-line communications to dramatically increase the volume of information flow. This was illustrated, when in 1993, the White House announced the availability of direct electronic mail access to President Clinton and Vice President Gore[5]. Part of the 'Americans Communicating Electronically' (ACE) project of several federal agencies to increase information access, White House e-mail did not mean Bill Clinton read your message. Rather, the White House selected from among several software packages which "read" e-mail and responded with the electronic equivalent of form letters. Although form letter responses had long dominated White House mail operations, up to then at least some human being had actually examined each incoming letter. The new on-line system increased access to the White House but that access was reduced to poll-like tally results calculated by e-mail software.

Figure 2: Mini-Case: PEN Brings Electronic Democracy to Santa Barbara, California

The Public Electronic Network (PEN) was established in Santa Monica to allow citizens to contact officials and each other electronically (Dutton and Guthrie, 1991). Available on a 24-hour basis from 35 public terminals in libraries, parks, and neighborhood centers, PEN acquired 1,300 users within its first four months in 1989 and had grown to 3,000 registered users and 300 online discussion groups by the following year (Pitta, 1990). It now reaches 7,000 callers per month (Kantor, 1992).

Upon dialing in using a computer with a modem, the citizen is presented with four menu choices:

* "City Hall" gives access to city meeting agendas, minutes, staff reports, and public documents, along with trash collection schedules and other information.

* "Community Center" provides a city social services directory, the public library card catalog, listings of civic and sporting events, and special interest news (e.g., senior citizens).

* "Mailroom" provides electronic mail to officials or other citizens. Citizens can submit comments to city officials and get an answer within 24 hours.

* "Conference Center" allows citizens to read and comment upon ongoing public bulletin-board discussions on topics like crime and planning. The system remembers when a given citizen last logged on and highlights new entries since then.

PEN has been used to report construction sites operating beyond legal hours, to protest against erecting a parking garage, and to alert people to the operations of a con man (Antonoff, 1989b). Being city-sponsored, PEN prohibits political campaigning but efforts have been undertaken to involve poorer and less educated citizens as well as citizens who are already computer literate (*New York Times*, 1989: A14).

Electronic Democracy: Summary

Whether from the perspective of political activism or the more moderate viewpoint of civic democracy, "Bill of Rights" issues arise in many aspects of computing. The National Research and Education Network, a multi-million dollar government-university-corporate communications project), for instance, has sought to address explicitly many "Bill of Rights" issues see Figure 3). An illustration of such issues arose in 1991 when Communist regimes in Eastern Europe and the former USSR were in the process dissolving. The "Acceptable Use Policy" of the Corporation for Research and Educational Networking (CREN, which runs BitNet and other networks) defines the purpose of its networks to "facilitate the exchange of information consistent with the academic, educational and research purposes of its members". This policy holds uses to be "not acceptable" unless explicitly endorsed by CREN policy. Some have argued that these policies should have prohibited the use of its networks for political messages during the 1991 events in the former Communist Bloc (Goodman, 1992). Others, of course, saw such prohibition as censorship and denial of access rights.

While it is unlikely to lead to a massive upsurge in direct democracy, information systems inherently pose issues which are fundamental to democracy. NREN is particularly open to these issues because of being in a formative stage, because of the collegial culture of its university basis, and because of its dependence on massive public subsidy. Nonetheless, all major IS projects raise similar issues of control and democracy. While power and computing have always been intertwined, the popularization of computers in the last decade has heightened sensitivity to issues of computerization, telecommunications, and political control.

The Vision of a Network Nation

While revolution is not in the cards for the politics of society at large, many writers have seen in new technology the seeds for a strikingly different future which would revolutionize and democratize organizational structure. Three decades ago, Marshall McLuhan (1964) popularized computer technology and telecommunications as

Figure 3: Mini-Case: NREN Wrestles with Governing Electronic Democracy

The National Research and Education Network (NREN) was in the process of wrestling with governance issues in the early 1990s. Advocates of an "Electronic Bill of Rights" raised these democratic questions:

1. ***How will the network be governed and managed, and by whom?*** Special focus must be on equality of access to the network and its resources as well as on participation in the governance of the network by all classes of users.

2. ***Who will have the ability to influence and control decisions about the management of the network?*** Will all classes of end users have the right to voice their needs or to call decision makers to task? Who will decide the resources to be placed on the network, the pricing of these resources, and the access rights to them? The network should enable more access to government documents and resources, taking care not to disenfranchise those without network connections.

3. ***Will different users have different kinds of access right to network resources?*** Or will all users have the same access rights? Will pricing structures and incentives be the same for all classes of users?

4. ***How will the rights to free speech and privacy of network communications and data be balanced with other rights?*** These other rights include the need to ensure the security of the system (e.g., viruses), to prevent illegal activities (e.g., fraud, theft), and to regulate material that may be offensive to community or national standards (e.g., pornography, abusive communications, unwanted junk mail). Who will make these decisions? What kinds of due process rights will govern these issues? What rights, duties, and liabilities, if any, exist for end users?" (For further discussion, see Connolly, Gilbert, and Lyman, 1991: 54-55).

forces which were creating a "global village" uniting everyone, everywhere, to everything. Works which have popularized the notion of an organizational revolution rooted in telecommunications include Hiltz and Turoff's *The Network Nation* (1978) and Toffler's *The Third Wave* (1980). Toffler wrote, for example, "What is inescapably clear, however, whatever we choose to believe, is that we are altering our info-sphere fundamentally... we are adding a whole new strata of communication to the social system. The emerging Third Wave info-sphere makes that of the Second Wave era— dominated by its mass media, the post office, and the telephone—seem hopelessly primitive by contrast (Toffler, 1980: 172). In this section we look at two critical aspects of the "network nation": (1) telecommuting and the vision of the "electronic cottage", and (2) groupware as a new generation of software which supports interactive, collaborative work using computers and telecommunications. Both telecommuting and groupware harbor the belief that physical offices may be displaced in the future by "virtual offices" with employees located geographically anywhere.

Telecommuting and the Electronic Cottage

The possibility exists that telecommunications will lead to a vast expansion of telecommuting - employees who work at home on their computers and send in their work via telecommunications networks. Networks may lead to geographic dispersion, with managers and staff working in places which are physically remote from one another. Giuliano called this the displacement of the physical office by the "virtual office" (Giuliano, 1982). In addition to effects on organizational structure, some exponents of "the electronic cottage" predict broad social effects. Toffler (1980), for instance, forecasts a vast expansion of personal freedom arising from work at home rather than in the office or factory. This is not entirely a new prediction. Jack Nilles, a California consultant, coined the term "telecommuting" in 1973. He predicted that by 1993 it would cease to be an aberration and become a mainstream practice (Furger, 1989: 45). While that reality has not yet come about,telecommuting is a vision which has widespread popular support. A survey of 500 federal workers found that although the overwhelming majority were not permitted to do so, four out of five (83%) would like to work at home (Temin, 1992: 1).

Although telecommuting expansion has not been as rapid as predicted there has been a steady growth (see Figure 2-4). Estimates of telecommuting at the end of the 1980s, after networking and distributed processing were becoming widespread, optimistically place the number of telecommuters at one million workers (futurist Jack Nilles, quoted in Antonoff, 1989a: 165). More recent optimistic estimates of the Link Resources Corporation hold that in 1992 there were 6.6 million telecommuters in the United States, expanding at an annual rate of 19% (Violino and Stahl, 1993: 23).[6] Of these, some

Figure 4: Telecommuting: Selected Examples

*** Federal Telecommuting Experiments**
An experimental telecommuting program was begun in July 1990, involving 400 workers in 12 agencies. Representative Thomas McMillen (D, MD) has proposed a Telecommuting Act which would establish five federal telecommuting satellite offices coordinated by a new Office of Telecommuting in the National Telecommunications and Information Agency of the Commerce Department (Quindlen, 1992c).

*** U. S. Department of Health and Human Services (HHS)**
Remote-session software enables employees to work at home installing computer hardware and software anywhere in America (Olsen, 1989). Using remote session software the installation expert can "take control" of computers located on the other side of the country and confirm or change the installation at that site.

*** State of California**
The state of California began telecommuting experiments in the 1980s. Over 200 employees did word processing, accounting, and other tasks at home, saving the state an estimated $25 million annually in the cost of leasing office space, not to mention energy conservation, reduction of air pollution, reduction of traffic congestion, and other public benefits (Antanoff, 1985; Savage, 1988; Flemming, 1988; Altman, 1989b).

*** City of Los Angeles**
Fifteen staff members of the Office of Contract Monitoring of the City of Los Angeles operate almost totally by telecommuting, meeting face-to-face only in weekly staff meetings: some 1,700 other LA workers telecommute (Desky, 1991: 20).

*** Private Sector**
In the private sector there are even more experiments, such as those at IBM and U. S. West.

18% were in the public sector, health, and education. Others suggest the numbers are considerably smaller and growth is less than media hype suggests (*Telecommuting Review*. 1988). Although only about one in five telecommuters does works at home for 35 hours a week or more, many more workers want to do so than have been able.[7]

Other enthusiasts for electronic democracy such as Turoff and Hiltz recognize that the predicted telecommuting revolution is more like telecommuting evolution. Even the optimistic predictions of Link Resources Corporation project the number of full-time telecommuters at only a little over 2 million by 1995. Turoff and Hiltz place greater expectations on networking of individuals located *within* organiza-

Figure 5: Telecommuting: Pro

*** Improved Morale**
Wendell Joice, personnel resource psychologist at the U. S. Office of Personnel Management (OPM) argues that "Telecommuting improves morale and reduces cost in the long term" (Desky, 1991: 1).

*** Improved Productivity**
Economic benefits may include reduced absenteeism, reduced costs for office space, reduced travel costs, increased employee retention, and increased productivity. U. S. West, a Colorado telecommunications company which established telecommuting for 500 of its 70,000 employees, discovered productivity gains of up to 30% for some workers (Piturro, 1989b: 35). Direct costs of telecommuting are relatively minor, from about $2,000 to $10,000 per employee for equipment, software, and phone lines.

*** Social Benefits**
Societal side benefits of telecommuting include reduced traffic, reduced demand on day-care facilities, and increased support for family values.

tions. Straub and Wetherbe (1989: 1338) likewise write, "The office of the late 1990s can now be envisioned. Its staff of professionals and managers are surrounded by intelligent devices that speak, listen, or interact with them to determine what is to be accomplished and how it is to be done. Contacts with other departments, other divisions, customers, vendors, and other organizations are made with little effort and without human intervention." They emphasize, "This social change will be accompanied by vastly expanded communications links made possible by the networking technologies" (p. 1338).

It is interesting to note that Paul Cray, one of the authors of the first book predicting a telecommuting revolution (Nilles et al., 1976) now sees far less effect than expected, in spite of better technology. Although telecommuting has some major "pros", it also has some strong "cons" (see Figures 2-5 and 2-6). While some studies show telecommuters are more productive than fellow employees this may be due to self-selection. That is, telecommuters may be more productive individuals in the first place. Olson (1989b) found telecommuters were highly work-involved people who were also loners, with relatively low needs for either affiliation or dominance. Cray believes that only something like a gasoline crisis of severe and enduring propor-

Figure 6: Telecommuting: Con

*** Can Be Exploitative**
Telecommuting can be a device for the exploitation of women workers and others whose need to be at home makes them willing to work for less (Bailyn, 1989).

*** Can Harm Professional Relationships**
Clerical workers engaged in telecommuting have found that relationships with supervisors deteriorated, child care responsibilities intruded, and job satisfaction diminished.

*** May Merely Amplify Existing Tendencies**
Studies suggest that telecommuting amplifies existing tendencies: traditionally low-freedom clerical workers can be reduced to piece work in a sort of reversion to early industrial control mechanisms while relatively high-freedom professionals working at home may experience a greater sense of personal control (Olson and Primps, 1984).

*** Often Opposed by Unions**
Because of negatives such as these, belief that home work will undermine the capacity for employees to discuss issues and collectively bargain, and remembrance of their fight for anti-sweatshop legislation in the 1940s, labor unions have generally opposed telecommuting (Falbowski, 1987; Hamilton, 1987).

*** Raises Other Complex Problems and Issues**
Telecommuting raises a host of thorny issues: local zoning laws about work at home, the issue of overtime pay for home work, workmen compensation and homeowner insurance problems, discrimination issues vis-a-vis existing and prospective employees who do not own equipment needed for telecommuting, issues of the extent organizations should finance in-home office improvements for the homeowner, security needs, and family issues such as bringing the stress of work into the home.

tions could lead to general mass acceptance of telecommuting apart from an unrepresentative core group. Acceptance would be particularly difficult in the public sector where physical absence from the workplace seems in conflict with heavy emphasis on accountability (Cross and Raizman, 1986). Public employees fear becoming an "invisible worker," and hence, home computing is likely to be a supplement, not a replacement for on-site office work (Hiltz and Turoff, 1978; Mills, 1984). Likewise, in the private sector Olson (1989b) found evidence of resistance to telecommuting among managers charged with their supervision and also found little demonstrable benefit to the organizations themselves in spite of its appeal to certain types of workers for whom job satisfaction increased as a result of telecommuting.

In what has been called "the most complete research project on telecommuting in the country", the Washington State Energy Office in Seattle studied telecommuters in 25 public, private, and non-profit organizations over two years. The study revealed a number of negative impacts. One-third of supervisors reported lower productivity from telecommuters and higher workload for remaining at job-site workers. Some one-third of telecommuters dropped out of the program at some point. The proportion of managers rating their staff as "very good" or "excellent" declined from 76% to only 68% after telecommuting and the proportion stating that their employees "needed improvement" rose from 2% to 10% (Violino and Stahl, 1993: 24).

In spite of the possibilities, studies of telecommuting suggest that rather than increasing freedom for all workers, it may merely amplify existing tendencies: traditionally low-freedom clerical workers can be reduced to piece work in a sort of reversion to early industrial control mechanisms while relatively high-freedom professionals working at home may experience a greater sense of personal control (Olson and Primps, 1984). Forcing telecommuters to purchase their own home technology is another common throw-back to nineteenth-century work practices (Violino and Stahl, 1993: 24). Telecommuting can be a device for the exploitation of women workers and others whose need to be at home makes them willing to work for less (Bailyn, 1989). Clerical workers engaged in telecommuting have found that relationships with supervisors deteriorated, child care responsibilities intruded, and job satisfaction diminished.

Because of negatives such as these, the belief that telecommuting will undermine the capacity for employees to discuss issues and collectively bargain, and remembrance of their fight for anti-sweat-shop legislation in the 1940s, labor unions have generally opposed telecommuting (Falbowski, 1987; Hamilton, 1987). And telecommuting raises a host of thorny issues: local zoning laws about work at home, the issue of overtime pay for home work, workmen compensation and homeowner insurance problems, discrimination issues vis-a-vis existing and prospective employees who do not own equipment needed for telecommuting, issues of the extent organizations should finance in-home office improvements for the homeowner, security needs, and family issues such as bringing the stress of work into the home.

Even among professionals, telecommuting may lessen organizational commitment, or at least give that appearance and make it less likely managers will welcome it (Olson and Primps,1984). Perin (1991b) found that professionals' reluctance to telecommute stems partly from the widespread belief that physical distance from the office increases the social distance as well, attenuating management trust and eroding career standing. Gurstein (1990) found telecommuting greatly reduced opportunity for promotion in large organizations, leading home workers to a preference for part-time rather than full-time telecommuting. Managers and fellow employees may suspect the telecommuter, protected by the privacy of home, of shirking on office work. In general, the future success of telecommuting depends on reorienting traditional management culture and increasing the level of trust (and decreasing oversight) within the organization. That is, it depends on issues of implementation, team development, and changing organizational information cultures.

Groupware: Computer-Supported Cooperative Work

While telecommuting remains a distant goal for most workers, another aspect of the "network nation" vision is closer to realization. Computer-supported cooperative work (CSCW) reflects the belief that networking can be combined with applications software to transform the way many work groups go about their tasks (Galegher, Kraut, and Egido, 1990; Bowers and Benford, eds., 1991; Greenbaum and Kyng, eds., 1991; Greenberg, ed., 1991). Jan Mouritsen and Niels Bjorn-Anderson see in work group computing, which they call "orgware", the culmination of IS evolution. "Often office systems," they write, seem to fail because of an overemphasis on the technical and economic aspects of systems development and a relative neglect of sociopolitical concerns" (Mouritsen and Bjorn-Anderson, 1991: 308).

Mouritsen and Bjorn-Anderson argue that the first IS wave was the hardware stage with its tool perspective and focus on data processing. The second wave, epitomized by Macintosh's desktop icon metaphor, was the software stage with a communications perspective and a focus on communication media. The culmination, they believe, will be a third wave with a sociopolitical perspective focusing on conflict mediation using orgware to promote sharing information among groups, departments, and organizations.

In addition to the little-used "orgware" label, work group computing software is also known as groupware, computer-supported cooperative work (CSCW), productivity software, electronic meeting systems (EMS), and group decision support software (GDSS)[8]. Various authors have used "groupware" to refer broadly to any software designed to work in a distributed environment, which is to say, most major applications (databases, spreadsheets, statistical packages; cf. Dunkle, 1990). However, most reserve the term to refer to software which facilitates task-oriented interactions on a network. Robert Johansen of the Institute of the Future, a promoter of CSCW, has defined no fewer than 17 different meanings of groupware, including software for face-to-face meetings, support for remote electronic conferencing, and tool support between meetings (Karon, 1987b; Johansen, 1988). In practice, though, groupware may take the simple form of straightforward electronic mail systems which expedite organizational communications but do not change organizational structure and work practices.[9]

The Case for Computer-Supported Cooperative Work.

One of the foremost arguments for CSCW is that it replaces traditional serial work organization with a more complex, interactive process rich in feedback for the participants. In *Enterprise Networking: Working Together Apart* (1992), Digital Equipment Corporation marketing executive Ray Grenierand management consultant George Metes note that traditional work was divided among work groups who would serially undertake a series of steps such as product specification, design, assembling resources (people, tools, components, information), prototyping, testing and revision, production, and marketing.) The problem with serial work organization is lack of feedback from later steps to earlier ones.

Grenier and Metes discussed such concrete examples of serial work organization as the construction of a 45-story New York office building, where designers located heavy elevator equipment where builders had erected a floor incapable of bearing the load and where lights illuminating the building's copper roof could not be accessed by maintenance staff who were blocked by permanently sealed windows. In general, serial work organization can fail to provide information necessary to make effective decisions in such cases. This happens whenever the factors associated with work are such that "everything is related to everything else" rather than the simple situation where each stage is a self-contained problem with little bearing on later stages.

Because interrelatedness is the rule, not the exception, Grenier and Metes argue for a new organizational paradigm or organizing principle which they label "simultaneous distributed work" (SDW). Under SDW, all stakeholders in a work process from designers to consumers can work concurrently as a team throughout the life of a project. Distributed processing using groupware on networks allows the team to be at physically remote locations one from another. Through electronic mail, teleconferencing, hypermedia access to

Figure 7: Groupware in the Department of Defense

The Groupware Center for Functional Process Improvement implements computer-supported cooperative work (CSCW) in the Department of Defense. It is specifically designed to support group decision-making about the creation of new agency information systems.

Located at the Washington Navy Yard, it offers an electronic meeting system combined with capabilities for "what if" simulation. Users can collaboratively conduct "strategic vision" sessions, model new systems, document solutions, and create technical and data plans.

The core of the groupware process requires agency participants to define clearly and justify their roles. While this can be a source of resistance to using the Center, it is also central to its strategy for business systems improvement.

The Center uses *Group Systems V* software from the Ventana Corporation (Tucson, AZ). This software allows participants to brainstorm electronically and to cast votes. A human facilitator is provided by the Center to assist electronic meeting processes (e.g., editing documents to eliminate redundant input).

A component of the system is the Business Process Improvement Program (BPIP), created under Paul Strassman, a director of Defense information in the 1980s. BPIP provides a structured framework to help groups work through modeling their business processes with a view to their improvement or elimination (Endoso, 1993).

designs, group decision support utilities, and other work group computing tools, team members can be in perpetual interaction providing maximum feedback from each part of the team to each other.

Actual organizations involve many informal and unstructured groups, centers, channels, grapevines, cliques, gatekeepers, and other liaisons (Mintzberg, 1979). These are ignored by formal organizational structure but are potentially tied together in an effective working whole by groupware. Management's role under the new paradigm shifts from that of establishing and then enforcing a preconceived set of specifications and plans to that of shepherding a dynamic process of connectivity and interoperability.

Productivity is a second foundation stone of the case for computer-supported cooperative work, in addition to benefits of replacing serial work with simultaneous distributed work. Indeed, "productivity software" is sometimes used as a synonym for work group software. For instance, in a controlled experiment comparing decision-making in an ordinary conference room with face-to-face contact, a conference room augmented with electronic mail, and a conference room augmented with an electronic blackboard which could display everyone's input, outside evaluators found the electronic blackboard setting to yield the most ideas and to display the highest quality of decision-making. Traditional face-to-face conferencing scored the lowest (Rein and Ellis, 1989). Likewise, Bullen and Bennett (1991: 282) found that groupware could "reduce the volume and complexity of information so that managing the content and meaning of information could dominate managing volume." That is, the information channeling aspects of groupware can free managers to concentrate on analysis rather than just massaging.

Groupware has other productivity benefits. Among the easiest to document are travel and personnel time savings when electronic meetings replace regional or national conferences. The Army uses *GroupSystems V* (Ventana Corp., Tucson, AZ) to implement electronic meeting systems, even on a global basis. One report cited $125,000 savings in travel and personnel cost-avoidance in a project completed in 3.5 days rather than the usual four to six weeks (Olsen, 1992a: 27). IBM has an extensive electronic meeting systems (EMS) project used by over 15,000 people. It claims a 55% average improvement in group performance, with even more dramatic time savings (Grohowski, McGoff, Vogel, Martz, and Nunamaker, 1990).

Problems of Computer-Supported Cooperative Work.

Groupware does not always work as suggested in advertisements. Applications such as video-conferencing, on-line calendars, meeting schedulers, collaborative writing, weighted group decision-making, and other forms of CSCW which arose in the 1980s had an image of expensive, repeated failure (Grudin, 1988). Although electronic mail and on-line information services are now commonplace, specifically CSCW offerings such as group calendaring software are still rare (Bullen and Bennett, 1991). Few organizations have purchased specialized computer conferencing systems (Kling, 1991: 84). Successful groupware requires careful attention to a long list of social as well as technical factors (such as those enumerated by Ellis, Gibbs, and Rein, 1991), including turn-taking protocols, reversibility of decisions, handling concurrent attempts to control, employing an intuitive group interface, and so on. Because of its intertwined sociotechnical nature, the impact of groupware on an organization varies widely from setting to setting (Johnson-Lentz and Johnson-Lentz, 1982).

Given this background, many organizations have opted to delay installation of computer-supported cooperative work software or to

Figure 8: Groupware in the 1980s

* Conference on Computer-Supported Cooperative Work, 1986
The first major conference on CSCW is held in Austin, TX.

* An extensive literature developed, 1988-1989
Ex.: Carasik and Grantham, 1988; Greif, 1988; Olson, ed., 1989a.

* <u>Work-Group Computing Report</u>, 1989
A specialized journal arose to cover and promote what promised to be the "software revolution of the 1990s". It was believed that whereas the 1980s were marked by stand-alone use of word processors, spreadsheets, databases, and graphics packages, the 1990s would be characterized by counterparts which could be accessed on a group basis for collaborative work, seamlessly integrating them with electronic mail, decision support software, group calendar schedulers, and on-line help facilities.

Figure 9: Groupware in the 1990s

* National Science Foundation CSCW Grants, 1991
NSF's Computer and Information Science and Engineering Directorate established three programs to support CSCW (Rosenberg, 1991). The Coordination Theory and Collaboration Technology Special Initiative gave awards for "collaboratories" for work group computing. The Database and Expert Systems Program coordinated use of collaboratory designs for access to knowledge in large distributed databases. The Gigabit Network Project funded research on group collaboration using the new high-speed networks being funded by Congress and being coordinated by the NSF.

* COMDEX, 1991
At a major trade show, Intel's president emphasized groupware in a keynote address while Apple Computer's John Sculley said CSCW would play a critical role product designs for the 1990s (Wohl, 1991: 10). By 1991 most business and governmental PCs had become networked. On this basis, the "office of the future" was predicted to lead to flexible interaction of professionals electronically rather than through traditional contact.

* IBM Allies with Lotus Development Corporation, 1991
IBM and Lotus allied to include *Lotus Notes* workgroup software as part of IBM's *OfficeVision* desktop system. It supports network communications, shared memos and reports, adding comments, developing collaborative documents, and using the work group version of *Lotus 1-2-3* (*Tele-commuting Review*, 1991).

* Microsoft Corporation Enters the Competition, 1992
Microsoft Corporation, the largest software vendor, in late 1992 launched *Microsoft Windows for Workgroups* and a suite of 19 CSCW applications for group authoring of text and presentation graphics documents, upkeep of document libraries for networked users, electronic mail, and group memory applications (electronic bulletin boards, scheduling software, brainstorming software; see *PC Week*, 1992). *Windows NT* was released in 1993 as a 32-bit *Windows* systems for advanced networking applications involving workgroup computing.

go with simpler alternatives. Advocates (e.g., *Technology and Learning*, 1992) argue that workgroup computing will receive speedy acceptance because it is software which works, because there is agreement that collaborative skills are needed, and because local area networks are increasingly available. In spite of some successes, however, it is not clear that the groupware vision will be the "software revolution of the 1990s". Although a number of large organizations have begun experimentation with workgroup computing, there are alternatives such as simple use of local area networks for communications, teleconferencing rooms, and decision support rooms (using DSS software combined with other brainstorming and prioritizing aids) may prove equally or more attractive in the long run.

Even when groupware is selected as the preferred method, it suffers from a variety of other problems. One is the lack of e-mail standardization and the inability of most existing software distribution channels to provide the very high level of customer support that complex, networked groupware packages require (Nash, 1991). Groupware, unlike many other computer innovations, cannot be approached on an individual-by-individual basis. Rather there is a critical mass problem: before it is worth any person doing it, a majority of the work group must adopt it. Also, if it does elicit widespread use, groupware can burden a company's or agency's network and slow down other essential traffic. Finally, when used for collaborative writing, groupware raises thorny issues of copyright law, particularly is the collaborative document is to be used on more than an in-house basis (Ratcliffe, 1991).

Because the productivity of groupware cannot just be assumed, CSCW software may be required to prove its worth in terms of benefits outweighing costs. Hewlett-Packard, for instance, abandoned its worldwide teleconferencing system for R&D not because it did not work but because it was difficult to cost-justify when budget-cutting became necessary (Fanning and Raphael, 1986: 293). The difficulty of managers in documenting whether its costs are really recouped in greater productivity benefits is compounded by conversion costs associated with the sheer size of the base of installed users of stand-alone software. Resistance of employees to changing the way they work is a problem common in CSCW, and overcoming resistance involves costly investments in organization development, training, support staff, and sometimes even in direct incentives (Hayes, 1992).

What end-users did in the 1980s on a stand-alone basis has considerable inertia in the 1990s. Groupware will prove appealing in work settings where tasks already require active collaboration but may prove a "hard sell" when IS staff proposes changing existing work practices to take advantage of groupware. As Esther Dyson (1988: 21) has pointed out, groupware typically "is unlikely to be easily or universally accepted because it monitors what people are accomplishing, is explicit about the state of their work and their position in the work and company hierarchy, and is unforgiving regarding decision and timing requirements." It is hardly surprising, she concludes, that employees usually prefer traditional methods based on communications which provide a social buffer for the individual in the form of eufunctional ambiguity, interpersonal allowances, and evolving rather than fixed work commitments.

Computer-Supported Cooperative Work: A Summary

In general, groupware has been found to succeed in organizations which already support information sharing, whereas in unsupportive organizational cultures the introduction of groupware has little effect (Kydd and Jones, 1989). For instance, if individuals are working together closely on a project, electronic mail will be substituted for face-to-face contact but the mere existence of e-mail will not prompt other workers to communicate if that is not already an established pattern (Reder and Schwab, 1989). A study of one company's nationwide groupware found that it tended to succeed within homogenous groups, not groups differing in status, values and missions (Bikson, 1987: 171). Naturally, groupware has its greatest impact on teams whose members are widely scattered and who could rarely meet face to face without it (DeJean, 1988: 75). The enthusiasm of the group leader for the technology is a major factor in its success (Rein and Ellis, 1989). So too are good success stories, suggesting the wisdom of investing in support of early adopters (Francik, Rudman, Cooper, and Levine, 1991: 62).

Problems of groupware may lead to marketing disappointments to computer industry leaders, part of whose enthusiasm for groupware lies in the fact that, as Roger Moody, president of Coordination Technology, points out, "White collar workers spend sixty to eighty percent of their time in interaction. That's why seventy-five percent of them don't use PCs" (Wohl, 1992: 12). Groupware is intended to change that but its adoption, as narrowly defined, may prove slower than optimistic industry estimates were predicting in the early 1990s. On the other hand, networking, electronic mail, and distributed processing have already become well entrenched in American organizational life. In this broader sense, workgroup computing is becoming consolidated on a widespread basis in the 1990s.

The ascendency of electronic mail and electronic bulletin boards may be associated with a decline in face-to-face meetings in some organizations. Halachmi refers to this as the shift from "work group" to "workgroup". He writes, "As the workgroup replaces the work group, organizations must reinvest some of the productivity gains in the organization to compensate employees for the loss of opportunities to interact with each other" (Halachmi, 1992: 533). Dysfunctional information technology effects such as threats to privacy, security, and health of employees are problems and costs from a managerial viewpoint.

Extensive use of groupware often requires changing the information culture of the organization. As Sandler (1988) notes, if groupware is seen as part of a strategy of enhancing productivity through better information sharing and coordination, then access to information must be speeded up. Specifically, Sandler argues that information must become "everybody's right", free of political haggling over individual and group rights to information sources. This is similar to what Shoshana Zuboff has called the conversion from automating organizations to "informating" organizations (Zuboff, 1988a). However, knowledge is power. Groupware can be seen as an effort to redistribute that power and hence politics and resistance are to be expected.

The Network Nation: A Summary

Some believe that organizations as we know them will disappear in the coming "network nation." Virtual offices will replace physical offices as employees telecommute or at least participate in computer-supported cooperative work. Some even foresee that organizational hierarchies will give way to online information marketplaces which individual professionals accumulate credits according to the rate of use of their reports or other work. If not the "computer revolution of the 1990s", enough examples exist to show these trends bear watching. It seems likely that computing and telecommunications will lead to greater communications volume, more diverse patterns of intra- and inter-organizational communications, and less top management control over information flow.[10] Distributed processing is moving IS and organizations generally at least somewhat in the direction of satellite work centers linked to main offices by telecommunications (Olson, 1983).

On the other hand, the revolutionary predictions of organizational democracy through networks and computer-supported cooperative work are premature at best. The evidence to date is much more in the direction summarized by Kraemer and King (1986), that the organization's top management is, if anything, strengthened by its firm and growing central control over new information technologies. Although data centers are more supportive of end-user computing and client-server networks in the 1990s compared to a decade earlier, they are also far more centralized (Caldwell, 1992d).[11] Likewise, Kraut (1987c) found that telecommuting reinforced existing office structures and was not leading to structural change and innovation. The Cypress Semiconductor case (see Figure 2-10), likewise, shows anything but organizational democracy arising from computer-supported cooperative work. The network nation is coming, but it is coming much more slowly than some have predicted and with far less revolutionary consequences.

Figure 10: Mini-Case: CSCW at Cypress Semiconductor Corporation

Cypress Semiconductor Corporation (CSC) of San Jose, California, chose to implement computer-supported cooperative work in the late 1980s. CSC's management philosophy was guided by performance perfectionism, minimal bureaucracy, and a quest for ever-higher productivity per worker. It achieved an outstanding income record compared to competitors and credit for this has been given to groupware used by the firm (Govoni, 1992).

The CSC groupware system not only made information on every unit available to every other unit, it also broadcast data so the good and bad performance of each unit was publicized. Employee activities were monitored closely and performance measured in detail. A "goal management system" required employees to input explicit aims, priorities, and estimated task completion dates.

Under this system, employees with a goal-delinquency rate of 20% or more were singled out for attention. One aspect of the custom-written groupware was "killer software". The computer monitored unit inventory every four hours and if any unit was found to be slipping behind schedule then all computers in that unit were automatically shut down until the problem was corrected (e.g., until parts were finally moved to the production line). Likewise, killer software in purchasing stopped all raw materials from entering CSC when a supplier failed to deliver materials by the expected date.

CSC employees frequently felt the groupware system was too quantitative and intrusive, but the system was strongly supported by management, which was motivated by the apparent productivity success of the system.

Conclusion: Is Computing Democratizing America?

Even before the explosion of computer infrastructure in the 1980s, the issue of information technology and power had become a major concern (Mowshowitz, 1976; Weizenbaum, 1976). In spite of widespread concerns, computer and telecommunications technology is a moving target. Rapid change makes it difficult to discuss and evaluate. Trends anticipated for the remainder of the 1990s include very high bandwidth channels, development of interactive three-dimensional video, shape recognition cameras, virtual reality as a communication medium, and team workstations. Interactive television, real-time digital video transmission, and other networking breakthroughs are already technically possible, but implementation will depend on the extent corporations and perhaps governments invest in building a fiber optic national gigabit network (Thyfault, 1992b). Trends early in the twenty-first century may include computer-mediated high bandwidth global telecommunications, full-motion digital video, and 3D telepresence (Rheingold, 1991a).

As Danziger (1986) noted several years ago, a survey of research on present-day computing, telecommunications, and politics shows little evidence of significant impact. Yet emerging advanced information technologies such as those noted above may change this assessment. Perhaps the most important impact thus far is that cited by Tom Lehman (1991: 246), who observed, "We have gone from optimizing the technology to optimizing the people." That is, computer technology and telecommunications are not only advancing at a rapid pace but are increasingly focused on issues of human interaction. If computer technology is not democratizing America in any "revolutionary" sense, it has begun to change human interactions in many spheres and there is reason to think that future social impacts will be greater than has been the case up until now.

Speculating on future technological impacts is, well, speculative. For instance, regional Bell operating companies (RBOCs) have now been given permission to sell on-line services, but it will be a few years before we can really assess the effects of this court ruling. It is still too early to tell if telecommuting or computer-supported cooperative work software will have the impact their proponents predict. Moreover, forecasts are made more uncertainty because evaluative research is in short supply. More research is still needed on the effects of computing and telecommunications on such topics as productivity, organizational structure, democratic work practices, and equity in information access. Nonetheless, there are some observations we can make about computers, telecommunications, and political power.

Don't Expect Radical Change from Electronic Democracy

Some proposals, such as those to use computer technology to optimize democratic processes, would constitute radical changes if implemented. There is little doubt that some forms of "teledemocracy" are feasible when technological factors are considered alone. For instance, over two decades ago Flood (1978) detailed how interactive communication technology could be wedded to decision theory, social choice theory, and mathematical programming to create what he called "dynamic value voting" (a process in which group members express their preferences through an electronic market). The implementation of ISDN (integrated services digital networks, which permit voice/data/video transmission over a single phone line) and other communications advances make Flood's concepts more feasible than ever today, enabling two-way access through home workstations (Sussman, 1989). Flood suggested that universities might be a good place to test out such a system. However, it is significant that in the decades since Flood's work, no university has taken up the challenge. Technological factors cannot be considered alone when it comes to changing the political process. Teledemocracy requires much more than technological feasibility for adoption—factors such as addressing vested political interests in the present system, fostering civic education enabling and motivating citizens to use teledemocratic tools, and institutionalizing counterbalancing processes which compensate for the dangers inherent in decision-making by mass referenda.

Of course, examples can be cited where computers and telecommunications have been useful tools for democracy. During the pro-democracy upheavals in China in 1989, computer-based telecommunications played a key role in providing news about protests alternative to state-controlled broadcasts (Leitschuh, 1989; Lyons, 1989; Krasnoff, 1989). Ganley (1991) has detailed how information access through computer media has played a critical role in such modern events as the 1978-1979 Islamic revolution in Iran, the 1986 unseating of Ferdinand Marcos in the Philippines, the 1987-1988 attempt to remove General Manuel Noriega as leader of Panama, in 1988 efforts of opposition parties to obtain independent voting results in the Chilean plebiscite, and the 1989 pro-democracy movement in the People's Republic of China. On a lesser scale, the activist network EcoNet was instrumental in promoting Earth Day 1990 around the world (Richardson, 1990) and the women's movement is advanced by various on-line services (Atkinson and Hudson, eds., 1990).[12] Nonetheless, in spite of the assertions of some (e.g., Downing, 1989) that activist networks such as Peacenet in the U. S. are new options for democracy, such uses of telecommunications are dwarfed by conventional system-maintaining telecommunications uses by mainstream institutions. This prevents one from characterizing telecommunications as a whole as an instrument of disruption, empowerment, or structural change even though on occasions it may be.

In spite of the long history of impacts of communications on politics, it is difficult to summarize its net effects on political power. Communications technologies are tools, used by dictators and revolutionaries, incumbents and opponents, business and labor— everyone. To ask for a summary of the impact of telecommunications on political power is like asking how tools of power affect power. They are instruments by which political actions are taken. As the instruments become better, it is possible to take more actions faster at greater distance involving more actors. Improvement in communications tools, including computer-assisted telecommunications, has a tendency to accelerate political activity but not determine its direction or outcome. If there is a direction, it is to be understood, as Beniger (1986) has pointed out, in the context of media as part of a larger system of social control in an information society in which telecommunications, like other media, serve as control mechanisms. On-line access systems remain heavily biased in favor of large organizations and well-to-do individuals who can afford the equipment and charges involved (Newkirk, 1990), an inequity reinforced by the U. S. educational system (Smith-Gratto, 1989).

While radical transformation of American life through implementation of on-line direct democracy is not in the cards, the evidence is not yet in on the impact of computers and computer-assisted telecommunications with regard to everyday functions as part of civic life. In spite of grant programs sponsored by IBM and others, there has been relatively little actual experimentation with use of computers to enhance civic political processes. One exception to this generalization is the public access network instituted in February, 1989, by the city of Santa Monica for its citizens (Pitta, 1990; Varley, 1991). Expecting only a trickle of usage, within two days over 250 users were saturating the new network. "I couldn't believe the interest this generated all over the world,: Ken Phillips, head of Santa Monica's Department of Information Systems was quoted as saying (Wilkinson, 1989: 1). The system allowed residents to file complaints with City Hall officials and get electronic mail answers back on their screens, as well as to obtain information about business licenses, AIDS testing, and many other subjects. By the end of the first week, only 5 residents had gotten on the network and 400 were waiting. City officials were totally unprepared to cope with the level of citizen participation opened up by even this small experiment in "electronic democracy".

However, not all "electronic civics" experiments are successful. A California state legislative committee set up an electronic bulletin board like Santa Monica's in 1987. After a flurry of initial use by 1,000 citizens, it was found only 100 ever bothered to call back and usage dropped to a low level. Later the system was dropped. While the potential for impact is great, usage may be severely limited by lack of ownership of a computer (Santa Monica's mayor doesn't have one, for example), by technical difficulties of communications, by lack of interesting or unique information, by lack of response to messages, and other obstacles. The Santa Monica system seems to appeal to "an adventurous minority of residents" (Yarnall, 1989: 34) and is not the harbinger of profound political changes.

In summary, if we want to find ways in which computer and telecommunications technology is democratizing America, we need to look elsewhere than in the political arena itself. This is not to say computing lacks political effects. However, the suggestive but tiny experiments in electronic direct democracy and even in electronic civics are overwhelmed by the use of technology to reinforce existing political processes. The reinforcing effects of computers are visible from the use of computers in political direct mail fundraising, in daily campaign opinion-polling, in delegate tracking, and in virtually every other aspect of political life one could name. It might be said that computer technology has further democratized America in the sense that routine political processes, such mailings to voters during election campaigns, have become more efficient, targeted, and pervasive than ever. But to find ways in which computer technology seems poised to democratize America in the sense of changing rather than merely reinforcing structure, one must look beyond the formal politics of government an examine the politics of organizational life.

Middle Management Under Seige

One of the most often-cited impacts of computing on organization concerns the erosion of middle management positions. Middle managers took information from the shop-floor or street level and passed it on up the hierarchy in digested form for managers at the top. Computing and telecommunications have made it possible for those at the top to bypass middle managers and directly receive data, summaries, trend lines, aberration reports and other information emanating from lower organizational levels. Many believe this will have a profound effect on organization design much as the automobile changed urban design (e.g., Wigand, 1988: 311).[13]

Middle managers' role has been to collect, analyze, and make recommendations based upon data. Now, in networked setting, top management may find that these information functions may be performed as or more effectively by lower level staff using computers under a broad span of control. That is, networked IS enables top management to reap substantial profits by reducing the relative size of middle management and by reducing the number of levels of management in large organizations. Wigand (1988) has cited numerous examples of corporations reducing middle management in the 1980s as a result of new IS technology.

The one exception to hypothesized middle management shrinkage is the role of IS management itself. As lower-level end-user staff do more and more data collection and analysis on computers, reporting directly to top management, there is a greater and greater need for central IS support to provide assistance. In this way, the IS unit's information centers provide the means for a transition to flatter organizational hierarchies. In terms of organization design the traditional pyramid may give way to a diamond, with clerical positions being distributed organization-wide (Wigand, 1988: 317).

During the late 1970s through the mid 1980s, it seemed that middle management might be immune from the predicted effects of automation. In spite of rapid expansion of IS investment, the ranks of middle managers grew quickly. Indeed, implementing new information systems itself created many middle management positions, such as information center directors, network administrators, and jobs in expanded training departments. However, with economic recession and austerity budgets in the late 1980s and early 1990s, chief executives were pushed to make hard cutback management decisions. Often the choice was to reduce the ranks of middle managers on a permanent basis.

While the erosion of middle management does not necessarily translate into organizational democratization, it does have political implications. Thus Rolf Wigand wrote, "As organization charts are redesigned, chains of command are simplified, and new structures are implemented, the balance of power is changing and shifting in our organizations, largely as a result of information technology. Rigid, hierarchical structures are redesigned, resulting in leaner, more flexible and responsive organizations with fewer management levels and more direct information exchange between top and bottom layers" (Wigand, 1988: 318).

Team Management Comes of Age

Murray Turoff and Roxanne Starr Hiltz, authors of *The Network Nation* (1978), are among those who long ago predicted widespread democratic effects from computer and telecommunications technology. "We predict," they wrote, "that by the 1990s, we may see the emergence of a kind of internal marketplace within the organization. Individual employees may offer portions of their available time and allocate it to the highest internal bidder...Supply and demand would govern the allocation of information workers and the production of information services within the organization" (Turoff, Hiltz, and Mills, 1989; see Turoff, 1985). That is, organizational hierarchies would dissolve into a democratic marketplace of on-line marketing of professional services.

Though democratization of organizations has fallen well short of these predictions, computer and telecommunications technology can increase the total level of intra- and inter-organizational communications. It can create a far more open communications/influence/

decision process than that associated with traditional face-to-face committee systems. Glitman (1990) found that networked microcomputers cause managers and employees to work more closely together to improve productivity. Thus, in a suggestive study of the pulp and paper industry, which is computer-intensive, Glenday (1990) found there was strong empirical evidence that semiautonomous work groups were more important than in traditional enterprises which are not computer-driven.

Telecommunications has the potential to make nonsense of traditional pyramidal management structures, increase "span of control" greatly, and can create a far more open communications/influence/decision processes than those associated with traditional face-to-face committee systems (Sharp and Perkins, 1981). Networking makes possible the discussion, decision, and preliminary implementation of complex joint projects of multiple remote participants (e.g., in the study by Kiesler, Siegel, and McGuire, 1984).

In summary, increased levels of communication associated with networked IS leads to erosion of hierarchical rigidity (Johansen, 1984). An autocratic management style may no longer be appropriate to situations in which subordinates are at remote locations or telecommute from home. Managers cannot supervise as closely and are forced to rely more on facilitation, persuasion, delegation, and management by exception. Rather than mandate goals through directives, managers encounter the need to emphasize building trust and commitment in teams to assure that all members of the networked group understand and/or share common goals (Olson, 1983; Turoff, Hiltz, and Mills, 1989; Grohowski, McGoff, Vogel, Martz, and Nunamaker, 1990).

Summary

Networked computer/telecommunications systems harbor the potential for upheaval because information which was once accessible only by a few at the center becomes easily and widely available to all the actors in a system. While this can lead to better decision-making and improved productivity, it is also true that increasing the availability of information increases the opportunity for equity comparisons, for perceptions of relative deprivation, and for conflict. This assures that new technologies will pose challenges to existing political and

Figure 11: Mini-Case: IS Increases Conflict in Portland, Oregon

Sy Adler and Sheldon Edner studied the effects of installation of a new information system by the Portland, Oregon, Metropolitan Service District (Metro)—a regional transportation planning agency.

Whereas previously transportation models for the region were undertaken centrally by Metro, the new information system gave each local government and planning agency access to transportation data which each could use for their own analyses and models.

The result was a weakening of the political process which had hitherto forged consensus on regional transportation issues. "In general", the authors wrote, "as increasing numbers of planners work with the model, critiques of model assumptions and outputs become increasingly likely to surface" (Adler and Edner, 1988: 156).

At least for the Portland case, Adler and Edner concluded that the new IS system made it "more difficult for Metro to act as a comprehensive regional planner and to forge coalitions on regional-scale projects, particularly those focusing on downtown Portland." (p. 162).

organizational relationships, as numerous studies have shown (Danziger, Dutton, Kling, and Kraemer, 1982; Dutton and Kraemer, 1985; Adler, 1987).[14]

In the United States, computer-supported cooperative work software seems to raise the promise of cooperation, collaboration, and commitment. However, getting people to work together whether electronically or face-to-face can also involve competition, conflict, and control (Kling, 1991). Getting employees to change may involve all the turmoil of a social movement. A study of computer-aided urban land use models, for example, showed that computing (1) does indeed provide all the participants with more information on such matters as who gets what, which (2) heightens conflict and (3) slows decision-making. As a second illustration of the political implications of new technology, an internal study of electronic mail at Hewlett Packard found, "Some managers correctly foresee that such a system can be most upsetting to the current established order, and do not participate in it as a result" (Fanning and Raphael, 1986: 298). Therefore, ambiguity rather than the explicit and detailed clarity sought by most groupware packages may serve the organization better in terms of facilitating faster and smoother decision-making (Reder and Schwab, 1989).[15] On the other hand, some organizations may come to view heightened conflict as beneficial. Greater information and more conflict may mean better decisions are reached ultimately, but this is difficult to prove (Pack and Pack, 1977).

Telecommunications technology cuts both ways on the matters of organizational conflict. Computers and telecommunications also may play a critical role in conflict resolution as well as conflict generation. In an interesting study of international negotiations using a computer model, Koh (1984) found that computer mediation helped reduce the emotional involvement of the delegates and to facilitate compromise. That is, because facts pertinent to international decision were presented by the computer rather than other countries' delegates, it was easier to "back down" from original national positions. It may be that computer mediation of conflict has a generally defusing effect. This would be consistent with the common observation that computing can be used effectively by managers to place a mantle of neutrality and science over otherwise controversial decisions.

Advocates of "5th generation management" such as Savage (1990) believe the 21st century will be marked by organizations built around task-focusing teams rather than traditional hierarchies and that this shift in organizational structure will be linked intimately with computer use to increase peer-to-peer networking around changing sets of problems. Likewise other authors, such as Harvard Business School's Shoshana Zuboff (1988a), believe decentralized and distributed processing are breaking down traditional pyramidal structures in large businesses. She foresees the growth of employee roles defined not by hierarchical level so much as proximity to the customer and marketplace (O'Malley, 1989a: 74).

The widespread access to information made possible by distributed networks will mean that management functions may become assumed by many employees previously not considered "management". Zuboff ties decentralization trends in information processing closely with human resource development, viewing the former as providing a revolutionary opportunity for the latter. Likewise, in *Paradigm Shift* (1992), Don Tapscott and Art Caston argue that workgroup computing, distributed processing, and interorganizational networking (airline links to travel agents) are making the centralization-decentralization pendulum swing obsolete in modern organizations. Instant availability of information is turning hierarchical organization into a liability. Rather, in a competitive world, strategic advantage goes to firms and agencies which can take advantage of multidisciplinary problem-oriented teams that can exploit technological opportunities as they occur. The potential of computers to democratize American life lies in this area of organizations and teamwork, not in still-utopian visions of direct teledemocracy.

ENDNOTES

[1] HandsNet may be contacted at 20195 Stevens Creek Boulevard, Suite 120, Cupertino, CA 95014; 408-257-4500.

[2] Capitol Connection ended in 1988 due to lack of public interest, which in turn was partly based on the primitive software used for access (Fredell, 1988a).

[3] Electronic Democracy Conference, 1831 V. Street, Sacramento, CA 95818

[4] For information on PEN, call 310-458-8383.

[5] The e-mail addresses were PRESIDENT@WHITEHOUSE.GOV and VICE.PRESIDENT@WHITEHOUSE.GOV.

[6] Estimates of telecommuting vary widely. Link Resource Corporation's estimates are at the high end. The most conservative estimates place the number at about a tenth of the LRC estimates.

[7] Some additional increase in telecommuting also arises due to temporary needs as in the case of In-FLight Phone Corporation's "office in the sky" for business use during air travel (Berg, 1991).

[8] GDSS is illustrated by software originated by the Collaborative Management Workshop of the University of Arizona (LaPlante, 1989). The Workshop is a high-tech conference room with 48 microcomputer workstations tied together in a local area network, using the same group productivity software. Users record their thoughts and reactions to a specific problem under group discussion, and everything entered is sent automatically and anonymously to every other user. Everyone can "talk" at once rather than speak serially as in face-to-face conferences and anonymity prevents intimidation of junior participants by seniors and other inhibitory forces in face-to-face forums. Software components in the Workshop include the electronic brainstorming package discussed above, an issue analyzer to help form an agenda, prioritizing software to help define the relative importance of alternatives, and a text editor to help prepare group statements. In the 1987-89 period some 150 corporations have used the Workshop to improve decision-making.

[9] Among examples sometimes labeled CSCW or groupware is *Corporate Calendar*, groupware for scheduling. *Aspects* is software allowing multiple members of a work group to contribute to a document's development simultaneously. On the other hand, "groupware" usually includes any application which uses electronic mail or teleconferencing. *Lotus Notes*, for instance, is an oft-cited "groupware" package which combines electronic mail on LANs with forms which accessed online databases. It can also be used for such diverse purposes as publishing organizational newsletters, implementing in-house consultancies, document-sharing, or other office automation tasks. Other groupware products are extensions of electronic mail. Wang Laboratories' *Freestyle* software, for instance, combines image capture, voice recording, pen annotation, graphics, and e-mail so that what is sent is a voice recording synchronized to accompanying text, graphics, writing, and pointing which unfolds during playback.

[10] Likewise, Reynolds (1969) notes, the telephone was found to be a technology which enhanced communications but did not become a means for asserting more control.

[11] Caldwell cites data showing that between 1986 and 1992, one in ten data centers were closed. Among 150 surveyed, the number of firms with only one data center grew from one-third to over one-half. The Department of Defense, to take one example, is reducing its 170 data centers with 20 megacenters. This centralization is caused by new networking and operating software which makes centralization reliable and efficient, and by economic pressures to cut costs through consolidation. Often the CIO role in megacenters is one of gate-keeping in the traffic cop sense. Such centralization of data does not necessarily translate into centralization of power.

[12] EcoNet is managed by the Institute for Global Communications. For description of EcoNet and related on-line services, see Rittner (1992).

[13] This prediction dates from a classic article by Leavitt and Whisler (1958), reiterted in subsequent studies in the 1960's: Hoos, 1960; Kraut, 1962, Burck, 1964, Lee, 1964). Both Hoos and Burck had found empirical evidence for shrinkage of middle management, but both studies have been faulted for poor methodology and/or analysis (Federico, 1985: 10-11).

[14] Telecommunications can prove even more disruptive in Asian and other cultures which do not consider openness and directness in communications a virtue (Ho, Raman, and Watson, 1989).

[15] Reder and Schwab studies the groupware package called *The Coordinator*, software which attempted to remove ambiguity and obtain explicit commitments from participants in a decision-making process. Users found the software involved excessive keyboarding of commentary and preferred face-to-face communication. Other software which does not attempt to remove ambiguity has been found to be helpful in brainstorming during decision processes, in contrast.

CHAPTER III

Computer Technology and the Right to Privacy

Probably the most publicized policy issue pertaining to information systems (IS) is the issue of privacy from technological peeping Toms using computers. A whole new field of law is emerging out of efforts to balance the public's right to know, the individual's right to privacy, and government and corporate rights to secrecy (Tapper, 1990; Reed, ed., 1990).[1] Since the 1970s, employee complaints about computer invasion of privacy have become a significant organizational problem (Ewing, 1982). Computerized human resource databases in personnel departments, for instance, have been used for over a decade as evidence in lawsuits, particularly those involving discrimination (Mitsch, 1983: 37; Westin, 1979). Issues of privacy, security, and access are now common themes in popular books about the "computer age" (cf. Wessells, 1990). More recently, the Electronic Frontier Foundation has been funded with computer industry support to protect the First Amendment rights of computer and telecommunications users against abuse by government institutions (Boone, 1993; Lee, 1990a; Parker, 1990). EDUCOM, a coalition of hundreds of colleges seeking development of academic computing, has made privacy and information rights a major issue, embedded in a proposed "Bill of Rights" (*Educom Review*, 1993). A new Constitutional amendment has even been proposed by Harvard law professor Lawrence Tribe to protect privacy in the new technological era (Tribe,

1991).

At the same time, legislation has given employees and citizens more and more access to computer files containing information about them and has protected these data more and more from access by others. Many reformers believe these efforts are mainly symbolic and lack teeth. Calls for more sweeping reforms go way back. Nearly two decades ago Goldstein (1975) advocated that organizations prepare a "privacy impact statement," construct a comprehensive privacy plan, and make privacy a part of social responsibility programs. This would treat privacy issues in formal terms much as organizations must do for affirmative action plans or environmental impact statements. Although this particular proposal has never been implemented the subject continues to be of concern. For example, in 1990 the House Committee on Government Operations held hearings of a related sort on whether there is a need for legislation to establish a "Data Protection Board" or a "Privacy Protection Commission" to safeguard individual rights in the electronic information age (U. S. House of Representatives, 1990).

Unfortunately, there is an inherent trade-off between "the public's right to know" and individual privacy rights. In this chapter I review both sides of this trade-off. First access under the 1982 Freedom of Information Act is discussed, along with various federally-mandated access services. Then I look at the privacy side: the threat of electronic surveillance. In a third section, I look at the access/privacy issue from the point of view of information owners and see how ownership rights can be a threat to both access and privacy at various times. A final section takes a governmental viewpoint, first with a look at a major existing set of programs (computer matching in welfare, internal revenue, law enforcement, and other areas) and a major set of proposed programs (establishment of a 'National Data Bank'). The theme of the chapter is not that the "access" side or the "privacy" side is right but rather that -- as in each of the other policy issues discussed in later chapters -- the "right" solution must emerge from political rationality, not technical rationality. That is, answers have to come from political processes of conflict and compromise, not from imposition of technical solutions drafted by experts.

Computers and the Public's Right to Know

Computers could greatly enhance public access to data but such access is still more a goal than a reality (cf. Lohmann, 1990: 26). Progress is often stymied by a conflict over balancing the opposing rights of information providers versus those of information users. Obstacles also arise because of conflicts between advocates of government regulation versus advocates of reliance on market forces. The American Civil Liberties Union has an Information Technology Program which has long called for amending federal laws to provide citizen access to electronic data just as the Freedom of Information Act gave access to printed data. A June, 1989, report from the ACLU titled "Communications Policy and Public Access to Electronic Public Information" criticized existing information policies such as the Paperwork Reduction Act and OMB Circular A-130 for serving only the cause of efficiency. Access rights were not addressed, they stated, noting "In the same way citizens achieved access to published government information, public constituencies will have to make a political demand for access rights to electronic government information and address the legal barriers and public policy assumptions which today limit their ability to share the benefits of the emerging electronic government" (Grimm, 1989c: 84).

As electronic databases have proliferated at federal, state, and local levels, public information access has become an increasingly important issue. Early on, the General Accounting Office has responded by publishing the *Federal Information Sources and Systems Directory*. This access publication was part of the implementation of Title II of the Legislative Reorganization Act of 1970, as amended, "to develop, establish, and maintain an up-to-date inventory and directory of sources and information systems containing fiscal, budgetary, and program-related information (Comptroller General, 1977). More recently, in the 1990s the Federal Depository Electronic Dissemination Information Project of the Government Printing Office and the Joint Committee on Printing has attempted to create a system which would provide government information in electronic formats, but the project is small and underfunded. APDU, the Association of Public Data Users, is one of the very few interest groups which has pressured for such innovations, the nature of which has tended to keep them out of the public's mind and off the political agenda.[2] However, the access issue goes well beyond the matter of providing electronic equivalents of guides to government documents.

Access through the Freedom of Information Act of 1982

(FOIA, 5 U.S.C. Sec. 552): The Freedom of Information Act (FOIA) is thought by many to assure Americans' access to governmental data. Unfortunately, although FOIA has problems even for printed information, when it comes to computer-based data FOIA is largely irrelevant. FOIA representatives in federal departments tend to support computerization of their agencies' records but most FOIA responses are still completed manually in federal agencies (Commission on Freedom of Equality of Access to Information, 1986; Feinberg, 1986). Moreover, most federal agencies have taken the view that

Figure 1: What the Freedom of Information Act Does

* Agencies must designate an officer to handle information requests under FOIA.
* Agencies do not need to release data which are internal government communications before a policy decision is made, proprietary data in government contracts and proposals, or certain information which is protected by privacy legislation.
* Apart from these exemptions, agencies must provide government data which can be retrieved with reasonable effort.
* Agencies may set fees for searching, copying, and reviewing data for clearance.
* Individuals making a FOIA request must be specific as to content.
* Individuals making a FOIA request must be willing to incur the costs involved.
* Individuals making a FOIA request must state how the information will be used.
* Users fall in three categories: (1) news media, educational and non-commercial institutions; (2) commercial users; and (3) public interest groups and non-profit organizations. News media can be charged only duplication costs.

access to electronic information is not covered under the act. In 1988, the U. S. Office of Technology Assessment (OTA) issued a report, *Informing the Nation: Federal Information Dissemination in an Electronic Age*, noting the general failure of FOIA and related legislation to provide for access to electronic information. While some lawyers believe FOIA can be extended to computer information by contesting it in the courts, most reformers believe that an amendment to FOIA is necessary (Sorokin, 1991).

The Computer Security Act of 1987 (CSA) addressed this issue but proved to be an example of a "reform which does not reform". The CSA defined "sensitive information" and in so doing attempted to clarify what agencies might or might not withhold from FOIA information requests. Sensitive information was defined as "any information, the loss, misuse or unauthorized access to or modification of which could adversely affect the national interest of the conduct of federal programs" (Grimm, 1988f: 6). The CSA is enforced by the National Institute of Standards and Technology, which in turn relies on agency self-policing. This, together with vagueness in the CSA itself, meant little practical change[3], particularly since subsequent budget cuts led agencies to sacrifice security initiatives in favor of meeting basic missions (Power, 1992h).

The Office of Technology Assessment found that FOIA was used in the Department of Defense and elsewhere as a justification to deny public access on the ground that by definition providing electronic access goes beyond the clause in FOIA which stipulates that citizen access requests must be such that they can be fulfilled with "reasonable" effort (U. S. Office of Technology Assessment, 1988b: 18). In their report, the OTA concluded "Congress may wish to legislate a government-wide electronic information dissemination policy" (U. S. Office of Technology Assessment, 1988b: 17). Likewise, the 1991 White House Conference on Library and Information Services adopted a resolution favoring amending FOIA to include data stored in computer format. They further resolved that the Depository Library program should be expanded to include electronic information, and that there should be no fees for use in public libraries (Lunin, 1991: 16). As early 1993, however, Congress had not yet acted on the proposal.

The same access problems exist at the state level as at the national (Karasik, 1990). News media, for example, have tested state courts only to find that requesters cannot demand disclosure of information on computer tape (*Ohio ex rel. Recodat Co. v. Buchanan*, 46 Ohio 3rd 163, 189; see *News Media and the Law*, 1990). Klemanski and Maschke (1992) surveyed state-level enforcement of freedom of information laws and found that state-level administrators endorsed disclosure but lacked adequate training, time, and resources -- all forces acting against free disclosure.

When training, time, and resources are present, public access efforts can succeed. For instance, based on the FOIA model Minnesota launched the Minnesota State Information Systems Project (SISP). Operated by the state's Legislative Reference Library, SISP was created in 1983 with a mandate to create a comprehensive state information systems directory (Perkins, 1987). Sound strategy, in addition to resources, is also essential to success. For instance, in 1987 the North Carolina state legislature also chose to address the same problem as Minnesota. The NC strategy was to create a system of depository libraries to receive six copies of every state agency report, catalog, bulletin, newsletter, notice, and publication. This strategy seemed to provide citizen groups with physical access to printed documents, but in fact its plan to dump truckloads of printed matter in depositories was more akin to a *Guiness Book of Records* wastebasket than to a usable access system. Moreover, the unenforceable burden it placed on administrators led to immediate widespread non-compliance by public officials.[4]

Congressionally-Mandated Information Access Services

In the view of some, the public's right to information access should be virtually absolute. The Independent High Tech Party of Massachusetts, for instance, seeks to promote democracy through technology and supports placement of all government records on disks made available on computers in public areas (Anzovin, 1991). While current practice is remote from this ideal, Congress has acted from time to time to mandate public electronic information access. In fact, the federal government maintains over 400 computerized databases (Information USA, 1990) and over 100 electronic bulletin boards accessible to the public (Kantor, 1992).

In October, 1986, Congress passed the Emergency Planning and Community Right-to-Know Act (EPCRA). Though less known than

FOIA, EPCRA is more explicitly related to electronic information issues. It requires the federal government to take affirmative actions to create and distribute via telecommunications a large database on toxic releases. As such it is the first Congressionally-mandated on-line information system other than the on-line system for patent information (established in 1979). While dealing with a specialized area, EPCRA is important as a precedent affirming the importance of free flow of information over protecting the rights of bureaucratic agencies (Goldman, 1991: 25). Whereas FOIA applies only to information already held by government, the EPCRA requires government to collect and make available specific types of data relevant to community concerns.

Individual federal agencies have begun to provide expanded electronic access. A prominent example is the Client Information and Policy System (CIPS) of the Department of Housing and Urban Development (HUD). CIPS is scheduled to become operational in 1994, providing HUD clients with electronic access to about 90% of the department's policy documents and related legislation (Quindlen,

Figure 2: Selected Congressionally Mandated Access Services

* Electronic Bulletin Board, U.S. Department of Commerce.
A low-cost on-line service providing full-text documents and statistical files from Commerce, the Energy Information Administration, the Federal Reserve, the Census Bureau, the Treasury Department, and other agencies (Olsen, 1991a)

* AAMVAnet (Amer. Assoc. of Motor Vehicle Administrators)
Mandated by the 1986 Commercial Vehicle Safety Act as a tool for preventing commercial drivers from hiding violations through use of multiple licenses in different states (Richter, 1992d).

* Public Law 96-374
Mandated the Department of Education to establish an information clearinghouse for the handicapped.

* Public Law 98-362
Mandates the Small Business Administration to establish an information resource center on computer crime.

* Public Law 99-570
Mandated the Department of Health and Human Services to establish a clearinghouse for alcohol and drug abuse information.

1993d).

A recent effort to make government databases available to the public is the Wide Information Network for Data Online (WINDO) project of the U. S. Government Printing Office. WINDO is intended to provide the nation's 500 depository libraries with improved access to federal data in electronic form. At this writing a private sector initiative is planned for 1992 which would provide all libraries with similar access by broadcasting all public digital data by satellite, including numeric, text, and graphical information. Libraries should be able to specify information codes wanted to build up collections on topics of interest (Hilton, 1991).The Government Printing Office also established the Federal Bulletin Board (FBB) in 1992. The FBB provides direct citizen access to information files from a wide variety of agencies (e.g., Supreme Court opinions). Users pay a telecommunications charge plus a fee of $2 - $21 per file they download.[5]

Another recent effort to provide electronic access to the federal government is Fedworld. Fedworld is a pilot project of the National Technical Information Service (NTIS). It provides virtually direct PC access to computer files, databases, and programs in more than 50 federal agencies. Information can be accessed from the Departments of Agriculture, Commerce, Defense, Energy, and Justice, as well as agencies such as the National Science Foundation, NASA, the Library of Congress, and the Government Printing Office (Smith, 1993a). While much of this access can be accomplished by dialing in to individual agency bulletin boards directly, Fedworld consolidates the process and supports multi-agency access without the need for multiple log-ons. Initial response to the system was reflected in about 1,600 calls in the system's first three weeks of operation. As of 1993, however, the project was still experimental, could only support 40 simultaneous users, and was located in an agency whose services were fee-supported—characteristic of a design for access by commercial users, not the public.[6]

The cause of mandated information access took a giant step forward with the release in February, 1993, of the Clinton administration's policy paper, "Technology for America's Economic Growth, a New Direction to Build Economic Strength". In contrast to previous presidents, Clinton made dissemination of federal information a priority of his administration (Peters, 1993: 8). With this mandate, further momentum has been gathered recently through the formation of the Coalition for Networked Information (CNI), a public interest group mobilizing information professionals and in and out of government for projects focused on Internet and other on-line access to federal data.

The newest, mandated information access program is contained in the GPO Electronic Information Access Enhancement Act, signed by President Clinton in June, 1993. Under this act the Government Printing Office will provide on-line access to the *Federal Register*, the *Congressional Record*, and other government documents. "Reasonable fees" will be charged, but citizens can get free access through Federal Depository Libraries which will not be charged for the service. Initial access is scheduled for June, 1994, with public access later.

While the effects of GPO access, WINDO, FedWorld, and their counterparts remain to be seen, up till now in practice there is little effective public access to government information although determined individuals can root out the data if they are aware of its existence. Contrary to popular supposition that these individuals are primarily journalists and academics, most FOIA use comes from convicted felons and people involved in intelligence-gathering for business or for foreign governments (Aines, 1988b: 99). "Freedom of information" has had little to do with "average citizens" up until now.

Computers, Privacy, and Electronic Surveillance

The image of the government as a *1984*-type "Big Brother", operating through computer invasion of privacy, is a commonly articulated fear (Rule et al., 1980; Gardner and White, 1983; Rule, 1983:179; Rubin, 1987; Rubin and Dervin, eds., 1989). Some 80% of Americans are concerned about threats to their privacy posed by information technology (Betts, 1990). Bowers (1988), for instance, discusses "Computers and the Panopticon Society", likening computer surveillance to the 19th-century proposal for a circular prison centered on a guard able to view prisoners in all cells at any time. These fears are not without foundation. Extensive wiretapping of domestic targets is practiced not only by the FBI but by numerous government agencies. On the international front the National Security Administration (NSA) has a staff of 40,000 and is deeply involved with electronic surveillance. John Gilmore of the Electronic Frontier Foundation terms NSA's mission as one of "wire-tapping the world" (Barlow, 1992: 25). The National Association of Working Women, 9 to 5, estimates that some 26 million workers are now under electronic surveillance (McPartlin, 1990: 33; Nussbaum, 1992: 21).

Beyond this there is the threat of illegal electronic surveillance. Five NYC "hackers" were arrested in 1992, for instance, for selling information on how to obtain credit reports on-line without authorization (Thyfault, 1992a: 15). Some even argue that freedom of the press may become "technologically obsolete" as surveillance of electronic transmissions erodes Constitutional rights (Costikyan, 1991). In 1977 the Privacy Protection Study Commission recommended establishment of a 'Federal Privacy Board' to monitor trends and advise Congress (Privacy Protection Study Commission, 1977). Though never implemented, the controversy has continued to the present day (Christensen, 1986; Ermann, William, and Gutierrez,

Figure 3: Privacy Legislation

* The Fair Credit Reporting Act of 1970
Allowed consumers to review their records held by credit bureaus, but credit records could still be given to anyone with "a legitimate business need" and they remained notoriously difficult to have corrected. The act gives consumers the right to add a note to their credit files, but this right is rarely known, let alone used.

* The Privacy Act of 1974
Based on an HEW report (U. S. Department of Health, Education, and Welfare, 1973), this act restricted federal agencies to use of data solely for the purpose for which the data were collected; gave individuals a right to to get a copy of records pertaining to them; required agencies to keep records current and accurate; required employee training and security measures to safeguard personal data. Willful action to violate individual privacy rights was made subject to civil suit for damages. Agencies were required to publish in the *Federal Register* information about each system of records. The Office of Management and Budget was charged with responsibility for coordination. Coverage is limited to federal agencies.

The Privacy Act affected only outside access. Broad interagency data was allowed. Law enforcement agencies, the CIA, and certain other agencies were exempted. A report by the U. S. Office of Technology Assessment found that the Privacy Act "offers little protection to individuals who are subjects of computer matching" (U. S. Office of Technology Assessment, 1986b: 38).

1990; Parker, Swope, and Baker, 1990; LaPlante, 1990a; Dejoie, Fowler and Paradice, eds., 1991; McPartlin, 1992g).

Congress has long been concerned with issues of computing and privacy rights, particularly with regard to tax records. In 1968 the Internal Revenue Service initiated an effort to redesign its information system to give employees more direct access to tax account data. However, the effort never progressed beyond the conceptual design stage and was canceled due to Congressional concerns about protection of privacy rights. It was not until a quarter century later that a similar effort was undertaken on the third try (GAO, 1987b). Starting in the 1970s Congress undertook a number of initiatives seeking to expand privacy rights vis-a-vis emerging information systems (see Figure 3-3).

In spite of federal legislation, many have still felt that U. S. laws have not kept pace with new information technologies and practices. This was an explicit motivation behind the formation of the United

Figure 4: Privacy Legislation, Continued

* 1974-1978
After the Privacy Act of 1974, federal legislation often included provisions on computing with respect to access and confidentiality. By 1978 no fewer than 74 pieces of legislation contained such provisions (House Committee on House Administration, 1979).

The Privacy Act of 1982 and 1984 Supplement (U.S.C. Sec. 552a)
These acts further protected personal data on education, medical treatment, criminal records, employment history, and other matters. However, 11 exceptions were granted, including statistical reporting, law enforcement, courts, health and safety, Congress, GAO, GSA, and the National Archives. The Privacy Act raises legal issues about computer matching (e.g., of tax and welfare records), access by credit agencies, and access by individuals (e.g., criminals seeking likely victims) (Relyea, 1986; Levitan and Barth, 1987; Hernon and McClure, 1987).

The Electronic Communications Privacy Act of 1986
Protected users of telephones and communications equipment from wiretapping and like privacy violations on private, cooperative, and commercial networks (Caldwell, 1990c). To establish privacy violation, one must show security measures have been taken in the first place (Goode, 1986). The ECPA allows exceptions in law enforcement, with a court order. More important, the ECPA explicitly authorized employers to access employee communications and to deny privacy rights on corporate networks (Hernandez, 1987: 17-18). Privacy advocacy groups like the Electronic Frontier Foundation consider the ECPA to have been relatively ineffective (Barlow, 1992: 26).

States Privacy Council in 1991. This coalition of academic and industry representatives has called for a re-examination of privacy legislation with respect to IS issues. The group favors creation of a "Data Protection" agency at the federal level and opposes creation of a national identification card. Some of its members advocated a Constitutional amendment to extend First and Fourth Amendment protections explicitly to computing and telecommunications.

European countries often have gone further than the United States in seeking to guarantee privacy rights (Tuerkheimer, 1993). For instance, British data privacy laws have led to the establishment of a system of "data custodians" in agencies such as the U.K. Office of Population, Censuses, and Surveys. When a request is made for reports on cancer incidence and deaths, or whatever, data custodians work together to make sure that individuals cannot be identified, even in cases where data are drawn from multiple data files in different agencies. Data custodians also have responsibility for performing quality checks on new data files, including the power to send them back if data quality problems are found. Perhaps most important, British data custodians play an advocacy role on the privacy issue, using information and persuasion to bring about change (Kiely, 1992d).

Guidelines regulating computer applications' impingement on privacy are increasingly finding their way into state legislation and the formal ethics rules of various professional associations. This is particularly true of health-related applications (Romano, 1987), but the same principles are increasingly applied in other areas. New York adopted "Ethical Guidelines for Data Centers Handling Medical Records" nearly two decades ago, in 1975 (Gabrieli, 1985). Likewise, Colorado has adopted a set of ethical guidelines for computerized psychological assessments, and the American Psychological Association now refers to computer ethics in its "Standards for Educational and Psychological Tests" (Erdman and Foster, 1988: 72). Such ethics guidelines are well on the way toward becoming universal.

Client confidentiality is a major privacy issue within many organizations. Agencies receiving funds from the National Institutes on Drug Abuse, for instance, are required to establish special review committees to oversee professional ethics in surveys and other forms of data collection and storage. However, this is not a simple matter of "the more privacy, the better," Following precedents in medicine, for instance, some psychologists would like total privacy of computer records on the ground that only trained and certified professionals have the competence to interpret test results properly. Others, however, believe educators, employers, and other categories should be allowed access. Privacy can be raised as an issue not to truly protect the privacy rights of individuals but to protect organizations from outside scrutiny. Moreover, organizational employees may use the privacy ethics issue as a basis for resisting implementation of new information technologies altogether (Benbenishty, 1989: 83).

Widespread computerization complicates life for IS administrators seeking to fulfill responsibilities under state freedom of information acts and also under privacy regulations. Robert Brennan, president of the Massachusetts Municipal Data Processors Association and director of data processing for the city of Quincy, Mass., noted that commercial requestors can gain many public computer tapes for the cost of copying (*PA Times*, 1987). Brennan warned that there is the strong potential that private users may gain information about individuals. Criminals, for example, might gain useful data about potential victims. In addition, commercial users may make a profit through resale of data collected at great public expense.

Some officials respond to privacy demands by advocating restricting access to computer data to certain classes of users, such as academic researchers. Information industry attorneys, however, argue that governmental attempts to analyze the motives of requesters (e.g., commercial, academic, criminal) would violate the purpose of freedom of information acts. Because prevention of access may lead to freedom of information lawsuits, an increasing number of governmental jurisdictions simply seek to regulate access through user fees. This addresses commercial re-use fairness issues but does not prevent invasion of privacy and still can be challenged as an unfair levy on the right to access to which the freedom of information acts were addressed (*PA Times*, 1987: 1, 16).

Privacy issues are most intense in areas such as taxation, government benefits, and law enforcement. Clarke (1988: 505) has popularized the term "dataveillance" to describe the dangers of electronic surveillance of large numbers of individuals through programs like computer matching of welfare or tax records. These practices, which he calls "dataveillance", have adverse impacts for both the individual and for society. Dangers of mass dataveillance for the individual include arbitrariness in decision-making, merging data out of context, files with unknown accusations by unknown individuals, lack of due process in accessing or correcting records, and use of records for questionable activities ranging from selective advertising to covert operations. For society, dataveillance may contribute to a prevailing climate of suspicion, adversarial relationships with citizens, and even laying the basis for repressive potential in government.

Controversy has surrounded the FBI's National Crime Information Center (NCIC), which first came online on January 27, 1967. Former FBI director J. Edgar Hoover had inspector Jerome Daunt manage installation of NCIC in just six months. In its first year of operation it

Figure 5: Mini-case: The FBI Library Awareness Project

The government's efforts to control access to information sometimes provoke storms of controversy. Rep. Don Edwards (D-California) testified at a House Judiciary Subcommittee on Civil and Constitutional Rights, "Advanced computer and surveillance technologies offer major advantages to the FBI in complex investigations" so Congress must "pay close attention to this area because these powerful technologies make increasingly pervasive forms of surveillance possible" (Grimm, 1989a: 146).

An example is the FBI's "Library Awareness Program", under which FBI agents tried to enlist librarians in reporting "suspicious" activities by foreigners such as seeking assistance in gathering on-line information (*Database Searcher,* 1988: 37).

The American Library Association (ALA) attacked the FBI program as inimical to intellectual freedom and professional standards, noting that in 38 states and the District of Columbia it is illegal to interfere in the confidentiality of library records. The House Judiciary Committee, Subcommittee on Civil Rights, subsequently held hearings in which the FBI cited the need for counter-intelligence work, especially in the NYC area where United Nations delegations are headquartered.

In late 1989 Patricia Berger, president of the ALA, revealed based on newly released documents, that the FBI had "misrepresented their activities by conducting background investigations of librarians who refused to cooperate" (*Information Today*, Dec. 1989: 7). Whereas the ALA had been assured by the FBI that the Library Awareness Program visits to libraries had stopped in December, 1987, new documents revealed that continuing contacts occurred in 1988 and 1989. Although not a computing issue per se, the controversy was followed closely in the computer press because of its broad implications for privacy rights by those accessing information on-line.

had amassed 381,000 records and handled over 2 million transactions. By 1991 it had 24 million records and handled a million transactions every day (Quindlen, 1992a: 62; Robb, 1980c; Masud, 1988). In designing the NCIC 2000 upgraded data system, a panel of experts in computer science, criminal justice, and civil liberties was established specifically to address privacy concerns (McGraw, 1988b). The panel rejected proposals to link the NCIC with other government databases but, over the objections of the American Civil Liberties Union, allowed creation of tracking and investigative files on drug, murder, and kidnapping investigations.

Investigative files on suspects raise important privacy issues. Should government establish computer databases on suspects who, after all, are supposed to be innocent until proven guilty? The NCIC panel said yes. Proposals exist for adding suspects in cases of terrorism, arson, and organized crime. Police favor such investigative files for the help they provide in piecing together information pertaining to wanted criminals. Civil libertarians, on the other hand, see such files as a blank check for policemen to place any individual of interest into an electronic database containing speculative and possibly erroneous and damaging information. In 1989 the FBI dropped plans to create a National Crime Information Center (NCIC) database of suspects not yet charged, under pressure from the American Civil Liberties Union, the Computer Professionals for Social Responsibility, and others concerned with privacy rights (Grimm, 1989a). However, subsequent FBI budgets requested funds for improved data communications, artificial intelligence software designed to identify patterns of criminal activity, and physical and electronic surveillance activities (Grimm, 1989a). All these improvements, fingerprint matching and image transmission to/from patrol cars, interface with Canadian crime data, on-line access to parole and probation records, and other projects continue to expand the NCIC (Quindlen, 1993b: 1; Kiely, 1991: 27-28).

With the NCIC already handling over a million inquiries a day, up 50% just since 1988, from 20,000 access points with regard to 24 million records on file is it administratively realistic to think that suspect records can be overseen adequately from the point of view of Constitutional rights (McGraw, 1988b: 88)? Both the ACLU and the Computer Professionals for Social Responsibility (CPSR) fear that the new computerized fingerprint matching and the even newer (and less reliable) computerized mug shot matching software now being tested will result in false identifications.[7] The CPSR wants the FBI to assign each law enforcement user with an access code and to keep a complete audit trail of all accesses to the NCIC system. The ACLU wants the FBI to establish a Data Integrity Office to monitor data accuracy and to provide a mechanism for correcting data. Yet even if such safeguards were implemented they would function only as courses of redress for occasional cases. Systematic re-validation of data in the giant NCIC database and detailed analysis of access audit trails for possible abuse would be an enormous operating expense whose mission would be difficult to carry out effectively.

Moreover, NCIC, FBI, and other criminal database records are far from being always reliable. "At a time when increasing reliance is being placed on criminal history records for pre-employment background checks, lawmakers often overlook the poor quality of existing databases," Representative Don Edwards, chairman of the House Judiciary Subcommittee on Civil and Constitutional Rights, noted in 1991 (quoted in Quindlen, 1991: 6). Likewise, as many as half the arrests in the FBI criminal history file and a third of arrests in state files, are missing information on the final outcome of the cases (including verdicts of innocence) according to the Office of Technology Assessment (Quindlen, 1991).

When the government maintains massive files of unverified data on crime suspects and others, how can IS managers provide safeguards against database abuse? Abuse can be a major problem. For instance, in 1991 the FBI arrested 18 people in 14 states for theft of data from the FBI National Crime Information Center and the Social Security Administration databanks. Employees stole computer data to supply private investigators with information on criminal activities, employment histories, earnings, tax filings, and so on, for use in making decisions about job applications, dismissals, loans, and lawsuits (Moran, 1991: 14). Such abuse confirms fears Kenneth Laudon warned about specifically a decade earlier, writing that the Social Security system with its 30,000 partially distributed terminals required additional oversight because the traditional trial-and-error approach, he believed, would not work anymore (Laudon, 1980: 494).

Privacy safeguards might require elaborate bureaucratic clearances, cross-checks, rules and procedures. For instance, in the criminal justice area, measures might be needed to determine that an

Figure 6: Mini-case: The Other Terry Rogan

An Alabama state prison escapee, Bernard McKandes, obtained the birth certificate of one Terry Dean Rogan. Although Rogan had reported his identification papers missing, McKandes frequently used Rogan's name in his criminal undertakings. This led the Los Angeles Police Department to enter Rogan's name in the National Crime Information Center (NCIC) database for many of McKandes's crimes. As a consequence, Rogan was arrested no fewer than five times. This was not a unique case: fugitive Richard Skar was also confused by the NCIC with a UCLA professor (see Richards, 1989).

Did the police have the right to issue arrest warrants for McKandes in Rogan's name? Or was this a violation of Rogan's rights? The U. S. District court agreed with Rogan, holding the LAPD liable. After the courts granted a monetary award to Rogan, the NCIC decided to add a new field for "use of stolen identification" to the 'Most Wanted' file in its database. Under this principle Rogan was not entitled to prevent the police from listing his name in the database records pertaining to McKandes but he could insist that the same record contain clarifying information. Thus, the issue of privacy can involve too little data in computer records as well as too much data about individuals (McGraw, 1988b: 88).

investigation is officially "opened", that a crime in question is "terrorism". How is this to be defined, and by whom? Compare the 1988 criticisms of the FBI for harassing pro-Sandinista, anti-Contra Latin American peace groups. How does one assure that certain information is properly phrased so that allegation and speculation is not confused with fact. To enforce all this might require a huge bureaucracy devoted not to fighting crime, but to guaranteeing abuses will not occur. Perhaps, civil libertarians argue, if we can't afford the measures to "do it right" we should not create investigative databases at all.

The most recent major issue pertaining to electronic surveillance arises because commercial communications companies are introducing new technology which is making previous eavesdropping techniques obsolete. The FBI is alarmed that information transmission is shifting from easy-to-monitor analog systems like phone lines to nearly-impossible-to-monitor digital systems such as ISDN fiber optic cables. As a result it sought legislation in 1992 to maintain its ability to wiretap (the "Digital Telephony Proposal", sponsored by Senator Ernest Hollings). This legislation would force computer and communications equipment manufacturers to design methods of digital wiretapping into their products, passing the added costs on to consumers (Whitmore, 1992). Computer hardware, software, and telephone companies opposed this legislation on grounds of cost and development burden as well as because it would undermine the competitiveness of American technology in worldwide marketing of truly secure software systems (Murray, 1992).

Even if the FBI and its allies in the National Security Agency (NSA) get a digital wiretapping bill passed, they face the problem of dealing with increasingly sophisticated data encryption methods. To address this the FBI and the NSA are supporting a weak Digital Signature

Figure 7: Mini-case: Caller ID

Caller ID, one facet of ANI (automatic number identification), is a computer-supported telephone feature which displays the phone number of incoming calls. It can be used to fight harassing calls, improve policing of telecommunications networks, and compile lists for telemarketing. The American Civil Liberties Union and the Department of the Public Advocate of the State of New Jersey expressed opposition to this new service. Callers, they stated, might hesitate to call emergency hot lines. Confidential information might be leaked by the caller to others. The right to have an unpublished number might be lost.

Do civil liberties concerns justify banning caller ID? Should phone companies be forced to allow callers the option of suppressing display of their phone number ("number blocking")? If so, may a fee be charged for number blocking, or would this violate the rights of the poor? In July, 1990, Pennsylvania courts ruled that caller ID violated the state's wiretap laws and was an unconstitutional trespass on privacy rights. An administrative law judge in California has ruled that Caller ID is not in the public interest. In Washington the state utilities commission took much the same view and recommended updating the state's privacy laws (Powell, 1991: 24; Taff, 1988).

At present some states (NJ, TN, VA, WV) permit caller ID and do not provide number blocking. Southern Bell, in Atlanta, offers caller ID but restricts number blocking to "qualified organizations" such as police and social service organizations. Other states (KY, MD, NV, SC, ME) offer caller ID and either permit or require number blocking. Massachusetts, for instance, requires both per-call and per-line blocking options. Some states (ND, NE) offer free number blocking. As of 1992, of the 23 states who considered caller ID, nine have opted to require a blocking option (Richter, 1992a: 65). Caller ID issues suggest the need for a unified national policy on privacy in relation to telecommunications and computing.

Standard (DSS) developed by the National Institute of Standards for digital security applications precisely because they fear stronger standards, already available commercially, would prevent efforts to crack encrypted messages in the course of combatting crime and espionage (Power, 1992: 1). Industry spokespeople argue that the NIST standard constrains technological development and would be used only for transactions with the government, where a lower security standard was required. At this time the FBI has not sought legislation forcing the private sector to use the lower NIST DSS standard although the NSA wants to require wiretap capability on all ISDN transmissions. Congress must decide whether privacy or wire-tap capability is American national policy.

Information Ownership Rights

In the computer era information has become the paramount market good. The "commoditization" of reference databases and other information has been noted widely (e.g., Roszak, 1986; Mosco, 1988). Corporations have sought to maximize profits by selling information online, as is their ownership right, but this can have profound adverse effects in some circumstances. For instance, international financial problems have prevented access to on-line databases by Latin American scholars (Tenorio, 1988). Well-heeled American lobbies have grown stronger by on-line access to mailing lists that impoverished public interest group competitors cannot afford. Commoditization can also mean one corporate interest seeking to restrict access in the process of fighting off competitors. This happened, for example, when CompuServe (the leading general-purpose electronic network) went to court to prevent telephone companies from competing with it in the form of electronic mail (Rockwell, 1988). Although the CompuServe decision was reversed in 1991 (Webb, 1991), permitting on-line services from phone companies, it does illustrate that what is good for a particular information owner is not necessarily what is good for the country.

Ownership versus Access: The Commoditization Issue

Anyone who is an author is very aware that information is a commodity, ownership rights over which can become the subject of controversy. For instance, full-text databases now make available many articles by a given author, tantamount to a book, yet the author receives no royalties (Behar, 1989). Instead the information vendor receives the profits and the information seeker must pay for what in years past would have been obtained free in a library. Of course, free libraries still exist and commoditization of electronic information brings convenience of access. Since the on-line access service is very expensive to mount and maintain, vendors see substantial fees as a necessary part of business survival. However, it is already true (e.g., for *Sociology Abstracts*), that the electronic versions of databases are more comprehensive than the print versions found in libraries. In some cases information is *only* available online. In such circumstances, commoditization can restrict information access to affluent organizations and individuals.

Public data can be commoditized. An example is the contract which allows West Publishing, a private firm, to insert copyrighted information into the text of government decisions and laws which they provide in digitized form back to government. The federal government uses these digital records as part of its JURIS on-line system for legal information, serving 15,000 federal employees. JURIS is operated by the Department of Justice on government-owned software and computers under Executive Order 12146 (July 18, 1979). However, because of Westlaw copyrighted materials, the government does not fully own the information contained digitally in text records of its own laws. On this basis, the public is denied access to government information and is instead referred to very expensive on-line legal services available from Westlaw and similar firms. In 1993 the Taxpayer Assets Project launched a petition drive to force the Clinton administration to change the Westlaw contract to allow low-cost public access.[8]

Congress, moving to greater use of digitized online data, has ceased or curtailed print publication of many vital public documents. The *Digest of General Bills and Resolutions*, for example, was published in print five to ten times a year. Now, due to on-line use, the print version is only published once a year, for historical archiving, long after it may be of use to affected public interests. Frantzich writes of this, "We are rapidly developing two classes of users, those who can instantaneously search and analyze massive data banks (such as the full text of the *Congressional Record* online), and those citizens and scholars forced to use the traditional, cumbersome, and inefficient methods. The story of absolutely or relatively reduced access repeats itself across the whole range of government information" (Frantzich, 1989). Likewise, Newkirk (1990) reiterates the "two classes" theme, stating that the new "electronic democracy" is limited to computer buffs affluent enough to take advantage of the opportunities. Real public access, Newkirk argues, would require a system based on touch-tone phones, not computers, whose distribution is heavily skewed toward the well-to-do.

The Information Industry Association (IIA) vigorously defends commoditization of information. They argue that commoditization increases public access, not restricts it. Others contend that commoditization has an opposite effect, particularly in the case of governmental information. The basic position of the IIA, which represents commercial information services, is that the government should make data available to the business sector either for free or for low fees. However, the IIA argues, the government should not provide value added products or services which would enable the consumer to analyze and utilize government data.

In the IIA view, adding value is the role of the private sector. Government should not be in the business of deciding what value-added services are appropriate for users. "Such 'editorial' decisions should not be the role of the government in our society," Bob Simons, general counsel for Dialog Information Services and an IIA member, recently testified before the House Subcommittee on Government Information (*Information Today*, 1992: 23). That is, industry representatives argue that public access is best served by government providing raw data to business at subsidized rates. Then government should refraining from competing with business by not providing public access software and services which would enable the public to use governmental data without paying for it commercially.

The value-added debate is illustrated by the case of the Federal Maritime Commission (FMC). As of 1989 there were over 700,000 tariff filings annually with the FMC. Although these data are public, it has been so difficult to get at them that private firms have arisen which charge a fee for searching for specific tariff information. When the FMC proposed to automate the system to allow users to dial up a computer database and obtain tariff information for a nominal charge, these firms charged the government was competing unfairly with private enterprise. As of this writing, the FMC planned to go ahead with automation in spite of the vendors' organization (the Information Industries Association) but it stated that it would make sure its access services were "very rudimentary" so as to minimize competition with vendors (Grimm, 1989b). That is, the compromise was that public access should be provided, but only access to raw data, not analyzed data. Users would have to do their own analysis or pay for analytic reports from private vendors. Industry groups are fearful that agency user fees such as the FMC's would fund information access upgrades which would make public data access more competitive with costly private services (Power, 1992e: 88).

Commoditization reaches its epitome in the case of privately-owned telecommunications networks which assert full ownership over the networks they have created. This, of course, is opposite to the view that telecommunications networks, like phone networks, are public communications media subject to Constitutional protections of free speech. The assertion of full ownership rights is also opposite to the view that telecommunications networks should be utilities regulated by government commissions. As with phone lines, some control is essential. Few if any would disagree with the network owner's right to control, say, the dissemination of pornography on its networks as Central Washington University was forced to do in 1991 (Wilson, 1991a: A22). Failure to exercise such control would subject the owner to possible prosecution under sexual harassment legislation.

Cases involving control issues occur regularly. The Communications Secrecy Act of 1986 (CSA), Section 2511, makes it illegal intentionally to intercept and disclose oral, wire, or electronic communications (with some exceptions, such as ship distress signals). Companies have asserted ownership rights under this act, which they claim gives them the right to protect their networks from loss. Under this act, for instance, an Iowa long distance carrier named Teleconnect blocked user access to a computer BBS (bulletin board system) it suspected of posting access codes enabling users to make illegal free phone calls (Sexton, 1989: 33). This action was challenged before the FCC on the grounds that First Amendment rights outweigh ownership rights of the telephone lines. Would IBM's phone lines be blocked, it was asked, if a carrier thought IBM might have committed an infraction of the Communications Security Act? Or is it more proper to leave enforcement of the law to the government, not to the owners of communications lines?

A second case arose in 1990 on the Prodigy network, a public bulletin board service created by Sears and IBM. When Prodigy instituted a new, higher fee system it provoked a rebellion among its users, some of whom formed the Cooperative Defense Committee (CDC). CDC activists began protest activities on the Prodigy network only to find that the company suspended the accounts of ten activists. They did so on the grounds that they had received complaints from customers annoyed by receiving e-mail from angry CDC members (*Database Searcher*, 1990b: 7). That is, at present when owners

Figure 8: Mini-case: Dun and Bradstreet vs. the United Auto Workers

The conflict between ownership rights and rights to access arose in a 1987 action by Dun and Bradstreet Credit Services (D&B), cosponsor of Dun's Financial Records. D&B ordered DIALOG Information Services, which made their database available at a fee through the nation's largest on-line database service, to block access by 240 passwords (users). This reflected D&B's attempt to apply to telecommunications their previous policy of denying print versions of their database to labor unions or to the Internal Revenue Service.

The United Auto Workers wished to gain access to corporate information to understand better how much management could afford to give and how much they were bluffing and "poor-mouthing". UAW lawyer Jay Whitman led the effort to reverse D&B's policy. Whitman pointed out that labor's use of such data to determine in collective bargaining situations if companies were validly pleading poverty would not affect honest corporations. "Who benefits from this decision," he said. "Only the liars."

In a precedent-setting move with grave consequences for free public access, DIALOG in December, 1987, decided to implement D&B's policies by blocking access by certain users working for labor unions and government regulatory agencies *(Database Searcher,* 1987).

More recently, the ownership versus access issue was joined again in the courts when Microsoft Corporation sought a temporary restraining order to prevent disgruntled ex-employee Joan Brewer from using CompuServe, a public network, to send electronic mail to current Microsoft employees (Patton, 1991).

The UAW could not be blocked from viewing print data in a library and Brewer could not be restrained from calling an employee on the phone if harassment were not involved, yet rights assumed to be basic in older technologies are in dispute when it comes to computer and telecommunications technology.

exercise rights to deny access totally to users seeking to exercise free speech rights, the rights of the former outweigh the rights of the latter. Users have recourse only through the marketplace (by switching to other networks), not through the courts— at least for now.

One of the strongest and most controversial court tests of information ownership rights occurred when the University of California challenged narrow copyright laws written before the era of electronic media. In 1979 the 9th Circuit Court in *Mills Music Inc. vs. Arizona* had held that states could not use the Eleventh Amendment to claim immunity from the copyright act. In 1985, however, the U. S. Supreme Court ruled that the Eleventh Amendment applied unless expressly waived by states or unmistakably abrogated by Congress. Subsequent to this ruling, in 1987 a California District Court overruled Mills Music (*BV Engineering vs. Board of Regents of the University of California*, 9th Cir., 1988; see BloomBecker, 1988), holding that the University of California - Los Angeles did not violate the Copyright Act by buying one copy of a software package, then making additional copies. This ruling, of course, had profound negative implications for the software industry. Although UCLA won the lawsuit, the House Judicial Subcommittee on Courts, Civil Liberties, and the Administration of Justice initiated an investigation of the issues (Fishman, 1988). In 1990, legislation was passed which overturned the victories UCLA had won in the courts, ensuring that copyright fees would indeed apply to state governmental units.[9]

Privatization, reducing information services to commodity status, has remained national policy under the Reagan and Bush administrations. The Paperwork Reduction Act of 1980 reflected the drive of the Reagan administration to privatize government-produced data. This act gave commercial vendors the right to contract with federal agencies for exclusive distribution rights to electronic-based government information. As librarians have noted, "Depository libraries that previously received government information free of charge in print form can now incur a cost if they purchase the electronic version. With the addition of the distribution company's charges to an information vendor, the electronic product can also cost the user substantial fees disseminating governmental research reports, software, and other information products. Continuation of such trends could create gross inequalities in the ability of scholars, public interest groups, journalists, and other citizens to access critical information. Were such inequalities to become widespread, democracy would be weakened. In this light, Congress acted in the 1993 GPO Electronic Information Access Enhancement Act to specify that Federal Depository Libraries should not be charged for access to on-line Government Printing Office documents.

Ownership vs. Access: The Cost-Recovery Issue

In a society in which information has been associated with free public and university libraries, it can be a rude awakening to discover the often high cost of electronic information access—much like the "sticker shock" in buying a new car. Just as the now-outlawed poll tax was used to deprive citizens, often blacks, of the right to vote, so database fees can effectively remove the right of access for all but a few Americans. In fact, institution of such fees is sometimes suggested as a legal way to prevent information access when outright denial would violate the Freedom of Information Act. Moreover, as noted in a 1986 report from the U. S. Office of Technology Assessment, costs of electronic data threatens to price information out of the reach of even schools and colleges, let alone community groups and individual citizens (U. S. Office of Technology Assessment, 1986a).

Some legislation and public policies restrain the price of government data. The Paperwork Reduction Act of 1980 and OMB Circular A-130 which implements it prohibits government from competing with private information companies and stipulates that information

Figure 9: Mini-case: Recovering Costs of NY's On-line Legislative Service

The New York state legislature offers an on-line service covering proposed legislation. To recover costs it charges $1,500 per year plus $25 per hour in access fees.

Although activist community groups would like to access this service, they find its costs prohibitive. As a result, actual access is restricted to a select group of 120 subscribers, mostly corporate interest groups.

One analyst notes, "As government policy-makers enter into the information business—or alternatively privatize government information by turning it over to private sector information vendors—they also slam in the face of citizens important doors to a democratic information society." (McCullough, 1991: 12).

costs be kept to a minimum. The Title 44 of the U.S. Code requires the government to provide its publications free through 1,400 depository libraries throughout the United States. In many jurisdictions IS cost-recovery is also under constraints which prevent greater-than cost fees. Constraints may take the form of laws forbidding competition with business, laws stipulating set fees for open records access, equal treatment regulations which may be violated if charges prevent de facto usage by some groups, and rules requiring on-line data accessibility (which makes it difficult to retain proprietary and therefore vendable information rights) (Roitman, 1987).

There continues to be strong support for providing government information free or at least at very low cost. Situations such as that in New York (see Figure 3-9) have led public interest advocates to attack government policies for pricing data high. For instance, in testimony before a Congressional committee, taxpayer advocate James Love deplored the government's tendency to price electronic information at commercial market rates. He called on the SEC, for instance, to offer low-cost remote access to its financial databases. Love said a citizen should be able to get a single government account and have dial-up computer access to on-line government information in all agencies. Another public interest advocate has called on Congress to mandate that the Government Printing Office set up "a one-stop shopping center" for government-generated data (Olsen, 1991: 6).

However, in opposition to the traditional view that government should provide information on a free basis, the last fifteen years have seen the ascendancy of the view that government should not make information a "free good" with all the waste associated with free goods. In 1977 the Commission on Federal Paperwork wrote, "The real culprit of the paperwork burden is mismanagement of information resources. Government has tended to regard information as a relatively free and unlimited commodity, like air or sunshine, simply ours for the asking" (Commission on Federal Paperwork, 1977: 12). During the 1980's, pushed on by fiscal hard times, many agencies found virtue in selling their information rather than giving it away.

Public Technology, Inc., a non-profit membership organization for local governments and an arm of the National League of Cities, the International City and County Management Association, and the National Association of Counties, advocates sale of information as a creative way of generating revenues. Thus at the state level, Governor

Mario Cuomo of New York in 1990 submitted legislation "to establish fees for providing government records based on the commercial utility of the records" (*Information Today*, 1991: 54). The Maryland Motor Vehicles Association, like many counterparts in other states, regularly sells driver address and driving record data to anyone willing to pay the five-cents-a-name cost. Turning to the federal level, Census data tapes are not inexpensive now ($175 per tape; nearly a quarter million dollars if a researcher needs all 1990 Census tapes) and Congress recently held hearings considering significant fee increases (Rockwell, 1992).

Selling government information immediately runs up against (1) the need to make information products usable by information consumers and (2) the possibility of competing with competitors in the private sector. The Reagan and Bush administrations largely have followed the thinking on this of the billion dollar industry of firms like Knight-Ridder and Dow Jones, which purchase government data inexpensively and then charge mostly corporate customers hefty fees to access it. Lobbying for these interests, the Information Industry Association (IIA) in 1991 passed a major policy statement titled *Access Principles for State and Local Government Information.* The IIA resolution calls on governments to encourage diversity of information, guarantee public access rights regardless of data storage medium, assure equal and timely access to all persons, and seek prevention of monopolistic control of government information. The IIA states that fees for access should not exceed the marginal cost of dissemination—that is, the cost of disseminating additional copies or allowing electronic access, not counting the costs for databasing the information for internal government needs (IIA, 1991). It should be noted that the position of the IIA is not entirely public-spirited, however, since as an industry association one of its aims is to keep the cost of government information low for its corporate members while trying to keep government out of the information services business.

As the Reagan administration left office it issued a major proposal to prevent government agencies from developing information systems that would compete with private enterprise. This proposal led to strong protests from such groups as the Consumer Federation of America and the National Education Association, which were concerned the Reagan policy would prevent citizens from benefitting from the computer revolution of the 1980s (Margulius, 1989: 79).

Nonetheless, with strong support from the IIA, the Reagan proposal was implemented in a revised OMB Circular A-130, which called on agencies to place "maximum feasible reliance" on the private sector in disseminating governmental electronic information products.

The 1990 Census, for instance, contained a revolutionary new street-level mapping system called TIGER. While one can buy TIGER data files from the U. S. Census, to display TIGER data on an actual map requires purchasing an information system from a private vendor. By intention, the U. S. Census does not provide the means to utilize TIGER data directly. Where information services have not been given over to the private sector altogether, the effect of OMB A-130 has been to encourage agencies to move increasingly beyond simple cost recovery to pricing at commercial rates.

It should be recognized, however, that only one of the major obstacles to public access is information pricing by government directly in the form of user fees or indirectly through privatization and commercialization of government data. Another is sheer volume. With 75% of all federal transactions expected to be electronic by the year 2000, access paths such as the National Archives and Records Administration (NARA) are quickly being overwhelmed by the sheer amount of electronic data. Moreover, NARA finds that two-thirds of all computer files it receives have problems with documentation and use. As files get older, agency personnel who understood them may no longer be around to explain them. Eventually hardware obsolescence becomes an access problem. As of 1991, only two machines can still read tapes from the 1960 census: one is in Japan and the other in the Smithsonian Institution. While standardization such as EDI (electronic data interchange) helps with some access problems, technological innovation (e.g., object-oriented databases, relational geographic information systems) continually adds new layers of complexity to the problem of maintaining access to data.

In summary, cost recovery raises political issues of access, equity, and the role of the public sector. IS managers cannot assume cost-recovery is merely an "internal" matter with only accounting consequences. Indeed, political action may be required by virtue of legislation affecting such policies. To overcome such cost recovery constraints, it may be necessary to obtain authorizing legislation or in some instances simply a ruling that fees serve a permissible public purpose. Cost recovery, like so many other IS aspects, is ultimately a political rather than technical matter.

Ownership vs. Access: The Privacy Issue

While some lament the lack of public access to government data, others fear that computerized databases have already gone too far in eliminating privacy. This fear has been raised, for instance, with regard to the medical records of patients with AIDS (Cohen, 1990). Likewise, personally-identifiable records (e.g., motor vehicle records) are being sold by various agencies, the individuals involved usually are not informed. Robert Ellis Smith, publisher of the *Privacy Journal*, urges safeguards such as requiring the consent of the individual before computer cross-checking is undertaken, allowing people to remove their records from any list for sale or rent, and to bar any suspension of government services based solely on computer selection without human intervention (Desky, 1991: 1).

Privacy rights also have been raised frequently in the area of electronic mail (e-mail) (DeBenedictis, 1990). Is e-mail private, owned by the employee and subject to privacy considerations as with telephones? Or is anything on e-mail (and many systems archive *everything*) owned by the organization like everything in its hard-copy file cabinets? For instance, in the federal government the OMB's FIRMR regulations strictly curtain interception of telephone messages but pose no such restrictions on electronic mail. To take some actual cases, is it all right for the mayor of Colorado Springs to read the e-mail of city council members? Is it all right for Stanford University to suppress humor of which it disapproves on campus networks it owns? Is it all right for managers in Epson America, Inc., to read an employee's e-mail, then use this as a basis for firing the employee? Does that same employee have a right to sue the company for un-constitutional invasion of privacy?

In 1990, Alana Shoars filed suit against Epson, Inc. (a leading printer manufacturer) after she was fired because, she believed, she had challenged management's right to read electronic messages between employees. This suit was considered the first major legal test of privacy issues in electronic mail. The Shoars suit was a test of the Electronic Communications Privacy Act of 1986 (ECPA). The courts held that the California law Shoars cited to invoke protection of privacy did not cover e-mail. Most attorneys advise that there are no legal constraints on corporate access to electronic communications. In telephone-related matters, according to Lew Maltby, coordinator of the American Civil Liberties Union's task force on the workplace, employers may monitor calls but are required to "hang up immediately" once they discern a call is personal. However, one cannot "hang up" on a copy of an electronic mail message.

To take a university example, in 1990, the University of Wisconsin asserted the right to and did read "private" e-mail, citing their belief that the law permits reading of e-mail when the purpose is to protect property rights. Specifically, the university read dozens of e-mail messages to and from Professor Patricia Mansfield. They did this to gather evidence for a case that Mansfield had used university computers for commercial purposes, something prohibited by university policy. In contrast, the policy at some other universities (e.g., Virginia Polytechnic Institute and State University) is to permit reading of e-mail only upon a court order (Caldwell, 1990d).[10] Nonetheless, more stringent privacy policies such as VPI's are voluntary. In fact, the University of Wisconsin, at least at present, is correct in asserting that property rights outweigh privacy rights on telecommunications networks accessed by computer.

Legal issues surrounding electronic privacy have created new managerial responsibilities. At a minimum, managers of organizations with e-mail need to make sure that their organization has a written policy on privacy in electronic communication even if that policy is in favor of organizational ownership. For instance, the policy of owners of the Prodigy on-line network (created by Sears and IBM) asserts the right to read anything in the networks public areas but asserts e-mail is private, even for their own personnel (Flynn, 1990: 5). Managers also need to inform employees in writing if organization policy does not assure privacy of electronic communications. Two former Nissan Motor Corporation USA information specialists sued their company, for instance, for invasion of privacy after corporate snooping into their electronic mailboxes revealed objectionable exchanges with car dealerships. The employees stated that they would not have exchanged personal messages if they had known they were being monitored (Caldwell, 1991a). Likewise, if organization policy seeks to assure confidentiality, users of the e-mail system should be informed in writing of their specific responsibilities to take actions (e.g., deletion of files, use of passwords) which assure privacy

(Caldwell, 1990b).

Although there has been some legislation to protect privacy rights in this country (Figure 3-10), there is still no law directed specifically at *general* privacy rights vis-a-vis electronic media. National efforts to safeguard privacy have been implemented in other nations, however (Bennett, 1988, 1991). In 1980 the OECD issued its "Guidelines" document outlining minimum standards for data handling for privacy protection purposes. The United States has never become a signatory to these Guidelines, though over a hundred American companies voluntarily subscribed (Tuerkheimer, 1993: 71). In 1984 Britain's Data Protection Act was passed (Watson, 1989) and more recently the European Commission has framed a privacy protocol which is expected to take effect in 1994.

This protocol, called the Digital Data Services Protection Directive, Article 24, makes illegal the transfer and use of information on individuals without their explicit consent and authorizes EC member states to block transmission of electronic information not conforming to EC privacy standards (Rothfeder, 1992: 173-4). In addition, it prohibits the transfer of data on individuals into countries without

Figure 10: More Privacy Legislation

* The Family Educational Rights and Privacy Act of 1974
The "Buckley Amendment" set some restrictions on data collection and disclosure for students at federally-funded schools and gave students and parents access rights to educational records.

* The Right to Financial Privacy Act of 1978
Restricted the access of federal agencies to bank records, but the FBI and state and local agencies are exempted.

* The Electronic Funds Transfer Act of 1978
EFTA became effective in 1979-80 and set forth principles for electronic funds transfer but did little to prevent deception of consumers (Kling, 1980b).

* The Video Privacy Protection Act of 1988
Prevents disclosing records about what you rented at your video store, but you do not have the same protection about your medical and insurance records.

* The Computer Matching and Privacy Protection Act of 1988
Ostensibly regulated computer matching but was worded such that there was little real impact on matching programs.

adequate privacy protection legislation. Some believe this would include the United States. These forthcoming European-wide uniform privacy laws are in stark contrast to American practice, which has placed business efficiency ahead of individual privacy (Cassidy, 1991).

Computer Matching and National Computer Databases

Among existing government information efforts, the practice of "computer matching" has probably generated the greatest privacy concerns. Computer matching means, simply, correlating data across different databases, often in different departments. Most concern centers on law enforcement aspects, as when matching is used to uncover such things as unreported tax liabilities or duplicate benefit payments. However, matching is also used extensively simply for planning purposes, as in studies correlating public health indicators with government expenditure data. Some have called cross-database computer matching an invasion of privacy. Shattuck (1984), for instance, argued that computer matching was a violation of the Fourth Amendment's prohibition against unreasonable searches. Matching also may be said to violate the presumption of innocence when services are denied solely on the basis of a computer match (e.g., denial of welfare), placing the burden on the citizen to prove innocence. Moreover, Shattuck contended, matching violated the Privacy Act of 1974, which under HEW General Counsel Carl Goodman was ruled to restrict data use to "routine use" or "law enforcement". However, computer matching, which was anything but routine in 1974, is now standard practice. Agencies consider it routine use under the Privacy Act merely on the basis of published notice of the matching effort in the *Federal Register* or the like.

Does the government have the right to search through the records you file with the Internal Revenue Service and other agencies? Yes, they do, but the computers have changed the stakes in this policy issuc. What was once merely a hypothetical threat is now technologically feasible: to compile detailed dossiers on every citizen by drawing information from every form for every transaction every citizen has ever filed with a government agency, possibly even merging into vast credit information databases in the private sector as well. Although this spectre appears most menacing at the federal level, the issue of comprehensive databases arises in lesser governmental units as well. Butterfield (1986, 1988: 33-4), for example, noted that social service tracking systems in Florida, Kansas, and elsewhere "have the potential for telling practitioners much more about a client's behavior than may be necessary and desirable". He predicts those whose privacy rights have been violated will turn increasingly to litigation over such practices.

In this section I look at computer matching as perhaps the leading area of existing practice which has raised widespread concerns over privacy rights. I then also look at the comprehensive national databank concept, perhaps the leading threat to privacy in the future.

Government Policy on Computer Matching

Few would disagree that computer matching can benefit society. For instance, the Federal Aviation Administration used computer matching to uncover dozens of U. S. pilots who failed to report drug- and alcohol-related driving convictions in order to keep their pilot licenses (Grimm, 1988d: 3). In such cases the interest of public safety seems to outweigh the pilots' rights to privacy over their court records. Likewise, computer matching was used to reject an employment application from a convicted child molester who was seeking a job installing cable television in homes. As a third illustration, the Federal Tax Refund Offset program uses computer matching to enable agencies to deduct payments due from the tax refund checks of delinquent parents (Smith, 1989), helping enforce child support judgments.

Computer matching is something governments have come to feel they cannot afford to be without. Since 1975 the Department of Health and Human Services and its equivalents in the 50 states have collected nearly $30 billion in delinquent child support payments alone, using data retrieved from federal agency databases, mainly IRS and Social Security Administration. In fiscal 1988, computer matching returned $4 in funds for every dollar spent collecting it. Studies done in the mid-1980s suggest that the benefit-cost payoff of such matching programs is in the range of 1.19:1 to 2.67:1 (Greenberg and Wolf, 1985), saving taxpayers millions of dollars.

However, there are other instances where computer matching has aroused controversy. At the extreme there is the case cited by Vallee (1982) where French police, acting on an erroneous computer match, shot innocent victims to death. At other times citizens have lost welfare benefits and endured hardship due to computer matches based on erroneous information. The IRS, cognizant of privacy concerns and fearful that matching might inhibit the filing of truthful tax returns, has resisted welfare-type matching of corporate tax returns.

Computer matching has far broader implications than might be suggested by the frequently-cited cases of tracking down welfare fraud or tax evasion. Matching has become an important aspect of the American electoral process as direct-mail entrepreneurs have matched various lists against voter registration records to match voters to likely attitudes. For instance, Aristotle Industries matches subscribers to *Guns and Animals Magazine* to voter lists to obtain lists of voters likely to oppose gun control (Frenkel, 1988: 1177). Candidates then buy these matched lists in order to send appropriate mass mailings to appropriate individuals. This also enables candidates to omit mention of their positions on issues unpopular with given voters, varying what is omitted according to the matched list in use. This manipulation of the democratic process is now the rule rather than the exception.

Computer matching is, of course, linked to the threat of creation of an all-intrusive "National Data Bank" of the type discussed in the next section. Computer matching is also associated with problems of equity. Computer matching has been used primarily against lower-income (often minority) populations while at the same time the Internal Revenue Service has fought every effort to apply computer matching to corporate records, even though this is thought to have the potential to bring in an additional one billion dollars in tax revenue (Seaborn, 1991a).

Practical implementation brings a final group of computer matching problems. Even when computer matching is implemented, agencies cannot simply act on computer match information alone. Once overpayments are highlighted by computer matching, agencies must still follow up personally to validate the computer findings (Greenberg and Wolf, 1986), an investment not all agencies are willing to make (Gardiner and Lyman, 1984). That such investment is essential, however, is suggested by the high error rate of matching programs. For instance, Marx and Reichman found a New York matching program had an error rate over 50% due to timing problems alone (1984: 435).Rocheleau (1989: 11; 1991) reports that of 8,500 people matched as dead by Medicare files but alive and receiving benefits from Social Security, 6,000 were indeed dead and 2,500 were alive. The Office of Technology Assistance has reported that only 12% of agencies conduct record quality audits to assess such error factors (U. S. Office of Technology Assessment, 1986b: 12).

Congress has been aware of the controversies surrounding computer matching, leading to a succession of legislation (see Figure 3-11). This legislation has not changed the nature of computer matching programs appreciably. Contrary to what might be supposed from surface reading of its provisions, the Privacy Act of 1974 did not constrain computer matching activities. The "routine use" exception clause of the Privacy Act was reinterpreted in practice to regard computer matching as routine provided notice was printed in the *Federal Register*. Arguing that control of fraud and deception was part of the routine use of data in all government programs, agencies were able to ignore the Privacy Act almost completely insofar as computer matching programs were concerned (U. S. Senate, 1986: 333). Acceptance of computer matching was aided by its early association with control of welfare abuse, where popular belief held that in accepting government benefits welfare clients implicitly waived their rights to privacy (Keisling, 1984: 22).

While legislation culminating in the Computer Matching and Privacy Protection Act of 1988 (CMPPA) constituted steps toward safeguarding the rights of individuals, legislation to date has had little practical effect. CMPPA meant, for instance, that people filling out Social Security benefit statements from 1989 on might spot this notice on their instructions:

> How Do Computer Matching Programs Affect You? On forms that you fill out for us you give us information about yourself. Sometimes we check the information you, and others, give us. We use computer matching to do the checking. The law allows us to check this way even if you do not agree to it. We may also share information about you with other government agencies that pay benefits. They will use this information in their computer matching programs. (Social Security Form SSA-1099-SM [1-90]).

Figure 11: A Brief History of Federal Computer Matching

* PL 95-216, 1977
Congress mandates state welfare agencies to use state wage data for Aid for Dependent Children eligibility.

* Long Term Computer Matching Project, 1981
President Reagan's Council on Integrity and Efficiency (CIE) promoted matching efforts through a clearinghouse, newsletter, and encouragement of standardized data formats (Rocheleau, 1989: 3; 1991).

* Revision of OMB computer matching guidelines, 1982
CIE efforts led to new Office of Management and Budget guidelines which required public notice (e.g, *Federal Register*); safeguards on data; and return of data files to originating agencies (a precaution against formation of a national database; Kusserow, 1984).

* Deficit Reduction Act, 1984
Congress enacted a provision that authorized computer-matching for all need-based programs. States were required to implement matching as a condition for receiving federal welfare funds.

* The Computer Matching and Privacy Protection Act of 1988
Public Law 100-503 required agencies notify those affected by its computer matching; required agencies to have written agreements when exchanging information for matching; to have a data integrity board to review written agreements; to undertake a cost/benefit analysis of matching programs to determine if they are justified; and to provide for civilian notification procedures and an appeals process. Also required was a 30-day notice prior to cutting off benefits after computer matching indicates the need to do so.

Such pro-forma notices provided no real protections although the 30-day notice requirement did increase the length of time available for appeal in some states. As one analyst noted, even after PL 100-503, "there remain no substantive protections against matching" (Rocheleau, 1989: 22; 1991).

The Computer Matching and Privacy Protection Act can be interpreted as much as a Congressional sanction to implement computer matching as legislation to protect individual rights vis-a-vis computer matching, in spite of claims that it "would provide the subjects of matches with due process rights permitting them to know about matches involving them and to offer evidence rebutting any adverse information developed by matches" (Grimm, 1988c: 4). Compromises leading to its passage allowed agencies to provide periodic notices to those affected rather than notices each time, and exceptions to the notice requirement were allowed in the case of investigations by law enforcement agencies. Early agency fears that the CMPPA would disrupt computer matching programs or slow their growth have proved groundless.

The National Data Bank Issue

One of the most widespread popular fears regarding computing is that government may create an all-knowing national data bank system which would make possible unwanted control over the details of formerly private aspects of everyday life. At one time the "Law of Requisite Variety in Information Systems" (Clarke, 1988) was thought to prevent creation of such a centralized national databank. This "law" was rooted in the proposition that no single information system could serve all agencies economically since each agency needed unique data definitions, unique data format and structure, and unique data quality controls. However, as information systems have improved it has become increasingly feasible to envision such a national data bank. It is no longer necessary that data reside in a single location provided that connectivity and data standardization are adequate. For better or worse, great strides have been taken in both of these areas.

In the 1960s Congress held hearings on the proposal to establish a "National Data Center". Although never implemented as such, its purpose was to create a better foundation of data for measuring social indicators relevant to domestic legislation. However, many opposed it vigorously on the grounds that computer matching of data smacked of totalitarianism. Testifying before 1966-7 Congressional hearings, Representative Frank Horton stated, "One of the most practical of our present safeguards of privacy is the fragmented nature of the present system. It is scattered in little bits and pieces across the geography and years of our life. Retrieval is impractical and often impossible. A central data bank removes completely this safeguard" (quoted in Rule, McAdam, Stearns, and Uglow, eds., 1980: 56; see U. S. House of Representatives, 1968).

Some other countries have implemented just such national data banks. Thailand, for instance, established a Central Population Database Center (CPDC) using American technology.[11] Each of Thailand's

55 million citizens is assigned a computerized identity card which includes a facial photograph and thumbprint. The system is used not only to verify identity for voter registration, drivers' licenses, and passports, but also so law enforcement, social welfare, and other officials can track voting patterns, personal travel, and other hitherto private activities (Thomas Hoffman, 1990).

Privacy in relation to government technology is in some ways dwarfed by the issue of privacy in relation to financial and corporate computing. Database marketing systems and credit systems are being used to collect detailed information on individuals, including credit card purchase information, real estate records, voter registrations, court records, and other data which when collected in one place can yield extremely detailed profiles of almost any American citizen (Burnham, 1983; Rubin, 1987; Stevenson, 1988). In addition to raising issues of privacy, credit report agencies often carry inaccurate information which is difficult to rectify.

For instance, TRW (a major credit bureau) was once forced to purge all tax lien data for Vermont and three other states when it was shown one of its contractors incorrectly posted city-supplied lists of taxpayers as tax evaders. However, TRW initially stonewalled the issue until forced to act by media publicity (John Schwartz, 1991: 47). As another example, a Washington, D.C., private investigator's credit report listed his "former employment" as simply "PRISON". In fact the individual had been assistant commissioner of corrections for a large northeastern state (*Privacy Journal*, 1990: 1). Mistaken identities in a rental real estate database likewise prevented a Los Angeles woman from renting any apartment in over 100 attempts and caused a high-level Washington cable company executive to be fired for alleged cocaine convictions. However, ordinary use of private databanks quite apart from such mistakes raises major issues of privacy rights, as in the case of Ernest Trent, an oil rig worker kept out of the industry for six years because company personnel managers utilize a database which blacklists workers who have ever filed a workman's compensation claim— even though it is their legal right to do so (Rothfeder, 1990b; Garfinkel, 1990).

A new dimension to the credit report agency problem arose in 1991 with the announcement of a CD-ROM commercial product (*MarketPlace Households*, from Lotus Development Corporation and Equifax Corporation—one of the top three credit bureaus) containing personal information on 80 million Americans. This product was withdrawn after 30,000 individuals requested removal of their names from the database. The Lotus plan elicited the concern of the Scientific Freedom and Human Rights Committee of the ACM (Association for Computer Machinery). The ACM Code of Ethics, Section 1.7 (see Appendix I), drawn in response to such threats to privacy state, " It is the responsibility of professionals to maintain the privacy and integrity of data describing individuals. This includes taking precautions to ensure the accuracy of data, as well as protecting it from unauthorized access or accidental disclosure to inappropriate individuals. Furthermore, procedures must be established to allow individuals to review their records and correct inaccuracies. This imperative implies that only the necessary amount of personal information be collected in a system, that retention and disposal periods for that information be clearly defined and enforced, and that personal information gathered for a specific purpose not be used for other purposes without consent of the individual(s)" (White, 1991: 11). In terms of these guidelines, *MarketPlace Households* seemed to border on the unethical.

The *Marketplace Households* project was particularly objectionable in that its distribution on CD-ROM disks removed all possibilities of control over its use. However, other private sector initiatives toward creation of integrated national databases have gone a long way toward doing what the government, thus far, has been forbidden to do (see Figure 1-12). The ACM ethics code notwithstanding, private-sector national databanks rarely become public issues. Rather, they are taken as part of the normal way of doing business in the 1990s. It is reasonable to suppose that acceptance in the private sector will eventually be followed by legitimation of national data banks in the public arena. The issue is perhaps not so much "whether" as "when" and "how"—in particular how data quality checks and privacy safeguards will be implemented.

Conclusion: Information Systems as Political Process

At the start of this chapter it was stated that resolution of the three-way tension among access, privacy, and ownership rights needed to come from political processes, not technical solutions. One way to think about this is to consider what is apt to happen under purely technical or purely economic strategies. Technical and economic perspectives each has a role to play, but that role needs to supplement, not replace, a broader political process in which all relevant actors affected by information systems confront each other, seek their own goals, and in the end reach compromises in the form of governmental and organizational regulations over information systems.

A purely technical approach would envision elaborate, fail-safe systems of computer account privileges, passwords, privacy-protecting data filters, and other software system safeguards. The technical approach can mitigate access/privacy issues to some degree in some settings. But in the end, the fact is that there is a big demand for information others would just as soon keep private. As with prohibition policy on alcohol or drug policy on cocaine, it is difficult to suppress demand through better technical solutions. Bankers want to

Figure 12: Mini-case: National Data Banks in the Private Sector

PEP, the Personal Employee Profiling Service. Developed by the Human Resource Information Network, this national on-line database provides employers with consumer information, asset evaluation, property records, business background data, pre-employment reports, national motor vehicle information, criminal records, educational data, credit reports, and more. To gain access to this detailed information on an individual, a searcher need only respond, attest the information is sought for employment purposes, and that the candidate has signed a proper release form. Also, PEP sends postcards to searchers to verify their passwords. In the case of Fax transmissions, PEP asks the searcher to stand by the Fax machine so reports are not seen by unauthorized individuals (*Database Searcher*, 1990a: 10). In spite of these precautions, however, the opportunity exists for possible abuse of privacy.

SBS, the Strategic Banking System. This $100 million system created by Banc One and EDS provides salespeople with detailing information about bank customers. SBS was six years and 10 million lines of code in the making. It can provide as much as 12,000 pieces of data about a given customer: economic life histories of individuals, their ages, names and ages of their children, their salaries, retirement accounts, mortgages, loans, the number and kinds of cars that they own, and more (Layne, 1992). None of this data access is illegal or even new. What is new is how convenient systems like SBS make the process. SBS replaced 15 previously separate transaction processing systems and ties into 50 banking systems. Where earlier complexity had provided a certain likelihood of privacy, new integrated systems make full disclosure of all information convenient for anyone with access privileges.

know all your past dealings with business people, insurers want to know your past health history, and your employer wants to check out your past records from education to possible jail records. Politicians and marketers want to know your preferences and habits so they can target appeals to you. And if you are a public figure in any way, add the quest of reporters, your opponents, and the just plain curious who seek to know everything about you. Beyond this there is the major information demand coming from everyone from investors to corporate spies, to criminals seeking data that may turn to their advantage. Even we social scientists might like to know more about your political views, your religious practices, and even your sexual habits.

If information is valuable to someone, someone else will find a way to obtain it and sell it. During the 1992 election campaign, even leading presidential candidates were reported to have paid for and to have had no trouble obtaining detailed financial and other data about their key opponents and supporters alike. Earlier in 1992, widespread sale of information was reported in both the Social Security Administration and in the National Crime Information Center. Both had elaborate technical systems in place for protecting privacy, but "where there's a will there's a way". Technical safeguards may serve to convince the public and would-be regulators that "we've taken care of the problem". The aura of science confers tremendous legitimacy on the technical mentality but sole reliance on technology may paper over a problem, not bring it to the surface where it can be dealt with in a better way.

A purely economic approach fares no better. This is the mentality that every policy issue can be resolved by reliance on ownership rights in a free market environment. Our legal system tends to back up this perspective, conferring extraordinarily broad rights on the owners of information, just as it does the owners of the means of production. As we have seen in this chapter, ownership rights can conflict sharply with both rights of access and rights of privacy. Being legally entitled to assert "I own the information and I can do with it as I want" does not solve the problem that from a societal point of view information systems may be exacerbating problems we as a nation are trying to overcome. When the state of New York provides high-priced on-line legislative information to corporate lobbyists, effectively denying access to impoverished public interest groups, the mere fact that the law agrees this is legal under current ownership rights law does not in any way remove the policy issue at hand. Likewise, the Smithsonian is currently leaning toward commercial marketing of cultural information on optical media but critics charge that market access is much different from public access, which public goods deserve. The important concept of information as a public good is taken up again more extensively in our final chapter.

No single reform, whether it be mandating "information impact statements" for organizations or establishing a "Privacy Protection Commission" will end the inherent trade-off between access and privacy. But this does not at all mean reform is meaningless. The Emergency Planning and Community Right-to-Know Act (EPCRA) does help community groups seeking information access to respond to toxic pollution problems. The Paperwork Reduction Act of 1980 did get the ball rolling toward requiring federal agencies to develop explicit information policies with provisions on access and privacy. In spite of such reforms, however, concern remains over access and privacy as policy concerns. No reform will change the underlying demand for information or the likelihood that demand will be fulfilled in one way or another.

What is needed is not so much a single piece of legislation as it is greater public awareness that information access and privacy are issues that matter. The massive, rapidly-evolving world of information systems will be the subject of many reform efforts at organizational and governmental levels in the next decade. The real issue is not so much the specific reform proposals that are made as it is who will be the players in the political process which determines the rules of the information game. The technical perspective tells people that the players should be computer scientists, free from "political" influences. The economic perspective tells people to have faith in the corporate owners of information and their counterparts in government. Such viewpoints operate as ideologies to restrict who plays the game. From a societal point of view, however, the more diverse the players in conflicts over information rights, the better.

Many students and citizens come to the subject of information management expecting to be bored. They don't see their stake in it. They accept the ideologies which say it is the province of technical experts, corporate executives, and government officials. And more often than not, the politics of information systems -- a theme discussed throughout this book -- is fought out among a restricted group of information executives, suppliers, organizational clients, and other interested "insiders". However, control over information has everything to do with whether this nation will expand or restrict the freedom of its citizens, the productivity of its enterprises, and the effectiveness of implementation of its public policies. I end this chapter not with a solution but simply set forth the belief that it is the responsibility of students of information systems, whom I presume to be the primary readers of this book, to understand and make known the policy implications and issues of computing. As this happens the politics of information systems will become broader and more inclusive. Both organizations and society will benefit as a result.

ENDNOTES

[1] This field is covered by the monthly periodical, *The Computer Lawyer*, published by Prentice-Hall Law and Business, Englewood Cliffs, NJ.

[2] APDU, 87 Prospect Ave., Princeton, NJ 08544. Another organization with similar interests is the Government Relations and Fund Development program of the Special Libraries Association, 1700 18th Street NW, Washington, DC 20009.

[3] Although the CSA definition of "sensitve information" remained vague, it was considerably more restrictive than the sweeping policy of the National Security Decision Directive 145, which it overrode. NSDD 145 had required federal agencies and contractors to protect all "sensitive but unclassified" information. The CSA was seen as legislation undoing the excesses of NSDD 145, which in turn was seen as a directive gutting freedom of information initiatives (Head, 1988b).

[4] In a 1990 test, the author sent a written request to the system asking for (1) a major 1988-9 statistical report summarizing trends at the state's largest public university, and (2) a request for any holdings on use of "expert systems" by North Carolina state government agencies. The first turned out not to be a document on file with the system in spite of its importance, and with regard to the second the author was informed there was no way to determine if there wre any holdings of this nature.

[5] For information, call the GPO at 202-512-1530.

[6] For information on Fedworld, call 703-487-4650.

[7] Computerized fingerprint identification was considered and rejected by the U. S. in the 1970's. See U. S. Federal Advisory Committee on False Identification, *The Criminal Use of False Identification* (Washington, D.C.: Superintendent of Documents, 1976).

[8] Taxpayer Assets Project, POB 19367, Washington, DC 20036; 202-234-5176; juris@essential.org.

[9] An amendment to the Copyright Act, 17 USCS section 511, was added 15 Nov. 1990, PL 101-553, Sec. 2(A)(2), 104 Stat. 2749. This amendment makes it explicit that states and their employees are not immune from suit under the Copyright Act by virtue of the 11th Amendment.

[10] For instance, under the Electronic Communications Privacy Act of 1986, four things must be proved before a judge in order to obtain a court order: (1) probable cause that an individual has, is, or is about to commit a crime; (2) probable cause that access will provide evidence on the crime; (3) normal investigative procedures have failed to do not appear likely

to succeed; and (4) there is probable cause that the facilities where electronic mail access occurs are the facilities used or to be used by the person being investigated.

[11] Some 400 Sun Microsystems workstations are used, connected to three Cyber 960 mainframes and Cyber 830 multiprocessors, running IM/DM relational database software from Control Data Corporation of Minneapolis, MN.

CHAPTER IV

Computer Crime, Information Security, and Information Rights

Organizations quite naturally claim the right to combat crime and to keep secrets from competitors and unauthorized users. By nature, these rights have implications of central control. Central control for purposes of security and secrecy can conflict directly with rights to information access and to rights to privacy discussed in the previous chapter. For instance, in order to crack the famous "Hanover Hacker" computer espionage case described by Stoll (1989), Stoll had to eavesdrop on electronic mail of users who had stolen "superuser" network privileges. Likewise, the FBI in 1990 eavesdropped on hundreds of "hackers" and even set up a trap on an electronic bulletin board in its efforts to fight computer telecommunications crime (Sterling, 1992). Should court orders be necessary in such cases? Does the government's right to secrecy and its role in combatting electronic crime outweigh the rights of network users to privacy? At present, the pendulum is tipped heavily against the rights of privacy. However, the "Great Hacker Crackdown of 1990" was a factor behind creation of the Electronic Frontier Foundation, one of several groups now raising constitutional questions of this sort.

In this chapter I first look at the extent of the security/secrecy problem, focusing on computer crime. The case is made that far from being merely a fascinating news tidbit, computer crime is a major issue with national implications. I then look at organizational needs for computer security and secrecy. How are security objectives achieved and what national policies exist to assure success? A concluding section asks how information rights can be balanced against the needs for security and secrecy. I propose that codes of ethics may need to be made far more stringent than at present and we may need to continue to move toward (and possibly mandate by legislation) reforms such as establishment of a system of "data custodians" similar to that in some European countries.

Computer Crime

Computer crime has emerged as a much-publicized issue in newspapers, television, even motion pictures, and in books like Bill Landreth's *Out of the Inner Circle: The True Story of a Computer Intruder Capable of Cracking the Nation's Most Secure Computer Systems* (1989); Clifford Stoll's *The Cuckoo's Egg: Tracking a Spy Through the Maze of Computer Espionage* (1989); and Buck Bloombecker's *Spectacular Computer Crimes* (1990). Stoll, for example, traced the "Hanover Hacker" case, in which an astronomer turned system manager conducted a worldwide chase to catch a sophisticated computer spy who had broken into military and scientific systems around the globe. Likewise, Bequai (1986) has detailed the use of computers in international terrorism, political repression, organized crime, blackmail, sabotage, and industrial espionage.

USA Research Inc. estimated that in 1991, computer break-ins alone accounted for 164 million dollars in damage, double the amount in 1989. There were almost 700,000 reported attacks on U. S. workplace computers in 1991, again double the 1989 level (Violino, 1993a: 30, 35). All types of computer crime (e.g., software piracy, consumer fraud, program theft) probably bring total damages to over a billion dollars a year. A survey of 1,700 U.S. organizations found that 70% had experienced security breaches in the past year (Violino, 1993a: 30). On American campuses, a 1991 survey of academic computer center directors found that 43% reported unauthorized users who "hacked" their way onto a university computer, 70% noted illegal software copying, 71% reported harassing e-mail, 78% reported unauthorized use of accounts, 87% noted unauthorized sharing of passwords, and 91% reported virus infections (Stager, 1992: 28) -- all forms of computer crime in one way or another. A wider survey of primarily corporate users reported 58% had experienced computer viruses within the past year, with half reporting virus attacks were increasing and only 13% reporting a decreasing trend (*InformationWeek*, 1993: 25).

Computer crime is particularly threatening because organizations are often vulnerable. Information systems concentrate data far more than earlier paper systems, with the consequence that an amount of data that previously would require a truck can now be slipped into an employee's pocket and removed. The theft, alteration, or destruction of information resources, moreover, may itself be computerized so that the organization faces not one but thousands of criminal acts. Crime and abuse can be spread over vast amounts of data, as in schemes to allocate one tenth of one cent from all accounts into the account of the criminal. With earlier paper systems, of course, even the criminal would not find the paperwork involved worthwhile. Then, too, the rise of end-user and distributed computing in the 1980s has greatly dispersed the tools with which to commit computer crimes and abuses. Telecommunications networks have further exposed organizational vulnerability to individuals outside the organization, sometimes to anyone with a phone anywhere in the world. Even drug dealers, bookies, and other criminals have found uses for the instantaneity and relative privacy of electronic mail (Moran, 1990; Zimmerman, 1991), just as legitimate users have.

"Hacking" and computer viruses

There are popular images of teenage hackers telecommunicating computer viruses into national security networks (e.g., the Wisconsin '414 hackers' case in 1983, the *Wargames* movie, the *U.S. vs. Craig Neidorf* case in 1990[1] [see D. Denning, 1991; Haefner and Markoff, 1991]). Some such attacks have been politically based, as in the 1987 attack on Hebrew University by pro-Palestinians (Denning, 1988) or the 1989 attack on NASA by a group or individual using the name Worms Against Nuclear Killers (McCormick, 1989: 4).

Viruses are a non-trivial matter. New viruses appear at least once a week (Patrick Berry, 1991: 32). In 1992 an insurance industry expert reported that "The number of viruses has exploded exponentially. We used to see four or five viruses a month. Now we see that many each week" (*New York Times*, 1992: 8). Some viruses infect major installations such as HUD computers (the Department of Housing and Urban Development) (Schwartz, 1991b). In the U. S. Commerce Department records have been kept on viruses since 1988. These data show a skyrocketing in 1991. In October, 1991, Commerce Officials spent more time on virus recovery than in the entire previous year (Smith, 1991b: 1). A survey of 600 large companies found 40% reported viral problems in the third quarter, 1991, with the rate rising quickly (Violino, 1992a: 18). Over 1,100 distinct computer viruses had been identified by 1991, with approximately 10% of incidents being "disaster" class (affecting 25 or more stations). Managers increasingly call for full-time staff just to deal with viruses (Violino, 1992a). Some analyses of computer viruses estimate their cost will be $5 to $10 billion in the 1990-95 period (*PC Week*, 1990a).[2]

Telephone fraud by phone hackers ("phreaks") is at least a half-billion dollar problem. Telecommunications allows computer access to corporate PBX's and hence to racking up long distance phone calls by unauthorized individuals. To stop this financial hemorrhaging, AT&T has sued corporations to recover costs incurred by hackers (e.g., $528,000 at the N.Y. Human Resources Administration; over $1 million at the United Nations) (Thyfault, 1990). The airlines alone have incurred over a million dollars in liability due to phone hacking (Thyfault, 1991: 12).

Software Piracy

In terms of dollars, probably the biggest form of computer crime is software piracy. A poll of 900 *PC Computing* readers found 92% admitted to having used illegal software (Atelsek, 1992: 202). When multiplied over tens of millions of users, the costs of software piracy are staggering. However, costs are theoretical. The most common purpose for using illegal software is evaluation. Later, serious users are motivated abandon pirated copies in favor of purchasing software they find valuable in order to obtain manuals,technical support, and upgrades. Often illegal software are "home copies" of software purchased by an employer in situations where peoplc take work home but the fine print of software licenses disallows use on home machines. Were software piracy preventable, the increase in purchase of legitimate copies would be only a very small fraction of the total value of illegal software.

Embezzlement, Fraud, and Program Theft

These are the main forms of computer crime. They are white collar crimes by an organization's own employees rather than by hackers or criminals of the traditional type. The American Bar Association surveyed 148 firms in 1984, finding that computer crime occurred in 72 firms, with losses amounting to half a billion dollars (ABA, 1984). A survey by the National Center for Computer Crime Data (NCCD) found that 36% of computer crimes were for financial gain, 34% involved theft of computer services, and another 20% involved theft of or damage to software or data (Jennifer Smith, 1989: 18).

More recent estimates of computer crime range from a half-billion dollar a year problem (in America alone) to up to $5 billion (Loch, Carr, and Warkentin, 1991: 5). In 1985-1987, experts placed the average value of computer crime between $76,000 and $92,000 (Gilbert, 1989). The National Center for Computer Crime Data reports that more than half the cases involve less than $10,000, perhaps reflecting the diffusion of computer crime (Race, 1990). These statistics are guesses and may underestimate the true dimensions of the problem. Some have estimated that reported computer crimes may be only one-sixth of the actual amount (Bailey and Rothblatt, 1984).

Numerous examples of computer crime can be cited (see Figure 4-1). In response to computer crime, computer law has become a major field in its own right, taught in at least 65 law schools (Speer, 1992: 21). There are many support organizations for computer law as well (see Figure 4-2) and computer law also has emerged internationally (Wasik, 1991). In spite of the rise of computer law and computer crime support services (see Figure 4-3), most efforts to combat computer crime must rely on private security agencies, not legislation. A 1989 Justice Department study attributed this to the relative lack of qualified law enforcement personnel in the public sector (cf. Rosenblatt, 1990). Likewise, a whole new profession of computer crime fighting has been spawned. One computer crime investigator reports that in most cases he is called in as a preventative measure to check computer security, but in 80% of cases he uncovers some type of criminal activity not suspected by management, usually perpetrated by employees of the organization (Race, 1990). Nonetheless, Neumann (1992) found that most reported cases of computer fraud

Figure 1: Computer Crimes

*** Financial theft**
Stanley Rifkin robbed a Los Angeles bank of over $10 million simply by making several phone calls to its wire transfer room to direct money to a Swiss account. In a second instance, a bank IS employee sent an electronic message to Brinks to deliver 44 kilograms of gold to a remote site, collected it, and disappeared (Neumann, 1992: 154).

Allen Green, a former automated teller machine repairman and employee of a Philadelphia bank, used its ATM machine to withdraw illegally $2,900 in 1984. Since then there have been larger ATM thefts, including one for $350,000 in which both user authentification and withdrawal limits were bypassed (Neumann, 1992: 154).

*** Product theft**
In the ladies apparel industry, a company president and comptroller conspired to place orders and then cancel them too late to stop production but early enough to have the company computer automatically cancel the invoice. They were left with thousands of undocumented items of clothing to sell for personal profit (Race, 1990).

*** Information theft**
NASA records show that on dozens of occasions between 1981 and 1989, unauthorized users gained access to the Space Physics Analysis Network's computers and used them to gain access to other NASA and federal computers (GAO, 1989b).

*** Software theft**
Seattle engineering firm Parametrix was forced to pay $350,000 when caught using bootleg software by the Software Publishers Association (Soat and Garvey, 1991: 40).

Figure 2: Support Services for Computer Law

*** Computer Law Association**
A professional association with conferences and publications. CLA, 3028 Javier Road, Suite 500E, Fairfax, VA 22015; 703-560-7747.

*** Computer Law Institute**
Sponsored by the Practicing Law Institute, the CLI offers programs and publications. CLI, 810 7th Ave., NY, NY 10019; 212-765-5700.

* ***Computer Liability Report***
A bimonthly newslette on computer law cases and issues. CLR, Hagelshaw & Cole, 27 Maiden Lane, Suite 600, San Francisco, CA 94018; 415-296-0554.

*** Software Publishers Association**
A vendors group whose activities range from education on computer law issues to raids on organizations suspected of using pirated software. It offers a free audit disk which seeks out pirated software residing on hard drives. SPA, 1730 M Street NW, Suite 700, Washington, DC 20036-4510; 202-452-1600.

*** Electronic Mail Association**
Offers publications related to privacy and information rights. EMA, 1555 Wilson Boulevard, Suite 300, Arlington, VA 22209; 703-875-8620.

Figure 3: Support Services Dealing with Computer Crime

*** National Criminal Justice Computer Laboratory and Training Center (Washington, DC)**
Initiated in 1988 by the Criminal Justice Statistics Institute on a Justice Department grant. Provides training and technical assistance for police, prosecutors, court officials, and other criminal justice personnel.

*** Financial Fraud Institute**
U. S. Department of Treasury

*** Financial Crimes Enforcement Network**
U.S. Department of Treasury

*** Information Systems Security Association**
ISSA is a 1,600-member private sector association (Robb, 1990b)

*** National Center for Computer Crime Data**
A private sector resource for security professionals.

had been uncovered by chance and carelessness by thieves (e.g., exceeding withdrawal limits), not by systematic security efforts.

Program theft when committed by one organization vis-a-vis its competitor or by an organization vis-a-vis a software publisher is a clear and major form of computer crime. It should be noted, however, that when it comes to disputes between an organization and its employees, what the organization calls "program theft" may be viewed by the employee as "intellectual property rights" (see National Research Council, 1991b). Programmers in a firm or agency routinely sign waivers assigning to the organization all rights to programs they create. Even if they don't, such programs are viewed by the courts as "work for hire" and the property of the organization. However, in recent times application development has become an activity of computer enthusiasts throughout the organization, not just of programmers hired for the purpose. In general the law holds that programs created outside an employee's job description belong to the employee unless a specific waiver of rights has been signed (McPartlin, 1993b).

Organizations often choose to combat information system crime and abuse internally rather than rely on external regulation because such acts may be seen as evidence of poor security management, embarrassing the organization. This may lie behind findings that managers commit larger computer crimes but are less severely punished than are lower employees (Straub and Nance, 1989). One report estimates that businesses report only 6% of instances of computer crime (Loch, Carr, and Warkentin, 1991: 5).

Computer Crime by Corporate Policy

In the foregoing discussion, the focus was on individuals as criminals. However, as Kling (1980b) noted over a decade ago, computer crimes by individual criminals are dwarfed by abuses associated with common business practices. For instance, an executive of Borland International was recently charged with sending stolen trade secrets via electronic mail to competing computer firm, Symantec Corporation (Kelly, 1993). Theft is an illicit but apparently widespread corporate practice supporting an indeterminate number of "grey sector" operations. Being illegal, data is hard to come by but anecdotal evidence suggests information theft is not uncommon. One executive was quoted as saying, "Last week I got a call from some guy who said he could get me anything on anybody for $50. He had a shopping list of stuff he could get, a whole section on corporations. I hear from these people all the time" (Violino, 1993b: 49). Indeed, hiring hackers who were convicted of electronic crimes in order to test corporate information security is now a business in its own right.

Other practices which may constitute computer crime may include, for instance, deception of consumers about the capabilities of software or liabilities under electronic funds transfer (credit cards, debit cards, etc.). To take one example, research at UCLA found as much as a 5:1 bias in bar-code scanners used at check-out counters toward overcharging rather than undercharging errors. They estimated that this cost consumers an estimated $2.5 billion annually (Bartholomew, 1992a: 27). Though such practices are sometimes contested in civil suits, our society does not usually take them into account when "computer crime" is considered even though the amounts involved are an order of magnitude higher.

Computer Crime: A Conclusion

In the 1980s there was a growing recognition that computer crime was a national problem requiring a national public policy. The Computer Fraud and Abuse Act of 1986 (CFAA) reflected this growing awareness. By 1988, some 47 state statutes dealing with computer crime also were on the books. For instance, Texas's computer sabotage law was passed in 1985 and led to its first conviction in 1988—a fired insurance computer programmer who destroyed the firm's payroll records (*Insight*, 1988: 61). A survey of 657 IS executives, however, uncovered the fact that three out of five had no idea whether or not their state had computer laws ((Loch, Carr, and Warkentin, 1991: 6). Moreover, a survey of 33 state laws found them to have fundamental weaknesses due to unclear wording, lack of a simple trespass violation, jurisdictional problems, and interstate inconsistencies (Nycum, 1986).

Even though computer crime is a billion dollar national problem it was not until January 22, 1990 that the first person was convicted under the CFAA. The individual convicted was Robert Morris, a Cornell graduate student hacker who had originated a destructive "worm" or "virus" program which had caused networks connected to Internet and some defense systems to crash worldwide on Nov. 2, 1988 (Spafford, 1989). Damages were estimated to be over $200,000 (see Figure 4.4).

Was Morris typical of computer criminals? Among hackers there is some evidence from self-reporting surveys that destructive hacking of this type is associated with male status, lower socioeconomic background, larger family size, and coming from a culture where it is perceived that referent others undertake similar actions (Harrington,

Figure 4: The Internet Worm Case

"The virus—a sophisticated 50,000 line program—searched out valid user names, files, log-on procedures and passwords. It located any attached networks and compiled a list of target machines in those networks. It replicated itself until it used up the infected machine's available storage space, slowed legitimate processing to a crawl and then moved on to other targets.

The virus spread with frightening speed. Within minutes it had contaminated its way across the continent and had entered computers at Bellcore, Livingston, N.J. As soon as Bellcore researchers detected it, they shut their systems down. Hit at almost the same time, the National Aeronautics and Space Administration's Ames Research Center, in Mountain View, California, also shut down its systems. Two days later, the organization still had not restored service to its 53,000 computer users."

TPT/Networking Management, December, 1988: 10, 12.

1989: 34). In white collar computer crime, criminals are also white males between 18 and 30 but are more likely, as one would expect, to be middle class (Manzolillo and Cardinalli, 1990: 16). However, in terms of dollars Morris was hardly typical. White collar crime is popularly perceived in terms of images of graduate student hackers silently injecting viruses into defense computers in the middle of the night, just "for the hell of it". The larger reality, however, has to do with computer crime by organization insiders finding ways to make computer technology profitable, sometimes for themselves at the expense of the organization and sometimes for the organization at the expense of society.

In the end, any organization's members have to be motivated to 'do the right thing', and to regard violations as lapses into unprofessional or unethical behavior. Recognizing that computer security has a very human dimension, many organizations have turned to formal ethics programs, involving establishment of ethics codes, ethics training for employees, establishment of a system for reporting ethics violations, and creation of an in-house disciplinary process for violations (Green, 1990). Codes of ethical conduct do not replace the need for legislation such as the CFAA but, by the same token, legislation regarding computer crime will be far more effective if it is supported by the social infrastructure of well-thought-out codes of ethics which have meaningful organizational sanctions apart from the legal system itself. This theme is discussed further in the conclusion to this chapter.

National Policy on Computer Security

Legislation pertaining to electronic security goes back to World War II with concerns for protecting secret military and intelligence coding schemes and devices (see Figure 4-5). As business needs for electronic data encryption escalated in the 1980s and 1990s, governmental agencies like the NSA and the FBI came into conflict with the business and computer industry communities, which sought to market and utilize advanced encryption technologies which even these agencies could not crack.

Security also intensified as a policy issue in the second half of the 1980s in part because Microsoft and IBM, the leading PC operating system and PC manufacturers respectively, did not incorporate physi-

Figure 5: Roots of Computer Security Policy

*** Invention Secrecy Act of 1940 (ISA)**
Provided that discussion of new technologies for which a patent is sought could be prohibited or censored for a period of months. The ISA has been applied routinely to cryptographic applications.

*** International Traffic in Arms Regulation Act of 1943 (ITAR)**
Defined cryptographic encoding programs as "munitions" subject to export control.

*** National Security Act of 1947**
Used in conjunction with legislation above as a legal basis for governmental assertion of secrecy rights in cryptography and related technology.

*** National Security Agency (NSA)**
Established in 1952 by President Harry Truman as a secret government agency with the mission of protecting the government's ability to keep its own codes security and developing the ability to crack the codes of others (Murray, 1992: 13-14).

cal and data security systems into their products as did the originators of the more powerful UNIX operating system (which, as a consequence, is now finding increasing favor in government). For this reason, workstations which must be centrally controlled are sometimes advocated by those concerned with maximizing security in IS, both in the United States and in the former Soviet Union (Stone, 1987). Likewise, the National Security Agency's Project Overtake and Commercial Comsec Endorsement Program (CCEP) supports development of secure communications devices, such as encryption modules, the ability to remotely zero out modules which fall into the wrong hands, sensors to detect tampering, and alarms which indicate possible security problems (Sanders, 1989). Many federal sites use fingerprint identification devices to control access to premises as well (Hosinski, 1989).[3]

In the field of national defense, security is promoted by the National Security Agency's National Computer Security Center (NCSC) and the "Orange Book", a security bible titled *Defense Department's Trusted Computer System Evaluation Criteria* (Jander, 1989). The "Orange Book" and related TEMPEST security standards in defense are discussed extensively by Russell (1991). However, numerous other fields outside the defense area also require security to protect corporate secrets or to provide confidentiality and privacy.

The Computer Security Act of 1987 (CSA; PL 100-235) transferred authority for computer security from the National Security Agency, where 1984 National Security Decision Directive 145 had placed it, back to the National Bureau of Standards (now National Institute of Standards and Technology - NIST). The CSA meant that the federal government again would have two security standards: one for civilian agencies under the NBS and one for defense agencies under the NSA. The passage of the act reflected the interest group power of civilian IS groups opposed to defense-based security standards not perceived appropriate for civilian applications (Grimm, 1988b; see hearings on the CSA in U. S. House of Representatives, 1988).

Planning for computer security is now part of the management task of directors of all civilian agencies, which must submit their proposed security plans to the National Institute of Standards and Technology (NIST). Planning is supported by the Computer System Security and Privacy Board, a policy-making body established in 1989 within NIST and charged with identifying technical and management issues affecting computer security and privacy issues (Power, 1989: 81). After the passage of the CSA, the NIST reviewed security plans for 53,443 computer systems in 74 federal agencies (Grimm, 1988e: 1). In conjunction with the NIST and as mandated by the CSA, in 1989 the Office of Personnel Management implemented a basic course on computer security to assist agencies in meeting the training requirements of the Computer Security Act.[4] The NIST's National Computer Systems Laboratory also maintains the NCSL Computer Security Bulletin Board providing technical support to agencies seeking to implement CSA plans.[5]

In the aftermath of its passage, most observers reported that the CSA made little substantive difference in agency practice (Grimm, 1988f). A 1990 audit by the General Accounting Office reviewed a sampling of 22 security plans filed under the CSA. The GAO found that only 145 out of almost 400 security controls had even been planned by early 1989, and of these, only 38% had actually been installed (GAO, 1990f). Citing the inadequacies uncovered in this study, Representative Robert Torricelli (D-NJ) said, "The U. S. government remains a Third World country with respect to computer security" (Smith and Power, 1990: 93). Following the GAO report, the Office of Management and Budget issued OMB Bulletin

90-08, establishing a system of on-site visitation of agencies to review their security plans by representatives of the OMB, NIST, and National Security Agency (NSA).

Reacting to criticism such as this and to growing awareness of the extent and dangers of poor computer security, in 1993 the OMB revised Circular A-130, the leading federal policy document on information planning. The revision specified that only employees who have received security training courses can be allowed access to government networks. It also required all agencies to establish a computer incident reporting system, identify response capabilities for various types of incidents, and to test system contingency plans regularly (Power, 1993b: 65).

Recent policy debate has focused on data encryption, one of the commonest approaches to security. The FBI, frustrated by the difficulty of tapping multiplexed phone lines called, supported Senator Joseph Biden's 1991 Senate Bill 266, which declared "It is the sense of Congress that providers of electronic communications systems permit the government to obtain the plain text contents of voice, data, and other communications when appropriate authorized by law" (Barlow, 1991: 25). Similar wording was proposed for (but failed to pass) in the Omnibus Crime Act of 1991. Likewise, the National Security Agency (NSA) has proposed to the Federal Communications Commission that vendors be required to redo their encryption software to provide an electronic "back door" for NSA access (Gassee, 1992). Taken at their face meaning, these proposals would mean that communications vendors would be obliged to turn their encryption keys over to authorized government agents.[6]

The battle intensified in 1993 when the NSA pressed to make its own encryption software, embedded in ROM on a 'Key Escrow Chip' ("Clipper chip"), the basis for security. The chip would be embedded in telephones and other devices connected to the emerging 'National Information Infrastructure' (NII) proposed by the Clinton administration (see Chapter 8). Under the NSA plan, once contact was established between the sender's and receiver's devices, the chip would select from among millions of encoding keys for that particular transmission, making interception impossible—except that transmissions could be decoded by the NSA, FBI, and others who would have authorized access to "key-escrow" databases. Law enforcement agencies would have to obtain a court order to obtain decoding keys, each stored in two parts in two separate government agencies. Clinton endorsed this strategy and the underlying principle that government agencies must retain decoding capabilities, but he called for voluntary adoption, starting with implementation of the Clipper chip throughout the Department of Justice (White House, 1993; see also Wayner, 1993; Begley, 1993).

Corporate leaders opposed the Clinton plan on grounds that if government could decode information, competitors and criminals would learn ways to do so as well. Computer industry interests were also opposed on grounds that the Clinton plan would require separate American and foreign versions of products since foreign governments would not want to purchase technology designed to allow U.S. government 'snooping'. Finally, civil libertarians like the Electronic Frontier Foundation opposed the plan because it threatened Constitutional rights against illegal search and seizure (Mace and Willett, 1993).

In summary, the thrust of existing national policies on computer security are directed toward traditional defense-sector needs and considerations. A conflict between the defense and civilian sectors has arisen, articulated most sharply in conflict over cryptographic and telecommunications technology which would defeat the traditional defense-sector objective of having the means to keep American military transmissions secure while being able to monitor everyone else's transmissions. Business, however, particularly in a competitive global economy, wants and has sought out cryptographic software and telecommunications standards (e.g., ISDN— integrated systems development networks) which provide uncrackable security.

At this writing it is expected that the Clinton administration would modify Reagan-Bush policies in these matters and would take a more pro-industry stance than did Bush, himself a former CIA chief highly committed to the national security community (Stephens, 1992). Within government, the IS community in civilian departments became increasingly large and powerful in the 1980s, eventuating in their being set free to sail their own course under the Computer Security Act of 1987. Although the CSA forces agencies to have a security plan, there is no unified national policy on just what these plans should entail. The next section explores many of the management issues which arise in setting organizational security policies.

Managing Security Systems

The public policy aspects of computer crime, security, secrecy, and privacy rights are tied closely to questions involving the management of security systems. As data have been downloaded increasingly from mainframes to PCs the issue of data security has intensified, popularized in works such as Jay Tuck's *High-Tech Espionage* (1986). Although 'manager of computer security' was not a formal job classification of the U. S. Office of Personnel Management, by 1991 efforts were underway to make it one, reflecting the enormous growth of concern for computer security (Power, 1991b). Likewise, computer security is now well-established in university curricula, reflected in textbooks (e.g., Pfleeger, 1989).

While such security principles seem common sense, the are frequently violated in practice. As National Computer Security Center (NCSC) chief scientist Bob Morris has noted, "Any system can be insecure. All you have to do is stupidly manage it" (Stoll, 1989: 240). Using obvious passwords, sending access information in the mail, failure to examine automated security audit data, giving access information to subordinates and other unauthorized persons, and other human failures can compromise even an elaborate defense-sector computer security system. For instance, in 1992 the General Accounting Office took the Drug Enforcement Agency to task for putting classified information on informants and undercover operations at needless risk, potentially endangering lives and jeopardizing the war on drugs. The DEA, it noted, did not know what computers were processing national security information. DEA personnel were routinely processing classified information improperly on computers that are neither approved for such use nor appropriately safeguarded (GAO, 1992a).

Outside defense, computer security is often inadequate. The President's Council on Integrity and Efficiency (PCIE) audited computer systems at 10 federal agencies during 1986-1989 by having experts attempt to access supposedly secure databanks. PCIE Director John Lainhart later noted, "I didn't expect to penetrate every system as easily as we could. Managers were not paying attention to security because they thought it was technical. Worse, even though vendors told them how to protect software, the users installed packages without implementing all the security features" (Silver, 1989:

74). A 1990 General Services Administration study of the Department of Justice found many disturbing weaknesses in security and concluded that the Justice Department was not adequately protecting its highly sensitive computer systems. Justice lacked plans for handling disruption of computer services, lacked training of personnel in security, and had lax physical security in its facilities (GAO, 1990c). A 1991 GAO study found dozens of security lapses at the New York, American, and other stock exchanges (GAO, 1991a). To take another instance, 1991 Congressional hearings revealed that weak security measures in the U.S. Attorney's Office in Lexington, Kentucky, allowed sale of surplus computer equipment which still contained highly sensitive data. And during the Persian Gulf War, Dutch hackers were able to penetrate 34 Department of Defense sites due to poor password management, inadequate security training, and failure to maintain and analyze audit trails (GAO, 1991c).

To combat computer crime, organizations need to establish an information system which alerts executives to unusual transaction levels or types, flags duplicate transaction codes, and maintains a record of which stations initiated which transactions, as well as undertake other security measures noted above. Nonetheless, investigating computer crime can be complex, time-consuming, and costly, and many organizations simply lack the resources (Alexander, 1990).[7] A national study by Nance and Straub of over a thousand American organizations found that of computer abuse which was discovered, 41% was detected by accident and only half by formal system control (Dooley, 1988: 4).

Information systems managers face three main classes of problems. These are providing physical security, establishing access rules, and making security systems "user-friendly". The next three sections discuss each of these in turn.

Providing Physical Security

Computer security also has not only to do with protection against spies and criminals, but also against earthquakes, floods, and even such disasters as when a groundhog crawled into the transformer of the U. S. Navy's David Taylor Research Center (Dudek, 1989); when an electrical fire at the Securities Industry Automation Corporation caused the New York and the American Stock Exchanges not to open

Figure 6: A Checklist for Security Management

Security systems for IS are among the most complex challenges for managers. Martin (1981:584-585) has listed eleven major dimensions of IS security systems:

1. There must be a finite list of identifiable system users.

2. Each user must have network authorization.

3. Actions of each user on the system must be monitored.

4. Both hardware and software must be protected from alteration or damage.

5. Unauthorized users must be locked out.

6. If there is damage or loss to data, data must be reconstructible.

7. The network connecting users and computers must be tamper-proof ("failsafe").

8. Network transmissions must be private.

9. There must be a capacity to audit the data.

10. Computer centers themselves should be catastrophe-proof.

11. Computer centers, at least the critical ones, should have backup centers where IS process could be replicated if needed.

(Schmerken, 1990); when a short-circuit in the Burlington Northern Railroad's St. Paul, MN, data center shut down 25,000 miles of track for two hours; or when terrorists bombed New York's World Trade Center in 1993, causing hundreds of financial firms to scramble to assemble makeshift computer networks (McPartlin and Panettieri, 1993). Commercial computing's worst disaster to date was occurred in April, 1992, when a tunnel collapse sent 250 million gallons of water into tunnels and basements in Chicago's business district, setting off large-scale computer failures in over 30 companies (Caldwell, 1992a).

Likewise, IS managers must worry about facilities factors illustrated by NASA, which has stored over half of its 1.2 million magnetic tapes in substandard conditions, according to the GAO (Caldwell, 1990g: 48). Information systems security management covers risk analysis, physical security (intrusion, power lapse back-up generators, redundant power feeds, fire, lightning, flood), personnel security, regulations and laws (privacy, national security, international constraints), hardware security (physical access, electromagnetic radiation, wiretapping), software security (viruses, passwords and access controls, audit trails), and network security (encryption, digital signatures, hacking) (Borsook, 1993; Cooper, 1989).

IS security ranges from concerns over fire protection to electronic eavesdropping to espionage and terrorism. Measures may range from acquiring guard dogs to implementing elaborate electronic encryption and password systems. Some security consultants even recommend hiding the organization's data center by removing signs and directory listings (Krass, 1991a: 13). When, as is frequently the case, computer systems are distributed rather than centralized, security issues multiply exponentially. The fact that computer data must be backed up doubles the problem since the backup files must be secured as well. Frequently, organizations have given little thought to protecting the data on distributed systems (Fillon, 1992: 30). In the 1992 Chicago disaster, for example, of the 18 outages handled by Comdisco Disaster Recovery Services, only 7 involved mainframes.

Redundancy is the main approach to physical security at computer sites. It is estimated that some 28% of total processing downtime is associated with mismanagement of the site infrastructure, but ideal management is expensive (Puttre, 1990: 34). A model is the Newport Financial Center (Newport, N.J.), designed with a "fail-safe infrastructure". Features of this infrastructure are dual independent lines to the local electric utility; dual diesel generators for backup power; regular monitoring of all cabling; redundant telecommunications and cooling systems; centralized 24-hour monitoring of all environmental and security systems; a dual fire protection system; and a strict physical-access control system. Similarly, the National Computer Center of the Social Security Agency is protected by a $2 million uninterruptible power supply of 768 battery cells that kick in upon any power loss.

Though one might think that IS security was primarily a technical matter, Buck Bloombecker of the National Center for Computer Crime Data reports that of the typical corporate budget for computer security, 67% goes for security personnel. Only 10% goes for hardware and software. Some 23% is expended on outside services and other items. Overall, out of every $100 in a typical corporate budget,

$3 is spent on computer security and of this, $2 is spent on hiring security personnel (*Computer Technology Review*, 1990: 1). Most security problems in commercial IS are due to abuse of authority granted to employees, a sampling of 3,000 cases by the National Research Council revealed (1991a: 61, 159-60). Computer security investigators are therefore mainly concerned with assuring that properly authorized personnel do, in fact, follow appropriate procedures.

Determining Information Access Rules

What is the scope of data which may be accessed by various classes of users? This issue arose in a 1989 lawsuit filed by the National Security Archive, the Center for National Security Studies, and Public Citizen, to gain access to electronic records from the Reagan administration. The suit raised questions about the status of electronic files kept by federal agencies. While the Federal Records Act gives the national archivist power to prevent the destruction of federal records, the act is ambiguous on the definition of what a "record" is though clarifying legislation has been proposed.[8]

The lawsuit arose in connection with the Iran-Contra scandal, in which Colonel Oliver North was charged with illegal redirection of funds to support anti-Nicaraguan guerrillas. North had conducted much of his business on the White House electronic mail system using a software package called the Professional Office System (Profs). Profs recorded all transactions to a temporary file on disk, erasing these files automatically when backups were made. The White House normally kept backup tapes only six weeks. The lawsuit claimed these backup tapes were public documents within the meaning of FOIA. The White House said they weren't and maintained the information is not a record until printed in hard copy and placed in official White House files (Himelstein, 1990; Quindlen, 1993a).

In this case (*Armstrong vs. the Executive Office of the President*), not decided until 1993, U. S. District Court Judge Charles Richey ruled that White House e-mail did contain federal records.[9] Richey found the White House and the National Archives and Records Administration (NARA) in contempt for failing to preserve e-mail records and ordered them to disseminate new guidelines for managing federal electronic records. Fines and jail terms were stipulated if agencies failed to protect such electronic records. The incoming

Clinton administration took the same view as the Bush administration and appealed Richey's ruling to the Court of Appeals for the District of Columbia. Although NARA naturally followed presidential policy in this matter, many records managers in NARA and federal agencies would not agree personally with the government's position in this case (Quindlen, 1993c: 1).

There are numerous other cases of governmental agencies resisting public release of data. An example is the unsuccessful effort of hospitals to challenge the release of mortality data by the Department of Health and Human Services (HHS). One the one hand the news media assert the right of the public to know which hospitals have unusually high death rates. On the other hand hospitals, many operating on tenuous budgets, fear that such announcements could drive away patients and threaten their survival, all on the basis of easily misinterpreted statistics. A hospital might have a very high death rate, for instance, because it differed in the type of patients it admitted, not in the quality of its care. In this case the public's right to know seems to have prevailed, but the case illustrates the reasons why organizations may resist information disclosure (Droste, 1987; Robinson, 1988).

The increasing use of telecommunications for medical consultations among doctors plus the advent of medical expert systems which dispense computer-generated diagnoses online, raise other security and confidentiality issues in the sensitive medical area (Rozovsky, 1985). For instance, doctors were pitted against hospitals and insurance companies in the case of the National Practitioner Databank, mandated by a 1986 federal law to help hospitals avoid hiring incompetent practitioners (GAO, 1990e). The databank receives some 60,000 records per year on adverse actions against doctors and other medical providers. Some one million queries per year are made of the database, causing doctors to protest that their reputations are besmirched due to any suit against them even if no fault was ever proved (Caldwell, 1990a), or if they had settled for small amounts simply to avoid larger legal costs (GAO, 1992d). At its 1993 annual meeting, the American Medical Association called for the repeal of the 1986 act to remove the "hassle factor" from medicine. Are databanks responsible for such misinterpretations, however likely, of the data they house, if they themselves are careful in their own statements? So far, the answer is no. There is no legal basis for denying information access to public data simply on the ground that the data may be misinterpreted by users.

Information access may be denied, however, simply through control over selection of which information is to be posted online in the first place. In 1993 the University of Wisconsin at Eau Claire, a public university, exercised this power in disconnecting Robert E. McElwaine from the Internet network. McElwaine, a middle-aged physics student, was given to writing long, rambling discourses on perpetual motion, Bolshevik conspiracies, claims the Holocaust was a myth, and other topics which he would post on electronic bulletin boards which often were devoted to other purposes. The university, in disconnecting McElwaine, took the view that it had the right to control data posted from its segment of the network in the interests of protecting other users from the burden to viewing communications in which they were not likely to be interested. Others took the view that McElwaine's free speech rights had been violated.

A similar furor erupted at the Northeastern Ohio University's College of Medicine when a network administrator set up a computer program to automatically hang up on any network user it flagged as a "crank" or "prankster". Deciding where access rights end and computer abuse begins is a controversial call for administrators. Although the College of Medicine administrator, Dick Depew, withdrew the censor program, he cited the rise of newsgroups for erotic images, discussions of sex, and tasteless jokes alongside on-line bulletin boards for academic topics. "If we don't take a certain amount of responsibility for what goes on with our newsgroups, then some outside force may come in and impose some sort of control on us," Deplew noted (Wilson, 1993: A21). That is, threat of public policy regulating on-line communications can be given as a justification for voluntary imposition of self-censorship. Such voluntary action, however, requires an organizational consensus on the line between valid free speech and impressible behavior— a consensus missing at the College of Medicine and in many other organizations.

Making Security Systems User-Friendly

Perhaps the greatest challenge associated with security systems is the need to make them user-friendly. On the one hand, as Highland (1988: 91) notes, "The more secure the network, the less user-friendly it can be". To enhance security, computer network managers will hide the identity of the network one is accessing, hide information about what brand of hardware is being accessed, and will not provide a help screen to assist users in the access process. Often they will not provide clear prompts for the user name, ID, and password, instead assuming users will know the proper access sequence. Secure networks may give the user seeking access only one try to "get it right" or they may give very little time to enter the correct information.

On the other hand, when security systems make users feel that the system is unduly inflexible or unfriendly, they may not be motivated to take the precautions which make the system work. Ultimately, the users must feel good about the security system and they must make it work. This may mean that security systems also include employee involvement in their planning, employee education, a system to report security problems, and rewards and sanctions for security compliance or noncompliance (Palmer, 1987: 45). Employees must be encouraged to do such simple things as not leaving their stations without logging off, and not leaving their passwords on desks or otherwise in plain sight (Radding, 1991a). Training for security is a key component of a IS security system, and such training is mandated for federal agencies by the Computer Security Act of 1987 (GAO, 1989a).

An illustration of the problems on non-user-friendly security systems is reported by Jim Seymour, a well-known computer columnist. Seymour had loaned out his hard-disk laptop computer to a colleague who also writes about computers. The colleague was reviewing locking programs for personal computers and installed several on Seymour's machine, leaving one installed when he returned the laptop. Seymour, following the security package instructions, soon found that the vendor-assigned password would not open the program. After calling the vendor, it was determined that a hidden file containing a new password had been erased and Seymour's colleague, who might have known about it, was abroad and unlocatable. Seymour had to reformat his hard disk, destroying all of its data, in order to regain control of his machine. "That echoed everything I've written about needing user-friendly security," Seymour wrote (1989: 10). "Here was a system that couldn't protect itself—in other words, its user—from ordinary human frailties."[10]

In summary, good management of security systems requires a combination of different strategies, not just one and certainly not just

Figure 7: Basic Security Strategies

Passwords
Passwords are an inexpensive, nearly universal strategy for computer security. Different users can be given different levels of access (e.g., restricting some users to read-only, with no capacity to modify data). The system must not allow repeated attempts to enter a password since computers can be programmed to try all combinations. Users tend to pick easy-to-guess passwords such as their initials (Highland, 1990: 61), they leave passwords near their stations or in wallets which become lost, they allow people to look over their shoulder as they enter passwords, and passwords are sometimes given out over the phone. For instance, entry was gained to a Navy computer at the Jet Propulsion Laboratory because a lazy user violated the rules and used his own name as a password (Munro, 1988b: 61). Greater security is achieved when all passwords are generated randomly on a secure computer and assigned to users, without user ability to redefine passwords. Passwords must be changed frequently, which is an administrative problem.

Data Encryption
Encryption disguises data files using either hardware or software (Seberry, 1989). Software systems require a key file on disk, with the possibility that the key may be stolen. Hardware systems are faster and more secure. Use of DES-approved algorithms reduces the chance of deciphering encrypted data but does not eliminate it. Moreover, there have been attempts in Congress (e.g., the Violent Crime Control Act of 1991: see 1991: 25) to force communications vendors to turn encryption keys over to FBI and other governmental agencies seeking to monitor voice, data, and other electronic communications.

Object Reuse
You can clear sensitive data from memory and/or disk after use, set time-outs to disconnect inactive computers and network connections, and automatically reset file clearance levels to require new authorizations by the network administrator.

passwords. Strategies include passwords, encryption, electronic audit trails, physical lock-up, and redundancy (see Figures 4-7 and 4-8). In general, security strategy is based on deterrence theory: making prospective losses outweigh prospective benefits of information system abuse. Policy education around formal codes of conduct are aimed at general employees, some of whom may simply be ignorant of the ethics of information system use and abuse.[11] Detection and criminal prosecution efforts are directed at employee embezzlers and other white collar criminals. Access controls, such as password

Figure 8: Basic Security Strategies, Continued

Audit Trails
Auditing software increases security by keeping detailed usage data by user and/or station, including time and type of access. Since 80% of all security breeches are internal, often via computer networks, a key defense is good monitoring software which documents all IS access in minute detail (Schwartz, 1990). For instance, audit information tracing a data delete command to his terminal was a key piece of evidence against Marshall Williams, who faced up to 15 years' imprisonment for deleting files and causing $400,000 in lost business and downtime to his employer (March, 1989).

Physical Lock-Up
Removable cartridge storage systems allow files to be removed physically from the computer system when not in use. However this very removability can increase dangers of contamination (e.g., cigarette smoke can damage storage media) or actual theft. Physical keycards which must be inserted or electronic locks on computers also limit access, though these can be lost or stolen.

Redundancy
In the event a system is compromised for whatever reason some systems build in redundancy to assure continued operation. For example, WordPerfect Corporation has a service staff of 500 to service the 11,000 daily calls. To secure service of all stations it ran two independent sets of cabling to each station so if one became disabled, the other could serve as a backup at the flip of a switch.

systems, are directed toward control of system hackers and career criminals. Surveillance may be necessary where corruption of high officials and experts may be a problem. On top of all this the organization must perform routine equipment checks, fire inspections, and other maintenance—things all to often neglected (Kass, 1990a) and the system must provide backups so that the original database can be reconstructed when all else fails.

Managing the many dimensions of security requires establishment of a professional security function in larger organizations (Wybo and Straub, 1989). With all these managerial concerns it is hardly surprising that "soft" issues like privacy and information rights are pushed to the side. Balancing security needs with information rights is the subject of the concluding section of this chapter.

Conclusion: The Role of Ethics in Balancing Information Rights

What is the balance between various information rights? Where does the right and duty of governments and corporations to fight computer crime end and the right of employees and citizens not to be subject to electronic surveillance begin? On the one hand there is the government's right to gather data in order to make effective economic and social policy. On the other hand there is the right of corporations not to be unduly burdened with data-gathering paperwork of a scale with more impact than most legislation yet imposed by bureaucrats rather than Congress. What is the balance between the corporation's right to use information technology to improve sales and profits versus the rights of citizens to maintain privacy rights the which technological innovations might attack? In response to questions such as these some have argued for limiting the size and scope of information systems in order to preserve individual liberties (Rule et al., 1980). However, others argue that foregoing the benefits of technology would only mean less efficient government and corporate systems with fewer services which are less humane (Laudon, 1980).

Many issues pertaining to computers and telecommunications will inevitably remain matters of judgment, not legislation. Gelder (1985) has reported an illustration of this. CompuServe, the largest general-purpose public network, provides as one of its services a "CB channel" which allows on-line "chatting". The anonymity provided by this service allowed a male to pose as a handicapped woman and carry on a series of electronic conversations over a long period of time with others on the network, many of who felt betrayed and harmed when the subscriber's gender eventually became known. Is this a matter of privacy rights of the male subscriber, a psychologist who wanted to explore reactions to a female persona? Is this "computer crime"? To what extent does CompuServe as a network have an overriding interest in preventing fraudulent transactions? To what extent does CompuServe have managerial responsibilities in matters such as this?

When considering computer crimes and transgressions, a prior question is "Does the public care about information rights in the first place?" The answer is yes, many studies show that the public is concerned with issues of privacy in relation to computer operations. A summary of opinion surveys from 1974 through 1983 showed that over half of all Americans (53%) felt computers were "an actual threat to personal privacy." A 1985 national survey by the Opinion Research Corporation showed 55% of Americans were "very concerned" about private information stored in computer databases.[12] Will information rights issues become more important in the future? On the one hand, the rapid increase in computer ownership makes the public more comfortable with computing and is therefore expected to diminish concern with and fear of computer threats to civil liberties (Dutton and Meadow, 1987: 166). On the other hand, others predict that "As more decision rules are automated in expert systems, perceptions of these problems may be amplified as mistakes are inexorably carried to their logical conclusion...which could trigger incidents that create perceptions of unacceptable intrusiveness" (McFarlan, 1990: 84).

It is still too early to tell if increased use will lead to increased acceptance or increased outrage. However, when the diffuse interests of the public in privacy and due process are weighed against specific opposing interests of corporations and government in secrecy, security, and ownership rights, the likely outcome is not difficult to predict. As Coates (1987) has argued forcefully, ethical standards in computing are routinely adapted to economic necessity. In general, specific interests usually overcome diffuse interests in the political arena. A danger exists, therefore, that a double standard will emerge, with large specific-interest information-oriented institutions successfully championing information access for themselves while frustrating the diffuse interests of the public. Likewise, one may see information-based institutions successfully defending information security for themselves while increasingly eroding privacy for ordinary individuals.

While most Americans are concerned with information rights issues of this type, a substantial minority are not. Moreover, while concern exists, many other issues take precedence in the minds of voters so that information rights is almost never an issue in election campaigns, nor is there much media priority given to information policy issues. Policy makers and information managers who seek to balance information rights must do so more on the basis of ethical standards than on the basis of popular mandates.

This is part of the reason why codes of ethics have become a major topic of discussion and action in professional associations related to information systems. This goes back a long ways in the health field, where confidentiality is regarded as critical, security provisions have been mandated for two decades in states such as New York, whose

"Ethical Guidelines for Data Centers Handling Medical Records" was finalized in 1974 by the Joint Task Group on Confidentiality of Computerized Medical Records and adopted by the House of Delegates of the Medical Society of the State of New York in March 1975 (Gabrieli, 1985). Outside the health arena no such comprehensive national approach to IS ethics exists, but organizations such as the Association of the Institute for Certification of Computer Professionals have been moved to create codes of ethics for the first time (McPartlin, 1992g: 31). Reformers such as Glastonbury and LaMendola (1992) have called for a formal "Bill of Rights for the Information Age" and for establishment of industry institutions to carry it out.

The largest American computing group, the Association for Computer Machinery (ACM) "Code of Professional Conduct" was updated in 1992.[13] As drafted by the ACM, Section 1.1 of this code says members "must attempt to ensure that the products of their efforts will be used in socially responsible ways, will meet social needs, and will avoid harmful effects to health and welfare" (see Appendix I). Section 1.7, on privacy, states "It is the responsibility of professionals to maintain the privacy and integrity of data describing individuals. This includes taking precautions to ensure the accuracy of data, as well as protecting it from unauthorized access or accidental disclosure to inappropriate individuals. Furthermore, procedures must be established to allow individuals to review their records and correct inaccuracies. This imperative implies that only the necessary amount of personal information be collected in a system, that retention and disposal periods for that information be clearly defined and enforced, and that personal information gathered for a specific purpose not be used for other purposes without consent of the individual(s)."

However, section 1.2 of the ACM Code "prohibits use of computing technology in ways that result in harm to any of the following: users, the general public, employees, employers." What happens when protection of privacy rights of the general public conflicts with mandated objectives of employers? Authors associated with the ACM Code of Ethics suggest computer professionals will cancel contracts and resign where, for example, employers opt for weak privacy security systems (Anderson, Johnson, Gotterbarn, and Perrolle, 1993: 100). However, one wonders if they will not use Section 1.2 to rationalize their service anyway on the grounds that two of the three named groups were served— the best that could be done. Likewise, Section 1.3 bars ACM members from making false statements, but one has to wonder what happens when they are interviewed about advertising claims of products or services produced by their employers.

A code of ethics is also published by the International Federation of Information Processing (IFIP), an association of national IS societies (Sackman, 1991). The IFIP code says IS professionals must work to improve the quality of working life. Does this mean that IS professionals must oppose computer surveillance of employees, universally regarded as a stressful practice eroding the quality of working life? The emergence of IS codes of ethics in the last decade is a sign of increasing recognition of human rights problems in computing but it is doubtful whether self-policing alone will solve the far-reaching problems involved.

This is not to say that codes of ethics are just window dressing. As Webster (1992: 19) notes, "Campuses whose codes of conduct do not include acceptable 'computer behavior' have a hard time justifying

Figure 9: Data Stewardship at North Carolina State University

NCSU policy, established in 1990, required all authorized users to complete a "Data Access Compliance Statement" which:

* Spells out confidentiality rules on what information is public and what is private.

* Makes it an offense subject to organizational disciplinary action to access data outside of one's assigned duties.

* Makes it an offense to release private information without authorization.

* Makes it an offense to publicly discuss university data records in a way that allows individuals to be identified, to share computer passwords, and so on.

* An enforcement structure is created from the chancellor through named "data trustees" (e.g., the Vice Chancellor for Finance and Business) to "data stewards" (department-level officials) to "data custodians" (computer support staff) to individual users (Winstead, 1990).

The NCSU policy is not unusual. Increasingly, agencies and companies are organizing to implement similar structures and procedures which assign responsibility to all levels of users of computerized data, with particular emphasis on the privacy rights of individuals.

disciplinary or punitive actions they take in response to violations. Students will claim they didn't understand, didn't know, didn't think about it because it wasn't mentioned. Some will say that if it wasn't forbidden, it must be allowed. Their litigious parents and the parents' lawyers will try to drive through the loophole. Some administrators fear being sued if they take a stand against behavior that isn't explicitly mentioned in an official publication." Rezmierski (1992: 26) suggests organizations can develop control policies or they can "develop processes to clarify community values, stimulate individual social growth, and increase the value placed on diversity". While creating codes of ethics can be constructive, it may be more effective in the long run to undertake activities which build a desirable information culture in an organization.

Public and private organizations have become attuned to the importance of ethical codes for information systems if only due to their fear of civil liability or even criminal penalty for possible transgressions of rights. At the author's institution (North Carolina State University), for instance, ethical guidelines were formalized in a data management policy centered on "data stewards", established in 1990 (see Figure 4-9). This is similar to the system of "data custodians" in the United Kingdom under British privacy acts (Kiely, 1992d). Data stewards or custodians do not resolve the tension between managing security concerns and maintaining privacy and access rights. But at least they locate responsibility for decisions on these matters. The concept of stewardship is that information is a resource maintained for the common good of the organization or, at the federal level, of society.

The data steward is responsible for protecting the organization's interests in combatting electronic crime. However the same individual is responsible for maintaining whatever privacy and access rights the organization has deemed fit to establish. Indeed, some of the same technology at the steward's disposal for monitoring networks to detect computer crime may be used to protect privacy rights against access by unauthorized individuals. Security, access, and privacy are sometimes complementary, sometimes in contention. As the data steward deals with issues sure to arise under these conditions, firm grounding in a code of ethical conduct is an important asset. It is even more of an asset if the organization has undergone the political process of bringing out into the open, raising conflicts about, and ultimately deciding collectively what it wants to consider ethical and what it wants to consider an offense. In this way politics must sanction ethics.

ENDNOTES

[1] Craig Neidorf, a University of Missouri student, was indicted on interstate wire fraud and transportation of stolen property due to his having published information about Bellsouth's 911 system. However, the government dropped the case and issued an apology when it became clear that Neidorf had not stolen anything but only published information that had been stolen by another party. His defense attorneys had likened his action to *The New York Times* having published *The Pentagon Papers*, a then-classified document illegally taken and released to them by Daniel Ellsberg, who was prosecuted.

[2] For Additional reading on viruses, see Denning (1990), Hoffman (1990), and Levin (1990).

[3] Examples of fingerprint security devices are *TouchSafe* (Indentic, Palo Alto, CA), *Thumbscan* (Thumbscan Inc., Oakbrook Terrace, IL), and *Ridge Reader Mint 11* (Fingermatrix Inc., North White Plains, NJ).

[4] For information on independent study courses, disk-based tutorials, and videos on security planning, contact OPM National Independent Study Center, 303-236-4097.

[5] To access this service, dial 301-948-5717 and type <Enter> twice after the CONNECT message is displayed. Access is 8-N-1 or 7-E-1 at 300 to 2400 baud. For example, one may download the Data Encryption Standard (DES) file spelling out mandatory encryption guidelines.

[6] A debate over the relative merits of the Department of Justice/FBI proposals for electronic wiretapping is reflected in a pro-FBI article by Denning (1993) and commentary by a variety of scholars and practitioners in a symposium in *Communications of the ACM*, March 1993 issue: 24-45.

[7] A manual has been issued to assist agencies without computer crime unites in such investigations (Kondos, 1988; Conly, 1989).

[8] Senatos John Glenn (D-Ohio) and David Prior (D-Ark) proposed such legislation in 1992-1993.

[9] A 1991 District of Columbia Circuit Court bars judicial review of presidential record-keeping. Thus Richey's order does not apply to electronic records of presidential advisors and other records which are strictly presidential rather than having a broader federal nature (Quindlen and McCarthy, 1993).

[10] Seymour now recommends an approach with lower absolute security but greater capacity for handling "frailties". An example at the personal computer level is SecretDisk II Administrator, a $500 program that creates one or more hidden virtual drives on one's hard disk, in which all files are encrypted and accessible only through passwords. The package also lets the security administrator retrieve lost or forgotten passwords.

[11] The case for an outline of ethics education on computing is found in the writings of sociologist Joseph E. Behar (1993, 1988).

[12] A computer search of POLL, the on-line database of all items asked in national polls such as those of Roper, Gallup, ABC News, etc., was conducted by the author in October, 1991. It revealed only two items: (1) a 1984 Harris poll showing 68% of Americans believed "it will be increasingly possible to use computer databanks to infringe upon personal privacy"; and (2) a 1974 Harris poll which showed 54% of Americans thought it was possible to "devise systems to safeguard the privacy of the individual against wiretapping, electronic surveillance, and the illegal use of computer tapes". The small number of survey items on this topic is itself evidence of the marginal public interest in this topic.

[13] The code is reprinted in Charles Dunlop and Rob Kling, eds., *Computers and Controversy: Value Conflicts and Social Choices* (1991): 693-697.

CHAPTER V

Social Impacts of Information Systems

When it comes to computing, human factors on the input side and social impacts on the output side are commonly more important than technical variables. A large literature has developed on the social impacts and human factors associated with information systems (e.g., Noble, 1984; Clark, McLoughlin, and Rose, 1988; Rosenberg, 1992). Although computing has had broad, primarily beneficial effects in economic, cultural, and political life, these impacts have elicited a range of charges that society may be harmed in one way or another by the rise of information technology.

In one sense, all impacts of computers are "social" since human beings provide the input to information systems and also receive the output. However, there is a narrower meaning of the term "social impact" associated with computing. As commonly encountered in the literature, social impacts have to do with effects of information technology which have societal consequences that go beyond political impacts and economic impacts. Because social impacts can be so numerous and so diverse, this chapter makes no pretense at being comprehensive or tightly integrated. Instead, five important but relatively unrelated social impact topics are examined.

First I discuss the symbolic uses of computing— the extent to which computing is used for functions of mystification and legitimation of predetermined policies rather than as a substantive tool for improving decision-making and increasing productivity. Second, I examine charges that computer technology is biased or even discriminatory on the basis of gender, race, ethnicity, class, and age. Third, I discuss the extent to which information managers may be held legally liable for the effects of their work. Fourth, I look at occupational safety issues associated with computing and at charges that challenge the common assumption that computer work has no inherent dangers for information workers. Finally, quality of work life (QWL) issues are discussed, emphasizing the sociotechnical nature of computing and inventorying the social variables which constitute success factors in implementing information systems.

The Symbolic Uses of Computing

There is an argument that discussions of the social impacts of computing should begin with an understanding that computing is primarily used for the power of its symbolism—for the scientific aura which it throws around matters to which it is applied. This argument seems to be supported by the common observation that the bulk of computer-generated reports wind up gathering dust on shelves. If computer information systems were really to keep decision-makers "in the loop", earlier scholars predicted, then their offices would become like "war rooms", with graphic terminals displaying on-line summary information in real time (Krauss, 1970). This vision of every top management office becoming an electronic war room for decision-making has not materialized. Does this signify a failure of the hopes that computing would profoundly improve organizational decision-making, and an implicit admission that in actuality computers are used not for actual decision-making but rather for decision legitimation? Similarly, some have even argued that top managers, distant from operating data at the bottom of the organization, have information systems established not so much for decision-making per se as simply for reducing managerial isolation and loneliness (Burlingame, 1961).

The Scientific Aura of Computing

Smart managers have long known that computers lend a mantle of scientific credibility to decisions they would have made anyway. In the heralded case in which computer-based program management (PERT) was implemented on the Polaris submarine, the admiral in charge later said PERT was used less for its ostensible functions than for its symbolic uses. That is, PERT created the appearance of progress on schedule, keeping overseers off the back of project leaders (Sapolsky, 1972). It may be not so much that computers improve decision-making as it is that they make people feel good about decision processes.

Theodore Roszak has argued that "a significant, well-financed segment of the technical and scientific community — the specialists in artificial intelligence and cognitive science— has lent the computer model of the mind the sanction of a deep metaphysical proposition" (Roszak, 1986: 218). That is, computers can be and are used for purposes of mystification, as "ideology machines" which produce hegemony for dominant powers (Mothe, 1987). People tend to have faith in what appears in a computer printout even though informal calculations might accomplish the same purpose. Even managers place too much credence on reports which are generated by a computer (Long, 1989).

This point is articulated by a federal policy analyst cited in Kraemer, Dickhoven, Tierney and King (1987: 92): "Basically, you can't fight or compete with numbers coming out of a computer with numbers you've generated off the back of an envelope. Since the opponents are going to use models, you have to do it too, to defend yourself. You can't just stand up and argue (and win) that simple calculations are as good as computer models, even if they may in fact be." Such recognition of the symbolic uses of computing is widely recognized among politicians and policy analysts. It may be a major force behind the increased use of computer modeling and other computer techniques in government (see Figure 5-1).

As Ashley Montague has commented, the old adage about GIGO (garbage in - garbage out) can become transmuted to mean "Garbage In - Gospel Out" (Roszak, 1986: 120). The increasing use of computers in schools may be reinforcing cultural assumptions that computer-based information is more objective and more authoritative than is information arising from reasoning, intuition, and insight (Bowers, 1988). Part of computer mystification may be a greater acceptance of determinism if not fatalism, implying passive acceptance of the supposed inevitability of computer results (Muir, 1988a, 1988b; see

Figure 1: Why Budget Officers Use Computer-Based Evaluations

Are computer information systems most likely to be used in the evaluation of public programs when it is necessary to invoke the power of their mystical aura?

A study of members of the National Association of State Budget Officers (NASBO) found that one of the most significant variables in explaining the degree of usage of computer-based evaluation was the degree of perceived public demand for accountability ($r = .49, p < .001$). See Stevens and LaPlante, 1986: 527, Table 2.

The correlation of use of computers with perceived need for accountability suggests that the motivation to use computers in budget evaluations may differ from what is commonly assumed. That is, the need to prove one's agency is accountable to accepted procedures, not necessarily need for the computer per se, may be behind use of computers in evaluating public programs.

This is consistent with the work of those who argue that computers are widely used to provide a mantle of science and impartiality for bureaucratic decision-makers. That is, in addition to whatever improvement in actual decision-making may be brought about by computing, IS may also serve to legitimate decisions — a role particularly important in the public sector where the demand for accountability can be high.

also Skinner, 1971). Some have even argued that "a two-caste system, with possible intra-caste differentiation, will evolve from current relatively ambiguous classes" as upper-class computer "haves" use information technology to mystify and control lower-class computer "have-nots" (Muir, 1987: 21).

The symbolic potential of computer-based decision support lends itself to manipulation of the ill-informed. Users with low computer experience - the largest number of users - are those most likely to give more credence to computer-generated analyses compared to the same analysis in traditional paper form (Luthans and Koester, 1976; Hansen, McKell, and Heitger, 1977; Koester and Luthans, 1979; Neumann and Hadass, 1980; Koh, 1984; Komsky, 1986; Kraemer, Dickhoven, Tierney, and King, 1987; Perrolle, 1987a, 1988b). Some fear that the control functions of computing as symbolic action will lead to cultural homogenization in which a depthless hyper-reality will constitute the postmodern cultural logic of late capitalism (Jameson, 1984; Habermas, 1983).

Research on the Symbolic Uses of Computing

There has been a good deal of research done on the symbolic dimensions of IS (information systems) (Boland, 1978; Boland and Day, 1982) and there is little doubt that this is an important aspect of information systems management. Dreyfus(1979:235-255) has called this phenomenon the "disembodiment" of data by computers: creating the illusion that data are purely objective, untainted by human value decisions, biases, and interests.[1] Computer-based reporting may strip truths of their context, selectively distorting perceptions and undermining the basis for informal logical and political analysis (Lyotard, 1984; Ess, 1987: 33-4; Murphy, 1988: 176).

Unthinking acceptance of computer-generated analyses may bias an organization in fundamental ways. "Although data may be objectified, they may simultaneously be rendered socially irrelevant" (Murphy and Pardeck, 1988: 130) as the categories used by data managers strip data of their social meaning in context. For example, computers in human resource management may appear to be used neutrally and objectively, yet the data that are collected about employees may focus entirely on day-to-day concerns with efficiency and entirely overlook the social context of team relations in organizational development and long-term success.

Some have sought to make the case that organizational biases of computing has led to a technological imperative which even displaces the profit motive. Contributing to technological advances and being knowledgeable enough to discuss them gives managers a sense of accomplishment and worth, Wuthnow (1982) argues. In this new status system it is technology rather than the marketplace that is the basis for organizational status. He warns against going to this extreme, instead advocating balancing technological morality with the profit motive, avoiding making the technological imperative an end in itself.

However, that computers may add legitimacy to decisions, and that computing may even be initiated for reasons of symbolism rather than substance does not demonstrate that computer assistance of decision-making is a facade. In fact, one must ask how long the legitimation mystique of computing would last if its results were demonstrably in error. That is, when it comes to decision-making, computing may be both symbol *and* substance. Later, in Chapter 7, I take up the question of how much computing contributes to increased productivity rather than merely to symbolic effects. There are real questions about whether computer investment has a genuine payoff in productivity terms or whether it is a technological boondoggle. Evidence discussed in Chapter 7 supports the conclusion that computing can serve both substantive productivity objectives as well as symbolic purposes having little to do with actual productivity. All of this, of course, is in line with the theme of this book, that computing is thoroughly enmeshed in political processes.

Is Computer Technology Associated with Gender, Racial, Class, or Age Bias?

It might be supposed that information technology is a "neutral" concept characterized by universalistic applicability to everyone regardless of personal attributes other than ability. However, many writers consider computing to be anything but neutral when it comes to discrimination and bias issues. Charges of this sort are heard most frequently in the area of gender bias (e.g., Bruce and Kirkup, 1986), but computing has not been immune to suspicion that it augments discriminatory patterns in other dimensions as well. In this section I look at questions of gender bias, racial discrimination, class differentials, and impacts on senior citizens.

Gender Bias Issues

Computing does have role models for women, such as Grace Hopper, the creator of COBOL, the first major computer language for business applications. Moreover, computing is used on a widespread basis to advance women's issues (Eastman, 1991). Nonetheless, computing raises important gender issues. In the computer arena, gender bias against women starts in childhood (see Figure 5-2) and continues right on through life. Research shows that in each of four major institutional arenas (leisure industry, media, education, and the family) males receive greater support and encouragement to be computer users (Reisman, 1990: 45). Evidence of gender bias is easy to find.

For instance, Demetriulias and Rosenthal (1985) studied micro-

Figure 2: Computing Favors Males from an Early Age

* The earliest computer software products (e.g., most Nintendo games) that children are exposed to are designed to appeal to boys (Pearl et al., 1990).

* Many studies arising from educational settings show male students are more likely to use computers, own computers, and to have more experience with computers (Lockheed and Frakt, 1984; Sanders, 1984; Schubert and Bakke, 1984; Chen, 1986; Becker, 1987; Gattiker and Nelligan, 1988; Badagliacco and Tannenbaum, 1989; Badagliacco, 1990).

* Boys outnumber girls at computer camps by 4:1, a disproportion camp directors attribute to parental attitudes (Muira and Hess, 1984). Kreinberg and Stage (1983) found parents were less likely to think computer camps would be an enjoyable experience for their daughters.

* Parents are more likely to make a computer available for boys' access than girls regardless of income (Kohl and Harman, 1986), a phenomenon which may be tied to the fact that fathers are more likely than mothers to make computer purchases (Linn, 1985).

computer advertisements and found boys constituted 61% of children shown and men were 75% of adult models. This is corroborated by Marshall and Bannon (1988), who found both gender and racial bias in computer advertising. Ware and Stuck (1985) similarly studied gender roles in three mass-market computer magazines and found males were illustrated twice as often as women. When women were illustrated, it was often as clerical workers, sex objects, or in other passive roles. Only women were shown in roles rejecting computer technology, whereas males were overrepresented in roles such as managers, experts, and repair technicians. Other obstacles to computer involvement for women include lack of role models, gender bias in software, and sexual harassment in a male-dominated curriculum and profession (Frenkel, 1990c).

Gender bias in computing is reinforced, not mitigated, by the educational experience. One study of school children found that while as many girls as boys liked computers, many more girls ardently disliked them (Hattie and Fitzgerald, 1987). Among incoming business students, women had less computer experience and in spite of having a greater perception that computer skills were needed for their careers, women were less willing to purchase a computer than were males (Morahan-Martin, Olinsky, and Schumacher, 1992).

Gender effects are related to a constellation of factors such as taking computer courses in high school and majoring in science or engineering, which, along with being male, are related to positive experiences with computer science (Sproull, Zubrow, and Kiesler, 1985). Some 85% of children using computers in schools are males (Erdman and Foster, 1988). While over one-third (37%) of undergraduate degrees in computer science are awarded to women, but only 28% of Master's degrees and 10% of doctorates go to women (Snyder, 1988).

Women are significantly less likely to become computer science majors but differences in college computer use outside computer science courses has not been found to differ (Chen, 1986). Temple and Lips (1989: 215) found college women were as likely as men to have a personal interest in computing but they were inhibited from taking computer training or becoming a computer science major because of "the communication, by male peers, of the attitude that women are less capable than men of learning about computers." When women do enroll in computer programming courses they perform, on average, as well as or better than males (Linn, 1985; Mandinach and Linn, 1987). Moreover, students who show greater computer anxiety, women or men, may nonetheless be equally able to complete computer tasks in spite of attitudinal differences (Lambert and Lenthall, 1989). In summary, in school settings males may use computers more not because of more favorable attitudes toward computing but for other reasons, perhaps more role models or other encouragement (Fuchs, 1986). It does not appear that intrinsic sex-related reasons justify gender discrimination in computer-related tasks.

Lack of experience is both a cause and effect of women having significantly less favorable attitudes toward computers (Griswold, 1985; Kay, 1989; Badagliacco, 1990). Less opportunity to engage in computing also adversely affects computer attitudes among women (Schubert, 1986). Many authors have shown that computer experience, which men have more of, leads directly to more positive attitudes toward computing (e.g., Koohang, 1989: 148). Most studies of the subject find women have less favorable attitudes toward computing (e.g., Vrendenburg, 1984; Collis, 1985; Dambrot et al., 1985; Davis, 1985; Webb, 1985; Wilder, Mackie, and Cooper, 1985; Collis and Ollila, 1986; Chen, 1986; Nickell and Pinto, 1986; Smith, 1987; Bradley, 1988; Badagliacco and Tannenbaum, 1989; for contrary findings see Loyd and Gressard, 1984; Baylor, 1985). Moreover, studies assembled by the Women's Bureau of the U. S. Department of Labor show that clerical workers, overwhelmingly women, are often excluded from planning and implementation processes involving technological change, further excerbating lack of involvement and dissatisfaction (Women's Bureau, 1985).

Self-confidence is an issue. Wilder, Mackie, and Cooper (1985) found women rated their computer skills lower than males. Most studies have found women to have more computer anxiety (Heinssen, Galss and Knight, 1984; Gilroy and Desai, 1986; Rosen, Sears, and Weil, 1987; for contrary findings, see Heinssen, Glass, and Knight, 1984; Smith, 1986).

However, once women do become involved in computing, there is some evidence that they do not evaluate computing less favorably than males (Shields, 1985).[2] At least one study found that even controlling for occupational status, women may be much more satisfied with their experiences in computerized offices than are men (Gutek and Bikson, 1985: 134).

Interestingly, regardless of the amount or type of computer experience, women are more likely to be concerned about the social impacts of computers (Wu and Morgan, 1989). Some of the findings about less favorable attitudes toward computing among women may simply reflect greater sensitivity to many of the valid social issues which surround the subject. Moreover, while most studies show a significant correlation between male gender and favorable computing attitudes, the magnitude of these differences is often not large or is absent altogether (e.g., Loyd and Gressard, 1984; Gutek and Bikson, 1985: 133; Lockheed, 1985; Nickell et al., 1987; Gressard and Loyd, 1987; Hattie and Fitzgerald, 1987; Gattiker, Gutek, and Berger, 1988; Morris, 1988; Norris, 1992).

Some studies even find women have more favorable computing attitudes (Loyd, Loyd, and Gressard, 1987; Norris, 1992). Temple and Lips (1989) studied university students and found that men had taken more computer science courses, were more knowledgeable about programming, and had more favorable computing attitudes. However, Temple and Lips also found men and women did not differ in their reported personal interest in and enjoyment of computers. Likewise, Chen (1986) found that when amount of computer experience is controlled, attitudes toward computing were similar between men and women. Moreover, in some areas computing has improved career opportunities for women, notably in the military where women's increasing presence as soldiers has been made possible in part by computer technology's ability to uncouple warfare from physical strength (Edwards, 1990).

The gender differences found in educational settings may be reflected in the workplace. In contrast to public schools, use of computers by women is much more common at work (Erdman and Foster, 1988: 83). Adele Platter (1988) studied 1980 data on 15,151 high school sophomores and seniors, comparing responses of the same individuals four years later when they were in college or the workplace. Platter found computing experience in work, school, and home is related to gender, race, socioeconomic status, father's education, and family income. Moreover, gender had control effects on

Figure 3: Mini-Case: Women in the Information Industry

*** Discrimination no, bias yes**
A December 1987 survey of 300 female and 700 male members of the International Communications Association found few women who felt they had been discriminated against in their careers, but two-thirds felt they were not moving up fast enough (Wexler, 1988).

*** "Old Boys Network"**
Women cited barriers in this computer-intensive profession such as the prevalence of an "old boys' network" and stereotyping women into clerical roles. In this survey some 29% of women were staff and 26% were managers but only 8% were directors, creating charges that women were stuck "at the third rung" in their careers.

*** Lower Pay**
Studies show that the computer industry pays women less than it pays men with comparable education and job responsibilities (Wright, 1987). Women are under-represented in high-paying and over-represented in low-paying IS jobs, regardless of being white, black, or Hispanic (Altman, 1989a: 25; Banks and Ackerman, 1990). Because of this, when broad IS work categories are considered (e.g., "computer programmers", "computer systems analysts"), women's earnings are 75% to 87% those of men in the same category.

*** Not "Ready for Management"**
A 1990 survey shows only 2.3% of CIO's (Chief Information Officers) were women. However, this discouraging finding still compares favorably to less than half of 1% women among the highest-paid officers and directors of 799 companies (mostly outside the information industry) surveyed by *Fortune* magazine (Myers, 1990: 38-9).

several of these relationships. That is, the relationship disappeared or was mitigated when gender was taken into account. Citing women's work roles and health needs, some authors have taken the view that governmental and business organizations have a responsibility to provide special programs for workers, particularly women, when computers are part of the work environment (Bradley, 1988). This issue has become the subject of public policy in Sweden.

There is little reason to assume the gender differential will improve soon. Frenkel (1990c: 35) notes, "studies show that girls from grade school to high school are losing interest in computing." Badagliacco advocates affirmative steps by educational institutions to provide role models and other incentives to avoid this social outcome. Unfortunately, many women in computing drop out of the academic pipeline, choose not to get advanced degrees, or go to work for industry, leaving disproportionately low numbers of women to serve as computing role models in education (Frenkel, 1990c: 35; Etkowitz, Kemelgor, Neuschat, and Uzzi, 1990). Likewise, Smith's longitudinal study of journalism students showed the gender gap on computer use and attitudes had worsened significantly between 1989 and 1992 (Smith, 1993: 13).

Studies show that the number of women heading into IS careers is dwindling (Savage, 1990). This may reflect bias problems encountered by women in the information industry (see Figure 5-3).[3] By reinforcing male dominance, "far from revolutionizing society, the computer has conformed to society, becoming another element of the status quo" (Reisman, 1990: 45). It should be noted that these problems have been widely noted and various ameliorative efforts have been undertaken, such as the National Science Foundation's funding of the 'Mentoring of Women and Minorities in Computer Science' project of the ACM (Association for Computing Machinery) (*Communications of the ACM*, 1992b).

Computers and Racial Discrimination

As with gender, race and ethnicity have been linked to less favorable attitudes toward and less experience with computers (Badagliacco, 1990). It is charged plausibly that wealthy school districts may familiarize white students more with computers than can be done in inner-city districts populated by minority ethnic groups. In this way computerization may be exacerbating cultural differentials in America (Ibrahim, 1985). Dutton et al. (1987c) have found that formal education, which is significantly lower among minorities, is a strong factor in explaining the adoption and use of computers in the home. Race also appears as a correlate of computing experience in other studies (e.g., Gattiker and Nelligan, 1988; Platter, 1988). On the other hand, computer technology may reduce cultural differences as well. Some authors, for example, have found fewer interracial differences when intelligence tests are administered by computers rather than by humans.

Like gender bias, racial effects can become self-perpetuating. "The fact that computer-related activities are seen as white and male may influence and discourage women and minorities from making an academic commitment to careers for which high-technology skills are essential," Joanne Badagliacco (1990: 42) writes. Badagliacco's study of 1,420 students found computer experience varied with ethnicity, with Hispanics having the least. Correspondingly, attitudes toward computers vary by race and ethnicity. The result, she warns, may be formation of a "technological underclass" (p. 59) of women and minority workers who are disadvantaged in terms of computer technology.

The effects of gender, class, and race are cumulative, so that disadvantaged status in two or three categories is worse than disadvantaged status in any one. Thus poor black women are the most disadvantaged in computing (Frenkel, 1990a:45). However, once minorities are inside the information industry, racial effects are different. Using "Current Population Survey" data from 1972 to 1983, for example, Glenn and Tolbert (1987) found minority men and women and white women working in the computing industry experienced, if anything, slight gains compared to other industries, but as with industry in general, they were concentrated in lower paid job categories. The concentration of blacks and Hispanics in lower-paid categories of information services is also documented by Banks and Ackerman (1990).

Chambers and Clarke (1987) likewise found that the effects of ethnicity, socioeconomic status, gender, and school ability disadvantage were cumulative. More disadvantaged students participated less in class computing, gained lower computing knowledge, and had less positive attitudes toward computing. That is, computing increased rather than reduced inequities. The relative lack of use of computers by black children is particularly regrettable in view of studies which show computing can be effective in matching black children's learning styles and the curriculum (Lee, 1986).

Computing and Social Class Differentials

It is not cheap to have a computer in the home. Similarly, private and affluent schools are more likely to emphasize computing. Wealthier school districts, usually serving higher socioeconomic status families, routinely provide greater computer access (Johnson, 1982; Lacina, 1983). Kohl and Harman (1986), while documenting gender differentials in computing, have found economic causes to constitute the greater barrier. Computer use in education declines dramatically when students are from families with low socioeconomic status (Becker, 1983; McGee, 1987).

The correlation of computing and social class has been documented in other countries as well. For instance, in a study of Israeli society Levy, Navon, and Shapira (1991) found that contrary to expectation, introduction of computers into the schools widened the gap of social and economic inequities by class. Race and ethnicity, of course, correlate with socioeconomic status. Badagliacco and Tannenbaum (1989), for instance, found that at an American college ethnicity was correlated with computer experience and attitudes, with whites having the most experience and most favorable attitudes and Hispanics having the least, even controlling for gender and number of credit hours.

During the 1980s over a billion dollars was invested in helping public schools compete technologically. As a result, sharp class and racial disparities noted early in the decade seemed to have largely disappeared by 1989. A sharp narrowing of disparities between the rich and poor and between public and private schools seemed to demonstrate great progress had been made (Piller, 1992: 218). However, closer investigation shows that even when inner-city and rural school districts in poor neighborhoods have computers, skills and resources to maintain and make use of this equipment is commonly lacking. One journalist concluded, "For every technological success story, impoverished schools suffer a hundred setbacks. The links between a generation of American students and the technological future grow increasingly tenuous" (Piller, 1992: 230).

Computing and Older Americans

AARP surveys indicate that seniors hold positive attitudes toward computing (Edwards and Englehardt, 1989). Controlled experiments demonstrate the computer capabilities of older Americans (see review by Ogozalek, 1991). Weisman (1983) found nursing home residents benefitted from feelings of mastery resulting from use of computers, not to mention benefits in the form of computerized health care technology (Levy and Gordon, 1988). Telecommunications services such as SeniorNet also serve to provide friendships as well as practical services for the elderly (Beck and Joseph, 1992: 64). While computerization is sometimes cast as a "youth issue", evidence suggests that elders are not discriminated against by IS technology and have the potential to benefit disproportionately. The *International Journal of Technology and Aging* was created in 1988 to cover many of these issues.

Computing and Bias: A Summary

Computer technology has the potential to reduce social discrimination in many dimensions. Technologically, it is associated with a range of higher status occupations which must be filled largely on the basis of ability and usually cannot be allocated to unqualified relatives, friends, and social peers. Politically, it is an avenue of power and access to higher decision-making within organizations. Socially, it is similar to engineering, long a preferred career avenue for first-generation students rising from the ranks of working class families where parents lack college educations. The wealth of computer-mediated information resources specializing in issues pertaining to women or minorities should make computer technology of interest to those groups.

The reality is that computer technology, in spite of its potential, more often reinforces existing patterns of social bias than it alleviates them. Although overt discrimination is not a problem, serious issues exist in the areas of gender, race, and class bias. "Agism" seems not to be a problem, however. There is a self-perpetuating dynamic which associates white collar white males with greater computer experience and more favorable computing attitudes. This dynamic shows no evidence of weakening with time and may, in fact, be becoming stronger than ever. To break the circle of bias will require affirmative organizational and perhaps public policies rather than simple reliance on marketplace forces.

Managerial Liability for Information Systems

In addition to the questions pertaining to the symbolic uses and social bias of computing, a third major social issue has to do with the extent to which IS managers may be held liable for harm that derives from their work. Although harm may take the direct form of occupational hazards in the literal sense or theft in the form of electronic copyright abuse[4], most discussion of liability has focused on harm coming from reliance on data derived from flawed information systems. Information managers supervise the collecting, archiving,

Figure 4: Liability in Computing

* A computer program error in the controller of Thorac-25, a machine to administer radiation doses, killed two and injured others in 1986-1987 (Reece, 1990: 60). An analysis concluded "Software that controlled devices critical to human safety was being developed in a haphazard, unsystematic fashion, and receiving little meaningful review from regulatory agencies" (Jacky, 1991: 613).

* The Government Accounting Office found that deficiencies in the information system used by the Environmental Protection Agency were responsible for the EPA's failure to recognize potential birth defect hazards associated with a California chemical spill (Smith, 1991a: 58).

* In 1989 the warden at the Washington State Reformatory in Monroe, Washington, seized 30 computers owned by inmates. He took this action after his legal counsel advised him of the possibility of illegal phone taps or transmissions, pirated software, and other liabilities which the prison staff lacked resources to monitor.

* Because inaccurate weather information from a National Weather Service computer was held responsible for a crew member washing overboard in a storm, the NWS was sued for $3.2 million (Stair, 1992: 639).

and the providing of data used for a wide variety of public and private purposes. Financial and even life-determining decisions may well be based on such data. When data are in error and losses occur as a result, who is liable?

Basis of Liability

The range of possible liabilities is enormous. Example areas include faulty concepts resulting in faulty applications, knowledge-base content errors, failure to trap input errors to avoid wrong output, inadequate training, corruption of magnetic media, failure to update properly, inadequate speed to meet application requirements, failure to include critical elements in documentation, program bugs, hardware deficiencies, and so on. A liability example with broad implications was the case of *Aetna Casualty and Surety vs. Jepperson and Co.* (642 F. 2d 339, 9th Cir., 1981). In this case a corporate pilot was killed in a crash due to reliance on computer-generated charts which had wrongly labelled scales. While the court held that "the professional ... will be expected to use his or her professional judgment in evaluating the information and not to rely blindly on what he or she is told by the computer or charts", nonetheless the chart maker was held at fault. While Jepperson was a private sector firm, government agencies produce similar computerized map databases and the same principles would apply. Numerous other examples of IS-related liability can be cited (see Figure 5-4).

Legal remedy for failed software involves disputes over software as a good or as a service. American law provides different remedies depending on whether a good or a service is involved. Software manufacturers prefer to view software as a service since this places the matter under common law where plaintiffs must prove negligence. In contrast, Article 2 of the Uniform Commercial Code, was designed to protect consumers of goods. It defines precise rights and obligations of vendors and purchasers, and plaintiffs only have to prove injury. Common law has no such specific protections and relies on interpretation of the contract, a document generally prepared by and for the benefit of the software vendor. Courts may hold software to be either a good or service, but in general, off-the-shelf software is a good requiring only proof of injury. Likewise, in general custom software is a service requiring proof of negligence (Joyce, 1987; Massey,

1988).

It is well-established that agencies and employees can be sued on grounds of negligence. Negligence suits assume employees had an implicit duty of care to the user or others affected - a computer version of the professional malpractice suit. *Black's Law Dictionary* defines negligence as "the failure to observe, for the protection of the interests of another person, that degree of care, precaution, and vigilance which the circumstances justly demand, whereby such other person suffers injury" (Tuthill, 1991: 49). Failure to adhere to commonly accepted standards is an obvious area of negligence. In *Diversified Graphics v. Groves Ltd.* (1989), IS consultants here held liable for malpractice because the system the developed for their client, Diversified Graphics, failed to conform to the standards of the Management Advisory Services Practice Standards of the American Institute of Certified Public Accountants.

If claims of expertise have been made, then the manager can be held to a standard that reflects this superior knowledge. This may be a special problem in the area of expert systems software, a form of "artificial intelligence" in which computer software incorporates knowledge of domain experts for purposes of automated decision-making such as diagnosis of disease. Legal experts advise manager not to oversell the abilities or accuracy of expert systems, to warn users against excessive reliance on the expert system, and to have a good tort attorney in the wings in case of malpractice suits (Myktyn and Myktyn, 1991: 44-45). While past cases such as *Triangle Underwriters v. Honeywell, Inc.* (1979) and *Chatlos Systems v. National Cash Register Corp.* (1979) rejected malpractice because the software provider/user relationship was deemed to lack the degree of professional trust characteristic of medicine, it may be that expert systems will be viewed as being sufficiently integrated with professional knowledge so as to make malpractice applicable.

Responsibilities of Information Managers

In spite of dramatic incidents, the courts are not likely to hold information managers to a standard of error-free computer databases. However, liability may result if reasonable care is not exercised in database management (Nimmer and Krauthaus, 1986). Reasonable care may well mean that data gatherers, coders, and entry personnel must receive training, and that some system of error-checking, proofing, and/or cross-reference checking must be undertaken for data verification. The IS manager needs to assure that there is an established system for handling reported errors and that data deficiencies are made known to data users in some known and publicized manner (Nycum and Lowell, 1981; Epstein and Roitman, 1987). To protect against liability, the manager may need to be able to document that reasonable precautions have been taken on a systematic basis in each of these areas (Tuthill, 1991).

Information managers involved in database services have the responsibility to establish a cost-effective data accuracy standard and adhere to it. Total avoidance of errors is not required or possible but managers can and should track the error rate and take steps when it rises above a reasonable standard. Although no court cases arose because of it, the Equal Employment Opportunity Commission (EEOC) was formally criticized by the General Accounting Office (GAO) in 1989 for failing to establish such an error standard. The EEOC's Charge Data System was found to have been partly responsible for age discrimination complaints exceeding the statute of limitations before the EEOC had even completed its investigations, primarily because

Figure 5: Strategies to Limit Software Liability

Statements about how a software system works and what it will do can be seen as a legally enforceable implicit contract with the user unless one or more of four strategies have been pursued by the software manager:

* **Integration clauses:** Even if the software is distributed free of charge, users can be required to sign a contract to obtain it and the contact can have an integration clause which states that the contract contains the entire agreement between the supplier and the user.

* **Disclaimer of warranties:** A standard clause states that there are no implied warranties.

* **Limitation on remedies:** Another standard clause states explicitly that the only remedy for claims against the software is repair or replacement of the software.

* **Limitation on liability:** A more generous alternative clause states that one can only recover such direct damage costs as purchase, installation, and conversion costs and not indirect or consequential costs.

EEOC staff failed to verify adequately the accuracy or completeness of data entered into the databases and failed to update its databases with new and revised data (GAO, 1989b).

Information managers involved in software services have additional liability responsibilities. Software producers should be aware that statements not only in contracts and written agreements, but also in sales literature, brochures, manuals, and even in oral communications can be used in breach of warranties suits. In principle, both the agency and the individual employee who is negligent can held liable. Although managers can pursue various strategies for protecting themselves against lawsuits (see Figure 5-5), carefully drawn contracts limiting liability do not fully protect the organization which produces software or electronic data since the entire contract can be attacked on grounds of fraud or misrepresentation. Disclaimers of express warranty, implied warranty of merchantability, and implied warrantee of fitness for a particular purpose are commonly used, but courts not infrequently set aside such disclaimers when the court finds such clauses "unconscionable" when considering the rights of the buyer. State tort laws vary on conditions under which contractual limitations and disclaimers are rendered void.

Ultimately, there is no sure way a manager of an agency which provides database services or produces software can be assured of protection from lawsuit. Beyond careful contracting, the manager should provide warnings about what the system can and cannot do especially in medical or other risk-associated fields. Liability for negligence is linked to a standard of ordinary or reasonable care or the conduct of an ordinary or reasonably prudent person in like circumstance. The manager should also implement formal procedures to test and debug programs and prior to release should be implemented. In summary, information managers have the responsibility to take affirmative actions which establish and enforce a standard or reasonable care. And it might not be a bad idea to purchase liability insurance as well (see Reece, 1990)!

Occupational Safety Issues

It is not obvious that computers are safe. Here I am not talking about the fact that computers embedded in vehicles, traffic light controllers,

Figure 6: Mini-Case: Repetitive Stress Injury at the *Los Angeles Times*

A *Los Angeles Times* reporter noticed in the late 1980s that he was experiencing pain in his finger joints. He tried to ignore the problem but it became worse. Doctor visits led him to take anti-inflammation drugs and he was advised to undergo physical therapy. By the early 1990s, he was wearing wrist splints at work and had to stop use of the computer every 15 minutes to do therapeutic exercises to prevent further repetitive strain injury (RSI) (Bartholomew, 1992b: 40).

Similarly, another *Los Angeles Times* employee suffered numbness and pain in fingers, back, and neck due to extended VDT use requiring medical attention (Pasternak, 1992). After numerous similar worker complaints, the *Los Angeles Times* asked the National Institute for Occupational Safety and Health (NIOSH) to study the problem.

The two-year NIOSH research found that two out of every five workers at the *Los Angeles Times* suffered moderate to severe RSI symptoms.

As a result, the *Los Angeles Times* has had to create alternative jobs for reporters disabled from apparent computer-related repetitive strain injury. It has also spent nearly two million dollars on ergonomic furniture and equipment in an attempt to ameliorate RSI problems.

boiler regulators, and the like may fail with disastrous results (they do, see Leveson, 1991). Nor am I talking about the fact that computer and communications equipment manufacturing plays a role in toxic waste and the depletion of the ozone layer (EPA studies show it accounts for 12% of chlorofluorocarbons: Hoffman, 1989; Reinhardt, Perratore, Redfern, and Malloy, 1992). Rather, I am referring to direct threats to the occupational health and safety of information workers. From the employee's point of view, there are health issues pertaining to exposure to computers for long periods. Harmful effects to individuals may lead to computer system failures, making a personal issue into an organizational one. For example, can air traffic controllers be harmed by staring at monitors too long, and can this lead to disastrous mistakes? Possible damaging health effects include eye strain, illness, and even miscarriages and birth defects.

Repetitive Stress Injury (RSI)

Sitting at the keyboard for prolonged periods can cause nerve damage in the hands in certain situations. Data entry operators and newspaper reporters, for instance, may strike their keyboards up to 25,000 times an hour, creating a high risk that these many little shocks will accumulate into tendinitis (inflamed tendons) or carpal tunnel syndrome (damage to the nerve running through the wrist's carpal bones), and other related bodily damage (Fritz, 1991: 22). Symptoms such as hand numbness may indicate damage and can involve the need for surgery. The outward bending of the hands over keyboards can also cause problems in the forearm muscles (Nakaseko, Grandjean, Hunting and Grier, 1985).

As a result of concerns over RSI, ergonomic safety standards were set by the Human Factors Society in the 1980s. Studies have reported few effects of such standards, however (*ERGO*, 1987). Ergonomically superior keyboards, chairs, and other assists are now available which reduce the threat of RSI, but they are still rarely seen in the officeplace (Adler, 1992). The controversy has continued in the pages of specialized journals such as *VDT News* (NY). By the late 1980's, ergonomic standards became more important as the courts looked with increasing favor on employees' suits arising from repetitive stress claims. By the 1990s, RSI had become a $20 billion a year problem for American industry according to Aetna Life and Casualty Co. A decade earlier it was not considered to be a part of managing information systems, surveys showed three out of four information managers now consider RSI policies to be an IS issue, if not part of their jobs as well (Bartholomew, 1992b: 33).

Repetitive stress injuries have led American firms to invest in new ergonomic computer furniture and other strategies (Goff, 1989). On the public sector side, in Congressional hearings in 1991, the American Postal Workers Union testified that carpal tunnel syndrome claims had doubled between 1989 and 1990 due to the introduction of new technology in the Postal Service. Supporting this, the Occupational Safety and Health Administration (OSHA) has found excessive ergonomic stress among operators of the Postal Service's new Computer Forwarding System (Seaborn, 1991: 112).

RSI has become the leading cause of job-related injury in the 1990s, rising from 18% of injuries recorded by the Department of Labor in 1982 to 55% a decade later (Bartholomew, 1992b: 33). Carpal tunnel syndrome affects almost 2 million American workers and tendinitis twice that many. Almost one in ten organizations surveyed in a 1992 *InformationWeek* poll of information industry respondents has been faced with RSI-related lawsuits. Fifty percent have paid workers' compensation claims and sixty percent report lowered productivity as a result of RSI (Bartholomew, 1992b: 36, 44).

While RSI is not limited to information workers, 46 million Americans worked at computers in 1990 according to the Bureau of Labor Statistics, and many of them are at risk of RSI injury. When you multiply the average $29,000 cost of compensating an RSI victim by the millions of workers affected, RSI can be seen not as a "how about that?" curiosity but rather as a major drain on the productivity of the American economy. For this reason, it has been suggested that Americans follow the lead of some European countries in formulating a national public policy on RSI and legislation to enforce it. The *InformationWeek* survey mentioned above showed that more information industry respondents than not favor such legislation (48% to 45%; Bartholomew, 1992b: 40).

Eye Strain

There is a long history of research and legislation regarding video display terminals (VDT's) used by computers (and other devices). This topic has become increasingly important as the number of affected workers has grown. The Communications Workers of America has 10,000 VDT employee members in the early 1980s, a figure which mushroomed to 425,000 by 1990 (McPartlin, 1993a: 52).

Behavioral optometrists have warned about visual stress, recommending ergonomic design and employee training in stress-reducing visual exercises. Eye strain problems have led organizations to invest in monitor glare shields, eye-care insurance policies, and training (Goff, 1989). In 1989, Suffolk County, New York, became the first American jurisdiction to pass legislation on such matters. Suffolk County's law regulates VDT usage by making training mandatory for situations where employees use VDT's more than 26 hours per week. Mandated training must include informing new employees within 30 days how to recognize VDT-related symptoms and how to take measures to alleviate them. Though limited in nature and successfully challenged in court, the Suffolk County law may be the tip of the iceberg. For instance, it has also been proposed that Suffolk County also pay for eye exams and correction of visual problems. In December 1990, San Francisco passed legislation requiring adjustable furniture, detachable keyboards, anti-glare screens, and 15-minute breaks every two hours.

Electromagnetic Emissions

In addition to eye strain, electromagnetic VDT emissions may have other harmful health effects. Monitors, particularly color monitors, emit ELF (extremely low frequency) and VLF (very low frequency) electric and electromagnetic fields. The electric fields are largely shielded in recent computers, but harmful levels may occur if care is not taken to sit at least 28" from the front of the monitor and at least 4' from the rear or sides of other monitors. However, magnetic fields are considered to be the more harmful aspect of ELF and these are not shielded. Although some manufacturers, including IBM, design reduced-ELF monitors, it has not been proved that even the reduced fields are safe.

Some research suggests that magnetic fields promote cancer. Animal research has established that low frequency magnetic fields such as those associated with computers can cause changes in DNA synthesis and RNA transcription, affect the response of normal cells to signaling molecules (including hormones and growth factors), and have effects on some cellular biochemical reactions. These effects might lead to cancer or birth defects but the linkage has not been proved (Fritz, 1991: 17). However, Swedish studies have linked magnetic fields with abnormal pregnancies as did a 1988 study by Kaiser-Permanente Medical Care of San Francisco (see Rosch, 1989). The U. S. Environmental Protection Agency issued a report in 1990 branding EMF emissions as "a possible human carcinogen" (Roberts, 1990: 85).

Studies abroad led the U. S. Office of Technology Assessment to issue a report in May 1989 titled *Biological Effects of Power Frequency Electric and Magnetic Fields*, urging that the matter be studied further. Animal studies, some funded by the computer industry in its own defense, found no link between VDT emissions and spontaneous abortion (Rosch, 1989: 276). The Swedish and Kaiser-Permanente studies have since been criticized on methodological grounds and are contradicted by Teresa Schnoor's 1991 *New England Journal of Medicine* article documenting a NIOSH (National Institute for Occupational Safety and Health) study which found no link to spontaneous abortions in women.

Technostress

Beyond the direct threats to physical health in the form of VDT usage, there is the issue of "technostress". Technostress is, of course, only one aspect of stress on the job. Job stress is increasingly recognized as a major organizational problem. The National Council on Compensation Insurance has found that stress accounts for 10% of occupational illness claims, averaging $15,000 each. This rate doubled in the 1980's (McPartlin, 1990: 30). British studies suggest that 10% of GNP is consumed by the effects of stress, and computer-related jobs are near the top of the list of stressful occupations (McPartlin, 1993a: 52).

While only a portion of job stress is attributable to technostress, computing contributes its share. Workers who are subject to computer monitoring exhibit significantly higher levels of tension, exhaustion, and muscle pain than do non-monitored workers (Betts, 1991). There also is evidence that computer use, even apart from monitoring contributes to higher blood pressure and mood responses similar to "anger" components of certain psychological tests (Emurian, 1989). Coined by Craig Brod, a psychologist and author of *Technostress: The Human Cost of the Computer Revolution* (1982), technostress is characterized by high-intensity involvement with computing leading to any interaction with humans producing stress in the computer-involved individual. A number of studies have shown that computer projects may fail because the expected productivity benefits are countervailed by the effects of heightened stress (e.g., in the case of an automated case management system in human services: Bowes, Kenny, and Pearson, 1993).

For many workers, the intense human-machine relationship is both draining and addictive, leading to "keyed up" behavior, expecting machine-like immediate results from co-workers, and intolerance toward non-logical social and "grey area" aspects of the work environment.[5] Other studies have shown that increased stress among VDT workers led to increased menstrual problems in women workers (Rosch, 1989: 287). Remedies for technostress include task rotation (Ebel, 1987), work breaks and flexible work weeks (Lasden, 1982), stress-reduction exercises (Frew, 1985), and a variety of ergonomic changes such as adjusting chair height and comfort, reducing glare, and improving environmental aesthetics (Mason, 1983; Sutton and Rafaeli, 1987).

Occupational Safety in Computing: A Summary

In summary, there are a variety of ways in which computing raises occupational health and safety issues. Ergonomics, a research field in the study of human factors of this sort, has emerged as a major field of study interfacing psychology and computer science (Bailey, 1982/

Figure 7: Mini-Case: The IRS Entity Systems Meets Employee Resistance

To improve management control over tax investigations, the U. S. Internal Revenue Service attempted to implement the "Entity" computer system in the 1980s (see McGraw, 1987a).

Entity software assigned priorities to IRS officers' cases on the basis of all tax forms and all tax years related to a single business or individual as an entity. Although it could have been used for decision support for the officers, in fact it was used to remove officers' discretion and force case assignment upon them.

Prior to Entity, IRS officers could prioritize cases partly on the basis of their analysis of ability to pay and establishment of payment schedules. Entity tended toward lock-step case assignment which some officials found resulted in overly harsh enforcement and in taxes going uncollected because the "wrong" cases were given priority.

In addition to being de-professionalizing, Entity was a form of quantitative reporting of officers' casework. Like other quantitative performance accounting efforts, Entity created stiff resistance. One reported, "I have found nothing in this system that enhances the quality of my work. It is a time reporting system, plain and simple. The emphasis is on our time and what we do with our time..." (McGraw, 1986: 2).

Based on employee complaints such as these, the National Treasury Employees Union mounted a campaign in 1987 to stop the spread of Entity from its experimental site in Hartford, Connecticut, to application throughout the federal system (McGraw, 1987a: 2).

Although eventually resolved by taking greater account of human factors, the Entity issue illustrates the temptation to use computing to enforce quantitative performance measurement on employees - an old concept pre-dating computers and one which has frequently been counter-productive. Management must decide if computing will be designed to enhance staff decision-making or whether it will be used to de-professionalize staff by withdrawing discretion over decisions.

1989; Singleton, 1989). While widely ignored by managers, ergonomic and medical awareness of the risks of computing has increased steadily in the last decade to the point where some communities have enacted protective legislation.

Much more has been done abroad, where a stronger labor movement has made it an issue. In 1984, meeting in Geneva, the International Federation of Commercial, Clerical, Professional and Technical Employees passed a guideline stating "Many of the physical and psychological problems which arise in VDT work could be drastically improved by reducing the total amount of working time workers spend operating VDTs, by limiting the workload and workplace of VDT work and by preventing VDTs from being used automatically to monitor the performance or behavior of individual employees" (Bureau of National Affairs, 1984).

Similar recommendations are heard in this country, as in suggestions that VDT use be limited to half of the work day or when the Communications Workers of America called attention to the plight of fired U. S. West operators, terminated because repetitive motion syndrome prevented them for completing a directory assistance call every 24 seconds (Snoddy, 1989). However, in spite of union pressure and exemplary local legislation there are no commonly accepted health and safety standards in the United States regarding VDT use nor is national legislation in the immediate future as of this writing.

Quality of Work Life Issues

Employee resistance and even sabotage can be associated with the computerization of work. Many of the problems associated with computer systems are attributable to subtle sabotage by employees dissatisfied with computerization (Metz, 1986). Just as the Luddites resisted the introduction of machinery in the dawn of the industrial revolution, so many workers find ways to resist the perceived threat of automation. Sometimes this can be overt as in the instance of a financial analyst with the District of Columbia decided, after policy disagreements with superiors, to change the computer access code to the District's financial database. He then "forgot" the new code, causing many days of turmoil in city administration. (McGraw,

1988a: 7).[6] However, in most cases, resistance is more subtle. Employees may resist retraining and revert to pre-computer methods whenever possible. The amount of desktop computing hardware that goes largely unused is a major productivity problem in America. Workers may also fail to uphold data entry quality controls, the blame computers for ensuing problems. New York City's multi-million dollar welfare system automation project was largely undermined in this way (see Figure 5-8). More broadly, employee resistance can take the form of debilitating griping and loss of morale, disinterest in finding new ways to be productive with new technology, and social pressures against peers who start to embrace information technology.

Quality of Work Life Issues and IS Success Factors

What are quality of work life issues from an employee viewpoint are IS implementation issues from a management viewpoint. Most problems associated with failed IS systems — and these are much more common than commonly realized— are human factors problems of an essentially non-technological sort. Tom DeMarco and Timothy Lister, for example, collected data on nearly five hundred management information systems projects and found that among the larger ones, fully 25% failed to ever complete. "We've been contacting whoever is left of the project staff to find out what went wrong. For the overwhelming majority of the bankrupt projects we studied," they wrote, "*there was not a single technological issue to explain the failure*" (DeMarco and Lister, 1987: 4; emphasis in original). Improving the quality of working life with regard to computing goes hand in hand with establishing success factors for good information systems.

Probably the single biggest QWL factor associated with computing is workers' feeling that IS systems are being foisted on them "from above", stripping their jobs of valued elements without any chance to help shape the new systems under which they will work. Feelings of disempowerment result from failure to consult end-users of computer services, especially when new IS systems are being implemented. Severe information systems problems can arise due to the failure to take account of the fact that in the end it is human beings who have to run them and use their results. The need to consult end-users and to take their views of what makes for quality in their working lives is illustrated in a General Accounting Office report on the National

Figure 8: Mini-Case: Automating New York City's Welfare System Without Consulting Users

In 1976, the New York state legislature mandated automation through what was called the NYC Welfare Management System (WMS). This efficiency measure was to be designed around a massive, centralized multi-purpose integrated database. WMS was implemented in a top-down manner. NYC had only written input to the contractor.

Subsequent testing in the field over two years later yielded some 3,000 errors. Worse, the welfare service error rate rose from 1-2% to an unacceptable 20% after WMS implementation. What had gone wrong? WMS's major problems were traced to not taking account of the capacities and motivation of the end users responsible for data input. From the point of view of NYC social workers, WMS was too big, too complex.

WMS's size and complexity satisfied the legislature's desire to create a giant integrated system for an entire jurisdiction, centered on a database holding all data which might be used by dozens of agencies for quite varied purposes.

However, reality was reflected in a 1987 report on the NYC experience, which stated, "The chaos and rampant error rates in NYC's new Welfare Management System appear to be due to a tremendous increase in the number of codes it requires for data entry and the consequent difficulty for users in learning to use it" (Roman, 1987: 1).

The new system consolidated welfare databases across the city but it also dramatically increased error rates. To provide full integration, it was necessary to create a system with over 100 data screens. Social work staff had to enter codes from long lists: employee codes, client codes, case codes, and so on.

WMS lacked an appreciation for human nature. Employees who were not concerned with certain aspects of the database chose to ignore or speedily and arbitrarily dispose those data entry fields not of interest to their own work. While it is conceivable that training, oversight, and rewards are salvaging the NYC system, its early failures illustrate that sociotechnical management is needed to take account of the needs of the staff who actually control data at its entry point. IS design is not separable from broader concerns of organization design and the quality of working life (Roman, 1987: 1, 17).

Institutes of Health (NIH), which was faulted for failing to consult its scientists before investing in a $800 million mainframe-based computer system when scientists wanted a much less expensive PC-based system (*Communications of the ACM*, 1992a: 9).

The Need for Sociotechnical Management

It is said that "To err is human, but to really foul things up takes a computer." However, on inspection it is often found that computer systems problems are traceable primarily to human factors. Information system failures are rarely limited to technical factors. Rather, they often involve human and even political dimensions (see Morgan and Soden, 1973; Lucas, 1975). Likewise, Buchanan (1988) found most computer network system failures to be traceable to administrative error. Noted computer scientists Carl Hammer told a governmental IS conference, "Let us look at the all too frequently mentioned 'computer goofs'. Upon closer examination they always turn out to be human errors which greatly upset the life and tranquility of the office" (quoted in McGraw, 1988a: 7). Hammer cited a number of illustrations of his point, to which we can add others illustrating such human factors as improper organizational work procedures, failure to consult end users, neglect of information systems investment, and employee resistance and sabotage.

Although information systems (IS) problems may be divided among those dealing with technical, data, conceptual, people, and complexity dimensions (Alter, 1980), in fact even technical and data problems may well involve people factors. Psychological factors associated with computing have been studied at least since the early 1970's (Weinberg, 1971; Shneiderman, 1980; Minsky, 1986). Studies have shown that most information systems problems are nontechnical in nature. They are conceptual (people have selected software which is inappropriate for the problem), social (personnel and interpersonal problems), and complexity-related (people find the system is too difficult to understand and use) (Lucas, 1975; Alter, 1980; Lyytinen, 1987b). For these reasons, behavioral science, rather than computer science, may be most relevant to understanding and addressing the problem of "computer foul-ups" (Turner, 1982; Dawson, Cummings, and Ryan, 1987). Sociotechnical systems (STS) management is an action-oriented methodology used by researchers and practitioners who seek to apply behavioral principles to IS implementation.

The traditional approach to planning IS systems is the systems development life cycle (SDLC) method.[7] Although traditionally associated with authoritarian top-down management orientations, SDLC in recent years has moved toward recognition of sociotechnical concerns.

Is planners increasingly recognize that information systems are sociotechnical systems. In spite of the importance of technical factors[8] and investment in technology[9], human factors in computing have been the subject of a burgeoning body of literature. Literature reviews include Attewell and Rule (1984), Anderson (1985), Kaplinsky (1987), and the U. S. Office of Technology Assessment (1985, 1987, 1988), as well as syllabi and course descriptions on the subject (Shapiro and Macdonald, 1987; Behar, 1988). Anthologies include Kraut, ed. (1987a), Cyert and Mowery, eds. (1987), and Hartman et al., eds. (1987). The result is that the IS literature, now more often than not, urges managers to display concern for employees' needs and attitudes recognizing these may affect the "bottom line" more than technical factors (Currid, 1990).

The sociotechnical perspective may be summarized by observing that what is technically optimal may not be sociotechnically optimal. Weick gives an obvious example from air traffic control, where information technology can outstrip human capabilities. "If automated control," he wrote, "allows planes to fly closer together (e.g., separated by 10 seconds), the problem is that when the control fails, humans will not be able to pick up the pieces because they are not smart enough or fast enough...Automation, however, is not at fault. Automation makes a 10-second separation possible. But just because such a separation is possible, doesn't mean it has to be implemented. That remains a human decision. The heightened capacity isn't dumb, but the decision to heighten capacity may be" (Weick, 1987: 122-123). Sociotechnical management seeks to improve both organizational effectiveness and the quality of working life through a design process which integrates technical and social concerns.[10]

QWL and IS Success: A Summary

Jacques Vallee (1982) cited a case where French police, acting on an erroneous computer match of an alleged criminal, were led to a confrontation in which innocent victims were shot to death. Yet few would argue that this is a "computer problem". Rather it is the quite common problem of treating everything which emanates from a computer as indisputably correct, not needing the back-up of human reasoning. In this case police failed to follow normal investigative procedures having nothing to do with computing per se.

Banker (1988) reports another case showing how "computer problems" are based on human factors. Shortly after the 1984 election, the Democratic Party sent thank-you letters to thousands of individuals who had contributed. In no time complaints and questions came flooding back from individuals who had been addressed "Rabbi", "Colonel", or by some other title which did not apply to them. It turned out that the Democrats had used a computerized mailing list which was dependent on entering a code for the desired title (e.g., '02' was 'Mrs.' and '20' was 'Rabbi'), as well as for other fields. If the keypunch operator started with an extra character, say a space, then all the codes were displaced by one character, in many cases causing 'Mrs.' to be coded as 'Rabbi'. A similar problem resulted in exclusion of Hartford, CT, citizens from federal jury selection. The U. S. District Court computer considered all Hartford residents to be dead because the "d" in "Hartford" was systematically misaligned into the wrong column, where it was interpreted as meaning the person was deceased (Associated Press, 1992b).

In both cases, the problem was partly technical: better error-trapping in the mailing list software could have helped the data entry clerks to be more careful. But it was also a management problem: the systems assumed there would be no data entry mistakes or at least that it was not worth paying anyone to perform a quality control role. With human beings making mistakes on the input side and with no human check on the output side, "computer foul-ups" are inevitable.

These examples illustrate how human and technical factors are intertwined. Such examples are hardly exceptional. It is not surprising that DeMarco and Lister, cited earlier, found few technological and many human critical factors in the hundreds of implementation disasters they studied. The point, however, is not to pit technological factors and human factors against each other in some sort of straw-man debate to vindicate one point of view or the other. Rather the purpose of this section has been to emphasize the integrated, *sociotechnical* nature of computing.[11] The two dimensions cannot be separated and a joint emphasis on both may lead to a more effective work process and a higher quality of working life than either perspective could yield on its own (Taylor and Asadorian, 1985: 14).[12]

Computer problems are not merely inconveniences. From the employee viewpoint, there is a major issue having to do with the quality of working life, being consulted rather than disempowered. From the management viewpoint, the major issue is getting those who implement information systems to act on the reality that human factors, not technological ones, are the crucial success factors for IS. And from a social viewpoint, the major issue is whether the national productivity potential of information technology will continue to be sapped by inattention to and underinvestment in the human side of the sociotechnical equation.

Conclusion: The Social Impacts of Computing

This chapter has examined five important but only loosely related questions about the social impacts of computing. The first had to do with the symbolic aspects of computing and issues of policy manipulation. The second pertained to social aspects of computing and issues of discrimination and bias. The third dealt with the legal aspects of computing and issues of social liability. The fourth concerned health aspects of computing and issues of occupational safety. Last, the fifth topic dealt with management aspects of computing and issues pertaining to the quality of work life.

Are the main effects of computing symbolic rather than substantive? Belief that the answer is "Yes" rests on the fact that, like other forms of staff support, computer reports are more apt to be used to justify decisions made than to change patterns of decision-making or alter power. Those who answer "Yes" are likely to emphasize the inherent limits to computing, as reflecting in four common fallacies about the subject: (1) wrongly assuming that the mind can be seen as a series of on/off switches (the biological fallacy); (2) wrongly assuming that reality is processed by the mind as a series of bits to which formal rules may be applied (the psychological fallacy); (3) wrongly holding the belief that knowledge can be formalized without significantly distorting it (the epistemological fallacy); and (4) wrongly holding the belief that knowledge is empirical and additive (the sum of its parts—the ontological fallacy) (Dreyfus, 1979: 155-227). Writers of this school of thought have explored how digitization of reality fosters the illusion that computing can be value-free yet manipulate the world for any technologically feasible end (Baudrillard, 1983; Lyotard, 1984; Guattari, 1984; Murphy and Pardeck, 1989; see also Dreyfus and Dreyfus, 1986).

In Chapter 7, I examine the issue of whether information technology is apt to live up to its claim to being the key essential ingredient in preparing Americans for 21st-century global competition; I look at the extent to which computer investment has paid off in productivity terms. In spite of widespread popular faith in the value of computing, there is a lively issue among serious analysts about whether IT investment may be highly over-rated. Those who argue that computing is primarily symbolic and manipulative would agree that it is indeed overrated. These writers are not surprised at the substantial amount of evidence that large-scale investment in information technology has not paid off. However, there is also substantial evidence that computing investment can increase productivity.

It is trite, but true to say, that in this case the truth lies in the middle. As will be discussed in Chapter 7, if information technology may not be America's economic salvation in the next century, at least it is clear that a revival of an anti-technological modern-day Ludditism would threaten grave harm. In this chapter, however, the argument was made that computer enthusiasts are wrong if they fail to recognize that a great deal of what is done in the name of information systems serves predominantly symbolic purposes which may, at times, even be used to mystify and manipulate those not privy to the interests using computing for essentially political purposes. Second, this chapter asked if the gender, racial, ethnic, class, and age impacts of computing constitute bias or discrimination? While agism seems not to be a problem, the evidence for gender, race, and class bias in computing is overwhelming. In this sense, too, computing is deeply political. Discrimination, however, has to do with intent, whereas bias has to do with effect. While there are some charges of "old boys' networks" in computing as in other economic areas, there is little documentation of overt discrimination. Rather discussion has centered on such topics as the need to invest in human resources, to create role models in computing for women, to fund mentoring systems for minorities, to upgrade teacher computing skills in low-income schools, and so on. Returning again to the theme of this book, discussion of this topic brings one back to debates over sociopolitical policies and interest group conflict over alternative resource allocations.

Third, this chapter raised the question of the extent to which information managers can or should be held legally liable for their work. My answers were "Yes" and "Yes". Although legal liability for information services is only now being defined by the courts, managers and public officials ignore liability issues at their peril. While my message is not "information can kill", it has been recognized in the courts that information managers cannot rely on the defense that "I only provide the data, I don't make the decisions". The novelty of electronic liability as an issue has led some to look upon it merely as an interesting curiosity. However, the potential for liability lawsuits in the information sector is large and growing. In time this can be expected to have major implications for national productivity if managers fail to do what the courts now expect: take affirmative actions to implement a standard of "reasonable care" to prevent damages which might otherwise arise from their services. Existing legislation does apply to information managers and there is reason to expect that the political process will bring yet more legislation imposing higher standards of social responsibility.

Fourth, in this chapter I investigated whether computing is occupationally safe for information workers. Contrary to popular perceptions, information work is not devoid of issues of occupational safety. It is true that some suspected risks such as possible effects of electromagnetic radiation have not been established to be significant, at least not yet. At the other extreme, repetitive motion strain (RMS) has quickly become a recognized national problem with large-scale implications for business, insurance, and national productivity. In between are other risks ranging from eye strain to psychological technostress, which have become accepted as real and significant but which have yet to assume the economic importance of RMS. As in other social impact areas, discussions of computing and occupational safety lead directly in a political direction. Even if America does not emulate European legislation on occupational safety for information workers, it is safe to say that this will be the subject of public policy debate into the next century.

Fifth and finally, this chapter raised the question of how computing affects the quality of working life and whether there is a synergy between QWL concerns and successful approaches to IS implementation. I argued that IS failures have been found to be attributable primarily to human rather than technological factors. By the same token, the human dimension provides the most important success factors for good IS implementation — as I will discuss further in the next chapter on computing and human behavior. Usually, the engineering-based SDLC (systems development life cycle) approach to IS planning is contrasted with the psychology-based STS (sociotechnical systems) approach. A closer reading of the literature suggests, however, that IS planners are merging these two traditions, and for good reason. Information professionals need sociotechnical management, with its recognition that human factors cannot be dismissed as "irrational" or "political". IS approaches which seek to ignore or suppress human factors are destined for failure. Instead, IS success requires acceptance of the sociopolitical nature of human beings and requires designs which work with rather than against this nature.

In summary, whether one considers the symbolic uses of computing, bias questions, liability concerns, occupational safety questions, or quality of work life problems, it is found that the key issues of computing are essentially sociopolitical, not technological. Sometimes information engineers treat politics as a form of corruption of the IS process, to be eliminated wherever possible. However, politics keeps rearing its head for the simple reason that computing affects the interests of different constituencies differently. The heterogeneity of the social impacts of computing assures conflicts of interest. With a tongue-in-cheek bow to logicians, we may say that "Computing is differential social impact. Differential impact is conflict. Conflict is politics. Therefore computing is politics."

ENDNOTES

[1] Habermas's (1973: 268-276) concept of "technological rationality"is closely related, referring to the treatment of all phenomena as material objectifications which can be quantified and organized in a neutral manner, stripped of their context in social space.

[2] When women do become involved with computing they are more apt to be oriented toward packaged applications, not programming (Turkle, 1984: 49).

[3] For instance, while most non-professional information workers (e.g., data processors) are women, only 29% of systems analysts are female (Tembeck and Meisch, 1987).

[4] Federal law prohibits copyright of software and other computer models developed by public agencies. This has meant that private enterprise has been at liberty to appropriate Census and other agency computer products and sell them to the public at an even lower price than the government's own low prices, thereby undermining cost recovery efforts. Moreover, businesses are reluctant to undertake joint software development projects with public agencies because of uncertainties about copyright protection over whatever products might be developed. For these reasons, federal IS managers often advocate copyrights for government-developed computer products, a concept which thus far has fallen on deaf ears in Congress (GAO, 1990b). A similar issue has arisen in the private sector since the U.S. Supreme Court in *Feist Publications vs. Rural Telephone Service* (1991), held that telephone white pages can be copied freely by competitors since they contain no "original expression" in selection and compilation of facts (Samuelson, 1992). Although sure to provoke litigation,

the *Feist* ruling holds that compilations of facts, even in the private sector, are not copyrightable if those who appropriate and resell the contents take the small effort involved in rearranging the information. For a general discussion of copyrights and fair use with regard to computer media, see Bergen (1992).

[5] For a review of these issues, see Grandjean (1987).

[6] In a similar case, the State of North Carolina received a computer system as a donation to its Department of Commerce but was unable to use it for four months because the donor had lost track of the password which had been installed. *News and Observer* (Raleigh, NC), 4/8/89: 1A.

[7] The SDLC model has been a staple in IS texts since the 1960's (Cf. Davis and Olson, 1985; Ahituv and Neumann, 1986) and is based on the idea of a product life cycle (Hammer, 1981). It can be summarized as a linear checklist of activities which must be undertaken in a series of phases which begin with planning and end with system termination. To put it another way, SDLC is a planning process which decomposes an IS system problem into its constituent parts, treats each step separately, recomposing the whole at the end (Langfors, 1973). Different authors include different labels for the step in SDLC, but the underlying common idea is that "there exists a generic, structured, linear, and iterative process for computer systems development" (Overman, 1988: 57). In general, the SDLC model evolves from an engineering background which has traditionally not given human factors a major place in planning priorities, although this is changing. These has been increasing recognition of the need for flexibility in applying SDLC methods (e.g., Ahituv, Neumann, and Hadass, 1984; Rubin, 1986).

SDLC assumes rational planning by decision-makers, emphasizing such values as stability, predictability, and control. The systems development life cycle (SDLC) concept is not static but has evolved in the direction on feedback loops from later stages to earlier ones, implying an iterative approach. The concepts of emphasis on feedback and iteration open SDLC to the possiblities of teamwork, participation, and other concepts associated with the organization development tradition. A second concept adopted relatively recently in SDLC thinking is prototyping. Prototyping is explicitly purposed for feedback objectives. It is seen as a team process overcoming earlier and simpler versions of SDLC. These earlier SDLC models are now seen as too liner, lacking a group planning orientation, and not reflecting actual experience in the real world. Factors which facilitate successful SDLC implementations are those common in organizational change generally. The situational perspective common in OD seems almost inevitably to be the applicable viewpoint for SDLC as well, a viewpoint which moves it not a small distance from the engineering to the social and behavioral sciences.

[8] Not all IS problems are rooted in human factors. In 1960, a false computer alarm wrongly saw a large fleet of Soviet missiles attacking the United States. Fortunately, because tensions were low at the time and because the Soviet leader was in New York at the time, no response was undertaken and it later turned out that lunar reflections were to blame (Berkeley, 1962: 175-177). Perrow (1984) reported numerous military mishaps involving computers. Our NORAD missile defense system was registering 10 false alarms a day in 1980. The largest American military loss in the 1991 Desert Storm war with Iraq was attributed to a technical computer glitch which failed to activate an anti-missile system (New York Times News Service, 1991). Likewise, on January 16, 1990, a computer code bug caused millions of Americans to receive the message "Sorry, all lines are busy." when they tried to dial long distance on the AT&T system. Other computer code bugs in the Ada language used by the Defense Department have created major problems in the development of "smart" weapons (Morrison, 1989). In general, most software contain "bugs" which cause a greater or lesser degree of harm or threat of harm.

Some shortcomings of IS can be ameliorated simply through improved technology. The NCIC (National Crime Information Center) database, for example, was much criticized for "false hits". That is, too many innocent individuals were matched to the descriptions of criminals in the databases. Consequently, in 1987 the NCIC board approved proposals to allow transmission of fingerprint images, photos, and composite drawings along with the descriptive text. Such approaches require vast increases in data storage and transmission speed, technology not theretofore available at an affordable cost. Indeed, full automation of FBI fingerprint files itself requires new technology and is still a goal of the NCIC 2000 project. However, no amount of improved technology will ever fully "solve" the problems of government databases in relation to individual rights, only build in greater safeguards (McGraw, 1988b). Moreover, many systems which seem to be technology-driven, such as the efficient Japanese just-in-time inventory system, on closer inspection turn out to depend critically on social bonds and relationships, not just computer hardware and software (Minabe, 1986). The larger and more integrated the IS system (and this is the direction of the times), the more critical becomes planning for human factors becomes (Walton and Susman, 1987).

[9] Neglect of investment in information technology itself can be a problem, just as can be lack of investment in associated human resources. In 1989 it was reported by the General Accounting Office that for over four years Customs Service officials had known their accounting software was defective and had been unable to account for $54 million in duty fees because the agency's Automated Commercial System lacked adequate accounting controls. "The Customs Service is basically saying," the GAO noted, "they have taken checks or cash under their control and sometime before that money was deposited with a bank, they have lost control. It appears, I underline appears, they have lost the money." Customs officials were reported in agreement that poor software was to blame. At one level, this is a technical problem having to do with software design and its lack of proper provisions for audit trails, cross-checks, and other controls. At another level, however, this fiasco reflects an agency so preoccupied with drug enforcement that IS was placed at the bottom of its priorities. Lack of rigorous software acceptance procedures, ongoing IS evaluation, and just plain lack of investment characterized IS in Customs. This is a problem which can be viewed as a technical problem, but is was also a management and people problem (Grimm, 1989d).

Another example of problems arising from false savings on IS investment was illustrated by the loss of the Phobos 1 satellite, launched by the Soviet Union in 1988 to gather information about Mars, went into a tumble and became lost. The error was traced to the transmission of a single character in a complex series of digital commands. This character triggered a test sequence meant to be activated only while the satellite was on the ground, before launch. Some labelled the error "bad luck" while others blamed system design for allowing minor code errors to translate into major and disastrous outcomes. Requiring verfication of key commands, for instance, could have avoided the satellite becoming lost. The disaster was at one level a design error, but it was also a human factors problem -- failure to design for the error-prone ways of human beings (Waldrop, 1989).

[10] Four common attributes of sociotechnical management are (1) reliance on small 'action groups' in a bottom-up, user-oriented process of design specification, experiments sanctioned by higher management; a team approach; (2) skills development as an organizational objective (as opposed to acceptance of de-skilling); encouragement of and use of autonomous work groups when possible; (3) structuring the reward system to encourage participation in productivity planning and implementation; encouragement of self-inspection; provision of feedback on performance; and (4) introduction of new technologies under a facilitative (as opposed to command-driven) leadership. These and other STS management principles are outlined by writers such as Trist (1973, 1981), Blackler and Oborne (1987), and Chisholm (1988).

[11] For an example of sociotechnical analysis of computing issues, see McInerney, 1989.

[12] This should hardly be surprising to academics since it has often been shown that how people use a computer, and not the machine's inherent features, determines how a computer

will be used (in education, for instance: see Mehan, 1989). If this seems an obvious point, IS literature still sometimes approaches implementation in terms of how to accomplish code conversation from one machine to another (e.g., Ayer and Patrinostro, 1986) or assumes equivalent technical perspectives which ignore human factors (see Skinner, 1979, for a critique of this traditional orientation).

CHAPTER VI

Computing and Organizational Change

Computers tend to change the way we relate to each other. As a consequence, information technology has broad impacts on organizational change. This makes it a social issue. In this chapter, I first look at how one of the most pervasive aspects of information technology affects human behavior. This aspect is computer-based telecommunications, whether in the form of electronic mail, computerized database services, or teleconferencing. Second, I look at how the introduction of computer technology creates employee resistance and organizational change. In the concluding section, I inventory the many human behavioral success factors which must be recognized when implementing IS projects if technology is to be compatible with human social, political, and economic patterns.

Information Technology and Communication Patterns

The spectacular growth of telecommunications in the last decade has been taken surprisingly for granted by most Americans, even those who use computer-based on-line communications extensively. As social scientists, however, we must ask whether communicating on-line is merely a more efficient way of carrying on communications previously accomplished in a slower but essentially similar manner. If we choose to communicate on-line, what do we gain and what do we lose? Will it change the way people perceive us and the way we perceive others? Are there organizational consequences to policy decisions promoting the use of telecommunications? In this section I will argue that communicating on-line is not the same as conventional communication. On-line communication is characterized by powerful opportunities and significant problems.

Electronic Mail and Human Communication

Electronic mail (e-mail) provides an interesting and important example of how information technology can influence communications patterns. E-mail is much faster than ordinary postal mail, costs far less, and has become increasingly popular. The Electronic Mail Association estimates that within large companies (over $500 million annual revenue) alone, some 9 million workers use electronic mail. Electronic mail within networked business units quadrupled between 1988 and 1992 (Rothfeder, 1992: 168). The number of e-mail users may be 25 million by 1995 (Bomengen and Ulrich, 1991). With the growth of electronic mail, several impacts on human communication patterns are evident (see Figure 6-1).

Electronic mail has expanded rapidly primarily because of its economic advantages.[1] It improves documentation and creates search-

Figure 1: Impacts of Electronic Mail

* Improved economic efficiency in communications.
* Increased volume of interaction and feedback.
* Increased lateral communication and support for team-oriented management.
* Increased problems of miscommunication.
* Increased information overload as an organizational and individual problem.
* Information filtering becomes a central communications issue.

able archives already in word-processable form, not requiring the added expense of rekeying data. At the same time, e-mail provides speedy delivery and response. It saves travel costs. All in all, electronic mail is the cheapest form of communication, costing about 16 cents to send a one-page letter from New York to California, compared to $1.86 by fax, and $13 for overnight express mail (Rothfeder, 1992: 168). However, e-mail cannot be understood simply in economic terms.

One of the effects of electronic mail is that it increases the frequency and amount of information interchange (Kerr and Hiltz, 1982; Estrin, 1986). One study found 60% of messages sent on e-mail would not have been sent without it, often forming ties among people who would otherwise not be in touch (Feldman, 1986: 85). Increased electronic mail leads to increased information sharing, which in turn leads to increased organizational productivity (Crawford, 1982; Papa, 1990: 361).

Electronic mail is not only more prolific, it is different in nature. E-mail encourages upward and lateral communication. That is, e-mail encourages organizational members to contact one another directly rather than communicate only "through channels" (McKeown, 1990). By encouraging direct communications, electronic mail is a force for alteration of traditional hierarchical communications patterns. By improving direct communication, it is easier to be a member of and to operate as a team. Team members can interact more frequently and conveniently than is possible when face-to-face meetings or even telephone contact is required. Management can take advantage of this by relying more on task-oriented team-based methods of operation and less on top-down command-driven modes of the past.

Electronic mail opens up organizational processes to view by a wider public. Meyrowitz (1986) has analyzed this in terms of Erving Goffman's dramaturgical theories of social behavior, with its focus on "frontstage" and "backstage" differences in social relations. Meyrowitz argues that electronic media enhance information flow, exposing "backstage" behavior to public scrutiny and creating a new middle-stage region of behavior. Boone (1993: 30-33) discusses the tendency of electronic communications to open more of the backstage to view, noting the situational nature of this trend. Sometimes greater openness encourages organizational integration, communication satisfaction, and goal performance. In other circumstances, such as times of organizational crisis, the effects of openness can be disastrous.

Finally, there are also social effects of electronic mail. An interesting study by Eveland and Bikson (1988) compared a group of retired workers linked by e-mail with a control group meeting conventionally, and found the e-mail group displayed more contacts, more involvement, and better satisfaction. It may well be that communicating on-line conveys feelings of empowerment, participation, and involvement in organizational life.

Electronic mail has adverse as well as beneficial effects on human communications patterns. Because it appears in print on one's monitor or printer, electronic mail is often perceived as being more formal than verbal messages on the phone or face-to-face. A study of e-mail at the Digital Equipment Corporation found managers perceived e-mail messages as being too sterile, formal, and terse. This in turn conveyed the impression that a response was needed even though that may not have been the intent (Crawford, 1982). In general, on-line communication content tends to be more event-oriented and less people-oriented than face-to-face communication and can even involve less sensitivity to the perspectives of others (Gardner and Peluchette, 1991: 179).

The formality of electronic mail can be a particular problem when employees use colorful language to vent displeasures. Houser cites the case of an Army physician whose e-mail condemnations of a software system were picked up by newspapers and the *Congressional Record.* Houser warns, "E-mail messages can live forever...E-mail messages can reproduce uncontrollably... [when] sending a nasty-gram directly to the object of one's disaffection ... I recommend these encounters be oral, not written and readily reproduced" (Houser, 1992: 25; Machrone, 1992).

On-line communication brings the problem of *information overload* (Selnow, 1988). Electronic networks and their associated databases contain enormous amounts of information. When networking also involves the large numbers of individuals, often with each able to effortlessly disseminate their communications to many others, the volume of network traffic can become overwhelming. Klapp (1986) believes that the information glut associated with computing is not only an obstacle to effective communications but also can become a major factor behind increased boredom in everyday life. The balance between information access and information overload is not necessarily achieved naturally (for further discussion, see Quarterman, 1990).

Studies show that reading monitors is more stressful than reading print.[2] Although keyword searching is vastly more efficient, generalized scanning and browsing is often more difficult. Because of information overload, filtering becomes a communications problem. The very ease of e-mail broadcasting (sending the same message to multiple people) can jam electronic mailboxes. Subscription even to a few active interest groups on a network may elicit dozens of e-mail postings a day.

At the same time that communications volume increases, many people may feel that quality decreases. E-mail will bring you more mail which is more time-consuming to sort through.[3] Bruce Lewenstein of Cornell University studied an electronic bulletin board in physics from 1989 through 1992 and found, for instance, that such electronic communications services provide little real advantage for researchers. Lewenstein found the physics BBS to be dominated by "computer jockeys" carrying on non-technical discussions more akin to radio talk shows than to specialist forums. When researchers did find kindred colleagues on the network, they were likely to carry on further communications with them privately (*Chronicle of Higher Education*, 1993: A25).

In summary, network managers may have to exert great effort and care to facilitate and structure communications to achieve intended objectives and to minimize unnecessary overload (Hiltz and Turoff, 1985). For example, software can be designed to filter desired types of information and automatic filters can be set individualized to each user's needs, even to the point of posting selected materials automatically to the user's electronic mailbox. Software can also govern queuing rules to establish user priorities as appropriate to particular organizational settings and software can also utilize standard user interfaces to minimize learning time. In spite of such efforts, the many human behavioral aspects of electronic mail mean management must be prepared to fund substantial training and support costs when electronic mail systems are installed.

On-line Information Services and Anonymous Communication

In addition to electronic mail, a second type of telecommunications is the on-line bulletin board service (BBS) and its larger cousin, the on-line information service. BBS's exist for every purpose under the sun from technical support for particular word processing packages to social support for homosexuals. Whatever your professional field, there is probably at least one BBS dedicated to providing a variety of services to you. These services usually center on (1) discussion groups where a "conversation" is carried on by participants serially posting messages or documents to the bulletin board, where all can read them; and (2) a "library" of useful text or data files which members can download to their personal computers. Other features may include electronic mail, electronic shopping, travel and weather services, online surveys and balloting, and teleconferencing.

On-line information services provide users with instant access to vast amounts of textual, bibliographic, numeric, and other forms of data. While undoubtedly a powerful tool, such services have problems compared to making queries to a reference librarian face-to-face. Search requests are made by keyword, searching is by brute computer force, and most searches yield as much garbage as they do helpful information. An additional problem is that retrieval systems are not standardized, so users of many on-line systems are forced to learn many sets of retrieval commands (Hildreth, 1986). This problem can limit effective access to professional librarians and others who can afford the time investment involved.

From the viewpoint of organizational change, perhaps the most significant feature of on-line information services is that in most instances the user can be anonymous if he or she wishes. The anonymity often associated with BBS and other telecommunication services reduces apprehension about being evaluated and promotes candid discussion of issues. Moreover, anonymity makes people less defensive about criticism and more willing to explore the reasons why others disagree with them (Nunamaker et al., 1991: 58).

Anonymity was credited with underlying the success of U. S. Representative Bob Wise's (D-WV) Whistle Blower BBS, an electronic bulletin board which in 1991 received over 1,000 messages and led to 75 federal investigations of suspected waste, fraud, and corruption (Higgins, 1992).[4] Others have found that on-line communication increases the likelihood of personal information being disclosed, probably for reasons of anonymity (Kiesler and Sproull, 1986; Greist, Klein and VanCura, 1973). Likewise, in the area of social work, taking social histories by anonymous computer-administered methods have been found to collect more extreme responses and fewer factual discrepancies than human interviewing methods, suggesting that computers elicit more candidness (Ferriter, 1993).

Some have argued that anonymity in electronic communications can encourage inventive forms of interaction involving disguised identities. These altered identities may be adopted for exploratory purposes but in the long run may reflect a "postmodern de-centering of the self" as altered identities adopted for special purposes form the basis for fragmented personal relationships (Turkle, 1984; Steinmetz, 1988). In particular, the altering of social norms in on-line communication may involve de-individuation. That is, it may be argued that users become engrossed in the on-line media to the point of weakening internal values and norms and/or weakening the salience of peer- and social-originated values and norms. Thus Siegel, Dubrovsky, Kiesler, and McGuire (1986: 183) write, "people who are absorbed in computer-mediated communication might become 'de-individuated' ... submergence in a technology, and technologically induced anonymity and weak social feedback might also lead to feelings of a loss of identity and uninhibited behavior".

Matheson and Zanna (1990) examined the issue of de-individuation in a controlled experiment and found that computer-mediated communications involved significantly higher levels of self-awareness and only marginally lower levels of public awareness compared to face-to-face communicators, contrary to de-individuation theory. Matheson and Zanna (1990: 9) concluded that increased uninhibited behaviors in on-line communication do not reflect de-individuation and normlessness but rather reflect the correlation of self awareness with lowered propensity to be influenced by peer perceptions and greater resistance to and reactance against potentially coercive communications (e.g., attitude reversal through persuasive communication). They also speculate that heightened self-awareness underlies the tendency of on-line communication to generate large numbers of decision proposals while at the same time achieving consensus on-line tends to be slower and more difficult (cf. Gardner and Peulchette, 1991: 180-198).

A debate exists over the limits to be imposed on organizational bulletin boards and other telecommunications services. Use of such services for social chat and even game-playing is a common occurrence. These practices are encouraged by anonymity or at least lack of direct oversight characteristic of information services. Some organizations permit such social activities while others attempt to "pull the plug" (Zuboff, 1988a: ch. 10). Perrolle (1991a) argues for the wisdom of the former policy, holding that the effectiveness of communications in an organization depends on intangible interpersonal relationships which cannot flourish when communications are limited to strictly technical questions.

Conclusion: Information Services and Organizational Communications

Computer-based teleconferencing is sometimes advanced as a revolutionary new technology which will alter fundamentally the patterns of communication, decision-making, and power in modern organizations. Information services and on-line communications involve many pros and cons (see Figures 6-2 and 6-3), making it difficult to analyze IS impacts on organizational communications. While telecommunications is often promoted as a system for totally open communications, at the same time, as Perrolle (1991a: 351) notes, "computer-mediated communication can embody inequalities in social relationships and can limit conversational participation, serving as a technology *for* (emphasis in original) distorted commu-

Figure 2: Meeting On-line: Pros

* Teleconferencing promotes broader input into meeting processes and reduces the chance that a few people will dominate a meeting (Nunamaker et al., 1991: 58).

* Electronic meetings increase the number of decision proposals generated through group communication (Siegel, Dubrovsky, Kiesler, and McGuire, 1986; McGuire, Kiesler, and Siegel, 1987). This suggests meeting online may be particularly useful during the early brainstorming stages of decision-making.

* On-line conferencing also increases risk-taking and choice shift in some settings (e.g., in a lab setting with student subjects: Kiesler, Siegel, and McGuire, 1984).

* Electronic transcripts of teleconferences can be and usually are recorded automatically, creating a group memory often absent in face-to-face groups.

Figure 3: Meeting Online: Cons

* At least one study shows that people communicating on-line tend to evaluate each other less favorably than they were to communicate face-to-face (Kiesler, Zubrow, Moses, and Geller, 1985).

* On-line communication may lead to more uninhibited speech in the form of wearing, insults, name-calling, and hostile comments (Kiesler, Siegel, and McGuire, 1984; Siegel, Dubrovsky, Kiesler, and McGuire, 1986; McGuire, Kiesler, and Siegel, 1987). In general, telecommunications can alter social norms which enforce the social control over interactions (Kiesler, 1984; Kiesler and Sproull, 1986; Sheffield, 1989).

* Compared to face-to-face methods, computer conferencing takes *more* time to reach decisions, at least if travel time to meetings is not taken into account.

* For a given length of time, less consensus is achieved through teleconferencing than face-to-face meetings (Rice and Associates, eds., 1984: 185-215).

nication." We may add, managers may value telecommunications precisely to the extent that it preserves organizational statuses, not for the extent that it opens communication.

However, a particularly significant finding is that on-line communications decreases recognition of the status of any given participant. That is, on-line information services decrease the tendency of higher-status individuals to dominate low-status individuals, inhibiting or preventing the participation of the latter in conversation (Molotch and Boden, 1985; Sproull and Kiesler, 1986; Perrolle, 1987b).

Higher status individuals may feel threatened by the capacity of teleconferencing systems to provide organization and articulation to lower status employees. For instance, a teleconferencing system was employed by professional women in a pharmaceutical firm to discuss career options. Managers in the industrial relations and legal divisions of the firm monitored the conference because of fears it would lead to unionization, affirmative action demands, or other conflict. Management oversight of the conference squelched participation and effectively shut it down (Zuboff, 1988a: 382-383).

While on the one hand the status-equalizing tendencies of on-line communication might suggest its democratizing possibilities, in fact it is better interpreted as a breakdown in social and organizational norms which stands as a severe obstacle to using this technology for effective decision-making (Kiesler, 1984). Some have concluded that electronic communication is associated with lowered normative influence and hence with more extreme group behaviors, which in turn can polarize decision-making (Kiesler, Siegel, and McGuire, 1984).

Implementing on-line communications in ways which take account of the sensibilities of all concerned may require professional network facilitators. This is true not only for status reasons but for practical ones as well: it is harder to get attention without disrupting, harder to differentiate intent (e.g., understand what is satire and what is serious), harder to detect signs of lack of interest or agreement, and harder to perceive the need to adjust for audience reactions.

Even simple typing of what is to be communicated can be cumbersome. Tolerance for ungrammatical expression is the trade-off for rapid on-line communication. Managers may feel that such expression demeans their status, preferring to avoid telecommunications rather than expose themselves to the problems it holds. Moreover, sharing unformed ideas on networks where any communication can be downloaded as a permanent document of record is not always the best managerial wisdom. For these reasons, managers generally prefer the phone to on-line telecommunications networks. Though computer networking is on the rise, so too there are breakthroughs in phone technology, such as fax, voice mail, and video conferencing. Though it is not clear just what mix of technologies may prevail, telecommunications is intensifying the quantity of communications and changing communications qualitatively as well.

The reason why information managers themselves strongly preferred telephone communication over electronic mail was the loss of "soft" aspects of communications which allow inferences based on affect, intonation, and status cues (Gardner and Peluchette, 1991: 177; Olson, 1982: 77). In general, by eliminating some sensory information, telecommunications changes conversational patterns from what they otherwise would be (Reid, 1977; Olson and Lucas, 1982). Inhibitions about using new technology or fear that it may discriminate against certain groups are also significant obstacles.

Due to problems of teleconferencing, attempts to establish on-line systems sometimes fail. For instance, Dubinskas (1986) has described the total failure of a computer conferencing systems, whose end users eventually wound up using it for a bulletin board. That is, users preferred the on-line system for its value for posting and reading mail and notes but did not find useful its functions for direct communication involving two-way dialog. Ironically, on-line users tend to resent system efforts to improve this communication by regulating turn-taking, interruptions, and other controls (Kiesler, Siegel, and McGuire, 1984). Real-time teleconferencing via computers is still best limited to small groups.

Video-conferencing will overcome many of the problems of teleconferencing noted in research cited above. Text-based telecommunications is awkward, frustrating, and slow due to the typing skills involved (Siegel, Dubrovsky, Kiesler, and McGuire, 1986). It has been estimated that in normal face-to-face discussions, some 40% of the information conveyed occurs through non-verbal cures, body language, and visual aids. This information is lost in ordinary network communication but is made available through teleconferencing systems. Moreover, the price of video-conferencing is falling dramatically in the 1990s (Taylor, 1991).

Video-conferencing technology is already available and line costs are expected to be little more than for voice communications by the mid 1990s (Tobin, 1987). Eventually, video-conferencing software will be integrated with peripherals such as fax (facsimile transmission devices). From the user's viewpoint, a video-conference will appear as one window on a computer screen, with a second visual image (e.g., a graph) in another, and a database in a third, with hard copy transmittable instantly by fax and software allowing remote users to be capable of manipulating each other's database software simultaneously with video-conferencing. In such an environment, many of the conclusions from existing studies of far more cumbersome and limited technology may become irrelevant.

Information Technology and Organizational Change

Information systems literature now gives considerable weight to organizational change (Helander, 1988). The interaction of information technology and organization change can be discussed in terms of the natural tendency of employees to resist technological change, the importance of cognitive aspects of implementation, the need to approach IS projects as organizational problems in stakeholding, the important role of organizational change agents, the need for participative management, the challenge of creating an "information culture" supportive of technological initiatives, and the role of team management in this. These seven topics are discussed below.

Employee Resistance to Computerization

Employee resistance to information systems implementation has been noted since the dawn of the computer era. It was explored by organizational psychologists like Chris Argyris (see Figure 6-4) in the early 1970s. Employee resistance to computing was documented extensively in the mid-1970s in the work of Henry C. Lucas (1975a, 1975b, 1976). Lucas showed the importance of employee participation in bringing IS implementation to a successful conclusion. Lucas's

Figure 4: Chris Argyris on Employee Resistance to Computing

Chris Argyris, a leader in the field of organizational psychology, long ago described the syndrome of "psychological failure" associated with negative confrontations of individual employees with information systems projects (Chris Argyris, 'Management information systems: The challenge to rationality and emotionality'. *Management Science,* Vol. 17, No. 6 [1971]: B275-92.1971).

This syndrome is characterized by employee resistance, shielding, withdrawal, and self-orientation.

These dysfunctional behaviors result because automation may undermine employees' feelings of being essential or may restrict the freedom of movement of employees.

Managing information systems requires leadership based more on competence than formal authority, and this too may threaten the perceived status or promotion chances of the employee or manager.

Computerization efforts often require job redefinition and some employees may resent reduced (or increased) responsibilities. They may dislike being moved to another unit.

Some argue that from the start of an IS project, managers should acknowledge employee rights against displacement or de-skilling and should use this as a basis for participative implementation planning (e.g., Carson and Griffeth, 1990).

work reflected empirical findings. For instance, a typical survey of major firms showed that the primary problems arising in IS implementation were associated not with technical factors but with lack of top management support, poor planning, and/or employee opposition (Cerullo, 1979). Surveys of users also generally show negative employee attitudes toward organizational computer services (Lucas, 1981; Turner, 1982; Oskamp and Spacapan, eds., 1990; however, see Senn,1980). Consultants routinely find that organizational surveys of computer user satisfaction averages from only 5% to 40% satisfied, and are almost never above 50% (Reddit and Lodahl, 1989).

Employee resistance to IS change has been documented in all types of organizations, such as resistance to point-of-sales software in retailing (Dahm-Larsen, 1989) and resistance to instructional software in educational institutions (Talley, 1989). In human service agencies likewise, it has been found that employees who are alienated by information systems, perceive them as technical and non-clinical efforts developed for administrators rather than the "real" needs of clients and social workers (Brower and Mutschler,1985; Mutschler and Hasenfeld, 1986). In fact, in any organization people tend to resist change (Keen, 1981). The more the features of the IS differ from the features of the organizational setting in negatively valued ways, the more the resistance (Markus, 1984).

Because of employee resistance, managers cannot assume technological innovations will "catch on" simply by force of example. To illustrate, even though studies have shown that computer-assisted diagnosis is at least as effective as clinical diagnosis (Hedlund, Evenson, Sletten and Cho, 1980), resistance by practicing clinicians has severely impeded their utilization (Goodman, Gingerich, and Shazer, 1989: 65). Not only do IS projects not spread merely by example, but computer system implementation can become an occasion for breakdowns in employee morale or even for employee opposition to change (Frederickson, Riley and Myers, 1984). In some cases, employee resistance to the introduction of computer systems has led to their actual abandonment (Hedlund, Vieweg, and Cho, 1985). Because of such forms of resistance, there has arisen a large literature on dealing with resistance to factory automation and other information systems efforts (Majchrzak, 1988).

Returning to the theme of this book, resistance arises because changing information systems is a political act. Many studies confirm that employees, rightly or wrongly, perceive computerization as a tool for increasing control over workers and an obstacle to delivery of quality services (e.g., social workers in Mandell, 1987). For instance, a study of social workers' use of three computer-based technologies found "the factor that was considered to be most important in the decision-making process was the control over treatment" — the extent to which software did or did not diminish professional prerogatives of control over decisions Cwikel, 1993: 283).

Employees may dislike changes in the decision-making system resulting from new information systems. They may dislike the fact that computerization is being imposed from above in an autocratic manner. Ownership, control, and distribution of information can represent an individual's power base, and most employees will react defensively to protect it (Harvey, 1988). For instance, a major problem in implementing executive information systems (EIS) is employee resistance to chief executives being able to dig into databases hitherto controlled by middle managers and others (Raths, 1989).

Computing and Human Cognition

Overcoming employee resistance is a problem in influencing the way people perceive their environment. That is, it is a problem of cognitive change. There are four basic employee perceptions to overcome in implementation of information systems projects: (1) that automation is being mandated arbitrarily; (2) that the new computer system will be unreliable; (3) that the new system will decrease the quality of working life through increased burdens, de-skilling, tighter oversight, or other factors; and (4) that employees will not understand the new system or be able to operate it (see Mead and Trainor, 1985).Changing employee cognition is particularly important since word-of-mouth information and perspectives are a critical aspect of the process by which technological innovations are spread (Czepiel, 1974).

To illustrate, themes concerning cognition and employee resistance were prominent in a major study of IS implementation in three of Canada's provincial governments (Alberta, Saskatchewan, and Manitoba). Each had been making major IS investments. The study found computerization altered the flow and content of information,

Figure 5: Cognitive Obstacles in Information Systems

Donald A. Marchand and John C. Kresslein set forth six major cognitive obstacles to implementation of information systems projects:

(1) Conceptual: the belief that agency processes are too intangible and dynamic to lend themselves to automation, or that if automated, IS will lead to undue manipulation and centralization of power.

(2) Methodological: the belief that in IS, social values must predominate in decision-making, not measurable economic criteria, and therefore in all important matters computerization is largely irrelevant.

(3) Political: the belief that sunk costs in the status quo prevent the extensive changes that full implementation of IS concepts would involve.

(4) Structural-functional: the belief that rapid growth and flux associated with information technology prevent IS development.

(5) Fiscal: the belief that funds are not available to finance IS.

(6) Social: the belief that personal computer-phobia, fear of job loss, retraining obstacles, and other people issues will overwhelm IS development (Marchand and Kresslein, 1988: 429-433).

changed job content, and affected relationships between organizational members. A key finding in the Canadian study was that the primary issue was not computing itself but rather perceptions of the method of implementing it. That is, the real issue was changing human cognition, not changing hardware and software.

The intentions, philosophies, and values which come into play when computer-based systems are designed and implemented determine how IS is perceived (Alexander, 1987). Although this seems self-evident, it is not. Baker (1991), an anthropologist whose ethnographic study of IS innovation documented the importance of cultural values and symbols in organizations, found that in each of eleven prominent models of IS implementation in the information systems literature, there was a failure to give adequate attention to cognitive change in cultural context.

Researchers have found that the "origins of IS inadequacy lie in the failure to explicitly integrate information needs and cognitive expectations with the management activities and behaviors present in organizations" (Martin and Overman, 1988: 69). In one case involving automation of an existing compensation system, implementation went smoothly. In another case involving establishment of a new management information system to track salaries in terms of gender, implementation became mired in controversy and the system failed to become integrated into organizational decision-making. The difference lay in the extent that IS interventions threatened or seemed to threaten the prevailing system of employee values and expectations within complex organizations. These cognitive systems are ignored by IS managers at their own peril.

The cognitive change problem vis-a-vis top management is exacerbated by the fact that the IS implementation manager is often placed several levels removed from the top. When businesses create new product lines or governments create new agencies, the directors of these new units usually report directly to the top. They are on an equal reporting basis with older, established units and this provision for information flow from new units helps organizations adapt to change. However, the same is not true with regard to information technology. Work groups associated with new technologies are not placed in separate units with equal reporting access to the top. Instead they are typically subordinated within the organization structure below managers primarily responsible for current business and agency practices and current technologies (Wasson, 1990). This structural position of IS implementation creates a bias against effective cognitive change at the top.

Stakeholders in IS Projects

Successful IS implementation requires giving each all key individuals and units a stake in the outcome (Metz, 1986). As noted by Dickson, a pioneer in the study of human relations and IS, when it comes to management information systems it is essential to "involve people as a component, knowledge of their behavior as a part of the system is important to the success of the entire field" (Dickson, 1968: 24). Although employees' attitudes tend to be against change, if new technology is seen as bringing desired benefits, as is the intent in organization development efforts, then attitudes will adapt (Larwood, 1984).

Each person must feel the reward structure of the organization encourages collecting and sharing of information even when such efforts are not intrinsically part of one's job in the narrow sense. Majchrzak and Cotton (1988), for instance, in a longitudinal study of introduction of computer-automated batch production found the most important set of factors determining adjustment was actual changes to individual jobs. The central goal of IS implementation is to convince employees that the actual changes proposed will lead to beneficial results in the reward structure.

Rewards to stakeholders may include not only income but control over the task, information providing the "big picture", training, status, recognition, and other factors. An illustration is the practice of using the implementation of IS projects as the occasion to redefine and upgrade job descriptions of employees and managers, thereby giving them a direct career stake in the success of IS (redefining managerial roles during implementation has long been advocated, for example, by Horton, 1974). The stake may be as intangible as enhanced self-concept. Thus, if employees believe that computerization will make them more effective, they will more easily accept the change it involves (Gattiker and Larwood, 1986).

Stake-holding may account for findings that managers and professionals are significantly more positive in their perceptions of computers than are rank-and-file employees (Safayeni, Purdy, and Higgins, 1989). This is because the former are much more likely to be accorded a formal stake in IS projects than are the latter. An example of an intervention addressing this issue, described by Namm (1986), is the formation of interdepartmental planning groups whose mandate it is to develop "key reports" on data utilization for the organization as a whole, showing managers and professionals how computerization will benefit them individually.

Although frequently implemented only with respect to key managers, the stake-holding concept potentially can be applied to all employees. Joshi (1991) has shown how resistance to IS change is a function of employees' perceptions of gain or loss in equity status and relative outcomes vis-a-vis others. To develop favorable perceptions, Drummond and Landsberger (1989) have set forth a "shared vision methodology" for participative information systems planning, involving early formation of work groups which develop explicit scenarios depicting their vision of how their future work environment will be after implementation.

Examples of participatory design are common. The UTOPIA

project in Sweden and Denmark may be the best-known participatory project (Bjerknes, Ehn, and Kyng, 1987; Greenbaum and Kyng, eds., 1991; Greenbaum, 1992) involved close design collaboration with workers and unions. Other examples include SMOAP, the Self-Managed Office Automation Project to give Canadian university workers more control over automation (Clement, 1989); HCOSP, the Human Centered Office Systems Project to do the same for British librarians (Eriksson, Kitchenham, and Tijdens, eds., 1991); and PROTEVS, a Swedish project involving participatory design in local government and in a pharmaceutical industry (Friis, 1988).

"PD" — participatory design of information systems — is now commonly accepted, although it goes under a wide variety of labels and has many variants. Specific participatory methods include ethnographic methods (Greenbaum and Kyng, 1991), structured conferences (Bjerknes, Ehn, and Kyng, eds., 1987), collaborative prototyping (Muller, Kuhn, and Meskill, 1992), cooperative evaluation (Wright and Monk, 1992), theater for work impact (Boal, 1987), participatory ergonomics (Noro and Imada, eds., 1991), and many others. Muller, Wildman, and Whitge (1993) have developed a taxonomy of participatory approaches. They rank them on two dimensions: (1) from early to late intervention in the development cycle, and (2) from interventions where designers participate in the users' world(s) to interventions where users directly participate in information systems design. Ethnographic methods, for instance, are at one extreme: early interventions in which designers immerse themselves in the users' environment. Participatory ergonomics would be at another extreme: late interventions in which users participate directly in design activities. In its June 1993 issue, *Communications of the ACM* featured a symposium on participatory design, articulating many of these approaches.

Finally, it should be noted that the management of expectations is at the core of cognitive change. On the one hand it is essential that employees believe that IS will benefit them, that they have a stake in its success. However, it is equally important that expectations not be raised to levels which cannot be met. Patrick (1990) has warned how well-intentioned "true believers" in technology are a more insidious threat to IS implementation than are anti-technological traditionalists. The "true believers" hurt IS by exaggerating the problems of existing systems and glossing over problems of proposed new technologies. If their rosy view is allowed to dominate, then employees will feel betrayed later when problems do materialize. What may and may not be expected from new systems should be dealt with as openly, candidly, and as directly as possible.

The Role of Organizational Change Agents

Because human factors are so important in implementation of information systems, there is a role for generalists rather than technical specialists in IS implementation. Change agents have a double challenge. On one level there is creating an organizational culture which is supportive of information technology changes. But at another level often there is another problem: convincing top management that their own values and philosophies have a major bearing on

Figure 6: Mini-case: Generalists as Change Agents in Congress

John Ferro, microcomputer coordinator for the House Information System (HIS) in Congress, recognized the importance of generalists as change agents when he was developing IS strategy for the U. S. House of Representatives.

When faced with developing extensive new database applications for Congressional offices, Ferro decided not to use programmers for the bulk of his development. Instead he selected those with a broad, non-technical orientation toward management information systems.

"The office automation consultants we use are generalists," Ferro explained. "They know the work going on in the offices because that's where they usually came from and they listen. Experienced technicians have great strengths, too, but they generally prefer the cloistered life of a professional programmer" (Angus, 1987: 35).

After teaching a database system to a generalist, Ferro found the generalist was able to go into Congressional offices and work effectively with end users on implementation. In this work the generalist strongly encouraged end users to become intimately involved with issues such as designing the data entry screens and reports in order to encourage a strong sense of end-user ownership.

An important side benefit of this generalist approach to IS organization development was a more self-reliant universe of users, enabling Ferro to support 2,000 users with only eight staff - a 250:1 ratio considered unusually efficient by support service standards (Angus, 1987: 35; see also Callahan, 1985).

employee perceptions of IS implementation and hence on IS outcomes.

Because of his or her typically technical focus, information officers have usually been at a disadvantage in dealing with this problem. That disadvantage arises from their relative exclusion from the chief executive's trusted inner circle (Haase, 1981). During the 1980s there was increasing recognition that top IS positions needed to center on provision of managerial leadership and guidance (Blair, 1984) as well as education and experimentation (Sullivan, 1985). Generalists are in a better position to do this than are computer technicians.

A survey of the top 500 information systems companies found "In recent years IS has been trading its lab coat for a suit jacket. What began in the transistor age as a 'techie' career is now frequently the domain of executives whose understanding of economics and business plans exceeds their knowledge of MIPS and throughput...Companies are looking for renaissance men (and women) then, and not technical wizards for IS jobs" (*InformationWeek*, 1989a: 113, 120). The transformation of computing from data processing to multimedia processing of text, audio, images, and video has further reinforced the need for generalists in the 1990s (Wetmore, 1992: 30).

Whereas in 1980 only 15% of IS chiefs had not risen through MIS technical positions, by 1990 twice as many (over 30%) were from outside MIS and the trend was continuing (Caldwell, 1990h: 29). Managing IS is mainly a matter of managing people and planning for business and governmental needs, not technical problem-solving. IS managers may even need to stand up to chief executives when the latter want to "speed things up" by false economies such as skipping time and resource investment in organization development (OD) aspects of technology change. Generalists acting as IS change agents seek to integrate traditional systems development life cycle (SDLC) approaches with OD human relations techniques.

Participation and Technological Change

The leading organization development strategy for cognitive change is utilizing employee participation throughout the IS implementation process. Plans for technology change are more effectively implemented when communicated to employees in an open, informative, and plausible manner (Garson, 1987a). Free and open communications reduces employee resistance to technological change, as Elliot (1958) found over a quarter century ago in his study of computerization at the Detroit Edison Company. Likewise, Monnickendam and Eaglestein (1993: 409), in their study of human services, found that the key variable explaining acceptance of computerization was participation, not computerphobia or other employee traits. In fact, they found that even the perception of receptivity by the implementors, let alone actual participation, could effect acceptance. In contrast, top-down computer systems generated and influenced primarily by central management are often perceived as costly to create and to maintain while at the same time they may be viewed by individual managers as remote, inflexible, and autocratic.[5]

Participative techniques such as employee surveys, focus groups, and feedback from employee use of prototypes more than pays for itself in large technology projects. For instance, Mantei and Teory (1988) carefully costed out use of participative techniques and found major direct savings in the form of reduced training costs, error reduction costs[6], and savings from avoidance of last-minute IS design changes. They also found intangible benefits in the form of greater adoption of time-saving IS features, avoiding system sabotage problems, and enhancing the ability of employees to solve problems using the software system. Other studies show the importance of user participation in implementation as a way of securing involvement, commitment, and success (Baroudi, Olson, and Ives, 1986; Schuler and Namioka, 1992).

Participation fosters stake-holding in change. For instance, Rocheleau found in a study of acceptance of urban transportation models, "The same people who are skeptical of quantitative models and answers arising out of 'distant' centralized IS systems may be much less cautious about the models they themselves have developed on user-friendly microcomputers" (Rocheleau, 1985: 267).[7] Rocheleau found that, in contrast to remote mainframes, use of decentralized microcomputers under the direct control of planners led staff to develop a personal interest in the reliability and validity of data as well as favorable attitudes toward computer modeling for decision-making. Other implementation experience supports the view that productivity gains are associated with participative methods (Metz, 1986; Cardinali, 1990; Greenbaum and Kyng, 1991; Richter, 1993b).

It should be noted that there is a down side to participation. Among the dangers of participative strategies noted by Mantei and Teorey (1988: 436) was the "trap of overdesign". While user feedback can be invaluable, it can also be never-ending. At some point strong management control must override participation in the interest of actual implementation. Likewise, on cost grounds managers may have to resist user interface standards advanced by participatory groups. And because software developers are part of a distinct culture, there are decided communications costs when they carry on dialogues with participatory groups or even with change agents whose role is to interpret group priorities to developers. Nonetheless, Mantei and Teorey, like most researchers, find the benefits significantly outweigh the costs of participative strategies.

Fostering an Information Culture

Implementing technological change is not simply a matter of making technical decisions. Rather, the values and beliefs which make up the culture of the organization often have more impact on decision outcomes than do technical and structural factors. For instance, in a study of end-user computing in 46 American cities,

Figure 7: The Psychology of Participation

Psychologists sometimes divide people into those with an "external locus of control" and those with an "internal locus" (Rotter, 1966).

"External locus of control" individuals, to simplify, are individuals who believe events are under the control of luck, fate, powerful others, and are outside their own control.

Kay (1990) found a high correlation (r = .79) between having an internal locus of control and having a high degree of computer literacy among adult students age 22 - 55.

Numerous other studies have shown that individuals with an external locus of control are particularly likely to react negatively to computer environments (Swanson, 1974; Robey, 1979; Baroudi, Olson, and Ives, 1986).

However, when high user involvement is introduced, external-control individuals react the same as internal-control individuals (Hawk, 1989). That is, participation is instrumental to removing psychological predispositions against IS interventions.

Danziger, Kraemer, Dunkle, and King (1993) found that the most significant factor explaining the quality of end-user computing services was the existence of a service-oriented culture among computer specialists in the organization. Service-oriented culture was more important, for example, than technical factors like level of complexity of technological problems faced by the organization. It was also more important than structural factors like whether computing services were organized on a centralized or decentralized basis.

Organizational "information culture" is the value and belief system which provides the context for all perceptions of IS and its role. New information technology sets in motion a complex process of seeking and giving advice on appropriate reactions to change. This process of advice-giving may become institutionalized in formal structures (Barley, 1986). If implementation is poorly managed, organizations may reject new technologies or merely routinize them (accommodate to them but minimize their organizational impacts) rather than institutionalize them (provide organizational supports which help achieve higher levels of use) (Zmud and Apple, 1988).

Organization development (OD) is a branch of administration addressed to building on organizational culture to accomplish goals. OD applications useful for enhancing the IS team include goal clarification exercises, management style assessments, trust-building activities, sensitivity training, and democratic participation, to name a few possibilities. All OD strategies share the classic unfreeze-change-refreeze steps of innovation (cf. Albert, 1984; as applied to IS, Carson and Griffeth, 1990). To illustrate by reference to just one OD tactic, managers can use employee surveys to provide information useful not only for decision-making but also for organizational development. OD surveys can play a role in the critical first stage of change processes by providing information that makes explicit the beliefs associated with the existing information culture. By making beliefs explicit (e.g., beliefs outlined above in relation to cognitive aspects of IS implementation), the basis is laid for their discussion through participative groups in the workplace or other means.

Developing supportive information culture is often a goal of training programs. This is recognized, for instance, in the U. S. General Services Administration's Trail Boss program. This program focuses on training the IS manager responsible for acquiring information technology equipment and training of his or her team members.

It reflects the GSA's recognition that creating a large number of knowledgeable, well-trained teams is key to long-term improvement in governmental information systems. The purpose of training is to inculcate a sense of cooperation and common vision, something more effective than specifying policies in detailed regulations. The GSA has found that the success of the Trail Boss program is directly dependent on the agency's organizational culture. By the same token, successful Trail Boss programs have contributed substantially to fostering supportive information cultures in participating agencies (Houser, 1989). Unfortunately, investment in training has generally been inadequate, often wasting the possible benefits of automation (Richter, 1993a: 78).

Teams, Information Culture, and Organizational Change

Many contemporary management approaches emphasize the importance of teams in organization-building. One of the currently most popular is total quality management (TQM), an approach which calls for creation of quality teams whose task is to develop solutions to key organizational challenges. TQM consultants such as Jeffrey Tash, president of Database Decisions Inc., a Newton, Mass. consulting firm, suggest creation of such quality teams to bring together all those affected by an IS implementation, making the team responsible for defining the requirements of the new software to be adopted (Scheier, 1989b).

Team-building may involve restructuring the organization away from traditional hierarchical lines and toward "empowered teams", as when Motorola dropped chief information officers in favor of giving decision-making power over information systems to steering committees and teams of end-users (Pepper, 1992: 36). Similar directions are advocated in books such as Ray Grenier and George Metes, *Enterprise Networking: Working Together Apart* (1992), which discusses how face-to-face team-building at the Digital Equipment Corporation evolved into collaboration using electronic exchanges.

Savage (1990) goes so far as to advocate dismantling traditional organizational departmentalization in favor of task-oriented teams as part of what he calls "fifth generation management", making an analogy to fifth-generation computer software's association with parallel processing and artificial intelligence. In Savage's view,

Figure 8: Information Culture and Social Networks

Information culture is intertwined with social networks in the organization.

Psychologists have found that the need for affiliation and networking is a major motivation for employment. While computing can either enhance or disrupt social networks on the job, consideration of such networks is an important function of organization development planning for IS implementation.

In a study of the introduction of robots into a work environment, Argote, Goodman, and Schkade (1983) found that one of the reasons for working was to maintain social networks.

In another study, Kiesler (1987) found that the unofficial, social aspects of computer networking were among its most significant aspects.

Employees often prefer oral and personal information sources to computer-based media (e.g., social workers, Forrest and Williams, 1987: 3-10). However, an emphasis on the role of computer networking in supporting interpersonal communication may help lessen this cause of resistance.

computer networks of task-oriented teams can become the hub of organizational activity in the twenty-first century. However, one needn't embrace this revolutionary vision to acknowledge the importance of teams to fostering a more effective information culture.

The rise of "groupware" is a more modest version of this, operating through a variety of software tools for group decision support, computer-supported meetings, teleconferencing, screen sharing, electronic presentation, team calendars, project management, group writing, and other task-oriented functions (Ellis, Gibbs, and Rein, 1991; Leibs, 1991). Even without groupware, team approaches are important to IS implementation simply from a participative and cognitive viewpoint, as discussed in previous sections. However, networking software of many types may enhance team strategies in the coming decades.

Conclusion: Success Factors for Information Technology Change

When information technology projects are part of organizational

Figure 9: Roles for Structured Open Teams

Constantine (1990) advocates "structured open teams" in implementing technological change.

A 'Technical Leader/Project Manager' role still exists in such teams but decision-making is by consensus, treating all team members as equals.

A 'Scribe' role records the decision-making process of the group.

The 'Information Manager' role provides group memory.

The 'Facilitator' role helps keep meetings productive, avoiding side-tracking, encouraging participation, summarizing).

The 'Critic' role is commissioned to play devil's advocate.

Constantine's structured open team approach may slow implementation, but by using the resources of all group members, Constantine believes this approach will lead to better solutions as well as more "solution ownership", leading to better and faster development in the long run.

change strategies, success is not a foregone conclusion. To take just one example, in 1992 the U. S. General Accounting Office faulted the National Institutes of Health for awarding a $800 million contract without conducting a needs assessment of its scientific users and not integrating the acquisition into its strategic planning efforts (GAO, 1992g). Similar problems outlined by City of Santa Ana officials (see Figure 6-11) are common in many types of IS projects and dealing with them absorbs a significant amount of the time of IS managers. As one pair of scholars note, reasons for IS failures "include everything from poor data and inappropriate technology to entrenched policy-maker values, bad timing, reluctant users, faulty organizational design and structure, and even the weakness of frameworks for IS research" (Martin and Overman, 1988: 69; see also Banks and Rossini, 1987).

Factors which facilitate successful systems implementation are those common in organizational change generally, with a few special concerns added. Success factors fall in five broad categories — product, support, management, mobilization, and environmental factors. For convenience, success factors are presented in outline form below.

Figure 10: Mini-Case: Information Culture and Organizational Memory

The 'Group Memory' role advocated by Constantine (see text box) has more importance than is often realized because IS implementation frequently involves the attempt to recreate in one place a system which already exists in another place.

Rettig (1990: 26) cites the example of a regional telephone company attempting to do precisely that, relying only on word of mouth planning without formal group memory of the system which was to be replicated.

The project manager for the new facility to be created focused solely on technical aspects, ignoring organizational development aspects of the original implementation. IS managers at the new site were not even consulted. A formal group memory role would have prevented "soft" aspects of the original project implementation from being forgotten.

Formal group memory can prevent technical mistakes too. In the same example a particular software module, one that billed customers for installation charges, was inadvertently omitted. A technician installing the new system noticed something was missing but simply patched over the "hole" in the code. Customers, happy about not being charged, did not lodge complaints. For several months the phone company failed to bill for installations, an oversight that would have been prevented by a written plan emerging from formal group memory in the original project.

I. Product Factors

A. *Functionality*

1. The computer system must work and be seen as a valued tool enabling managers to carry out their functions, deliver services, and respond quickly to new demands (Fletcher et al., 1992).

B. *Appropriate technology*

1. The needed computer power and other technology must be available, appropriate to the task and accessible within the budget.
2. One must have high quality data and trained staff for the application in question (ideally and in-house development staff may be best— see Raymond, 1985).
3. Inadequate investment in input-output hardware has been a common bottleneck and cause of IS failures.
4. Some degree of standardization characterizes success projects (Swider, 1988). Two-thirds of the 50 "runaway systems"

Figure 11: Mini-Case: The Santa Ana Survey on Failure Factors

In surveying other cities prior to developing its own information system, IS planners in the city of Santa Ana, Texas, compiled the following description of a "classic wrong approach" to organizational change, based on a composite of experiences in other cities they investigated:

1. After a long selection process, the city hires a consultant to conduct a needs analysis of city departments.
2. The city then hires another consultant to conduct a nationwide analysis to choose the best software system. Selecting the consultant takes the city council three months, and another four months is taken to buy the chosen software from a supplier, time required to meet city council timing requirements.
3. Another long delay occurs while the city council purchases a central processing unit through competitive bidding.
4. After a long, complicated, competitive process, the city purchases some computer workstations which are inferior to less expensive models on the market by the time the city takes possession.
5. The city, which for efficiency reasons is chronically understaffed, after painful intense debate, accedes to hiring some new staff to operate the equipment it has purchased.
6. The city takes several months to come up with job descriptions for the new positions; the candidates eventually hired have no actual experience in the intended application but do meet the description prepared by the personnel department.
7. The city hires yet another consultant, with suspect credentials, to train the new staff.
8. The new staff head, amid outdated software and hardware not of his selection, calls other experienced units in other cities to get advice. He is advised to start all over with a new consultant.
9. A newly elected city council spots the program as an example of ineffectual boondoggling by its predecessor, demanding to see results. As there is nothing to show after three years of effort, the program is canceled on cost-benefit grounds.

Sound implausible? The Santa Ana officials found it was all too realistic a picture of IS implementation at the local level (Eichblatt, 1987: 215-216).

tackled by a leading consulting firm specializing in righting out-of-kilter computer projects had to do with botched attempts of systems integrators unable to make subsystems with different standards work together (Mehler, 1991: 20-21).

5. In the public sector, appropriateness may also be affected by legislative requirements (Newcomer and Caudle, 1991: 383).

C. User-Friendly Design

1. Software should be user-friendly in the eyes of the users (Rivard and Huff, 1988: 558).
2. Ergonomics and the human-machine interface should not be ignored.
3. It helps if end users already have experience with computers or at least have realistic information expectations (Lucas, 1989; Kim, 1990).

II. Support Factors

A. Reputation

1. Obtaining support is helped by having prestigious staff or at least staff with prestigious training. The perceived quality of the IS staff is a major determinant of attitudes toward IS implementation (Thomas, 1990). IS needs staff who transcend technical orientations and who can address managerial as well as technical IS concerns (Swider, 1988).
2. It helps if implementation is based on established, respected theories and models.
3. It helps if the IS project measures itself against the practices of the best in the field (Fletcher, 1992).
4. It also helps to have what is perceived to be a high quality IS product to sell.

B. Marketing

1. Obtaining support is facilitated if one has a conscious "sales" effort, tailoring what is to be implemented to the needs of the decision-makers first and also to the needs of the users. While some demand is spontaneous, IS staff must market to end-users, staff, and top management through visits, forums, newsletters, user support groups, seminars, executive briefings, tours, demonstrations, hotlines, surveys, and other outreaches (Swider, 1988).
2. Specific personnel should be designated who shepherd the development, sales, training, and maintenance efforts with a view to pleasing decision-makers and users.
3. Awareness and articulation of a felt need must be encouraged among both decision-makers and users. Top management must see the information to be provided as relevant, economical, accurate, and motivating users to promote the

organization's objectives.

C. Management Support

1. Obtaining strong top management support before and during implementation is the single most commonly-cited IS success factor (see Parsons, 1983; Bruwer, 1984; Sanders and Cortney, 1985; Dos Santos, 1986; Swider, 1988; Lucas, 1989; Kim, 1990; Thomas, 1990). A survey by Sethi and Lederer (1989) of strategic IS planning in 80 companies found, for instance, that over half of IS planners consider their greatest difficulty is getting top management support for implementation. This support has to do with top management values and priorities, not the actual participation of top managers in IS implementation (Jarvenpaa and Ives, 1991).
2. Projects need a high-level "champion" who appreciates what technology can do and makes the case to the rest of top management (Fletcher et al., 1992). For instance, Matheson (1993) found having an innovative champion was more important than access to resources or participatory implementation in explaining success in social welfare organizations.
3. It helps if the IS unit is highly placed within the organization in the first place.
4. It also helps if IS responsibilities are under a single unit rather than split among many.

D. Political Support

1. Obtain the support of key political actors, not limited to the CEO, who can be advocates for change. Often this means making sure that IS planning flows from organizational mission goals or other expressions of the vision of the organization's leadership.[8]
2. If possible, work with people who are already familiar with and predisposed to functions similar to what is to be implemented.
3. Avoid offending other powerful political actors.
4. Try to maintain a neutral stance in organizational politics. Use "neutral," third-party consultants to help ease politically difficult decisions. Information system design may require providing managers information on a need-to-

know basis (e.g., access only to data on one's own unit).

III. Management Factors

A. *Strong management*

1. Employ a strong project manager who has clear lines of responsibility with commensurate authority. The Sethi and Lederer (1989) study found that next to top management support, the greatest problem of implementation was that success depended greatly on the team leader and obtaining a well-qualified leader is often difficult.
2. The manager must be able to set limits on the information system not only to contain cost but also to prevent information overload and to tailor reports to needs as perceived by upper management.
3. Rivard and Huff (1988: 560) found that IS success was strongly linked to the IS department playing a leadership role rather than simply trying to respond to demand.
4. Goal clarification: Base planning on needs assessment of end users Swider, 1988). Develop clear, limited, achievable goals early in the planning process. Break goals down into objectives, such as a schedule of deliverables. Clarify what the system *won't* do to limit unrealistic expectations. Organizations need a charter, purpose, and mission in which results are more important than "noble purposes" (Currid, 1991b). Conveying a vision is related to the issue of top management support and strong IS management (Riley and Ickes, 1989: 280).[9]
5. Develop and use success measurement indicators to monitor and document your progress and justify your budget.
6. Later make sure there is a clear plan for evaluation.
7. Adequate budgeting of resources and time: Provide a budget for the planning process as well as later stages of implementation. Adequate budgeting is especially crucial at the beginning stages (Swider, 1988). Implementation on a shoestring may be worse than none at all. The budget must be set after the project is clearly delineated, as through a working prototype.
8. Treat different types of clients differently as appropriate

and take account of competitive alternatives.

9. Have a realistic time frame (e.g., at least a year) which does not require forcing end users to absorb too much too quickly (Riley and Ickes, 1989: 282). Releasing IS systems before they are ready can cause clients to reject them, even if later "fixes" are made (cf. a Bank of America fiasco, Frantz, 1988).
10. Flexibility: Allow a flexible process and seek consensus one step at a time. Avoid the all-or-nothing plan approval strategy.

IV. Mobilization Factors

A. Team Planning

1. Assemble a planning team representing management, technical staff, and end-users.
2. Give departments and users a chance to object and take protests seriously. Do invest in organizational development. Tolerance for some dissent is essential. User participation is related to later propensity to use the system beyond compulsory use (Kim, 1990).

B. Participation

1. Emphasize end-user participation, understanding that user involvement and commitment are critical (see Adelman, 1982; Ives and Olson, 1984; Burch, 1986; Fletcher et al., 1992). Rotate membership to assure widespread participation.
2. Make sure there is adequate released time to participate. Avoid top-down mandates.
3. It helps if team members have experience with computers and are knowledgeable about end user computing and other technological options (Thomas, 1990).
4. User influence over IS development can increase role conflict and job stress, however, if it is not combined with user control over job processes themselves (Kang, 1990). If users are too constrained by limited decision-making discretion and standard operating procedures, they may be unable to take advantage of IS initiatives (Sanders and Courtney, 1985).

C. Stake-holding

1. System incentives: Make sure critical users have the proper incentives as well as duties in the IS system. Ask if the staff who enter data have the incentive to take proper care in collecting and verifying them, or if their incentive is to minimize hassles by not worrying about such considerations. Perceived benefits are a major determinant of attitudes toward IS implementation (Lucas, 1989; Thomas, 1990).
2. Ideally, each person affected will have a personal stake in implementation, and one such stake is personal achievement associated with having a specific assignment in the implementation (Currid, 1991b). It is desirable that at least some benefits be immediate (Riley and Ickes, 1989: 281).
3. Fairness and equity: Consider departmental and interpersonal fairness and cost issues. Do productivity benefits of the overall IS system accrue fairly to the departments suffering the burden of work and change?

D. *Communication*

1. Lack of communication with end users has been found to be the second most important cause of system failure, exceeded only by failure to have a plan with appropriate scope (Keider, 1984).
2. Keep all affected departments informed. Give regularly scheduled formal reports. Have open meetings and minutes.
3. After implementation, user support groups are often helpful as are in-house experts for continuing support (Riley and Ickes, 1989: 283).
4. Organizational culture, which cannot be changed overnight, affects IS acceptance and is associated with how staff approach problems, how knowledgeable they are about IS options and their costs and benefits, and the quality of interaction between users and IS implementers (Lucas, 1989).

E. *Training*

1. Commit to a substantial investment in training employees. Identify employees to be impacted by the IS early and target special efforts toward them. Investment in training and support personnel has been found to be an important

cause of failure in IS implementation (Keider, 1984; Richter, 1993a). Reliance on end-user mutual support alone is a recipe for failure (Swider, 1988).

2. Avoid IS jargon and a "semantic gap" between implementers and the organizational rank and file (see DeBrabander and Thiers, 1984).

V. Environmental Factors

A. Complex Environment

1. There is more likely to be follow-through and success in IS implementation, for instance, if there are competitive pressures to adopt technology.
2. Public information systems have greater interdependence with other actors in their environment and require closer attention to legislative, media, interest group, and other political considerations (Bozeman and Bretschneider, 1986).

B. Dynamic Environment

1. Success is more likely if the organization and its resources are growing.
2. It helps if the environment is changing in terms of suppliers, clients, and or governmental regulations. Uncertainty creates receptivity to change (Matheson, 1993). Conversely, if the organization is successful in a stable uncompetitive environment, the "if it ain't broke, don't fix it" mentality tends to undermine change efforts including IS implementation.

All of these success factors for organizational change in IS projects simply indicate what has long been known—that IS is not just a technical area which can be managed adequately in terms of technical IS criteria. In this regard it is interesting to note that Drury (1984) studied data processing steering committees and found that they were most effective when their agenda items originated outside the IS department. Systems plans cannot be based solely or even mainly on technical factors. Instead this is an area where human factors are critical and organization development approaches are important in accomplishing change effectively in an environment where, unfortunately, objectives of managers and other key actors are often diverse and conflicting (Montague, 1986).

On the other hand, researchers have identified a very large number of success factor variables but there is no adequate underlying theory to relate them. As Martin and Overman note (1988: 56), "research on successful system development does not show any single set of factors to determine success or failure of computer systems" (on the limits to success factor studies, see Lyytinen, 1987: 25).[10] Although some efforts exist to develop contingency theories of success factors, their conclusions are at a quite general level. For instance, Thompson (1992) used state-level social services computing to show that equipment availability, software availability, software appropriateness, training, and ongoing support must all be present for success. Absence of one or more of the prerequisites was more apt to lead to failure rather than partial success.

Even when some success factors are identified as prerequisites and corequisites, the relative importance of different success factors may vary by situation. In any given situation, some factors may not be necessary at all and others of only marginal importance. For instance, Lee (1990) has found that success factors vary by the stage of development of information systems within business organizations. The situational perspective common in organization development (OD) seems almost inevitably to be the applicable viewpoint for systems development as well, a viewpoint which moves it not a small distance from the engineering to the political and social sciences.

Computing can have profound implications for organizational change. In terms of communications patterns, technology is reinforcing more decentralized, team-oriented approaches to decision-making and problem-solving. At the same time, a growing recognition of the intertwining of technical, social, and political factors has meant that the traditional, top-down systems development planning methods have increasingly given way to sociotechnical approaches. The constellation of success factors for organizational change in information technology projects are the building blocks for a supportive information culture. What starts with the "hard" science of microchips and computer science algorithms ends with political concerns for participation and stakeholding, historical concerns for organizational memory, psychological concerns for cognitive change, sociological concerns about team relationships, and even anthropological concerns for organizational culture.

ENDNOTES

[1] Of course, there are potential economic costs as well as efficiencies associated with electronic mail. E-mail users have become accustomed to free availability, even for personal messages, and attempts to impose cost-recovery are usually considered to create more problems than they solve (Booker, 1989). Costs can skyrocket when electronic storage magnifies the effects of natural disasters such as massive data loss due to power surges, hard disk failures, magnetic interference, and so on. The "paperless office" is still many years away and electronic mail documents are frequently printed anyway. Studies suggest that computing is associated with more, not less paper and all the costs associated with it.

[2] Of course, most e-mail systems make it easy to dump messages to one's printer, but this in turn is slow and is not normal practice for e-mail users.

[3] Some e-mail packages are better than others in this regard. For instance, *eMAIL for Windows* (DaVinci Systems) includes a "Browser" feature whereby as you scroll through the usual single-line listing of messages a window displays the first several lines of each, allowing quicker filtering.

[4] Telephone hot-lines for whistle blowers were perceived to lack anonymity and did not succeed according to Higgins (1992).

[5] This is one of the earliest and most documented findings about management information systems. For a review of the literature, see Federico (1985: 15-20).

[6] Human frailties cause more IS failures than do technical problems (Megginson, 1963; Holmes, 1970). Much is known about the nature of human error, the conditions which encourage error, and software designs which are error-resistant (Norman, 1983; Perrow, 1984; Petroski, 1985; Norman, D. A., 1990).

[7] Acceptance of IS is much more likely when computing is presented as complementary to human skills, enhancing rather than replacing them (Rosenbrock, 1977, 1981; Petheram, 1989).

[8] Ewusi-Mensah and Przasnyski (1991) surveyed cases of IS project abandonment and found the single most important set of factors to be political, behavioral, and organizational issues of implementation. Similar findings were reached by Weill and Olson (1989) in their study of the impact of IS investment on firm performance, emphasizing the importance of political factors such as unit power, support for change, and organizational culture. A corollary is that while political support is needed for information systems implementation, implementing information systems is *not* a good tool for political change. For instance, in the 1970s, HEW tried to create Information and Referral Systems to encourage local social service integration but local agencies never bought the concept (Kling, 1978a). Likewise, USAC sought to promote urban integrated databases for similar reasons but cities opted for more practical IS applications like revenue collection (Kraemer and King, 1979).

[9] Ability to frame goals and objectives in terms of an organization's goals in relation to its environment is superior to a focus on objectives having to do with technical proficiency (Halbrecht, 1989). Good planning contributes to future satisfaction with IS systems (Schleich, Corney, and Bow, 1990). Lack of a plan or inadequate definition of project scope have been found to be the most important causes of implementation failure (Keider, 1984).

[10] For an early influential inventory of 22 success factors, see Ein-Dor and Segev, 1978; on success factors as a way of structuring planning, see Boynton and Zmud, 1984; for a review of 16 studies of success factors, see Caudle, 1988; for a review of 26 factors, see Magal, Carr, and Watson, 1988.

CHAPTER VII

Information Technology and Global Competition

Information technology investment is an idea whose time has come. In *The Lever of Riches* (1990), Joel Mokyr made the argument that technology increases output beyond the cost and effort it requires. Technological innovation was said to be the key to understanding why some nations are richer than others. And it was viewed as the prime factor in assuring that rich nations will become richer. Bruce McConnell, chief of OMB's Information Policy Branch under the Bush administration, held that the nation's prosperity depends upon development of federal information technology policy (Power, 1992i). During the 1992 presidential campaign, then Governor Clinton's technology policy statement was titled, "Technology: The Engine of Economic Growth". It too reflected the view that technology investment was the key to American economic prosperity into the twenty-first century.

At the corporate level, many writers similarly have argued that companies can overcome limited growth and find strategic advantage over competitors through information technology (IT) (e.g., Rockart and Crescenzi, 1984; Applegate, Cash, and Mills, 1988). Similar views are found in *2020 Vision* (1991) by Stan Davis and Bill Davidson. Davis and Davidson argue that companies that fail to get on the information technology bandwagon will find themselves unable to compete successfully in the 1990s. Although some have tried to raise warning flags[1], advocates of IT investment believe American firms are shortsighted when they apply rigid cost-benefit standards to information systems projects, seeking to cut costs in the short term while losing out in the emerging "information economy" in the long term.

While these advocates of information technology investment are not addressing information systems technology alone, their views are compatible with those of many that computing is the essential ingredient in reviving productivity in the United States, Great Britain, and elsewhere. IBM, AT&T, DEC, and other computer manufacturers had this argument in mind when they purchased tens of thousands of copies of *2020 Vision* for distribution to their customers in an effort to promote sales (Caldwell, 1991b: 30). In talks to government officials, industry leaders like John Sculley actively promote the view that information technology can increase productivity, helping counteract shrinking public budgets (Fredell, 1988b: 82). However, such rosy views of computing and productivity have been sharply attacked for grossly exaggerating what computing can and cannot do (cf. Robins and Webster, 1989).

Productivity does not flow from IS investment like water from a spring. For instance, 35% of major computer systems projects become "runaways" — millions of dollars over budget and months or years behind schedule. Some surveys indicate nearly all Fortune 200 companies have a "runaway" in the works (Gullo, 1989b: 63). It is estimated that some 25% of larger IS projects (over 60,000 lines of code) are canceled before completion, let alone actually ever contribute to improving organizational productivity. The U. S. Army studied nine major federal IS projects and found 47% of the information systems delivered were never used at all. By the end of the 1980s, two-thirds of chief executive officers of *Fortune 1000* expressed the belief that they weren't getting their full money's worth from IS investments (Gantz, 1989b: 35). The slow pace of IS impacts in relation to the rapid expansion of raised expectations in the 1980s led to articles like "What Happened to the Computer Revolution?", published in the *Harvard Business Review* (Salerno, 1985).

Given concerns of this type, can information systems really provide "competitive advantage" on a national scale and create a "productivity revolution"? In this chapter, I first examine the most sweeping of the productivity claims for information technology—that it will be the key to American global competition in the twenty-first century.[2] This argument focuses on the case for establishing a national industrial policy in support of information technology. In a subsequent section, I look at the related subject of American telecommunications policy. Having examined the emergence of national policy, I then go back to examine the productivity premises of these policies. First the case against IS as an engine of productivity is presented, then the case for. A concluding section tries to make sense of the issues surrounding information technology investment and national productivity.

Information Technology and Global Competition

While analysts debate whether information technology is really the "lever of riches", it is clear that absence of information technology makes global competition nearly impossible. This was illustrated by the Russian economy after the dissolution of the Soviet Union. When Russia attempted to convert to a market economy following the fall of communism in the early 1990s, privatization created an overwhelming volume of stock. However, Russia lacked automated systems for handling stock exchanges and other economic transactions taken for granted in the West. Although Russia had large numbers of mainframe and desktop computers, through neglect, inefficiency, and a restrictive security-centered national policy, telecommunications links were woefully inadequate. Data communications were largely reserved for the military and communication outside a local area was in most cases essentially impossible. All of this constituted a staggering obstacle to reviving the Russian economy (Parady, 1991). Though a dramatic case, most modern industrial countries are being forced in one way or another to face up to the question of the role of government under global information economies.

Global Aspects of Information Technology

Corporations, linked by computer-based telecommunications, have become global, raising complex questions about national interests. A General Accounting Office report on "High Technology Competitiveness" found a mixed picture (GAO, 1992e: 5-6). The United States has maintained its lead in supercomputing for the last decade, though Japanese supercomputing firms improved their competitiveness. On the other hand, the last large-scale American robotics firm was bought out by foreign interests in 1990. The U.S. share of the semiconductor materials and equipment market has fallen steadily for the last decade. In telecommunications equipment there has also been market erosion, but mainly in the less technologically sophisticated areas. The GAO refrained from making recommendations, noting the difficulty of defining "U.S. interests" in a world marked by multinational firms like Siecor (a U.S./German fiber optics firm) and GMF (a U.S./Japanese robotics company).

Global competition creates pressure to ship information systems work oversees to cheaper subcontractors, as has happened in many fields of American manufacturing. Countries such as Ireland, the Philippines, Egypt, Israel, Colombia, Russia, and New Zealand regularly solicit Fortune 500 firms for such contracts. Global networking technology greatly facilitates the transfer of all types of data entry, programming, and information processing work to other na-

Figure 1: Caterpillar, IS, and Global Competition

Information systems are playing a major role in the efforts of Caterpillar Inc., known for its line of bulldozing equipment, to compete in a global economy.

Caterpillar's "Plant with a Future" project seeks to establish an on-going process of plant-floor automation, including state-of-the-art robotics. Customer orders are fed by satellite directly into an automated production planning process which has resulted in cutting in-process inventory by 60%, saving billions.

Caterpillar has also established a worldwide computer and communications system linking 70,000 terminals to support such value-added services for customers as a global parts network, "business television" and repair videos, and data access.

Some 90% of the company's workers can access corporate data on a network.

By 1993, red ink had turned to profits and Caterpillar was more than holding its own against foreign competitors. Over half of its products are sold abroad. Its leading competitor, Komatsu of Japan, was forced to shift its construction strategy away from bulldozers. Caterpillar attributes recent success to its IS efforts.

tions where employees are paid less (usually half or less compared to American pay rates of $45 or more for experienced applications programmers) (McPartlin, 1992b: 54).

American firms have developed subsidiaries specifically for work export, as in the case of Citicorp's Overseas Software Limited, competing with Japanese brokers such as Mitsubishi International's Global Software Services Division. One major computer systems manufacturer ships work started at its American location to Europe at the end of the American work day, then to Hong Kong at the end of the European work day, then back to America—thus allowing three workdays in a single 24-hour period (Oliva, 1990: 105). When a large portion of all work is information-related, global computer networks provide the means for companies to gain such efficiencies through the export of American jobs overseas. In spite of problems such as less effective intellectual property laws to protect against information theft, the trend toward export of American information-related jobs is growing in the 1990s.

Some other countries have taken a protectionist stance on data processing export. Canada's 1980 Banking Act prohibits processing data transactions outside the country unless government approval is obtained. Sweden prohibits offshore processing and storage of data. West Germany requires that data records on German nationals must be kept in Germany (Carper, 1992). At present, the United States takes a firm free trade stand on matters of transborder data flows.

At the same time, American workers may be failing to keep up with computer-era skills of workers in nations with which the United States competes. A major journalistic study of American investment in computer-based education for high-tech careers found that "America has slipped another notch lower on the ranks of global economies because of, among other things, its education base" (Borrell, 1992: 26). This study found complacency among Department of Education officials, who took comfort in statistics showing 50% of all children in grades one through eight use computers.

In contrast, the report noted, "What we found is a false dependence on statistical analysis and a reality so discouraging that it made us question how this situation has remained unremarked on for so long. Antiquated computers; unused computers; computers used for games and not for teaching; schools and teachers unprepared to use computers that they own; mismanaged or misdirected policies; and unknown hundreds of millions of dollars spent over the last decade for little return" (p. 25). The authors concluded that America lacks direction when it comes to building the educational infrastructure for global competition in contrast to Japan (Cassagne and Iioshi, 1992).

In the absence of any national policy to the contrary, the profit motive, viewed from the typically American short-term perspective, has driven American software manufacturers to price their export products at costs substantially higher than American businesses incur. This systematic policy of overcharging was documented in a five-month investigative report undertaken by *InformationWeek* magazine. The report found that "According to IS chiefs, consultants, market analysts, and even some vendor executives, the overcharges inhibit purchases, restrict corporate expansion efforts, and delay software standards efforts" (Greenbaum and Tate, 1992: 50). The present preeminence of U.S. software makes this pricing policy possible, but European regulation and Japanese competition are in the offing (Greenbaum and Tate, 1992: 60; Goldberg, 1992: 200). At this writing Microsoft Corporation, the dominant American software publisher, was moving toward a consistent global pricing structure for its products but it was too early to tell if this signaled a reversal in American corporate policy toward software export (Soat and Kelly, 1993). Nonetheless, top 100 American software firms increased worldwide sales by over 20% between 1991 and 1992, with foreign sales now approaching 50% of their market (Hodges and Melewski, 1993).

Use of information technology is now a central part of strategic planning by corporations seeking to engage in global competition (Selig, 1984; Miller. 1988). However, it does not necessarily follow that government should inaugurate a "Marshall Plan" to subsidize and encourage information technology firms on a massive basis. When the French computer firm Groupe Bull[3] lost $1 billion in revenues, the French government stepped in to bail it out. The French also impose taxes and duties on computer equipment and software and on information transfers (Carper, 1992: 443). However, some analysts (e.g., Schrage, 1991) argue that such actions merely promote inefficiency, whereas, what is needed is unsubsidized competition with each nation specializing in what it does best. The failure of protectionist legislation in Brazil is also cited in support of arguments against national IT industrial policy.[4]

European firms are seen by commentators like Schrage as being dependent on their national governments, promoting low productivity and in the long run undermining the ability of their nations to compete globally. While such arguments for a hands-off, laissez-faire approach are common, particularly in the United States, the worldwide trend is toward greater assertion of national industrial policies promoting information technology. This has led analysts to argue that the United States should "get on board" soon if it is not to fall behind.

The Call for a National Information Technology Policy

The argument is made that real strategic planning for information technology must be global in nature. In this "battle for the world of tomorrow" (see Warshofsky, 1989), governments are presumed to be actively seeking to position their nations in the information technology arena (Palvia, Palvia, and Zigli, 1992). The Japanese subsidize the "Fifth Generation" artificial intelligence project (Hsu and Kusnan, 1989) and their Human Frontier bio-computing project (Wood, 1988: 12) through their Ministry of International Trade and Industry (MITI). Taiwan and Korea seek to supplant Japan. Britain, an early but not always successful example of governmental computing policies (Hendry, 1989), now considers whether government subsidization of the computer industry might be the key out of its economic doldrums —or would lead to disemployment (see Laver, 1989: ch. 5; Rowlands and Vogel, 1991).

The European Economic Community (EEC) has developed models for information policy which some believe should be adopted in the United States as well. For instance, the Council of European Communities has established a plan for constructing a common information services market (decision of 7/26/88; see *Communications of the ACM*, 1990). The Commission of the European Communities has provided $1.5 billion to fund ESPRIT (European Strategic Programme of Research and Development in Information Technology). The ESPRIT initiative draws together industrial and academic institutions from all EEC countries to enhance abilities to design and produce IS systems that can compete in world markets (Roth, 1991).

Likewise, Japanese "keiretsu" are industrial combines which coordinate strategy to dominate supply, block foreign competition, and penetrate world markets, fostering Japanese information technology ascendancy. Noting this model, Ferguson (1990) has urged European and American firms to form opposing industrial groupings. However, the reality is that the Europeans are proceeding with information policies such as establishment of information technology quality standards which may well be an obstacle to U.S. competitiveness, yet industry seems to be ideologically opposed to government involvement even if it is needed to protect their interests abroad (Frenkel, 1990a: 51). Many analysts argue that the problem with U.S. competitiveness with Japan over information technology is primarily a problem of overcoming philosophical mind-sets in America (e.g., Greene, 1989; Hart, 1992).

Figure 2: Mini-Case: U. S. Memories, Inc.

In the late 1980s, a shortage of memory chips and dependence on Japanese suppliers led American computer firms to support U. S. Memories, Inc., a $500-million consortium with government and industry backing.

America's share of the chip market had fallen from 63% in 1980 to just 36% by 1988. U. S. Memories was intended to restore American competitiveness in the microchip industry and to provide low-cost chips keeping prices competitive for American computer manufacturers.

However, industrial sponsors withdrew their support from the project in fear that Japanese chip suppliers would cut off supply lines in retaliation. Others, such as T. J. Rogers of Cypress Semiconductor Corp., opposed the project on free enterprise grounds and fear of creating a government-backed competitor (Lyons, 1990).

In the early 1990s, American semi-conductor firms embraced their former "enemies" and undertook large-scale joint ventures with Japanese firms who will do most semiconductor manufacturing in this decade (Powell and Schwartz, 1992: 60).

In contrast, the Koreans launched a major chip effort in 1986 with government backing, invested billions, and soon posed a threat to Japanese manufacturers as well as American.

Perhaps an even more telling contrast, however, was the history of the American semiconductor industry itself, whose emergence in the 1940s and 1950s was heavily subsidized by Department of Defense pricing policies which had little to do with free markets (Noll and Cohen, 1988: 136).

While the American Memories initiative had pros and cons, its demise seemed to be further indication of American reluctance to pursue vigorously a national information policy.

The history of American information technology policy is a long but until now narrowly focused one. Science policy was a major issue in the aftermath of World War II, with the prevailing view articulated by Vannevar Bush in *Science: The Endless Frontier* (1945), which discussed provision of computing resources to scientists. After the Soviet launching of the Sputnik satellite, governments in many industrialized countries took new initiatives to promote science and technology (McDougall, 1985: 6-7; see also Rurak, 1976). The report of the National Academy of Sciences and the National Research Council, *The Race for the New Frontier: International Competition in Advanced Technology - Decisions for America* (NAS/NRC, 1984), was representative of these new perspectives.

Congressional task forces on science policy in the 1980s and 1990s have placed increasing emphasis on computing as a tool of global competition (Null, 1988). Most recently this has taken the form of supercomputer centers connected by networks such as NREN (National Research and Education Network, a $3 billion high-speed network subsidized by the federal government). NREN is part of the federal high-performance computing program, which has set forth some 20 "grand challenges", funding of which would enable computer-based breakthroughs in science and global competitiveness (Office of Science and Technology Policy, 1989). Another example is the creation of a new technology development center under the National Institute of Standards and Technology (NIST) (Power, 1992g: 83).

The United States, with its strong ideology of free enterprise, has dragged its feet on the question of whether computer development should be a matter of national policy, but with the erosion of American markets the issue becomes heard more loudly with each passing year. Japan, in contrast, has long had a national information policy, in part centered on "fifth-generation" languages which can use artificial intelligence.[5] American information policies have developed eclectically and many, such as those reflected in the Freedom of Information Act (FOIA), actually operate to American competitive disadvantage, allowing foreign access to American information without reciprocity (Aines, 1988b: 99). Likewise, American trade laws arguably failed to protect the semiconductor industry from unfair competition and subsequent sharp decline followed in the 1980s (Howell, 1986; Hart, 1992).

In 1985 Edward Feigenbaum and Pamela Corduck's *The Fifth Generation: Artificial Intelligence and Japan's Computer Challenge to the World* issued a call of alarm, stating "We are writing this book because we are worried...American needs a national plan of action, a kind of space shuttle program for the knowledge systems of the future" (p. xvii). This was followed in 1987 by *The Technology War*, in which David Brandin (president of Strategic Technologies Inc.) and U.C.-Berkeley professor Michael Harrison called for a wartime-like mobilization of American resources through formation of a new cabinet-level department aimed at global information technology competition. A Brookings Institution study likewise called for sharp cuts in military research and development funding in favor of financing cutting-edge information technology geared to global competitiveness (Flamm, 1987).

Similar views are found in the information industry press. For instance, a *PC Week* editorial stated, "the fact is that fewer and fewer American companies can afford the generous research and development outlays needed to drive the industry[6] and still retain U. S. ownership...the U.S. government should move quickly to divert at least part of its Star Wars research investments to commercial ends, with an eye to seizing the leadership of 21st century commercial computing" (Whitmore, 1990: 85). Citing the rise of Japanese computing, the 1989 sale of Zenith's computer division to a French firm, and other developments, the editorial led to the conclusion, "Failure to lead damns us to follow, and in this industry, once we follow we may never lead again." Numerous other scholars have made the case for the critical importance of strategic information systems in global competition (e.g., Palvia, Palvia, and Zigli, 1990: 52).

In late 1989 the chief executive officers from eleven leading American computer firms joined together to form the Computer Systems Policy Project (CSPP). The CSPP functions as a corporate interest group seeking to influence American technology policy and legislation. Kenneth Kay, the director of CSPP, stated "Our basic position is that we do not think federal investments in research are being made with as much commercially relevant advice as there ought to be" (cited in Crawford, 1991: 15).

In a July 1990 report the CSPP warned that America was in danger of seeing its position eroded in all of the sixteen critical computer technology areas studied. A spring 1991 report called on the federal government to increase industry involvement in federal R&D decision-making. The CSPP criticized the government for allocating only 2% of its R&D investment to computing whereas the computer industry conducts 21% of total U.S. private sector R&D. Specifically it called on government to better plan its $76 billion R&D expenditure program by emphasizing generically useful research instead of technologies with little commercial potential, such as most defense research and development.

With IBM laying off or forcing some 70,000 employees into early retirement in 1992-1993, some analysts have concluded that "this confirms the industry is in its greatest contraction since its birth" (Scannel,1992: 3). Reaction from the incoming Clinton administration was one of dismay, particularly at associated IBM cutbacks in research and development. With Democratic Party interest in industrial policy, most commentators expected new initiatives toward establishment of a national information technology policy to be forthcoming in the 1990s (Power, 1993a).

On the other hand, there were also forces gravitating against a strong Clinton administration policy of government investment in the information technology industry. The Japanese electronics industry, which had seemed so threatening in the 1980s, found itself in a crisis of its own in the early 1990s—a crisis which the government Ministry of International Trade and Industry (MITI) seemed unable to prevent. Their decade-long Fifth Generation Computer Systems project ended in June, 1992, in relative failure to impact global competition (Shapiro and Warren, 1993). MITI's concentration on hardware manufacture at a time when software dominance was building unprecedented economic empires for Microsoft's William Gates and others, seemed in the 1990s controversial at best and quite possibly a mistake.[7]

Likewise, European governmental policy has proved unable to stem the decline of the European semiconductor industry. In contrast, private sector initiatives without government funding racked up impressive advances. High-definition television, for instance, had seemed to be locked up by the Japanese at the end of the 1980s but General Instrument, an American firm, was able to announce the first digital HDTV system in 1991, rendering Japan's old-technology analog model obsolete. These factors, combined with conditions of budgetary austerity, acted to moderate policies of the Clinton administration in the IT area (Levinson, 1993).

National Electronic Communications Policy

In spite of its rapid growth, there has been little regulation of electronic networking. Regulatory precedents lie in broadcasting but broadcast networking itself is characterized by a relative lack of regulation. This is an arena dominated by the view that non-regulation or deregulation encourages international trade and development (Dutton, Blumler, and Kraemer, 1988a:18-20). Advocates of deregulation of television and other network services have been particularly strong in the United States, which is seen by other nations as an international vendor and exporter of information services. Privatization and deregulation is the tendency in Britain, Germany, and Japan as well as the United States as each moves toward greater use of the marketplace for network services (Dutton, Blumler, and Kraemer, 1988b: 469-471). Nonetheless, it is not at all clear yet whether electronic mail, networking of computer-based databanks, and other computer-based electronic communications services will follow the same pattern.

To some extent a national telecommunications policy already exists, if deregulation and reliance on market forces is interpreted as public policy. This philosophy is prevalent in the FCC which has not only continued to deregulate telecommunications but even seeks to obviate state-level and judicial regulation through use of the court system, holding quasi-judicial hearings on tariffs, seeking to take control of the Modified Final Judgment (the 1984 AT&T breakup: see Figure 7-3) from the U.S. District Court and place power in the FCC, and through other regulations (Pearce, 1990).

Privacy legislation constitutes the main area of national electronic communications policy thus far. The 1986 Electronic Communications Privacy Act (ECPA) made it illegal for people other than the sender or receiver to read e-mail sent over public networks (e.g., MCI). However, internal corporate electronic mail systems are explicitly exempted from the ECPA. That this may be a problem is suggested by a 1992 survey of *InformationWeek* readers which found that fewer than half reported that their employers had an official, stated ethics policy on electronic mail privacy, data ownership, and file access (*InformationWeek*, 1992b: 40). The 1992 Code of Ethics passed by the Association for Computing Machinery (ACM) may accelerate this process (see Appendix I).

Figure 3: Mini-Case: Telecommunications Policy in the Telephone Industry

Regulation of the telephone industry has not provided strong precedents for national electronic communications policy. The Federal Communications Commission (FCC) does not even require carriers other than AT&T to file tariffs and public schedules of rates (Anthes, 1992). Current FCC policy has reduced regulation of AT&T (e.g., removed price-cap regulation of commercial services) in favor of reliance on the market, not regulation, as much as possible (Anthes, 1991; Taff, 1991).

In contrast, state utility commissions are active in telephone rate regulation. Most support a policy in which higher business rates subsidize lower residential rates, something opposed by business lobbyists (Blegen, 1991). All 50 states have incentive regulations aimed at encouraging phone companies to deploy fiber optic networks. Some argue that state utility commissions should broaden their regulatory purview, as through incentive regulations to encourage support for telecommuting (Schrage, 1992).

Non-regulation encourages investment. The Consumer Federation of America has charged that seven regional Bell holding companies overcharged telephone customers by some $30 billion since 1984, reinvesting these funds in lightly-regulated businesses such as information services rather than reducing phone rates (Ramirez, 1991). While non-regulation may well have increased information service access in this way, consumer groups, nonetheless, favor rate regulation to prevent overcharging.

In the 1984 breakup of AT&T and later court review of regional Bell operating companies (RBOCs), Judge Harold Greene sought to prevent phone company profits from subsidizing entry into and creating possible monopoly over other electronic markets (Snyder and Zienert, 1990: 121-123). Telephone industry interests oppose this policy (Andrews, 1991).

On October 30, 1991, the U. S. Supreme Court ruled unanimously to allow RBOCs to vend information services. It is expected that RBOCs will start marketing on-line information services starting in 1993. The American Newspaper Publishers Association, Mead Data Central, MCI Communications, and others opposed to RBOC deregulation fear that their own on-line services will be disadvantaged by unfair competition since they must rely on phone lines owned by their new competitors for provision of their services (Webb, 1992).

Access considerations also bring attention to the need for government regulation over electronic communications. For instance, current plans call for NSFNet to be funded by user fees starting in 1996, but some groups such as the Electronic Frontier Foundation are lobbying for government subsidies of certain classes of users in order to maintain general access (Quindlen, 1992b). A second access issue concerns whether certain types of uses, like for-profit activities, should be barred from NREN as they are at present from InterNet. The Computer Systems Policy Project, an industry group funded by Apple, Cray, and other computer firms, has also lobbied for inclusion of schools, hospitals, and businesses in NREN, not just research institutions.[8] A third access issue concerns national policies and local interpretations of them, as when NSF had to negotiate with supercomputer university regarding the permissibility of access to strategic technology by foreign students (Weingarten and Garcia, 1988).[9]

In addition to privacy and access issues, calls for regulation and government intervention also arise for reasons of industrial policy. Today, computerized flow of information is clearly recognized as a potent force with profound economic and political implications. Both in Europe and in Third World nations governments have taken action to govern the international exchange of information (Buss, 1984; Tjoumas, 1987). These laws are now being strengthened to the point where they can hold up or even halt a company's overseas operations. Although created initially to protect individual privacy, some countries now seem to be using legislation to fortify their own positions in the burgeoning information processing market. In the United States, NREN and the High Performance Computer Act (HPCA) are seen explicitly as a way to "allow us to leapfrog the Germans and the Japanese", in the words of Senator Al Gore (D-TN) (Schwartz, 1992: 56). Gore and others see the HPCA as a key investment in twenty-first century economic infrastructure, allowing the United States to compete effectively in global markets.

Likewise the Council of the European Communities has advanced identical global competition reasons for building METRAN (the Managed European Transmission Network for high-speed transmissions and GEN, the Global European Network, and other efforts to promote an internal market for information services (Patel, 1992; Frenkel, 1990). Similar arguments for private sector investment in telecommunications infrastructure as a strategy for competitive advantage are found in works such as Peter Keen's *Using Telecommunications for Competitive Advantage* (1986, rev. ed. 1988).

At the same time, electronic funds transfer systems, stock exchanges, and other financial institutions are becoming computerized on a global basis, with vast implications for the nature of the capitalist economic system (Estabrooks, 1988). An American response has been the creation in 1989 of the Bureau of International Communications and Information Policy, with the mandate to be the policy link between the federal government and private industry on communications and information issues affecting foreign relations and national security. There is increasing recognition that the American mish-mash of deregulation, state regulation, and federal policies in a few areas like privacy and access does not make for good foreign economic policy. For instance, the diversity of state regulations and their occasional conflict with federal and court regulations has led some industry leaders like Ameritech's CEO William Weiss to advocate a national telecommunications policy to supplant state regulation (*Telephony*, 1991).

However, industrial policy for electronic communications can pit the government against American business.[10] For instance, U. S. policy holds telecommunications to be subject to strong trade regulations designed to limit export of American "strategic technology" to would-be foreign competitors. The United States is joined in this policy by the 17-nation Coordinating Committee for Multilateral Export Controls (COCOM). Business, represented through the Telecommunications Industry Association (TIA), often supports development of common standards needed for global commerce.[11] However, the TIA is relatively unconcerned with strategic national interests and instead wants to obtain sales now by relaxing trade policy to allow large-scale shipments of telecommunications equipment and software to Eastern European nations which desperately need to build a modern communications infrastructure for their economies. The TIA argues that the long-term interests of the United States lie in facilitating, not blocking, East European economic development (Robinson, 1992).

Productivity issues are at the center of debates within the Clinton administration over the role for government investment in information infrastructure in general and over the governance of the Clinton-sponsored "National Information Infrastructure" in particular. This infrastructure centers on the High Performance Computing Act (HPCA) and other legislative proposals discussed in Chapter 8. Even prior to the election of Clinton, however, the Internet—the core of the proposed infrastructure—had grown hyperbolicly to three quarter million connected computers by January, 1992. Initially a network of a few thousand college-based computers, educational hosts now account for only one-third of Internet. Corporate hosts have grown to 25% and international hosts to another 30%. As corporate and international users clamor for access and expanded services, universities fear their needs will be lost in the rush. In 1993, the incoming Clinton administration faced issues of where to invest to maximize productivity; how to balance government, industry, and educational sectors; how to conform to increasingly stringent formal ethics standards of national and international associations; and how to respond to the use of American telecommunications networks by America's trade partners and competitors abroad.

The Case for Information Technology Investment

Most arguments for establishment of a national information technology policy ultimately rest on the assumption that investment in computing will increase productivity and competitiveness. It is believed that investment in information technology, particular decision support systems, will lead to more information, more approaches to problems, more participation in problem-solving, better understanding of decisions, avoidance of a myopic rush to consensus on problems, reduction of individual domination, and acceleration of interactions and meetings concerning decisions (Rudolph and Schermerhorn, 1991: 289-291).

The growth of investment in information technology suggests that IT investment works. Surveys show people believe IT will enhance productivity and provide competitive advantage, both for firms and for nations (for a review of such opinion polls, see Palvia, Palvia, and Zigli, 1990: 34). This section first looks at productivity success stories which fuel such beliefs and then at research which supports the information technology equals productivity equation. After this limits to IT productivity are discussed, leading into a subsequent section which analyzes the case against information technology as an economic panacea.

Productivity Success Stories

Computing generates many success stories such as computer networking in banking (see Figure 7-4). Typical is Lutheran Hospital

Figure 4: IT Productivity Success Stories

In many areas the productivity of computing makes return to manual methods unthinkable.

- Cartography: Applications in navigation, surveying, decision support, and map publishing are now thoroughly computer-driven (Monmonier, 1985) and improvement of related decision-making is well documented (e.g., Zwart, 1988).

- Statistics: In fields such as statistical analysis, old manual methods are almost never used, not only due to their drudgery but also because they are much more prone to human error.

- Law: On-line systems have removed much of the tedium of retrieval of law case precedents, vastly accelerating the speed of legal research as well as extending its scope.

- Management: Project management, an acknowledged method for achieving cost efficiencies, has come into widespread use now that computerization makes it easy to implement (Harding, 1987).

- Agriculture: Computers have made possible a revolution in farming techniques, such as the output of 12,000 tomatoes from a single tomato plant administered heat, light, and water by computer control. Computers have increased tenfold the number of cattle that can be overseen by a single employee (Stewart, 1988: 11).

- Law Enforcement: Automation of fingerprint identification, use of electronic mug books, and numerous other law enforcement tasks would be impossible without computers (*Police Chief*, 1989; Housman, 1989: 50).

- Public Services: Many new automated systems also dramatically improve client services, such as the multi-lingual multimedia kiosk system sued by the Long Beach Municipal Court (CA) to allow citizens to choose traffic offense pleas, method of payment, and other options—often eliminating the need to spend a day waiting one's turn in court (Polilli, 1992: 19).

of La Crosse, Wisconsin (Santosus, 1992). In 1990 it installed a clinical information system running in a distributed client-server architecture. The result was that doctors and staff received ready access to instant, complete information with higher data integrity. There was a dramatic reduction in time-consuming clerical work by nurses, freeing them to spend more time on actual patient care. And the organization was able to eliminate costly overtime work as well.

Numerous such success stories in fields ranging from agriculture to urban crime are probably the main driving force behind increasing nationwide investment in computer technology.

Data storage and retrieval alone provide impressive productivity and efficiency gains. The FBI was able to discard 110,000,000 3"-by-5" index cards when it automated its criminal justice database, reducing search and retrieval time by several orders of magnitude (*Government Computer News*, 1992a: 14). David Lind, an IS officer for the U.S. Navy, helped introduce CD-ROM storage of Navy manuals, regulations, and other documents. A single CD-ROM disk can contain the equivalent of 270,000 pounds of paper regulations: mailing a CD-ROM saves the Navy $4,000 in mailing costs alone. A small battleship would normally have over 20 tons of paper and filing cabinets, all of which can be replaced by a computer, printer, and a set of CD-ROM discs. The Navy realized $288,000 in cost savings in the first year of operation (*SIGCAT Recap*, 1991: 1). In addition to the sheer transportation and storage savings, retrieval of information under the CD-ROM system is, of course, far faster and more sophisticated. Numerous similar examples could be cited.[12]

Transaction processing is the heart of computing's earliest claims to productivity. Today forms software eliminates the drudgery of filling out business forms. Software prints the forms themselves and fills them in from corporate databases. Inexpensive microcomputer packages now allow firms and agencies to design forms as well as have them filled in and printed. This eliminates costly print-shop design and even costlier (and error-prone) clerical data entry. For instance, forms software is used by Compliance Specialists, a firm which assists California wineries, to do everything from printing bottle labels to filling in the paperwork associated with alcoholic beverage control (Kleinschrod, 1990). Computerization of traditional, centralized purchasing operations through electronic data interchange (EDI) forms, bar coding, handheld order-entry terminals, e-mail, and expert systems software, for instance, allowed Pacific Bell to reduce the cost of processing a transaction from $72 to $5 (O'Leary, 1993: 33).

In another instance, automated food stamp distribution saved Cuyahoga County, Ohio, some $900,000 annually and improved services for clients as well (*Government Computer News*, 1988c). In a more advanced transactions processing example, the Customs

Service saved about $300,000 annually when it found a way to use artificial intelligence to sort through half a million financial transactions from the six largest states to meet reporting requirements imposed by legislation (*Government Computer News*, 1988: 43). The American Hospital Supply Corporation (now Baxter Health-Care Corporation) is considered to have developed a strategic advantage over competitors by creating the first automated order entry system in its line of business (*Wall Street Journal*, 1990), and the McKesson Corporation used IT to redefine service standards for drug wholesaling, simultaneously raising the investment ante required of any future would-be competitors (Keyes, 1993).

Data communications likewise has led to striking productivity improvements. Computer-enabled touchtone telephone registration,

Figure 5: Mini-Case: The Richmond Savings Credit Union

The Richmond Savings Credit Union is a typical case example of the computing success story.

In 1983 the Richmond Federal Savings Credit Union was nearly bankrupt. Competing banks simply offered more services and convenience. "To compete we had to go beyond everyday banking offered by the competition," stated its president, Don Tuline.

To accomplish this, Tuline installed a system of networked microcomputers which allowed customers to use any branch, allowed branches to communicate transactions to one another, allowed instant analyses of what credit union customers were buying, and allowed each customer to have a personal banker with instant access to relevant data from all of the customer's accounts.

Moreover, by using microcomputers rather than mainframes the credit union saved $150,000 annually on computer operations and $200,000 annually on marketing expenses. It also generated $500,000 in annual fee income from new computerized services and by 1987 was able to return more than $1 million in profits to its members (Dressler, 1989).

In general, because of computing branch banks no longer do their own bookkeeping, many transactions are paperless, and automatic tellers and telephone banking have provided 24-hour financial services. Electronic data interchange (EDI), now becoming increasingly adopted as a standard for financial documents, promises even greater productivity gains in the future.

for instance, has eliminated the long lines of students in college gymnasiums and registration halls around the country. Electronic registration is not only a convenience for students but it also provides more efficient use of faculty, curriculum, and classroom space (Spencer, 1991). More broadly, electronic mail has brought the speed and convenience of the phone to the world of letters and documents, creating a productivity gain that is almost universally acclaimed by employees who now enjoy this type of service. A different type of success is illustrated in the microcomputer-based network operated by the U. S. Sentencing Commission to exchange information among prisons and courts to help reduce disparities in the sentencing of criminals (*Government Computer News*, 1987b: 74).

Even areas not thought of in the same breath as computing provide illustrations of IT productivity. This is the case of human resource management (HRM). HRM information systems are particularly critical in government since personnel costs are often 70% to 90% of an agency's entire budget. IS can assist in cost containment through reduction of paperwork, assist in affirmative action by maintaining information on the minority job applicant pool, assist in career counseling, and help with productivity programs by providing better tracking of employee performance data (Harty, 1985; Decker and Plumlee, 1985; on computer counseling, see Glaize and Myrick, 1984). In more sophisticated HRM analyses simulation may be used to model career patterns in relation to changers in the labor market (Kelleher, 1985; Ledvinka and Hildreth, 1984). Many newer applications such as the job skills databank (which keeps a computerized inventory of employees' and job applicants' skills for use in later recruiting and promotion decisions) are impossible to implement without extensive IS investment in computers, software, and staff training (Garson, 1986). IS is rapidly increasing in importance in human resource management and will continue to do so into the next century (Darany, 1984).

Use of computers for competitive advantage is illustrated in the food distribution industry by City Provisioners, a firm which provides its sales force with mobile laptop computers. The representatives in the field can use computers not only to take and transmit orders, but also to show customers how specific menus and food items will translate into the profit margin of the customer. In this way the sales representative becomes a welcomed management consultant for food industry customers, providing a service not available from other firms (O'Malley, 1989b). Other examples of competitive advantage using computers include SABRE electronic reservation system, a $340 million investment from the 1960s through the 1980s, widely credited with giving a proprietary edge to the American Airlines.[13] SABRE was then imitated in the Confirm system used by Marriott, Hilton, and Budget Rent-a-Car to seek competitive advantage (Keyes, 1993).

In other competitive advantage illustrations, CitiBank tripled its NYC market share by being the first to widely install automated tellers. Metpath Inc., a clinical laboratory, is said to have gained competitive advantage by installing its terminals and customer help system directly in physicians' offices. Otis Elevator has maintained distinction for reliability by installing an information system to track repairs in detail and plan for rapid restoration of services. Hertz provided on-the-spot printed directions to clients' destinations. Federal Express created its COSMOS system to tie 65,000 computers to track all of its packages in real time, enabling it to maintain a 40% market share in the express mail business in spite of charging higher rates than competitors. Progressive Insurance gained from computerized claims processing which enabled issuing claims checks at the site of an accident (Keyes, 1993). Conrail used radio-equipped notebook computers on 70 locomotives to track information on schedules, pricing, shipment status, arrival times, and billing in real time - one of many firms seeking strategic advantage through point-of-sales and other "liberation technology" systems which place computers where the organization's customers and clients are located (Santosus, 1993a).

Finally, computing makes possible one of the great competitive advantage strategies of the last decade—just-in-time manufacturing and just-in-time inventories (see Figure 7-6). Federal Express used just-in-time inventory software to transform itself from a delivery service to a firm which takes over the warehousing/inventory functions of many businesses (Porter and Millar, 1985; King, Grover, and Hufnagel, 1989; Zawrotny, 1989). Companies like Black and Dekker, manufacturer of power tools for the consumer market, have built worldwide integrated information systems which enable them to relate information about the current state of store shelves to inventory levels and production schedules. Through computers, just-in-time management seeks to eliminate overproduction and excess inventory costs. For instance, stockless operation of hospitals lowers personnel

Figure 6: Bar Code Technology and Just-in-Time Inventories

Just-in-time production and just-in-time local inventories are perhaps the most profound productivity advance in the American economy in the last decade.

These management innovations are based directly on computer-based barcode readers, which now do things such as radioing inventory information directly to computers tracking delivery. Point-of-sale bar coded merchandise helps retailers track local inventories (Parker, 1991).

To illustrate, the American textile industry has long been in decline due to overseas competition. However, now bar-coded apparel tags make computerized inventory control and sales tracking possible. This information is then used to get hot-selling apparel items to market much faster than foreign competitors.

Computers have allowed U.S. manufacturers to cut production time and to link production much more closely with changing sales patterns. American firms are thus able to supply retailers with small, fast-moving inventories better tailored to changing fashions.

Retailers are in the position of committing themselves, for instance, to buying 1,000 lower-cost coats nine months in advance, or committing themselves to buying a smaller number at a higher price from an American supplier but getting them far sooner and being able to reorder if the need arises.

Though the foreign price is cheaper, the risk is far less with American goods in many situations, enabling U.S. textile firms to compete more successfully than in the past (Jerome, 1989).

Bar-coding has revolutionized public sector programs as well, as in the use of hand-held computers in St. Louis Park, MN, to scan barcodes on residents' recycling bins. Scanned data is then used to lower trash collection bills of residents who recycle, a factor which increased participation from 45% to 90% of the population (*PA Times*, 1992: 2).

and space costs at hospitals, but it requires just-in-time computer-controlled distribution from hospital suppliers like Baxter International (Caldwell, 1991d). One consultant noted, "If you can't move to some version of just-in-time manufacturing, you won't be in the ball game in five years" (Caldwell, 1991c: 30). Many companies, such as Owens Corning Fiberglass, attribute competitive advantage to such computer integration of order entry, manufacturing planning, and distribution (Baker, 1990).

Research Supporting IT Investment Efficacy

Studies such as that by the Diebold Group (see Figure 7-7) document the groundswell of business management literature and opinion emphasizing the importance of recognizing the role of information in gaining competitive advantage (Porter, 1980, 1985; Porter and Millar, 1985). Likewise, in the public sector, 37 American city governments were studied over the 1976 to 1988 period by Northrop, Kraemer, Dunkle, and King (1990). They found that technical payoffs to computing existed though they often took years to reach fruition. Norris's study of 65 local government units found time savings of 25% to 300% on computerized tasks as well as ability to do work that had not been feasible before (Norris, 1989: 143). Northrop et al. found that the clearest productivity payoffs occurred in the areas of fiscal control, cost avoidance, and better interaction with the public. In other areas, such as better information for planning and for administrative control, managers surveyed did not feel that computing had resulted in the benefits which had been expected.[14] For instance, Oregon's Department of General Services saved over $100,000 in mailing costs, $8 million is estimated savings through lower bids, and eliminated 14 clerical positions when it replaced mail bids with online bidding (O'Leary, 1993: 36).

At the federal level, the FBI reports that it is 32% more efficient in case management due to automation. Its overall efficiency has increased 40% to 50% (Masud, 1988: 16). However, productivity gains of this magnitude to not apply to all areas. In a study of a public utility customer service department, it was found that introduction of a computerized records system enhanced productivity by making routine tasks easier. However, non-routine tasks became more difficult under the newly computerized system (Kraut, Dumais, and Koch, 1989). Similarly, a study of IS in a human service agency found decreased costs, increased quality of care, and improved working conditions. However, the agency was sometimes unable to cope with the quantity and quality of work generated under the automated system, partly because of increased time spent on computer-related matters (Gardner, Souza, Scabbia, and Breuer, 1986).

Computing itself is becoming more efficient as shown in a study of structured programming, a set of techniques widely heralded as fundamental to efficiency in computer programming, particularly in

Figure 7: The Diebold Group Study of IT and Competitive Advantage

The New York-based Diebold Group studied some 300 corporate annual reports describing the use of computers, seeking to understand the relationship of IT investment to subsequent economic advantage over competitors.

The Diebold study concluded that companies gain competitive advantage through IS in four areas:

(1) *productivity* (optimizing resource use, shortening development);

(2) *customer service* (reducing the customer's cost of doing business; strengthening ties to customers);

(3) *product innovation* (enhancing products or services; developing new products or services); and

(4) *pricing* (assessing and responding to market changes; better promotion).

The Diebold Study found corporations were increasingly willing to incur short-term costs in order to get maximum competitive advantage through IS. Whereas these competitive benefits were often "byproducts" of office automation in early IS, the study found such objectives had become primary objectives by the mid-1980s (Venner, 1988: 16-17).

For instance, electronic mail was often a byproduct of establishing networks to link PCs to mainframes, laser printers, and other common resources. But research has found that by speeding up organizational communications and feedback, electronic mail systems can have a significant positive effect on productivity and are now often established for their own sake (Crawford, 1982; Papa, 1990).

maintaining programs. In the past, some 70% of total life-cycle costs of major systems lay in maintenance, flagging it as major area for efficiency improvement (Canning, 1977). An Infotech study of 1,000 companies regarding their use of the structured method of programming concluded that structuring could reduce programmer time by up to half, reduce implementation time up to 30%, and reduce software maintenance time up to 80%. Likewise, computer-aided software engineering (CASE) tools, which partially automate software development, are widely regarded by those who use them as having improved their productivity greatly (Norman and Nunamaker, 1989).

There is evidence that computing is associated with innovation, widely perceived to be an important dimension of productivity improvement. Rule and Attewell (1989) surveyed 184 financial, construction, wholesale, and other private organizations in New York and found that acquisition of the first computer and the development of applications for it was connected to innovation. Managers in these firms experimented with new ideas and approaches which would not have been considered if computers were not available. Some 44% stated that the existence of computers had led them to search for new ways to utilize its capacities. Moreover, Rule and Attewell found that some 30% of applications were "transformative". That is, they were not just data storage and simple calculation programs but instead generated value added, as in programs for tax preparation, computer-assisted design, market analysis and other software that performed tasks hitherto requiring the labor of human professionals. The authors believe that the transformative proportion was increasing over time, indicating a growth of innovation as computers became more firmly entrenched in these organizations.

A 1987 report by Wharton School researchers Eric Clemons and Steven Kimbrough (Bonner, 1987) found that information systems did provide demonstrable productivity benefits. However, information technology investment may not give sustainable long-term advantage vis-a-vis competitors because competitors find ways to catch up - much like the effect of new military technologies in arms races. The banking industry illustrates the short term/long term problem. Banks first to introduce automated teller machines enjoyed a brief competitive advantage but once all banks had ATMs market shares did not change. To compete, banks must have ATMs, but there is no competitive advantage gained by the investment. Other investments, like home banking, proved not cost-effective at all. These findings are also consistent with various reviews of the literature which have found a generally positive relationship of IT investment to productivity gains (e.g., Federico, 1985: 35-6) but not necessarily to effectiveness or long-range organizational outcomes.

Measuring productivity effects is expensive and highly problematic. Managers know this and are rarely willing to invest in productivity studies, whether or not they support IS investment. Cost-benefit studies are far and few between. Most examples, moreover, are suspect because they were prepared by IS departments seeking to justify IS investment. Illustrative is the Army Corps of Engineers

Construction Engineering Research Laboratory analysis of four technologies (text and graphics scanners, voice mail, fax cards, and form-generation software). The Corps found that technological investment could increase productivity in a year's time as much as adding a full-time employee to each of its offices (Olsen, 1992b: 86). Unfortunately, cost-benefit studies vary widely in the extent to which indirect, long-term, and overhead factors (e.g., training) are included on the cost side of the equation, and the extent diffuse, qualitative, and long-term factors (e.g., job satisfaction) are included on the benefit side. Debate over what is to be included and what is not tends to make cost-benefit studies less valuable than one might expect.

In many areas of computing and productivity, the evidence simply isn't in yet. For example, the causal relationship of technological innovation to worker productivity, turnover, and absenteeism has been studied but with inconclusive results (Pfeffer, 1982: ch. 9). While the service sector is high in computer investment and low in productivity gains, other industries paint a different picture. A study of the insurance industry, for instance, found that 97% of the most profitable were in the top quarter of computer technology spending, investing some 20% of expenses to IS in comparison to only 10% among the least profitable companies (Karon, 1987a: 64).

Finally, there is evidence of a subjective element in the relationship of computing to productivity. Starr Roxanne Hiltz examined how four different computer conferencing systems altered group productivity. Hiltz found "The strongest correlates of productivity improvements for all four systems are pre-use expectations about whether the system would increase productivity" (Hiltz, 1988: 1449). Expecting that IS will be productive does not guarantee it will be so, but information systems projects are unlikely to succeed unless there is strong support from top management reflecting a belief in their worth.

Limits to Computer Enhancement of Productivity

Since the 1980s it has become common to believe that information technology is creating a productivity revolution. Nations and organizations that know how to take advantage of it are presumed to gain a competitive edge over others. Writers such as Peter Drucker, F. Warren McFarlan, Lynda Applegate, James Cash, Michael Porter,

Figure 8: IT Productivity Failure Stories

* The Florida On-Line Recipient Data Access system (FLORIDA) for welfare management was initiated in a 3-year, $85 million contract in June 1989. EDS undertakes to build a huge mainframe system with 84 databases, 1,390 programs, 12,000 terminals, and 5.5 million on-line transactions daily. EDS concluded the state's design requirements were not feasible and turned FLORIDA over to the state in June 1992. Evaluation found human and computer error resulted in $260 million in overpayments and $58 million in underpayments in 1992 alone. Moreover, FLORIDA severely hampered emergency efforts arising from Hurrican Andrew devastation that August (Caldwell and Appleby, 1993).

* The Pentagon has $40 billion in spare computer parts it doesn't need because Army and Navy computers cannot communicate with each other (Greve, 1993: 14A).

* Westpac Banking Group's CS90 project was intended to create a showcase system of decentralized IS using expert systems and artificial intelligence. In December, 1991, *InformationWeek* reported "Last month, more than three years after CS90 was begun, Westpac reluctantly ponied up to the worst: the project is out of control. CS90 has already drained nearly $150 million from Westpac's coffers -and the bank has virtually nothing to show for it" (Mehler, 1991: 20).

* The Westpac experience is not uncommon. A 1990 Gartner Group consulting study of *Fortune* 500 companies found that 40% had experienced "runaway" or "near-runaway" IS projects (Mehler, 1991: 21).

* Public and private organizations are now questioning the value they have gotten from their IS investments (Alexander, 1987; Weil, 1988). As recently as 1987 a survey of several hundred manufacturing executives showed over 60% believed in the value of their firm's IS spending, whereas by 1990 fewer than 30% believed their company received an adequate return on IS investment (Caldwell, 1990f: 20).

and others viewed IS with excitement and wrote extensively on the subject in the *Harvard Business Review* and other publications (see *Harvard Business Review*, Ed., 1990). For instance, Porter's 1985 essay emphasized "How Information Gives You Competitive Advantage", a theme echoed in the same period by Cash and McFarlan. Drucker predicted in 1988 that within twenty years information technology would lead to more efficient organizations with half the levels of management compared to the present. McFarlan's "Information Technology Changes the Way You Compete" argued that information technology could even determine the success or failure of an organization.

However, doubts about the effectiveness of information systems investment are commonplace (cf. Williams, 1991). As noted by Paul Strassmann in his book *Information Payoff* (1985), the 1970s and 1980s generated several studies which cast IT investment in a more negative light. These studies showed little or no value added as measured by productivity or company profitability after investment in and introduction of technology. In particular, the question was raised whether IT investment was effective as well as efficient.

For instance, in education computers have had little impact and it is difficult to establish that particular examples of computer-based instruction are more effective than traditional methods (Kling and Iacono, 1991). In general, input-output efficiency studies routinely show computers can crunch a lot of numbers, process a lot of words, and print endless forms, students of both public and business management alike have long rejected input-output efficiency studies as missing the main point, which is effectiveness vis-a-vis organizational values and goals. Strassman, a former Xerox executive, doubted the vision of the all-computerized "paperless office" and instead called for a critical, empirical study of value added measures of effectiveness of IS investment (Strassmann, 1985; how to do such studies is detailed in Strassman, 1990).

Research Casting Doubt on IT Investment Efficacy

Computing generates failure stories as well as success stories (see Figure 7-8). Empirical research does not necessarily lead to the conclusion that automation improves productivity. Stephen Roach, senior economist at a New York investment bank, studied the correlation of investment in information technology with productivity gains as measured by the U. S. Bureau of Labor Statistics (Zarley, 1988c: 41). Roach found that the service and financial sectors of the economy were by far the largest investors in information technology yet they consistently showed the lowest productivity gains per worker.[15] Some 80% of all computer investment through 1985 was concentrated in the service sector. The service industries that have invested the most have consistently shown the lowest rate of productivity growth (Karon, 1987a: 64; Boroughs et al., 1990).

It is difficult to show that white collar workers, often high-profile users of computer technology, actually benefit from it in terms of productivity. Noonan (1991: 25) found for white-collar work, introduction of new office technology was associated with 20% longer work weeks and an actual decline in white-collar productivity. One reason for lowered productivity was suggested by the findings of Schellhardt (1990), whose research showed that middle managers spent an increasing proportion of their time on activities formerly performed by secretaries and support personnel. Television advertising by Apple Computer and others routinely shows presumably highly-paid executives being rewarded organizationally for having used their PCs to produce flashy reports— but do effective organizations really want to devote upper management resources to honing desktop publishing techniques? Such questions arise because, as Schellhardt notes, in a world of user-operated word processors, e-mail, and fax machines, middle managers might spend only 27% of their time on actual management tasks.

There are, of course, problems with drawing conclusions about individual worker productivity from aggregate data since IS investments may indeed be making workers more productive, yet other factors may be limiting productivity gains in the financial and service sectors overall. However, the absence of a general correlation of IT investment with productivity increase does not stand as the only evidence that IT investment is not always an "engine of growth" and "lever of riches".

Failure is a rule, not an exception in large-scale information systems projects. A survey by Gladden (1982), for example, found that 75% of all systems development projects were never completed or, if completed, were never used, often because needs change too rapidly for the development process. Likewise, a study of *Fortune* 500 firms by the National Training and Computers Project found microcomputer managers reported over half of their users either underused or had entirely abandoned the software that was supposed to increase their productivity on the job (Watt, 1989). Even when computer systems are implemented, they may remain underutilized. In studying local government officials who did use computers, Kraemer and Northrop (1984, 1989) found that managers were using only about 10% of the capabilities of their software.

Ironically, the glowing reputation of IT investment sometimes compounds failure. Because IT investment is often justified on optimistic cost-cutting grounds, after the investment is made there can be considerable pressure to cut costs through staff reductions even when productivity gains do not warrant this. Such face-saving cuts can hurt organizational effectiveness and productivity, as illustrated by the case of the Customs Service. Customs used investment in its automation projects (e.g., identification of high risk illicit cargos) to justify significant staff reductions even though many, including the General Accounting Office, found the automated systems were largely useless and even though investment in staff more than paid for itself in recovered revenues (Grimm, 1988h: 12).

Computerization tends to lead to rising demands for computer services and to a rising total volume of work. Computers tend to create new demands for hardware, software, training, maintenance, telecommunications, and other forms of support. Because computerization makes mass mailing easy, for instance, more organizations do more mass mailings more frequently.[16] Because computerization makes reporting easier, more organizations have more reports more often for more managers. Total costs rise even though per-unit processing cost may go down. Thus in Frantzich's study of Congress, computerized mail meant per-letter efficiency but overall greater costs as Congressional representatives mailed many more letters. Likewise, electronic voting meant many more roll call votes (Frantzich, 1987).

The demand-push phenomenon occurs within computing itself. Joe Celko, a computer scientist at Northrup University, has noted that increased efficiency in writing software can easily mean that organizations create more software. In this sense, productivity strategies in computing like structured programming may not save money in absolute terms. In fact, maintenance costs may rise because the number of programs in use may rise as more efficient programming techniques are introduced. Since Celko estimates it takes two programmers for every five systems, software maintenance costs may tend to rise. This is consistent with findings showing computing tends not to reduce costs but to increase demand for computer services. That is, organizations become more efficient at higher volume levels and higher costs (Celko, 1987).

Increasing computer services, however efficient, do not necessarily improve the organization's productivity in terms of a "bottom line". The relation of investment in information technology to profits finds that American consumption of paper increased 320% whereas real gross national product increased only 280%. Moreover, the fastest rise in paper consumption came in the 1980s as microcomputers came onto employees' desks (Tenner, 1988: 23-24). Correlation

Figure 9: Seven Factors Limiting IT Productivity

1. **Goal-setting problems:** Computers can be effective only in relation to organizational goals, yet goal-setting is intrinsically political rather than computational in nature.

2. **Subjectivity problems:** Effectiveness varies by management style and other subjective elements.

3. **Complexity problems**: Effectiveness often is contingent on complex interactive processes with many unpredictable elements.

4. **Cost problems:** The cost/benefit ratio of IT investment contains many large and often unrecognized costs in the numerator.

5. **Motivation problems**: Those who must implement IT often are given inadequate incentives to do so or to do so well.

6. **Human resource deficiencies:** Those who must implement IT often are not those qualified to do so.

7. **Human error factor:** Those who implement IT, however well qualified and motivated, still make mistakes.

in the private sector is very ambiguous. Thomas Steiner blames falling profit margins in the financial sector on information technology. Specifically, he argues that IT investment is associated with chronic system overcapacity. Moreover, as computerization improved information flow, price competition became more intense. Although consumers benefitted and although any given bank needs to computerize extensively to stay in the competitive game, the industry itself found lower profit margins were a structural component of the "computer age" (Krass and Caldwell, 1991).[17]

The case even can be made that the "information revolution" associated with computing is broadly counter-productive. Around 1980 it was often predicted that computing would bring a "paperless society", with all important information stored online for computer access. However, if one looks at the period in which computers became institutionalized in American organizations, 1959 - 1986, one does not prove causation, but one has to wonder whether computerization explodes paperwork in the form of more frequent reports, lists, memos, junk mail, desktop published materials, and the like. Additional paperwork and the time consumed in producing, processing, and digesting it is seen by many as a force against productivity, perhaps one factor behind the slow-down in U.S. GNP growth.

Perhaps the most definitive summary of the productivity question to date comes from the "Management in the 1990s Research Program", run by the MIT Sloan School of Management from 1984 to 1990. Their conclusions are contained in Michael S. Scott Morton's anthology, *The Corporation of the 1990s: Information Technology and Organizational Transformation* (1990). Lester Thurow, an economist and Sloan School dean, found "there is no clear evidence that these new technologies have raised productivity...or profitability" and in fact "precisely the opposite is true" (Krass, 1991: 33).

In summary, information technology success stories are not always what they are cracked up to be. Probably the single most-publicized example of gaining "competitive advantage" through computing was American Airlines' SABRE system, which automated AA reservation systems and tied into services to over 14,000 travel agents. Some 8,000 operators at five regional sites handle half a million calls a day from travel agency locations in 47 countries. Although initiated in the late 1960s, the SABRE system did not achieve profitability until 1983 (Borovits and Neumann, 1988).

More recently, however, American Airlines' Vice President for Information Systems, Max Hopper, asserted that contrary to conventional wisdom, SABRE had done little for American Airline's market share (Freedman, 1991: 42). Hopper argued that SABRE was merely one part of a complex set of capabilities developed over a long period of time. Benefits came over a period of years due to new business practices, not IT as a stand-alone force.[18] Moreover, although still a profit center, SABRE lost key accounts and became embroiled in lawsuits with former partners in a major hotel and car-rental program gone bust (Caldwell, 1993b: 39). Because competitors can often duplicate IT advances, competitive advantage comes in the long run not from technology per se but by having managers and employees who are better able to act on information systems results than can corresponding personnel in other organizations.

In a similar vein, the Sloan School project discussed above also suggests that new approaches to productivity must be taken at least after the initial productivity gains reaped from automating obvious manual tasks. Their conclusion is that new organizational forms may be needed to exploit fully IS technology. Information systems must be used to obliterate existing business practices in favor of wholly new strategies rather than passively automate existing business procedures (Hammer, 1990). That is, the Sloan School project argues that the real impact of IS on productivity will come in the future as new, more flexible forms of organization are put in place capable of utilizing massive, instantaneous information flow rich in tactical and strategic planning implications.

Forces Limiting Productivity Improvement through IT Investment

Beyond technical issues of hardware and software availability and compatibility, in general it can be said that there are seven major limitations on productivity results from IS initiatives. These fall under the headings of goal-setting problems, subjectivity problems, com-

Figure 10: IT Productivity and Goal-Setting at Pepperidge Farms

Pepperidge Farms used to take a week to process orders but after installation of a system based on handheld computers, orders could be accepted at 3:00 p.m. for bread to bake at 7:00 p.m. and be delivered at 11:00 p.m. the same night (Oliva, 1990: 100).

In this way Pepperidge Farms received a competitive advantage which boosted its market share from 3.5% to 25% in the 1985-1990 period.

However, once this technology is installed by all providers, is it not likely that, as with ATM machines in banking, there will be better service (fresher bread for consumers) but no overall profitability improvement. Might not the only overall industry effect be to drive out small competitors unable to mount this technology, reducing competitiveness in the industry?

Many point-of-service automated order-processing systems provide temporary competitive advantage for a firm, but once installed in an industry generally, serve simply to raise client expectations about faster service without changing profitability. Indeed, profitability may go down due to the cost of the automated system.

Computing constantly raises such issues about just which values we want to maximize in order to be considered "productive" — productive of *what?* Who benefits?

plexity problems, cost problems, motivation problems, human resource deficiencies, and the human error factor (see Figure 7-9). These seven factors limiting productivity improvement through IT investment are discussed serially in this section.

Goal-Setting

Software can only yield productivity in relation to organizational goals, yet goal-setting is intrinsically political - a dimension computers cannot resolve. In any given organization there are many possible goals, some in tension with one another. Frequently management lacks clear goal priorities and seeks to foster the myth that the organization is seeking to maximize all goals. However, an IS system designed to promote the maximization of one goal may do so at the expense of another. IS will be seen as a productivity factor with regard to the first goal and unproductive with regard to the second. To be correlated with "productivity", IS investment must be directed toward systems which support the particular goals by which productivity happens to be defined in a given organization, industry, or society.[19]

Thus before computers can be successful 'engines of productivity', IS managers face the problem of defining which statistical indicators are to be taken as measures of progress toward goals. Such definitions are controversial. A well-known example is the unemployment index. Conservatives have favored a stringent definition of unemployment so as to cause unemployment to be reported low. Liberals, in contrast, have favored a broader definition taking into account people who have given up looking for work or who are under-employed, so as to cause unemployment levels to be reported higher and thus become a more important issue on the national agenda.

Measurement poses political issues in the case of every statistical indicator, including productivity measures (Carr, 1989c). In the context of a government agency, for instance, there may be political differences about such goals as maximizing service, minimizing costs, achieving service equity, maximizing client satisfaction, maximizing public satisfaction, maximizing the satisfaction of legislators, and so on. For instance, instances exist where computing improves the goal of job satisfaction but not the goal of economic productivity, or increases the quantity of communications with clients without increasing the number of clients served (Frederickson and Riley, 1985).

Managers must agree on the indicators to be tracked and maximized through an information system if IS is expected to yield major productivity gains.[20]

The goal-setting problem is related to the difference between efficiency and effectiveness. Computing routinely increases the quantity of output and therefore almost always improves efficiency, which is defined by the ratio of inputs to outputs. Effectiveness, on the other hand, has to do with the degree of goal-attainment, not how much paperwork is pushed across how many desks. Congress itself provides an illustration. "The darker side of the efficiency question is the fact that while computers were introduced to help (Congress) members respond to constituent requests and expression of opinion, the capacity for creating targeted mailing lists and the ease of responding to incoming mail have led to increased outreach and cost" (Frantzich, 1987a: 37). That is, computing made individualized mass mailings easy for Congressional representatives. Was more mail sent more efficiently? Yes. Were there cost savings? No, the opposite. Were democratic goals of a better informed citizenry achieved, or was the public underwriting the costs of re-election PR efforts that should have come from campaign funds? It depends on your viewpoint.

Contrary to popular belief, here as in most cases, automation rarely cuts costs through labor savings reflected in the overall personnel bill of the organization. When Deere and Co. moved its engineers to computer-aided design (CAD) it expected major savings. Instead it was found that engineers often overused CAD, experimenting with the numerous possibilities CAD made possible. The increased quantity of engineering designs reduced the anticipated productivity increase (Scheier, 1990c). Likewise, accounting department staffs have continued to increase at the same time accounting has become increasingly computerized (Livingston, 1987: 62). Improved staff capabilities through computer tools do not mean smaller staff nor are productivity gains for the organization assured even though efficiency gains for the employee are very likely.

Subjectivity

In addition to goal-setting obstacles, a second limit to computing has to do with managerial subjectivity. That is, particularly as it applies to increasing productivity through better decision-making, different managers make decisions differently. Individual styles of decision-making lead different administrators to follow different courses yet they may arrive at equally effective results. In particular a major drawback of computerized decision-making support is the threat it poses to decision-makers' "autonomy to use their intuitions, hunches, and practice wisdom" when these subjective factors run counter to generalizations based on computer analysis of aggregated data ((Oyserman and Benbenishty, 1993: 437).

Inappropriate managerial styles also may frustrate productivity gains through computing. This can occur in the case of productivity software used by authoritarian managers to monitor individual performance in the style of a nineteenth-century sweatshop. "When computer technology is used as an electronic whip to make people work faster, to intrude on their personal privacy, to judge them on subjective criteria, and to single out and punish substandard performance, good organizational results are hard to imagine" (Piturro, 1990: 31).[21]

If a manager tries to adopt a decision-making pattern that is not appropriate for him or her, poor results may follow. Managers often find computer tools do not fit their management style. While there has been some attempt in the area of expert systems and decision support software to take account of cognitive and personality differences in decision-making, the subjective element in productivity is a significant obstacle in many computer applications in management, most of which assume all managers can use identical software (Bariff and Lusk, 1977; Zmud, 1979).

Complexity

The complex contingencies of decision-making are a third obstacle to achieving productivity through IS investments. Collins (1992: 79) notes, "In the realm of complex planning of interactive processes with many unpredictable factors, computers can do no better than humans." In fact, management decision-making and hence the success of decision support depends not only on political and subjective factors but also on many other considerations. Ginzberg and Ariav, for example, list no less that eight classes of factors on which decision-making is contingent (1986; see also Ariav and Ginzberg, 1982).[22]

Without rejecting the possibility of a contingency theory of decision support which would take all these dimensions into account within the context of a computerized decision support system (DSS), the least that can be said is that (1) the multi-dimensional nature of decision-making is an obstacle to success, and (2) the very many contingencies involved increase the chance a manager-user will apply any given DSS software package inappropriately.

While some believe that expert systems and artificial intelligence will overcome these limitations (Boden, 1977; Haugeland, 1981; Goldkind, 1987), current evidence is that such software is most useful for routine expertise on well-understood problems. Contrary to public belief that the sentient robots of popular movies are near at hand or perhaps already exist in military laboratories, the relative consensus in the literature is that machines cannot "think" and that progress toward such a goal will be slow or impossible (Weizenbaum, 1976; Dreyfus and Dreyfus, 1986). Complexity remains a formidable obstacle to achieving productivity through computing.

Cost

Fourth, there are obvious financial limits and problems associated with reaping productivity benefits from computing. To be truly productive, computing must not only provide savings which pay for new computers but also for printers and other peripherals and supplies, networks, software, software upgrades, training, technical support, employee time, and depreciation. An organization may suddenly find it needs an additional position to provide training, one to provide maintenance, and even one just to support local area networking to connect computers together. In social work, for instance, "most agencies have restricted budgets which are controlled by outside funding agencies, [so] the massive expenditures required to computerize social work practice as well as questions about the effectiveness of such a move deter agency administrators from supporting such an innovative initiative (Cnaan, 1989: 6).

Even national organizations often lack funds for critical tasks. This was the case in the New York Stock Exchange, whose computer system was unable to detect and thus enable the Exchange to regulate computerized program trading, a factor thought to be a potential destabilizing force at critical junctures in the American economy, even though the computer systems used by individual member firms of the Exchange usually had this capability (GAO, 1988).

New technologies require extensive investment of management and employee time in rule formation, organization development, and the wear and tear of conflict that usually accompanies change. Given that most new technologies have little advantage over existing ones in their initial phases, it is common that financial constraints prevent many organizations from reaching the necessary critical mass insofar as information technology investment is concerned. For instance, EDI (electronic data interchange, a standard for electronic transmission of payments and other financial paperwork) has led to significant productivity gains, but only the largest banks can afford to institute EDI, slowing its diffusion significantly (Gullo, 1989a: 20).

Motivation

A fifth obstacle to IT productivity, human motivation limits computing's potential. For instance, when computers were introduced for word processing there was an opportunity to replace the inefficient typewriter-like QWERTY keyboard with a more efficient one, but "no one was willing to face the resistance of tens of millions of secretaries, typists, and others who had learned to type on a QWERTY keyboard" (Westrum, 1991: 206). Likewise, in studying human service organizations Kling (1978a) found that information was a "weak integrator". That is, in spite of the rational reasons for establishing computer-based information exchanges to coordinate and integrate multi-agency services to clients, in fact attempts to move in this direction are routinely frustrated.

Information is a public good and suffers the problems of other public goods. A particular problem is that what is in the good of all may not be in any particular person's interest. For instance, while it is in everyone's interest to integrate information using computers and networks, it may not be sufficiently in each actor's individual interest to make the expenditures of time and resources to do this. Thus Kling (1978a: 491) found that service agencies joined an integrated information system when the United Way made it a condition of receiving funds but then dropped out when this incentive was removed. Likewise, many cities established integrated urban databases using Housing and Urban Development grants in the 1970s but dropped these projects once grant money ran out (Kraemer and King, 1979).

The lesson seems to be that information sharing is not an adequate motivator in and of itself. More broadly, productivity may fail to materialize from IS initiatives because managers receive status and even compensation from the size of the budgets and number of personnel the supervise, giving them strong incentives not to turn productivity gains into reduced budgets or reduced labor requirements.

Human resources

A sixth obstacle to IT productivity is human resource deficiencies of one type or another. End users frequently lack training for computer use while IS specialists within the organization are often too ignorant of the substantive functions of the organization (e.g., strategic planning) to be of much assistance (Swain and White, 1992: 654-655). Managers are reluctant to invest the large sums required for retraining or restaffing but instead often seek to cut corners by laying information systems on unready users. More broadly, IT investment for global competition requires what Cheney and Kasper (1993) call the "development of the global IS professional", a type of individual currently in short supply.

Human error

Even when no other obstacle exists, people are prone to make mistakes. Vendors routinely encourage organizations to over-invest in IS technology cf. Garvey, 1990. Worse, a study by the Association for Computer Training and Support (ACTS) found that productivity software tends to be underutilized due to wrong software purchase decisions resulting in seeking to apply software which is not even capable of meeting users' needs (Pane, 1990). Banks which accepted overblown claims for electronic home banking and AI-based talking automatic teller machines, for instance, found their investments in these IS initiatives to be wasteful.

Decisions based on computer models are not infrequently flawed because the state of the art of human knowledge on given topics is not high or because of outright mistakes. Neumann (1993: 124) cites several illustrative cases. In 1991 a Tital 4 rocket booster blew up because extensive 3D simulation testing had failed to reveal stresses that full-scale testing might have. In the 1987 crash of Northwest Flight 255, which killed 156 people, it was later found that a crucial warning indicator worked correctly in the simulator but not in the actual aircraft. The collapse of the Salt Lake City Shopping Mall was due to failure of the computer model to take into account extreme conditions and due to other incorrect model assumptions. The selection of an inappropriate computer model also led to incorrect beam connections which led to the collapse of the Hartford Civic Center Coliseum.

At the employee level, lack of training may undermine possible productivity gains the employee might otherwise make, or the employee may waste time on trivial applications (e.g., computer games), inefficient applications (e.g., electronic calendars which are less versatile than printed pocket calendars), and inappropriate applications (e.g., when highly paid managers spend hours at desktop publishing better performed by graphic designers and other staff).

Trying to avoid human error, as in software selection, can be compounded in the form of what one writer has called "analysis paralysis": "the steps we went through were something like this: get literature from five vendors, read the literature, discuss the literature among ourselves, make a list of the good and bad points about each product, talk to the vendors about their products, determine how the tool would be used in the organization, attempt to match the product characteristics to the needs of the organization, develop a rating system, rate the products, discuss the scores, get more information from the vendors, have a preliminary discussion with out colleagues, get more information from the vendors. The result of this process is that we suffered a collective case of analysis paralysis" (Perry, 1989: 79).

Summary

Word processing provides a familiar example illustrating the pros and cons of computers as a means to productivity. Word processing is commonly cited as the single biggest and most immediate way most professionals can increase personal productivity using computers. Yet not everyone agrees. In his essay, "Why I Am Not Going to Buy a Computer", Wendell Berry (1991) argues that compared to pencil-and-paper, computers cost more, are less repairable, use more energy from a conservation viewpoint, and disrupt family life more. Yet, he argues, word processing won't help you write any better. We may ask, if word processing doesn't make you a more productive writer, why is it most professionals now use it? Why do surveys of secretaries, for instance, show that they like it and feel it is an area of accomplishment? Which side is right?

Early research on word processing among scholars tended to pit the humanists versus the technicists, with the former viewing computerized writing as dehumanizing and alienating.[23] Word processing has had a significant effect on productivity in writing. Word processing has been found to lead to writing more, revising more, and sharing writing results more. There is considerable evidence that word processing improves writing by facilitating the revision process. Making the revision process easier, in turn, has broad implications for how writers look at collaborative efforts (Crawford, 1988). Pamela Farrell (1987), for example, has found that among peer tutors and writers in a college writing lab, while working with the computer, the varying social, ethnic, and educational backgrounds of the participants "vanished" and a new relationship developed. Word processing can be associated with increased collaboration in writing in classroom situations, if instructors provide for and encourage this.

In spite of its undoubted advantages, in many settings it is difficult to show that word processing has increased productivity. Word processing, like other software, needs to correspond to the way professionals actually work. If it does not, however technologically sophisticated it may be, it may not be used extensively. The capabilities of computer software are far in excess of most professionals' capacity to find the time and resources to take advantage of it so its fit with actual work styles must be close if it is to be utilized. For example, S. K. Kinnell (1988) found news editorial writers did not take advantage of computer software of which they were aware, in spite of need for research being a commonly cited problem and in spite of the availability of full-text databases providing research answers. Lack of fit to editorial work styles was found to be the reason. In fact, advanced desktop publishing and other word processing features can be counter-productive, causing employees to waste valuable organizational time experimenting with fonts, sizes, layouts, colors, only to achieve mediocre results attributable to going outside their writing competencies into the field of graphic design, for which they lack experience or talent (Feretic, 1988: 7).

Word processing, wonderful as it is, has its limits. Some, such as

Gerald Grow (1988), argued that whereas typed manuscripts encouraged *editing*, word processing encourages *rethinking* and *revision.* However there is little evidence word processing enhances thinking. Carolyn Mullins (1988), for example, found that an experimental group using word processors did not differ significantly from a control group using manual writing tools.[24] William Snizek studied university scientists and engineers, finding that word processing and other microcomputing was associated with increased family tensions over time spent microcomputing in the home and in the office, with devolving clerical work onto faculty, and with difficulty in reaching closure on manuscripts (capacity for easy multiple revisions becomes expectation of multiple revisions) (Snizek, 1987).[25]

While word processing *can* improve writing by making revision easier, it tends toward the efficiencies of editing corrections. Effectiveness requires challenging the writer to revise not in the sense of copy editing but in the sense of rethinking and reorganizing. There is nothing inherent in the nature of word processing which does this. There is some evidence that word processing increases enjoyment of the writing process (Georgas, 1984; Naiman, 1985). If the dysfunctional effects predicted by Lyman are not likely to materialize, neither are improvements in the writing of graduate students and faculty. It would be a mistake to look to word processing as a solution to the issue of effectiveness in writing, though it does contribute to efficiency.

Word processing is used here as an illustration because it is a familiar one thought to have strong productivity effects. However, in many settings the introduction of word processors does not reduce the size of support staff and may even increase it. Word processing does not necessarily relate to any particular organizational goal such as labor savings, improved written content, or improved effect of what is written on the recipient of word processed materials. Both positive and negative effects are possible in any given setting, ranging from vast improvements in information retrieval to vast waste of organizational resources in increased document-passing. However, word processing is most likely to be effective when it is related to clear management goals, fits in with the style of those using it, comes with motivational incentives for users, operates under a cost containment strategy, is supported by human resource development efforts, and in general addresses the several obstacles to IT productivity discussed in this section.

Conclusion: Computing, Efficiency, and Effectiveness

> Fifteen years and billions of dollars into the computer revolution, a debate still surrounds one key question: Has the huge investment in computers paid off? Some business observers have answered with a resounding "No," a conclusion they say is evidenced by the government's economic statistics, which seem to provide no support to the theory that increased spending on computer technology results in improved productivity.—Karon, 1987a: 64

Several years later, nothing much has happened to diminish Paul Karon's questions about IT investment and productivity payoffs. In her book *Infotrends* (1993: xiii), Jessica Keyes notes "Technology does not necessarity beget competitive advantage any more than painting a canvas begets a Van Gogh." Support for across-the-board blanket investments in IT has given way to mangerial insistence on selective investment. If a selected IT investment is to be justified there must be a measurable value added resulting from the activities of the data processing unit.[26]The early benefits of giving word processors to secretaries or spreadsheets to financial managers were so obvious the evaluation issue did not seem relevant. Later investments in other areas where effects are more difficult to analyze, however, have brought the evaluation issue to the fore. Increasingly, cost justifications are required for IS projects, particularly in the private sector (Weil, 1988; Scheier, 1989a). However, all too often data processing units are so swamped with day-to-day activities that there is no time for gathering the data needed to justify their own budgets.

Although obtaining productivity information is difficult, management still needs to have an idea of the ballpark in which it is playing when it comes to IS investment. Costs of a single personal computer workstation, for example, include not only the equipment but also hooking the station into a network, purchase of software, training costs, and maintenance costs, to name a few factors. A 1984 study by brokerage firm Lehman Hutton found the first-year costs for each PC averaged $12,000 - far more than the costs of the computer itself. Management consultants Nolan, Norton, and Co., estimate the average to be $18,000.[27] Moreover, some analyses suggest that perhaps as little as only half of installed computers are actually put to useful work, further tilting the cost-benefit ratio in the wrong direction (Menkus, 1987: 49).

It is entirely possible for an agency or company to make huge investments in IS without fully realizing the magnitudes involved. This is because information technology expenditures, particularly for personal computers, are often decentralized to the department or field office level. From a top management viewpoint there may never by a total cost figure presented in the budget the CEO sees. Moreover, training and maintenance costs may never be calculated specifically for IS functions. These large costs may also remain hidden from top management. Time costs of personnel are also rarely investigated, allowing possible excessive preoccupation with computing for its own sake, refining desktop publishing layouts unnecessarily, using high-cost executives as computer technician trouble-shooters, and other wastes of human resource investment.

While many organizations do an annual inventory of computer equipment, this is from an asset viewpoint. Few ever seek to measure what the equipment is used for, much less measure the value added in relation to total cost. Other "hidden" costs such as electricity are almost always ignored. Often investments in IS are made to "stay on the cutting edge" and acquire prestige rather than to go with appropriate technology justified on a cost effectiveness basis (Meyer and Boone, 1987).

A common underlying problem associated with IS inefficiencies is the common practice of making information services a "free good" rather than maintaining an internal market through user charges. When the data processing unit was part of the accounting department, as was often the case in the early days of computing, service charges to users of computer accounting services were common. In contrast, when information centers proliferated in the mid 1980s, most services were "free" to end users. Computer services as a free good encourages abuse and waste (e.g., use of office computers for video gaming: Levy, 1984, 34-37). However, user charges may discourage use and diffusion of new technology, undercutting the purpose of IS initiatives. By the late 1980s, many information centers were reappraising the merits of user charges and considering at least nominal fees (Sommer, 1988a: 38) as increasing numbers of top managers refused simply to assume that investment in computing was inherently cost-effective.

Finally, of course, management information systems cannot make organizations more productive if they are not used. There is an astonishing gap between what IS is capable of doing in the realm of productivity and what actually gets done. For example, a 1987 Government Accounting Office study centering on the Reagan administration's "Reform `88" plan to consolidate federal financial systems found that federal agencies were very slow to take advantage of existing computerized audit tools (GAO, 1987a)—even though follow-up with such systems would have far more than paid for itself in recaptured savings. Utilization of sunk IS investment requires yet more investment—in people. The above-cited study of computing in the insurance industry, for instance, found that the most productive firms spent aggressively on the personnel side of the equation, in training, in applications programming, and in support of end users.

Probably the most common overall conclusion about productivity is summed up in a report on productivity effects of the billions of federal dollars poured into governmental computing. "The old reports get done faster," Olsen (1992: 1) wrote, "but managers keep asking for new reports and better reports than were possible before." It is difficult to demonstrate that there have been productivity gains in the traditional definition of ratio of dollars invested to value of goods and services produced. During the 1982-1990 period, when government invested billions in microcomputers and local area networks, government output grew at a rate of only 0.8% per year according to the Bureau of Labor Statistics (Olsen, 1992: 86). This was significantly lower than the rate in the 1967-1982 period. However, traditional productivity measures reflect changes arising from many causes and fail to measure many quality and service effects of computing. Most agencies argue computing investment has been very productive in spite of the difficulty of measuring productivity effects.

Obvious automation gains such as transaction processing (e.g., payroll) and word processing are now almost universally established. Full use of information systems tools in the future increasingly requires reshaping core organizational processes, not just automating pre-existing business practices (Davis and Davidson, 1991). For instance, Lincoln National Corporation, the nation's seventh-largest insurance holding company, began in 1989 to install the IBM *ImagePlus* system in the expectation that claims adjusters' productivity would be increased 20% to 40%. In 1991 they quietly killed the project when productivity gains failed to materialize. They concluded that to meet their productivity goals they would have had to re-engineer claims processing to eliminate paper altogether, not just use image processing to move paper (Krass, 1991c: 37).

The strategic use of information requires that management understand the cost effectiveness of information technology investments. As one analyst noted, "Though PCs are the biggest capital asset at many companies, few firms are tracking these expenditures". The result can be a rude awakening and cause an anti-IT backlash when huge cumulative costs eventually become an organizational issue (Zarley, 1988c: 41). Rather than allow such crises to follow their

Figure 11: IT Investment: It's Not How Much, It's How Management Uses It

Computers in and of themselves are tools. The existence of tools does not guarantee productivity. The question is not whether computer investment leads to productivity but rather whether management policies have used computer tools productively.

Hospital information systems provide an illustration. Until 1984 most hospitals had, in essence, two independent computer systems—one for billing and one for patient diagnostic information. The former was used by the business office and the latter by the medical staff.

After 1984, however, health care computing changed. That was the year in which the Health Care Financing Administration (HCFA) established DRG (diagnosis-related groups) funding.

Under the new plan, hospitals received payments based on the diagnosis, pocketing as profit (or absorbing as loss) the difference between the payment rate for the diagnosis and the hospital's cost for treatment. Suddenly hospitals had to integrate their business and clinical records, enabling a sophisticated form of performance accounting which can track costs in relation to medical functions.

The new systems are generally acknowledged to be far superior to the old in allowing hospital managers and their governmental regulators to make intelligent decisions to control costs and improve productivity.

However, it was not computer investment per se but rather the way computer tools were used that led to increased productivity (Traska, 1988; Desmond, 1990).

Like any tool, abuses can set in to erode productivity gains, as in the perception that hospitals have tended to give a higher proportion of high-payment diagnoses since the advent of DRG funding, simply to obtain greater remuneration (Dimborg, 1988).

course there is a need for justifying IS investments as they are made. Former Harvard Business School professor Stan Davis warns, however, against assessing IT projects for short-run cost savings because their primary value is often long-term information advantage (Davis and Davidson, 1991; *Government Computer News*, 1992b).

A similar point is made by Rothschild (1993), who notes that it took two decades before Thomas Edison's invention of the light bulb in 1879 and the first electric lighting of an entire city at the Paris Exposition of 1900. Likewise, he argues, it will take years for computing to overthrow the inefficient organizational designs by which workers were co-located in urban office towers. Eventually electronic mail, teleconferencing, and other technologies like fax will

Figure 12: Strategic Initiatives for Organizational Transformation

In 1993 the Program for Strategic Computing and Telecommunications in the Public Sector, part of Harvard University's John F. Kennedy School of Government, organized its 1993 national conference around five aopproaches to utilizing the strategic potential of information technologies.

1. Redesigning client services
American Airlines' Sabre reservation service; welfare ATM networks in the public sector.

2. Redesigning communications patterns
E-mail and voice mail in multi-national construction firms or in political campaigns.

3. Redistributing knowledge
Expert systems for financial investments or for enviornmental permitting in the public sector.

4. Using databases to add value, not just cut costs compared to manual methods
Mailing list segmentation in marketing or case management tools in the public sector.

5. Changing the internal culture of the organization
Redesigning information systems for end-user computing in the public or private sectors.

The conference organizers emphasized that each of these strategic applications fundamentally reshaped how an organization relates to its employees, clients, and other groups. Each committed the organization to transformational change.

remove today's barriers to interpersonal communication, unleashing a true revolution in productivity — the main gains for which come from rendering middle management functions unneeded. That is, Rothschild argues, the organizational transformations predicted by computing may yet come, but on a slower schedule than early enthusiasts believed.

Advocating changes like purging middle management, dispersing the central office, or eliminating paper is "thinking the unthinkable" for many managers. Organizational factors are critical to implementation of new information technology and frequently call for just such changes in organizational structure (Rocheleau, 1988). Often full strategic use of IS requires major organizational restructuring (McFarlan and McKenney, 1983b). Richard Walton, a Harvard Business School professor and author of *Up and Running: Integrating Information Technology and the Organization* (1989), calls attention to an MIT study of five auto assembly plants with different mixes of technology and organizational innovation. The plant with advanced technology but low innovation was no more productive than the traditional low-tech plant.

Achieving substantial productivity gains through information technology investment now often requires not only investment itself but also extensive organizational reforms. Change at the heart of the way an organization works requires sociotechnical approaches to organizational development, not mere technological planning. This topic is all the more important since, as IS leaders like John Scully, head of Apple Computer, point out, "the most significant productivity gains will come from putting computers as tools into the hands of the non-experts"—that is, into the hands of all organizational employees, not just IS staff (Fredell, 1988b: 82).

When there is discussion of the role of information technology and global competition, debate is apt to be cast in terms of whether America should or should not launch some sort of massive "Manhattan Project" or "Marshall Plan" to subsidize research and development of computer-related projects. Some have even proposed subsidy of existing efforts, as in calls to come to the aid of the floundering IBM Corporation after its stock values dramatically fell to half their former value in 1992. Although no truly massive effort has yet been undertaken, present initiatives such as the National Science Foundation's "grand challenge" multi-million dollar projects are traditional research grants in areas such as development of computational models in molecular biology.[28] The Commerce Department's Advanced Technology Program (ATP) likewise spent $68 million in 1993 for technology research. A broader effort is the High Performance Computer Act, which seeks to put in place a high-speed data transmission infrastructure linking academic, governmental, and other researchers.

What tends not to figure prominently in the discussion of information technology investment and global competition is precisely what the evidence on computing and productivity shows to be most important— organizational change. The lesson that emerges from examination of this evidence is that while IT investment sometimes has great payoffs, these success stories are not a good way to summarize the overall picture. There are serious questions about the likelihood that IT investment will lead to fundamental improvements in either organizational or national productivity.

What needs to be prominent in discussions of global competition is a recognition that the proper question is not whether to invest or not invest in information technology. Rather the critical question is, 'Under what circumstances is IT investment most likely to achieve the desired results?" Numerous success factors for information systems projects were outlined in the concluding section of the previous chapter. Beyond these particular factors, however, is the argument that the fundamental core of an IT investment strategy must go beyond automating existing work practices. This is particularly true of transnational firms, where it has been found that what is a good information system in operations in one country may be very inappropriate in another (Alter, 1992; Ein-Dor, Segev, and Orgad, 1993).[29]

To yield strategic advantage IT investment strategy must focus on the use of computing and telecommunications to transform the nature of work and the structure of organizations. For instance, Harvard University's 1993 national conference on "Identifying Strategic Opportunities for Information Technologies in the Public Sector" identified five such strategic initiatives (see Figure 7-12). Although this view has gained increasing acceptance and is perhaps today dominant among management analysts, structural change is something unthinkable for most chief executives. It is certainly not something government officials feel comfortable with as a focus for national policy. It is not in the interest of the information industry either.

Process re-engineering, a management technique which has become popular in the early 1990s, is closely allied with this perspective (Hammer and Champy, 1993). Re-engineering organizations involves such concepts as using advanced technology to handle information in new ways which eliminate "buffer" and "handoff" positions typical of traditional sequential processes where Clerk A turns paperwork over to Clerk B, who does more on it before passing it off to Clerk C, and so on. An example of a process re-engineering reform is the state of Oregon's replacement of its mail-based RFP (request for proposals) purchasing system with an on-line one. The result eliminate 15 jobs of clerks who had stuffed envelopes and updated mailing databases while effectiveness increased due to greater vendor access to RFP information (Martin, 1993). Process re-engineering is not limited to computing but its implementation is frequently computer-related. As a management technique it is based on the belief that the productivity benefits of technology require a radical transformation in organizational processes.

A focus on organizational transformation requires an acceptance of the fundamentally political nature of information systems and that acceptance does not come easily. Statements in support of national information technology policy systematically avoid its political and even management dimensions. This is true, for instance, of the "Computing the Future" statement of the Computer Science and Telecommunications Board of the National Research Council (NRC), funded by NSF and the Association for Computer Machinery (Hartmanis, 1992). The NRC policy statement endorsed infrastructure initiatives like the High Performance Computing and Communications Act and called for greater federal funding of computer science. However, notable in its absence was any discussion of management and organizational transformation. Rather the assumption is that massively more investment in information technology will in itself serve American strategic needs for global competition in the next century.

As a result it is therefore hardly surprising that national information technology policy, such as it is, focuses on the hardware of creating "information highways". Likewise the Civilian Technology Corporation (CTS) bill before Congress in 1993 would direct $5 billion for technology research. Quite apart from the "extreme danger of pork barrel politics" admitted even by some advocates of this type of national technology policy (Higgins, 1993: 7), what is really the danger is missing a focus on changing how managers and organizations use information technology.[30] Unfortunately, that is where the payoff lies. A national policy which fails to place changing the information culture and structure of organizations foremost is apt to be a policy which fails to place America in the strategic economic position to which it aspires in the twenty-first century.

ENDNOTES

[1] For instance, even when it is successful, information technology investment can lead to negative consequences, as Michael Vitale (1986) noted in his article, "The growing risks of information systems success". Vitale matched five "areas of opportunity" with five corresponding "catastrophes". The opportunity to change the basis of competition, as through automated inventories, can lead to the catastrophe of imitation by better-funded competitors who can outdo the original innovative organization. The opportunity to create entry barriers in the form of large IT investments required for start-up can backfire if competitors have unused IT capacity, as in the case of national hotel chains threatening to get into the telephone business. The opportunity to gain strategic advantage may, as in the case of American Airlines' reservation system, lead to efforts to regulate the industry to restore competition. The opportunity to tie in closely with clients, as Federal Express did by installing faxes for customers, can lead to customers gaining the capacity to do without the original innovating organization -- in this case buying their own fax technology not tied to Federal Express. The fifth opportunity to provide more customer services can backfire too, as when a NYC banking system to switch funds to higher-interest accounts more easily led to customers doing just that, reducing bank profits.

[2] For an overview of global competition in 11 American industries, see GAO (1992e).

[3] Groupe Bulle, among other things, owns the Zenith Computer Corporation in this country.

[4] Brazil provides another example of failed national IT industrial policy. Brazilian telecommunications legislation so restricted transborder data flow that businessmen had diskettes confiscated on international flights. Nationalist legislation required all datasets to be kept, at least in archival backups, physically within Brazil, and government approval was needed prior to installing or purchasing any data processing system. This legislation greatly impeded global data communications and led to Brazil's increasing isolation within an increasingly global economic world. Likewise, Brazilian "Law of Similars" legislation designed to force purchase of locally-produced microcomputers and operating systems led to a protected industry with inferior products which could not compete in world markets (Conger, 1993).

[5] Unger (1987) argues that Japanese interest in AI is motivated less by international competitive advantage than by the need to overcome their cultural disadvantage due to the difficulty of computerizing data entry using the complex mixture of Chinese and syllabic characters that comprise the Japanese language.

[6] This was noted by the incoming Clinton administration in December, 1992, noting that IBM Corporation's decision to cut back on R&D was "exactly what we don't want" (ABC World New, 12/16/92).

[7] An informative and interesting debate over MITI and Japanese industrial policy by

leading writers is found in the "Letters" section of *Policy Review*, No, 65 (Summer, 1993): 84-95.

[8] Apple's CEO John Sculley, for instance, envisions such a network as the infrastructure needed to sell home computers which would use voice rather than keyboard commands to answer phone calls, schedule appointments, and research information (Associate Press, 1992). Others fear that well-funded businesses will find little problem with increasing user fees, at the same time squeezing out non-profit users.

[9] Publicists for NREN paint a bright picture of its benefits. Schwartz (1992: 56) writes that after its establishment, "The Everyman, and his sister, the physicist, will be able to dip into anything from the stacks of Harvard Yard to the video archives of the Home Shopping Network." But in fact communications costs money and the government is unlikely to make NREN a free good. Beyond the issue of user fees, the enormous cost of carrying computer cable to faculty and student desktops is beyond the means of many colleges, virtually assuring that there will be great inequities in benefits under the National Research and Education Network (Wilson, 1991b). Are regulations and subsidies needed to rectify inequity or is the marketplace the most effective allocator of communications services? The Electronic Frontier Foundation (EFF), a major public interest group seeking public access, fears that an exclusive focus on a national fiber optic network such as NREN "could break the country into information haves and have-nots" (Webb, 1992: 20). Instead EFF favors emphasis on wedding ISDN (integrated services digital network) technology with existing copper phone lines to provide multimedia services to household phone subscribers.

[10] Hart (1992) argues that international competitiveness in the semiconductor and in other industries was advanced by the business-state alliance in Japan and the labor-state alliance in West Germany, whereas competitiveness has been hurt in nations in which one actor is dominant (business in the US, labor in the UK, and the state in France). Attempts to assert industrial policy in the US are seen as a threat by American business rather than as a desirable effort to establish a partnership.

[11] Needs to assure compatibility of transmissions is a significant force for electronic communications regulation and self-regulation. OSI (Open Systems Interconnect) is a set of international standards for telecommunication, particularly important to governments and large corporations which engage in telecommunications in volume. OSI is credited, for example, with making possible large network systems such as the Air Force's ULANA system. As of 1989 telecommunications with Europe required modems capable of meeting separate European communications standards. Nonetheless, with a suitable modem anyone who could connect to the Telenet or Tymnet packet-switch networks available in all sizable communities in the U.S., could also connect to any of Europe's national packet networks via the International Packet Switching System (IPSS). It is anticipated, however, that the various national networks will be seamlessly connected to InfoNet, an international carrier with equity participation by the various national networks, by the proposed lowering of European trade barriers in 1992 (Page, 1989).

The standards issue also involves assurances of service quality. For instance, should telecommunications companies have to meet certain criteria about transmission error rates or provide backup capacities so traffic will not be lost when outages occur? Currently the Federal Communications Commission (FCC) takes the view that marketplace competition combined with current regulations are adequate to assure quality. Other analysts such as Moir (1991) fear that users have no existing remedy when they encounter information traffic problems.

[12] Computer-related technologies for data storage, retrieval, and transmission can yield enormous savings in many settings. For instance, the United Services Automobile Association of San Antonio, TX, saved $750,000 annually by replacing its 40,000 square foot file cabinet office area with a system in which all incoming mail was stored on optical discs (*PC Computing*, 1989a: 68). Costing in 1989 from $4,000 to $45,000, optical imaging systems

allows users to access enormous amounts of data almost instantly, greatly reducing costs of information retrieval from file cabinets as well as increasing data integrity. The American Red Cross, for instance, uses an imaging system to store photos, fingerprints, birth certificates, letters, and other information on missing persons. The U. S. Navy uses computer imaging to maintain a library on 500,000 ship parts and supplies. Arthur Young uses optical imaging to scan trial documents, then later retrieve them while preparing briefs or even display them by projection for an entire courtroom to see; the firm expects to recover its $700,000 investment in a year and a half, mostly through reduced photocopying expenses.

[13] A similar system is Apollo by United Airlines.

[14] King, Danziger, Dunkle, and Kraemer (1992), also studying local governments, found that microcomputer-using managers reported the greatest overall increases in job effectiveness compared to mainframe users and managers who used computers only indirectly. But these authors also found that there were sound reasons why managers should delegate much 'hands-on' computer use to subordinates and that the image of the 'knowledge executive' as a hands-on user was overrated. Thus, survey research in local government does suggest productivity gains but it also suggests certain limitations and qualifications to the simple equation of "the more IS, the more productivity".

[15] Although low in productivity compared to other industries, banking productivity in the 1980s grew at about 2% per year compared to .25% annually in the 1973-79 period (Baily, 1989: 139). One can argue this corresponds, very roughly, to the rise of banking investment in IS. During the 1980s, the service industry capital investment in hardware and software was about $9,000 per employee and the rate of productivity increase was a minimal .2% annually, compared to 5% annually in manufacturing, where IT investment was less than half as much.

[16] Electronic mail typically reduces per-message costs but overall communications costs rise within the organization, often sharply. While electronic mail gives better service than conventional mail, it may not be obvious that the investment it requires leads to increased profits to pay for it.

[17] A Canadian study of five banks found investment in information technology corresponded to a period of slight increase of profitability. However, the main effect of IS investment was input substitution (e.g., displacing tellers with ATMs) with no large productivity effects (Parsons, 1990).

[18] Official measures of productivity often reflect goal-setting problems. For instance, the productivity of an airline might be measured in terms of return on investment (e.g., number of passengers per $100,000 invested). Yet such economic indicators may ignore major improvements in goal-achievement in other areas, such as passenger satisfaction. American Airlines' famed Sabre reservation system, which has spread to other airlines, set a new standard for booking tickets quickly and conveniently. Today it is virtually unimaginable to think of a reservation system which did not employ Sabre technology or some variation. American Airlines soon lost its ability to seek competitive advantage by having its Sabre system list AA flights first (AA hoped travel agents wouldn't bother looking lower on the listings for competitors' flights). Competing airlines were able to convince the courts this was an unfair trade practice and courts ordered American Airlines to randomize the order of airline listings. Moreover, Sabre may not have added a single passenger to the airlines industry and thus may not be counted as having contributed to the productivity of that industry.

[19] Peter Drucker (1992a: 10; 1992b), a leading management analyst, notes that information work requires a new, goal-oriented approach to productivity measurement. He writes, "In making and moving things the focus in increasing productivity is on work. In knowledge and service work it has to be on performance. Thus increasing productivity in knowledge and service work requires thinking through into which category of performance a given job belongs. Only then do we know what needs to be analyzed, what needs to be improved, what needs to be changed. For only then do we know what productivity means in a specific

knowledge or service job." That is, measurement of productivity in knowledge jobs depends on specification of goals and performance expectations related to them.

[20] As another example of the political nature of defining statistical indicators, consider the 1984-7 revision of the Standard Industrial Codes (SIC). SIC classify businesses into categories about which the government collects data, such as the County Business Patterns census. A participant to the process of revision noted, "The revised SIC reflects a long series of compromises" (Schmitt and Rossetti, 1987: 18). Older agencies opposed change in order to minimize disruption of long-standing time series. New agencies pressed to separate out new industries under their aegis, such as telecommunications. Consumer groups pressed for smaller industry groupings across the board so they might obtain more detailed information for purposes of lobbying. Different constituencies support different goals and what is "productive" for one group may be "counter-productive" for another.

[21] Piturro recommends using productivity software to measure performance at the work group, not individual, level and to provide long-term trend feedback rather than daily output monitoring.

[22] The eight factors discussed by Ginzberg and Ariav are these:

1. how structured the task is
2. the level of the task
3. the phase of the decision process
4. the functional area of the decision
5. the modes of interaction with the user
6. the nature of the user community
7. the relationship to other computer systems
8. the level of support for the system.

[23] Peter Lyman interviewed 155 Stanford University humanities faculty and discerned such alleged trends associated with word processing as a shift from the paragraph to the sentence as a unit of meaning, a shift from emphasis on interpretation to emphasis on information, and a shift from craftsmanship to technique in scholarly writing. Though no follow-up study was done, Lyman's findings probably reflected only a temporary artifact. There are humanistic and technical camps among scholars. The former were probably slower to adopt word processing. However, by now word processing is nearly universal and it is doubtful that the humanists interviewed by Lyman in 1984 would now insist that abandonment of the pencil in favor of the word processor diminished their sense of craftsmanship or their belief in the primacy of interpretive writing over descriptive information. James N. Danziger (1988), for instance, later surveyed 42 social science faculty and found microcomputer use to average 24 hours a week, mostly word processing, resulting in perceptions of modest improvements in the quantity and quality of written work, not the radical transformation of social science work patterns earlier predicted by some.

Early phases of computerization frequently arouse fears of dehumanization and alienation of work. In the case of word processing, Peter Lyman discerned a shift from interpretive craftsmanship to mere techniques of information retrieval, diminishing the status and authority of the writer. Lyman (1982), in earlier work, set forth a moral basis for his critique of social science reason as a cloak for professional-technical hegemony. Reason, Lyman argued, is not only a mode of thought but also a social relation of domination and subordination. In this view, the technical rationality of social science, especially the computerized variety, is an "angry" mode of discourse that creates social control by imposing shame on those not partaking of its methods. That anger is the pathos of social science is indicated by its transformation of people into things by devaluing experience and discourse in favor of data and technical rationality. Rens (1984) has carried similar views even further, superseding Marxist emphasis on control of the means of production with a new world view of dialectic determinism based on control over the means of communication, of which computerized information is emerging as the leading form.

These phenomenologists seem to have scholars selecting sides in a struggle of profound proportions when they choose to use a word processor. Ironically, Marxist scholars like Siegel (1986) agree with leading students of the social impacts of computing such as Kraemer, Dickhoven, Tierney, and King (1987) that no such hegemonic struggle is involved. In the Marxist view, computing and microcomputing are tools, like typing. Although the ruling class has larger and more sophisticated tools, whether computers or printing presses, those who oppose them also use the same tools to put out newsletters, generate mailing lists, edit radical magazines, assist the Marxist government of Nicaragua with data processing, and otherwise oppose the powers-that-be.

[24] Of course, as Mullins acknowledges, word processing is now so widespread such experiments may be undermined because of difficulties in establishing a true control group.

[25] In spite of these dysfunctions, Snizek also found scientists reported that microcomputing increased their productivity.

[26] In their book *The Information Edge* (1987), Meyer and Boone have presented many case examples of value added measurement. They cite its importance as part of obtaining top management recognition of information as a strategic resource worth investment. Some authors such as Venner (1988) have developed the concept of the "software portfolio" to encourage management to think of investments in software analogously to any other form of investment. However, a major limitation comes from information managers themselves. Even chief information officers (CIOs) are apt to look inward toward company/agency managers and staff as clients, whereas chief executive officers (CEOs) tend to look outward to focus on customers and suppliers (Pepper, 1991: 36). This aspect of "information culture" certainly is not inevitable but it is commonplace and frustrates true strategic planning with regard to information resources.

[27] Although computer costs have tended to decline, users have also tended to add more option boards and buy more kinds of software (needing more training and maintenance) so there has not been a corresponding decline in costs per station (see Zarley, 1988c: 41).

[28] The NSF "grand challenge" projects for 1992-1997 support computer models, algorithms, and software for high performance computing systems which are consistent with the goals of the federal High Performance Computing and Communications program. The projects receiving funding included The High Performance Computing for Learning Project, Massachusetts Institute of Technology; High Performance Computational Methods for Coupled Field Problems and GAFD Turbulence, University of Colorado at Boulder; A Distributed Computational System for Large Scale Environmental Modeling (chemistry), Carnegie Mellon University; and Computational Biomolecular Design, University of Houston.

[29] Alter discusses global operations of Toys 'R Us as a major example of this point.

[30] The Institute for Information Studies, a joint program of Northern Telecom Inc. and the Aspen Institute, warned against premature implementation of vast IT infrastructure projects. The Institute found claims that such investments would increase productivity and U.S. international competitiveness were unprovable. The Institute called for greater focus on human resource investment to close the "knowledge gap" between the computer literate and the computer illiterate, citing this as having potentially more payoff than direct investments in technology alone (Caldwell, 1993a: 23).

CHAPTER VIII

Public Policy for Information Technology

The status of information as a public good rather than solely as a private one provides the philosophical underpinning for public policy about information technology (IT). This chapter examines the theory that information is a public good. The chapter also looks at some empirical findings about the differences between handling information policy through public channels as opposed to through the private government of corporations and associations. After establishing the premise that information technology is a valid subject for public policy, two other subjects are treated in this chapter. The first is the nature and history of information policy planning in government agencies. The second focuses on the corresponding trends in public legislation. A summary section concludes by relating public policy for information technology to the theme of this book: how information technology is fundamentally political in nature.

Information as a Public Good

If information systems have a large public component then it is legitimate to believe they should be subject to public policy. But what is "public"? Do information systems have enough "publicness" to warrant government regulation? Before we can answer these questions with regard to information systems we need to consider our definition of terms.

In common terminology what is public *is* what is governmental. In reality, however, when one comes to classify things on a private sector/governmental sector basis one often finds that this dichotomy does not serve analysis well. Many scholars have criticized defining publicness solely on the basis of governmental legal ownership.[1] Such definitions ignore political influences on privately owned organizations, efforts to privatize governmental functions, and organizations which do not fall neatly under the labels of "governmental" or "private".[2] Research development laboratories, for instance, technically are either private or governmental but over the past few decades the clear distinction between public and private has become blurred.

Analysts such as Crow (1985; Emmert and Crow, 1988) have instead turned to other definitions of publicness that have to do with the relative levels of governmental and market influence. Likewise, Coursey and Bozeman (1990) have found that publicness as measured by degree of external political control accounts for organizational differences beyond those attributable to simple legal ownership (governmental or private). This perspective underlies the title of Bozeman's 1987 work, *All Organizations Are Public* and may be referred to as an environmental definition of publicness:[3] "Publicness is a dimension that varies from total market influence (zero publicness) to total political influence (pure publicness) over the environment defining the organization's activities (see Bozeman, 1984, building on the political economy approach of Wamsley and Zald, 1973). This dimensional aspect of publicness is a realistic and important conceptual extension of public goods theory, which traditionally has treated publicness unrealistically as a dichotomy determined by legal ownership.[4]

Public Goods Theory

The basic theory of public goods is straight-forward. Markets have difficulty distributing goods when achieving excludability is difficult. Excludability has to do with situations in which consumption cannot be limited to those meeting the vendor's terms, as in the classic case of lighthouses. Markets also have difficulty when subtractibility is low. Subtractibility relates to situations where one individual's consumption of the goods, nonetheless, leaves the goods intact for the next consumer, as in the case of weather forecasts. In public goods theory, private goods tend to be consumed subtractibly on an excludable basis (e.g., automobiles) while public goods are consumed jointly on a non-excludable basis (e.g., efforts to control organized crime) (Ostrom and Ostrom, 1977).

Defense is a public good because defense expenditures protect all Americans, not just selected individuals. If selected individuals were to pay for defense and others not, all would be protected anyway because of the collective nature of consumption of defense services. Public goods theory carries the normative suggestion that political influence should be greatest and market influence least to the extent that goods are public rather than private. Other examples of public goods are earthquake forecasts, pollution control, and mosquito abatement.

Pure public goods such as defense cannot be divided into marketable portions because consumption is almost entirely collective. Pure public goods therefore have a 'free rider' effect: if purchased privately, the rational median voter would not choose to expend funds on the public good because the benefit will be conferred anyway. To take a private sector example, collective bargaining representation confers collective benefits on entire work groups. Rational workers have no incentive to pay union dues since they will be represented anyway. The publicness of collective bargaining justifies political influence such as regulations forcing employees to pay dues in order to avoid free riders.

However, most goods are not purely public or purely private. Classic public goods theory usually spoke in terms of such a dichotomy, but the "publicness" of most goods is dimensional, not dichotomous. That is, many goods, including major information systems, are mixed goods with both public goods and private goods aspects. For instance, in the case of information systems, for instance, impacts of IS on privacy rights are an important public goods aspect. At the same time, information is routinely marketed as a private goods commodity, much like soap or automobiles.

Special problems arise when goods are mixed rather than being purely public or purely private. Consider another mixed good, education, as provided by a hypothetical economy in which that service is distributed solely on a market basis. Public policy discussion centers on the question of whether the education service levels provided by the sum of individual market decisions are the same as what would occur if the services were provided publicly. Ordinarily there will be a difference or gap between privatized service patterns and public.

Mixed goods are characterized by a gap (the "publicness surplus" between service levels when distributed by market economics and service levels when distributed by public policies (see Figure 8-1). In the case of education, for instance, a pure market approach might yield lower overall levels of educational service, adversely affect equity by increasing choices for the affluent while restricting choices for the poor. Likewise privatization might displace generalist curricula with occupational curricula more closely tied to immediate payoffs. In the recreational area it is similarly commonly assumed that state parks and the like have benefits to the commonweal which transcend uses by fee-payers. In other areas, such as public libraries, a pure market approach might find the level of demand inadequate to support a

Figure 1: The Publicness Surplus

There is a surplus associated with publicness in the consumption of mixed goods.

Consider a hypothetical economy which distributes a public or partially public good on a private basis. Then consider an otherwise identical economy which distributes the good on a public consumption basis.

The publicness surplus is the amount that would have to be added to the hypothetical (first) economy if all of its members are to be as well off as they would be in the second economy under which they are provided with public goods.

Distributive equity suggests all agents in the economy should have equal claim on the publicness surplus as well as on the public good itself.

Some have sought to deal with distributive justice through systems which impose higher taxes on those who value the public good more highly (Lindahl systems). However, under such systems the surplus from publicness is appropriated privately and fails to be equitably distributed in Lindahl equilibria. Instead, an income redistribution policy is necessary to optimize equity under these conditions (Otsuki, 1992).

That is, when a publicness surplus exists, distributive equity cannot be achieved without a public policy involving redistribution of resources through regulation, taxation, or other public policies.

purely fee-based service altogether, as has been found by numerous public transportation companies which have experimented with a self-supporting fee basis. In the area of information access, the surplus is the amount that would have to be provided in the form of income redistribution to enable all citizens to be as well off as they would be under an economy in which information access were provided publicly. A privatized information access culture has appropriated the publicness surplus to private organizations, the profitability of which may be contingent on perpetuating distributive injustice.

Those goods and services which achieve their optimal distribution solely through market forces should be and usually are private. Those that require subsidy, taxation, or regulation to achieve their optimal allocation, in contrast, have a strong element of publicness. Indeed, the degree of taxation/subsidy deviation from marketplace equilibria is a standard measure of publicness in public goods theory (e.g., in education, see Wyckoff, 1982).[5] Considerable research has been done on optimization of distributive equity in public as well as private goods (e.g., Otsuki, 1992).[6]

Publicness Applied to Information Access

With public goods theory as background, how does the concept of "publicness" relate specifically to information systems? Information access is a mixed good. It is neither a purely public nor a wholly private good. Access can be linked to the consumption of particular users who may be charged fees like other private goods. However, information access is also a public good in the sense that public libraries are. That is, although particular units of information can be consumed individually and thus can be private goods, information usually is not subtractible (one person's use leaves information intact for the next user) and information access infrastructure taken as a whole is consumed collectively. For instance, credit bureaus may sell consumer information as a private good on a record by record basis but if the credit bureau has instituted privacy safeguard procedures normally these protect privacy regardless of payment or nonpayment of fees. Lack of subtractability and presence of collective consumption aspects bring information systems closer to public goods status. The larger and more information-inclusive the information system, the more it has an element of "publicness".

The collective aspects of information access are diffuse because they involve *social* impacts. For instance, one such aspect is the benefit to democratic values of assurance that the transactions of business and governmental organizations can be held to public scrutiny. The fundamental collective and therefore public aspect of information access is the essential role it plays not only in citizenship but also in lifelong education, whether occupational, avocational, social, or intrinsic. The telecommunications aspects of IS are associated with collective consumption of basic freedoms of expression and thus bear the same publicness as public utilities such as telephone systems. And, of course, publicness is also affected by the negative public goods aspect of information systems in their capacity to pose a threat to privacy rights.

Information systems and the access they provide are strongly imbued with publicness. At the same time IS services are mixed goods which can be decomposed into finite modules and marketed at a fee to end users. That is, IS access can be privatized. It is important to note that privatization does not make such services any the less public in nature. Privatizing information access systems does not remove their publicness nor make them any less subject to public policy debate than would privatizing national parks or public schools. What makes information access systems subject to public policy is their publicness in nature, not whether their present legal ownership is in the public or the private sector.

The normative aspects of the analysis of information access as a public good can be rephrased in the more traditional language of the "public interest". Robert MacIver, in *The Web of Government*, described the modern industrial polity in terms of conflicting interest groups. However, he argued that general welfare was not simply the brute force outcome of this conflict. Instead, he wrote, "government cannot afford to sit by while the disputants bring economic pressure to bear on one another...In the public interest it must devise whatever measures are expedient to prevent the disruption of vital services" (MacIver, [1947] 1963: 350). What is "vital" can be considered to go beyond simply avoiding potential service crises.

The courts have held that "Public interest means something in which the public, the community at large, has some pecuniary interest, or some interest by which their legal rights or liabilities are affected"

(*State v. Crochett*, 206 Pac 816, 817). That pecuniary interest is the publicness surplus. More broadly, the Supreme Court has held "Property does become clothed with a public interest when used in a manner to make it of public consequence, and affect the community at large...When...one devotes his property to a use in which the public has an interest, he...must submit to be controlled by the public for the common good" (*Munn v. Illinois*, 94 U.S. 113, 126). In this light, large-scale information access systems would seem to be developments of strong public consequence and community effect, opening the door to public control as, for example, through resource redistribution linked to public goods, whether rendered by a government agency or by a corporation.

Administering Public Goods through Private Government

That large-scale information systems are imbued with a strong public goods aspect does not mean that they need be administered through government regulation. In fact, many public goods (e.g., network television entertainment) are delivered commercially. However, mixed goods endowed with a strong element of publicness raise the need for governance, whether through literal public government or through the "private government" of corporations. The issue is not whether government is needed but only whether it is best constituted as private government or public government in each particular instance.[7]

The publicness of mixed goods calls for governance in the form of subsidies, taxation, and/or regulation. This governance may be provided publicly by government or through private organizations, in which case it may be labeled private government. The concept of private government has a long tradition in political analysis (e.g., Heclo and Wildavsky, 1974; Miller, 1976; Thompson, 1983). In particular, self-governing professions possess authority delegated by the state to prescribe and police rules pertaining to that profession. This authority is a form of private government which in other policy domains has focused attention on the internal political processes of the profession.

In medicine, law, and other professional areas, private government is the preferred form of governance in America, even over public goods matters. However, this preference is associated with certain tendencies. As noted by Tuohy (1976), the private government of self-governing professions has tended toward the establishment of property rights in their respective skills, be it the medical, legal, or other professions. Tuohy further notes that the tendency of private government to establish professional property rights has been challenged increasingly by governments. The rise of highly interdependent technologies is a major factor in tension with the medieval-like segmentation of professional property rights. Technological interdependence raises issues of cross-professional access to productive resources which may hitherto have been claimed as exclusive property rights. As will be discussed shortly, information systems management as a profession asserts private property rights, creating the same controversies.

Lulofs (1981), applying microeconomic price theory, argues that the rise of professional associations providing divisible public goods, as information systems do, centers on striving for market control. Specifically, the tendency of private professional associations is to seek strict delimitation of markets for separate professional services. Enforcement is often sought by government regulations creating professional property rights. The process tends toward the development of a professional market order characterized by limited freedom of price fixing and strict prohibition of competitive behavior.

That is, private government of public goods is associated with ordered competition between and within professional associations as a substitute for market competition. Through formal and informal codes of conduct the cost of deviant behavior is increased so that individual professionals are induced to adhere to market rules. In a mature professional market order, consumer preferences are influenced heavily by the characteristics of the market order, diminishing market responsiveness to clients. Other studies also show serious systemic problems arising from administering public goods through private governments alone (see Figure 8-2). Needless to say, this empirical tendency flies in the face of theories about the benefits of free markets.[8]

Compared to other professions, information systems is new to the game just described. However, there is little dispute that IS seeks to be a self-regulating profession highly interested in protection of private property rights (cf. ACM, 1992).[9] Indeed, "Honor property rights" is "Moral Imperitive" 1.5 in the ACM Code of Ethics (see

Figure 2: Aspects of Managing Public Goods through Private Governments

Findings of a doctoral study on publicness in 234 technology-related research and development organizations in various industrialized countries (Stephen Loveless, 1985):

1. Controlling for country, discipline, technology, and unit size, that political dependence of the unit was associated with increased external and professional control, increased external information sharing, innovativeness, and increased quality of output.

2. Private property rights were associated with increased control by the organizational leadership, proprietary rather than social goals and output, conflict, dissatisfaction, and emphasis on quantity rather than quality of output.

Findings of another doctoral dissertation by Schlesinger (1984) revealed there systematic and significant ownership-based differences in organizational behavior:

1. Compared to their for-profit counterparts, public and private nonprofit organizations deliver more services yielding community-wide benefits and are less likely to provide very low- quality services.

2. Moreover, nonprofit firms react more quickly to changing technology and decision-makers in nonproprietary organizations are more readily trusted by clients.

3. Schlesinger concluded that under certain conditions ownership-based interventions are preferable to other public policy options for reaching socially valued goals.

Appendix I). Through organizations such as the Information Industry Association (IIA), the IS community seeks vigorously to protect such rights and to limit governmental regulation and competition. Currently, IS as a profession is enjoying great success in going down the path of private government. However, it will not be immune to the very same forces which dictate the dynamic in other professional domains. The IS drive toward private government will initially strengthen private professional property rights in information access. In the long run, though, technology-driven cross-professional interdependence will generate needs for resource access, in turn bringing challenges to private government in information systems. In a dialectic process, public governance of information access will be reasserted so that professional property may be treated in a way which recognizes its inherent publicness.[10]

In summary, the ownership of information, never a well-defined area, has become far more controversial in recent years as a result of the rapid expansion of computing and related telecommunications in the last decade. These issues have emerged largely in systems owned by corporate entities during a politically conservative era in which property rights are being vigorously reasserted and the concept of the public interest is on the defensive. When ownership rights are ascendant over opposing public interests, corporate entities assume policy-making powers which substitute for public processes.

This section has attempted to show the relevance of the literature on publicness to the issue of information systems in a democratic society. Information systems and the services they provide may be seen as mixed goods, often imbued with several aspects of publicness. The analysis of such public goods suggests that professions associated with them follow relatively predictable patterns which may be summarized by the concept of private government. In carrying out regulation of the publicness of information systems as a mixed good and doing so under private aegis, a form of private government develops which is prone to a number of dysfunctional tendencies among which are the development of vested professional property rights and ordered markets. Drawing on concepts from public goods theory and the concept of publicness, this section has sought to set forth the normative basis for recasting public goods theory in terms of public impact rather than public ownership, and has sought to use this as a basis for analysis of issues pertaining to information access in a democratic society.

Summary: Information, Public Goods, and Public Policy

The productive base of the American economy is changing. Over a quarter century ago, Machlup (1962) calculated that the production of information formed about a third of the American gross national product. By 1978, the proportion was estimated to be half (Porat, 1978). In the aftermath of the "microcomputer revolution" of the 1979-1985 period, the U. S. Office of Technology Assessment (1988) estimated that two dollars out of every five spent on new plant and equipment in the United States was going into computing and telecommunications. These changes give credence to those who state that America has shifted from a manufacturing economy to being an "information society." Just as the advent of the manufacturing economy brought Progressive legislative controls over the means of production, so it is predicted that the coming of the information society will be associated with parallel struggles for legislative oversight of the means of information.

To this contention, some say "What struggle?" Information systems can seem the epitomy of dull management, devoid of policy issues. At the other extreme are those who see information systems technology as having everything to do with the most momentous struggles of our time. For instance, Joseph Weizenbaum, author of *Computer Power and Human Reason* (1976), held that computer science shouldn't be just about computational skills. Instead, he wrote, it should hold out "a vision of what is possible for a man or a woman to become" (Weizenbaum, 1991: 741). Other critical theorists hold that there must be a radical reconstruction of the technological base of modern society if humanity and nature are to achieve liberation (Feenberg, 1991).

The values and perspectives with which we approach information systems (IS) problems are at the core of the information culture which determines what IS does in the case of any given person, organization,

Figure 3: Information is Power

That information is power — and therefore is an appropriate topic for public policy-making—is sometimes more recognized in other societies than our own.

In the 1920s, Trotsky had proposed a telephone system for the USSR. Stalin is said to have replied, "I can imagine no greater instrument of counter-revolution in our time." Even today Russia has only one phone for every 10 citizens.

In the late 1980s, Soviet leader Gorbachev's "Glasnost" (openness) campaign promised to double the number of telephones, to introduce computers and database access at all levels of the economy, and from grade school to train the next generation to be computer literate.

In a society which had posted guards at copying machines to restrict access, the concept of open telecommunications networks was revolutionary (see Hines, 1988; Dizzard and Swensrud, 1987). Though perhaps in a less dramatic manner issues of power and control over information systems (IS) are nonetheless equally important to democratic societies like our own.

or country. In the case of information systems, these values and perspectives revolve around the debate over whether information is to be understood largely in terms of traditional property rights theory, with all that implies for ownership rights as against various public interests in information. As we have seen in this section, this normative debate can be discussed in terms of two concepts with long traditions in political theory: "publicness" and "private government". "Publicness" is important because it establishes information systems as being within the proper scope of governmental regulation. "Private government" is important because it addresses problems that arise when private organizations assume the function of regulating the public aspects of large-scale information systems.

Public policy for information resource management has come to public attention mainly in the form of the issue of cost over-run scandals.[11] However, the more important public policy issues surrounding information technology have to do with attempts to assert democratic (which is to say, political) control over the information bureaucracy and, to a lesser extent, over the information industry itself. The 1980s witnessed a significant change in the political relationship between the career civil service and the appointed level. In the decade from the mid-1970s to the mid-1980s, Schedule C civil service positions, those subject to political appointment, increased some 84%. In the same period federal employment in general increased only 44%. In addition, the creation of the Senior Executive Service (SES) allowed 10% of these top-level positions to be politically appointed, as well as about 500 PAS positions (those requiring Senate confirmation). Though this situation applied to all policy areas in government, IS career servants were inclined to view their area as one in which it was particularly inappropriate to appoint a departmental leadership lacking in technical qualifications (Brooks, 1987: 22). It is in this context that Congress and presidential administrations have sought to control IS.

Public Policy-Making for Information Technology: A Brief Legislative History

The beginnings of federal public policy on information systems matters may be traced to efforts to coordinate the war effort in the

1940s. In response to concerns over the wartime growth in bureaucracy, the Federal Reports Act of 1942 tried to address paperwork burdens, but it was never effectively implemented. However, the war brought great improvements in data gathering and retrieval. National income accounts were standardized. Surveys became a widespread government tool (Duncan and Chelton, 1978). Later, the wartime Central Statistical Bureau was upgraded during the 1950s, becoming the Office of Statistical Standards (OSS). Nonetheless, in spite of progress in data collection, major reform efforts in post-WWII period such as the Hoover Commissions of 1947 and 1953 did not even recognize the need for treating information as a management problem.

This changed in the 1960s. When Kennedy's "New Frontier" and Johnson's "Great Society" agendas focused concern over socioeconomic issues, a push was undertaken to improve social and economic indicators. This culminated in a long-range information plan published in 1963, backed up by national surveys such as the National Housing Survey. In the 1970s, OSS was reorganized as the Office of Statistical Policy (OSP), emphasizing the view that IS required a strategic public policy.

As computing infiltrated from the private sector to the public in the 1960s, new issues arose prompting new public policies. Early legislation was reactive and narrowly focused on particular problems perceived to be associated with the new world of computing. The Brooks Act was passed in 1965 to give the General Services Administration (GSA) primary but narrow responsibility for procurement of the new mainframe computing systems then being acquired.[12] The Brooks Act, for instance, spelled out competitive bidding requirements. Although the Brooks Act's language envisioned coordinated, government-wide management of information systems, this aspect of the act remained in the realm of rhetoric (Carr, 1989b).

In this period Congress, when it paid attention to computing and information policy at all, was primarily concerned with eliminating obvious abuses. Thus in the 1970s and early 1980s computer crime became subject to regulation under the Privacy Act of 1974, the Foreign Corrupt Practices Act, and the Ribicoff Computer Crime Bill of 1978 (Becker, 1984).

Toward Public Policy on Information Systems: The Paperwork Reduction Act of 1980

Computer hardware became widespread in government long before a recognition arose that information systems might require broad public policy-making attention. For instance, in the early 1970s a White House Domestic Council committee asked major agencies to report their plans and policy statements on major information programs. Except for a hastily organized Commerce Department effort, it found no such plans existed (Aines, 1988a: 103). In the mid-1970s, however, the pendulum began to swing in favor of establishment of a national information resource management policy.

Public concern over national productivity was the wedge which brought information policy to the forefront of the public policy agenda. The Commission on Federal Paperwork (1975-1977) made information resource management (IRM) the subject of policy and legislative proposals. In considering these proposals, a report of the House Government Operations Committee held in 1976 that "A management system must be developed ... to bring the vast benefits of computer technology to bear in solving the many problems of government" (Carr, 1989b: 102).

Ironically, much of the force for formulation of a national public policy on information systems was motivated by the desire to restrict information-gathering. The Commerce Department viewed federal information gathering as a major productivity-impeding burden on American business. It lobbied to transfer the Office of Statistical Policy from the OMB to Commerce, where in 1977 it was reorganized as the Office of Federal Statistical Policy and Standards (OFSPS). The Department of Commerce positioned itself as a major force behind efforts which led to the Paperwork Reduction Act of 1980 and other policies to restrict information gathering.

In the late 1970s a growing conservatism, with its premise that government was too big, worked in favor of establishing an information policy. The Commerce Department thesis that information gathering impeded American productivity was seen as hostile to the purposes of the OFSPS and others interested in promulgating a positive national information policy. As the 1980 elections loomed, President Carter sought to use management reform as response to the conservative public mood.

Elmer Staats, Comptroller General under President Carter, was central to the strategy which developed. Staats urged creation of a high-level federal group which would implement statistical policy, records management, and reports clearance. Staats' view was that by controlling information policy, a lid could be put on the natural tendencies of bureaucracies to generate ever more largely unnecessary paperwork. The Paperwork Reduction Act of 1980 and the Paperwork Control Act of 1980 were both outcomes of this strategy. Although born of a conservative strategy to limit information gathering, these acts created the structure of public policy-making for information systems in the 1980s. They did not "eliminate bureaucracy" as conservatives wished but they did mandate comprehensive information policies in federal agencies for the first time.

Republicans opposed to then President Carter taking credit for paperwork reduction, the act was passed after Carter's defeat at the polls in November, 1980. The Paperwork Control Act sought to reduce the public burden of IS on small businesses and other organizations by requiring agencies to secure OMB clearance before instituting new information-gathering activities. However, some agencies, notably the Department of Defense and the Internal Revenue Service, disliked the Paperwork Control Act's clearance provisions and found ways of circumventing them. For instance, the IRS would wait to the last minute to request clearance, then state that failure to rubber-stamp its request would cost the federal government billions of dollars in lost tax revenues. Agencies can and do put their reporting and record-keeping requirements in the form of regulations or formal rules. As such they then go into effect after a 30-day waiting period for comment, evading the clearance requirement (Price, 1988: 26).

The Paperwork Reduction Act (PRA) was in many ways more important than the Paperwork Control Act. The core of the act required each federal agency to submit a five-year information technology plan to the OMB, which in turn formulated a government-wide five-year information policy plan. Agency performance was to be reviewed triennially. That is, the Paperwork Reduction Act established the institutional framework for formal public policy-making reflected in long-range federal agency information plans covering information access, security, privacy, and other public policy concerns.

The PRA also reinforced OMB authority originating in the Budget and Accounting Procedures Act of 1950 to regulate statistical and information policy. The Paperwork Reduction Act relocated the Office of Federal Statistical Policy and Standards back under OMB, where it became part of the Office of Information and Regulatory Affairs (OIRA), which was established to regulate the new planning process.

In spite of or perhaps because of its sweeping scope, the PRA was placed on the slow track for implementation. The OMB, opposite to the will of Congress, lumped the OIRA budget in with the rest of OMB and in its recommendations to Congress that year proposed cuts in every budget except its own. This policy on budget cuts was rejected by Congress and in the end OIRA received only $2.7 million of the $8 million estimated to be needed for its effective start-up. This caused some planned reorganizations, not to be implemented, such as transfer of agencies having to do with statistical policy (Price, 1988: 25). Due to Reagan Administration cutbacks, OIRA's staff had shrunk by 1985 compared to its forerunner, the OFSPS, from 25 in the 1970s to merely six. That is, six people were supposed to regulate $1.5 billion efforts of over 80 federal agencies to collect, process, analyze, and disseminate information.

In spite of the weak start of the Paperwork Reduction Act, by the time of the White House Conference on Productivity in 1983, information resource management (IRM) had become a central issue for administrative reform. In 1984 the President's Private Sector Survey on Cost Control, better known as the Grace Committee (named for its chair, J. Peter Grace) recommended a centralized, government-wide approach to IRM and greater reliance on private industry. The Reagan and Bush administrations endorsed major appropriations increases for information technology investment projects. Further legislation in the 1980s and 1990s consolidated IRM guidelines under the Paperwork Reduction Act.[13]

Information Systems Legislation in the 1980s

The 1985 National Computer Conference (NCC) typified increased recognition of information resource management, explicitly focusing on broad IRM themes rather than on traditional, narrow technical topics. Although the 1980s were marked by a series of legislative initiatives (see Figure 8-4; Sprehe, 1987a, 1987b; Miller, 1988), probably the most important apart from the PRA planning process itself concerned legislation on broad ethical and civil rights aspects of information technology.

Ethics legislation was embedded in the Office of Federal Procurement Policy Act Amendments of 1988 (FPPA), known as the "Procurement Integrity Act", reiterated in the Fiscal 1991 National Defense Authorization Act, was ethics legislation which had a significant effect on information agencies though it was not limited to them (Power and Green, 1990). The FPPA amendments prohibit officials from discussing post-government employment or accepting a job with a contractor for two years if the individual had been involved in a contract with them.

Pat Szervo, head of the General Services Administration's Information Resource Management service, was among many IS officials to leave government service because of the FPPA amendments, which were instigated by Pentagon procurement scandals in 1988. Robert Woods, director of IS for the Department of Transportation, stated "You ask these people to take on probably the most difficult jobs in any department or agency, and then when they're through you tell them they can't use that experience to make a living sometime in the future. That's just dumb. Who the hell's going to take these things on in the future?" (Power and Smith, 1989: 80).

On the civil rights front, IS was not immune to legislative initiatives pursued by the National Organization on Disabilities and other groups. Although the Rehabilitation Act of 1973 prohibited discrimination against the handicapped and its Section 504 required removal of barriers, real IS impacts frequently did not occur until the 1986 Rehabilitation Act Amendments (Section 508 of Public Law 99-506) required federal managers to make electronic equipment accessible to disabled employees 'with or without special peripherals' and to develop the necessary equipment modifications (U. S. National Institute on Disability and Rehabilitation Research, 1987; Power, 1988a). Specific guidelines were issued by the General Services Administration in September, 1988, as FIRMR (Federal Information Resources Management Regulations) Bulletin 56 (Power, 1988a: 6). In addition, the Technology Related Assistance for Individuals with Disabilities Act of 1988 (Public Law 100-407) further mandated access to computing facilities for persons with disabilities.

Figure 4: IS Legislation in the 1980s

*** The Semiconductor Chip Protection Act of 1984**
Reflected new awareness of the need to protect intellectual property rights as found in computing.

*** The Computer Fraud and Abuse Act of 1986**
Passed to close loopholes in existing criminal legislation which had not provided for electronic crimes. The first person indicted under this act was ex-Cornell graduate student Robert Morris, Jr., charged in 1989 with maliciously releasing a "worm" or "virus" into the Internet network used by many academic and research institutions.

*** The Electronic Communications Privacy Act of 1986 (ECPA)**
Protected privacy of electronic mail communications over public networks like MCI, but specifically exempted corporate e-mail systems from privacy protection.

*** The Computer Security Act (CSA) of 1987**
Replaced Reagan's National Security Directive 145, mandating a defense and a civilian system of security, and required all federal agencies to institute a formal system of security training (Grimm, 1988b; GAO, 1989a).

*** Reform '88**
A Reagan financial management initiative, endorsed the Standard General Ledger for all major agencies, defined core financial system requirements in the Joint Financial Management Improvement Program (JFMIP), and had the GSA issue a mandatory schedule for off-the-shelf financial software (Shields, 1990).

However, as of 1989 the GSA found vendors were dragging their feet on implementation of modifications for disabled workers in spite of research advances on technology to serve the disabled (Glinert and York, 1992). The GSA warned that it would make mandatory its 1988 guidelines if vendors did not improve (Power, 1989b).

The Americans with Disabilities Act of 1990 (ADA; Public Law 101-336)), popularly called the "Civil Rights Act for the Disabled", extended Rehabilitation Act requirements to the private sector and made suing for awards up to $50,000 for the first offense) much easier for the disabled. It also required that by January, 1993, institutions and businesses had to be in conformance with the law (Edwards, 1991). The ADA is not directed specifically at computing (though Title IV deals with telecommunications) but rather to "facilities". However, it is commonly thought that "facilities" comprehend making computer text displays accessible to the visually impaired and computer keyboards accessible to the dexterity impaired (Edwards, 1991; Wilson, 1992). Implementation of the 1986 and 1990 acts requires controversial decisions (Ladner, 1989). It remains to be seen if there will be serious attempts to assure that office computing will be made accessible to the disabled, and if so, to what extent of disability (e.g., to visually impaired? to dexterity impaired? to mentally retarded? to the blind?).

The Struggle Over IRM Priorities for the 1990s

A 1987 report of the National Academy of Public Administration and the General Services Administration found that broad IRM priorities of the 1980 Paperwork Reduction Act and Circular A-130 "have not penetrated very far across departments and down into bureau management" (Caudle, 1988a: 790). Information *technology* management, rooted in traditional data processing units, was found to dominate at the expense of information *resource* management. For example, discussions of technical connectivity among computers were found to be common whereas resource discussions about lack of information for public policy decision-making or about data integrity were not common.[14]

Often the Paperwork Reduction Act had led only to a relabeling of traditional offices and processes with little substantive change. In practice, implementation came to center merely on (1) getting OMB clearance for new information-collection instruments (e.g., surveys of business), and (2) complying with mandates to reduce the volume of paperwork. Priority was not placed, for example, on conducting information needs assessments or audits of data quality and timeliness.

Whereas the 1980 act envisioned planning for management of information as a valuable resource, Caudle found a narrower emphasis on hierarchial control for purposes of systems planning and clearance. Department-level IRM chiefs, were concerned with operational oversight and control over information technology, but bureau chiefs, merely stressed operational performance with only cursory regard for departmental concerns for clearance like compliance Similar criticizes have been raised against IS chiefs in the private-sector (Bryce and Bryce, 1988). Department IRM heads blamed bureau chiefs for lack of concern for clearance and compliance and bureau heads blamed department chiefs for trying to impose over-bureaucratic regulatory requirements of no use to the end-users they sought to serve. Neither department nor bureau chiefs displayed emphasis on broader IRM missions such as information needs assessments.

Whether the concept of information resources management would be cast broadly or narrowly, however, remained a critical question. Caudle found that IRM was "relatively invisible as a management concept outside of IRM offices" (Caudle, 1988a:796) and that it was widely associated with "a bureaucratic exercise with little meaning" (p. 797). This context is one which suggested the need for change but not necessarily the likelihood of it. That change might be reaction against rather than reform of IRM as federal policy.

A 1989 report, *The IRM Organization: Concepts and Considerations*, from the IRM Planning Support Center of the IRM Service of the General Services Administration, took up these themes. The report noted the preference of departments to focus on particular applications such as electronic filing systems because their productivity is more easily measured. Instead, the GSA report argued, agencies must define information priorities and clarify agency-wide responsibilities through IRM bureaus which support planning, evaluation, and systems design throughout a given organization (Power, 1989d).

An indication of what difference the IRM philosophy might make compared to older IS orientations arose in the reorganization of information services in the State Department in December, 1989. This reorganization centered on moving State's IRM section from its former location in the Bureau of Administration and Information Management to a new and upgraded structural home in State's Bureau of Diplomatic Security. The rationale was the desire to shift focus from computing systems to a concern for broader policy issues involved in protecting State Department communications and information systems worldwide. Another example of the new emphasis on information resource policy was the creation in 1989 of the Bureau of International Communications and Information Policy with the mandate to be the policy link between the federal government and private industry on communications and information issues affecting foreign relations and national security.

Ironically, as the IRM perspective gained ground in the IS community within federal agencies, in 1989 two of the Congressional leaders behind Congressional oversight initiatives were removed from the IS policy game. Senator Lawton Chiles (D-FL) retired and Representative Jack Brooks (D-TX) moved from the House Government Operations Committee to the Judiciary Committee. Representative John Conyers (D-MI), who replaced Brooks, helped draft a bill to alter the Office of Information and Regulatory Affairs (OIRA). OIRA is the OMB agency which oversees the Paperwork Reduction Act.

In essence, the Conyers bill would have weakened OIRA's rule-making authority and increased the role of Congress and the agencies in IS decision-making. On the Senate side, Jack Bingaman (D-NM) offered a bill which would centralize agency control over IS decisions by creating a single chief information officer in each agency and would increase OIRA's policy-making role. Both bills failed and OIRA's authorization expired at the end of September, 1989. Continuing resolutions kept it in existence but its director resigned and the agency went leaderless for four years.

With this background, the issue of whether to reauthorize the Paperwork Reduction Act of 1980 arose again in the spring of 1990. While the Bush administration proposed abolition of OIRA, Bush favored folding OIRA functions into the Council on Competitiveness, headed by Vice President Dan Quayle (Grimm and Power, 1990). Under the Bush plan, the Council on Competitiveness would have broad powers to review proposed regulations of all types, not just information technology regulations. This was viewed as part of a pattern of making the regulatory review process more overtly political (Power and Seaborn, 1991: 81). Others, such as Senator John Glenn (D-OH), opposed the Bush plan and a political deadlock continued until the incoming Clinton administration was able to appoint a new OIRA administrator in May, 1993.

Similar political considerations underlay the proposed Paperwork Reduction and Federal Information Resource Management Act of 1990 (PRFIRMA), which would have established a chief information resources officer (CIRO) in charge of information systems in each federal agency. The CIRO concept gained momentum from the precedent of the Chief Financial Officer Act of 1990, a Bush-supported reform which established CFO's in federal departments to improve management oversight. This reform was motivated by the frustration of not knowing who in an agency was responsible for the

1980 Act and a feeling responsibility was scattered among many political appointees primarily concerned with finance and other issues. It was anticipated that most CIRO's would be political appointees, as with the Department of Veterans Affairs, an agency which implemented a CIRO-type position in 1989.

Legislation for the renewal of the Paperwork Reduction Act remained deadlocked from 1990 into 1993. Trying to carry on, the OMB proposed in 1990 a draft revision of Circular A-130, its main policy statement implementing the Paperwork Reduction Act. Agencies rejected the draft's emphasis on private sector dissemination of government-collected data, stating public access would be harmed. A new version of Circular A-130 was issued in January, 1992, emphasized minimizing user fees for data. This benefitted both the public and private industry, which seeks to obtain government data free or cheaply, then resell it at a substantial mark-up.

The new A-130 draft also called for increased on-line data dissemination by government agencies, in contrast to the earlier draft's emphasis on relying on private industry for on-line services. The new draft specifically opposed government agencies entering agreement with private vendors where the agreement would undercut federal dissemination responsibilities by restricting use, resale, or redissemination. However, although seemingly a victory for those favoring inexpensive public access to government data, the draft Circular A-130s limitation on user fees might be used, for instance, to prevent the Federal Maritime Commission (FMC) from charging a nominal fee for accessing tariff rates through its automated system as an alternative to much higher cost access through a private reseller of government data. Those like the Information Industry Association oppose public access on grounds the government should not duplicate services offered by private industry. Others see the IIA as a lobby for public subsidy of private profits and are willing for agencies like the FMC to charge some small user fees to recover costs needed to finance a system which provides cheap public access compared to the for-profit sector (Power, 1992c).

Ken Allen, senior vice president for government relations for the Information Industry Association, stated of the deadlock, "Our interpretation is that there is a lack of interest in these issues" (Power, 1991c: 121). That is, although the IRM perspective had become common and perhaps dominant in the federal IS community it was not a major issue for the public, Congress, or the President. Indifference, combined with questions raised about the efficacy of the planning process (cf. Head, 1991), meant that IRM momentum gathered in the late 1980s seemed to stall as the nation moved into the 1990s. Bob Coakley, director of the Business Council on the Reduction of Paperwork, said that Richard Darman, OMB Director under the Bush Administration, "kept his hands off OIRA and the Paperwork Reduction Act, minimized his responsibilities under the law, and gave very little thought to the utility of IRM. The president's failure to carry out what his views were was a big problem" (J. M. Smith, 1992c: 75).

When the General Accounting Office prepared its information technology study as part of its transition series of reports for incoming President Clinton, it found that as of 1992, "There are hardly any agencies that are well managed with modern systems. There have been years of neglect" (Power, 1993a: 63). Related testimony of Senator John Glenn (D-Ohio) noted "Neglect, indifference, and turnover among top leadership perpetuates problems that, with proper attention, could be solved" (Power, 1993a: 63). In general, the GAO found agency IRM heads to be titular figures preoccupied with other matters, not functioning as genuine chief information resource officers.

Clinton Administration IT Policy

In contrast to the deadlock over control over IRM policy, in December, 1991, Congress passed and President Bush signed the High-Performance Computing Act (HPCA). The culmination of almost a decade of lobbying by academic and research institutions, the HPCA provided $3 billion in funding for development and installation of a fiber optic network connecting the nation's universities, research centers, and other institutions. The network, the National Research and Education Network (NREN), was sponsored by Senator Albert Gore (D-TN) and received bipartisan support.

The HPCA was widely viewed as a national investment in communications infrastructure necessary to keep America competitive into the 21st century. It also served to make the prior federal investment in supercomputer centers more productive by giving access to them to researchers at far-flung centers. Proponents termed it a "data highway", effectively making an analogy to another bipartisan public works program, the federal interstate highway program of the 1950s and 1960s. The HPCA also designated specific agencies responsible for specific areas of technology research and development, laying the groundwork for future industrial policy in the IT area.

In 1992, Senator Gore (D-TN)— soon to become Vice President of the United States in the new Clinton administration — put forward a sequel to the HPCA— the High Performance Computing and Communications (HPCC) bill. If passed, the HPCC would authorize over a billion dollars for a program of fostering "grand applications" of future technologies coordinated by the White House Office of Science and Technology Policy. The program, called the Information Infrastructure Development Program, funds such projects as the development of massive databases based on called digital library technology developed by the National Institute of Standards and the National Science Foundation. Digital libraries and other HPCC projects would be available through and would complement the NREN high performance networks funded by the HPCA. As with the HPCA, the HPCC is justified on grounds that it is investment in IS infrastructure needed to underlay American productivity and competitiveness into the next century (Gore, 1992; Quindlen, 1992d:86).

Because of Gore's close association with technology legislation, most observers in 1993 expected the incoming Clinton/Gore administration to take an activist role on information resource management issues. Under then-governor Clinton, Arkansas had been the first state to have an on-line interactive imaging system for geographic and other information. Under Governor Clinton, Arkansas also pioneered the Instructional Microcomputer Project for Arkansas Classrooms and Arkansas promoted collegiate access to the Internet under a Clinton appointee who put together ARKnet, a network of 20 colleges and universities tied together and to the national Internet network. As a presidential candidate, Clinton's IT plan was contained in a document titled "Technology: The Engine of Economic Growth". This document calls for six initiatives, including creation of high-tech "information superhighways" along the lines of Gore's HPCC. As a result, numerous computer industry chief executives broke Republican ranks and endorsed Clinton's successful bid for the presidency in 1992.

The Clinton position paper earmarked "a significant portion" of an $80-billion "Rebuild America" fund for IT investment, placing the concept of an industrial policy favoring government investment in information technology (see Chapter 7) before the public as a major public policy item. Laura Tyson, Clinton's nominee to chair the Council of Economic Advisors, was a University of California-Berkeley professor known to favor government support of high tech industries. Similar views were held by Craig Fields, Clinton's nominee for the top technology post in the Department of Commerce. This contrasted sharply with the prior Bush administration, which had fired Fields for championing an active government technology policy (Caldwell, 1993a: 23).

Because of economic recession and budget deficits, however, even during its transition period into office, the Clinton administration made it clear it would reject costly proposals such as formation of a federal cabinet-level Department of Technology and an NSF-proposed new Civilian Technology Corporation dispensing a $5 billion research fund (Higgins, 1993). Instead, the Clinton Administration advocated funding increases for the more modest Advanced Technology Program of the Commerce Department, perhaps as a civilian replacement for DARPA (the Defense Advanced Research Projects Agency). The new Secretary of Commerce, Ron Brown, fell short of endorsing a new national IT industrial policy—instead advocating only creation of a new cabinet-level National Information Infrastructure Council.[15] Clinton's belief in technology as the engine of growth were blunted by the higher priority he attached to reducing the deficit and finding solutions to the health care crisis.

In May 1993, a Clinton-Gore technology statement was issued titled, *Technology for America's Economic Growth, A New Direction to Build Economic Strength.*[16] It called for more information technology investment to strengthen global competitiveness, coordinate technology management across government agencies, and encourage government-university-private sector partnerships. The "reinvigorated" Office of Science and Technology Policy under Vice President Gore was named as the lead development group for Clinton technology policy development and the new National Economic Council was named as the monitoring group for implementation of new technology policies. Specific initiatives included permanent extension of the research and experimentation tax credit, investment in a National Information Infrastructure (NII, of which the HPCA is part; Gibbons, 1993), accelerated investment in advanced manufacturing technologies, technological investment in the automobile industry (esp. in relation to environmental hazard reduction), investment in energy-efficient federal buildings, and an increase in support for technology in education.

With radical innovations in information policy seemingly ruled out, debate in the early Clinton Administration focused on development of the "National Information Infrastructure" (NII) proposals associated with Gore's bills. Telephone companies and other commercial interests argued that the $11.5 million subsidy for NSFNet (the "backbone" of the Internet) and the $7 million subsidies for regional networks improperly pitted the government in competition against private enterprise. They favored limiting NSFNet to high performance transmissions among supercomputing centers, while private communications firms created a commercial network "backbone" for e-mail. For its part, the Internet dropped its ban on commercial us, jockeying for better position to compete with telephone and television companies in efforts to provide high-speed communications services for the emerging NII. As a result, commercial use of the Internet exploded in 1992-93, threatening to overwhelm traditional academic and government usage (Gerber, 1993).

Defending the Internet against privatization, university interests often argued that forcing colleges to purchase commercial services or privatizing the Internet would impose major cost increases which many could afford only by sacrificing much-needed educational services in other areas. Universities argue that even a program of federal subsidies to colleges to buy commercial services (as the Clinton administration favored) would limit network development, reduce technical support, and impair access equity compared to direct government-subsidized university operation of such networks. Robert Heterick, president of EDUCOM (an alliance of colleges interested in educational computing), raised this issue in noting the displacement of NREN (National Research and Education Network) by NII (National Information Infrastructure), stating "somewhere in our headlong rush to an NII we have to wonder where the 'E' went" (Heterick, 1993: 52).

Telephone companies, which favor privatization of governmental broadband networks and who are likely beneficiaries of privatization, are interested in one-way delivery of cable television services and may prove disinterested in developing the kind of switching capabilities of interest to academics presently using the Internet (Hart, Reed, and Bar, 1993: 46). As of Summer 1993, the Clinton administration had praised a yet-to-be-passed bill by Rep. Rick Boucher (D-VA) which would require privatization of Internet services which commercial firms wanted to take over within 18 months of passage of the bill (DeLoughry, 1993).

Planning Processes for Public Policy-Making on Information Technology

Strategic planning for public policy-making for information technology issues has traditionally been viewed by the federal government as a matter to be handled in a voluntary and cooperative way. In the 1970s, for instance, the General Services Administration (GSA) created the Federation of Government Information Processing Councils (FGIPC), which has persisted to the present day. FGIPC has served over the years as a forum for inter-agency information exchange and as a vehicle for sharing computing resources. Operating through ten regional councils it promoted considerable resource sharing in the 1970s when computing resources were more scarce and centralized. In the 1980s the diversification of computing combined with GSA budget cuts undermined the vitality of FGIPC. By the late 1980s the organization lacked a full-time director and at least three of the regional councils had become inactive while others were languishing. In spite of attempts in the late 1980s to reinvigorate FGIPC, as through formation of the Council of Data Center Directors as an affiliate, it had long become clear that the decentralized, bottom-up approach to federal IS planning was not likely to accomplish change broadly or rapidly.

Efforts to Establish Federal Strategic Planning for Information Technology

Other efforts to establish federal-wide strategic planning have also been relatively weak, depending heavily on voluntary cooperation of numerous federal agencies. The Interagency Committee on Information Resource Management (IAC/IRM) was chartered by the General Services Administration with the Office of Management and Budget. As of 1991 it drew membership from over 300 federal departments and agencies. However, the IAC/IRM only acts as a issues forum and vehicle for interagency communication and informal coordination on IS issues. It also publishes the *Federal IRM Directory*. However, the IAC/IRM is not intended to and does not function as a policy-setting planning group (*Government Computer News*, 1987a: 31).

A program designed to foster planning resources on a voluntary, cooperative basis in the federal government has been the General Services Administration's "Trail Boss" program. Starting in 1988, the GSA provided special training and later procurement authority to key officials designated to head major IS acquisition projects requiring special attention (Power, 1988d). While the "trail boss" program helped mold IS planners and was the GSA's largest information exchange initiative, it was not itself a strategic planning system.

In contrast to the weakness of policy planning processes in government, the lesson of the private sector, as simplified in reports such as those of the Grace Committee, seemed to point in the direction of a centralized approach to strategic information planning. Reflecting common private sector views, one authority on database management defined the strategic planning role in IS as follows:

> The data strategist is seen as creating the organization-wide strategy for the use of data. He must form a clear view of the corporation's future information requirements and must steer the evolution of data facilities so that the requirements become realizable (Martin, 1981: 381).

This view of strong, centralized strategic planning reflects traditional private-sector perspectives on planning. In spite of significant differences between planning in the public sector compared to the private[17], the vision of a unified federal strategic information policy planning process has been a recurrent theme since the 1980s.

In the 1980s it was common to find attacks on the "balkanization" of information policy-making in the federal government. Government reports such as the Office of Management and Budget's *Management of the U.S. Government* (1988) called for creating fully integrated management information systems in spite of the fact that industry had experimented with organization-wide unified databases in the 1970s, had largely rejected the concept, and was then moving toward diversified and distributed database management arrangements (Head, 1988d).[18] The call for integration and unification of information policy planning was also frequently associated with the concept of creating a new office—that of the chief information officer (CIO). The call for CIOs was in no small part a recognition of the fact that CEOs often fail to bring management attention to bear on the problems of managing information. For instance, a Government Accounting Office study of information resource management in the Department of Energy found that agency had wasted money creating information systems which overlapped or duplicated existing systems. Staff still lacked access to critical data with the result that the likelihood was increased that the public would be unnecessarily exposed to dangerous contaminants; that the safety and health of workers would not be adequately protected; and that outdated weapons components would continue to be manufactured and discarded. The GAO faulted the Department of Energy for failing to engage in a planning process that focused on information resource investments in terms of the department's strategic missions. Management disinterest was cited as the underlying problem (GAO, 1992f).

Of these functions set forth by the General Services Administration for CIOs, it is interesting to note that centralization was cast as a formal IRM responsibility (see role number six in the Figure 8-5). This reflected desires within the executive and legislative branches to assert greater control over information resources. Inherent in the IRM concept of agencies forming IS plans was the thought that these plans would be implemented in a coordinated and centralized manner. Though introduced at the same time as the wave of microcomputer-related decentralization of the early and mid-1980s, the IRM concept was part of an equally important counter-trend: the redefinition and consolidation of central IS roles in large organizations (Power, 1988b: 15). Although as of 1993 only four federal agencies formally had CIOs termed such, most departments had witnessed a growing executive-level focus on information resource management.[19]

Obstacles to Federal Strategic Planning for Information Technology

A unified approach to strategic planning of federal information resources faces a raft of obstacles which make its realization unlikely. For instance, Circular A-130 implementing the Paperwork Reduction

Figure 5: Roles of the Chief Information Officer

The emerging functions of the CIO as information resource manager were outlined in a 1988 report issued by the General Services Administration. Eight major roles were set forth:

1. Serve as agency representatives on IRM councils
2. Advise key IRM officials
3. Advise procurement officials
4. Sell IRM plans within the agency
5. Negotiate implementation
6. Develop MIS policies, including policies on upgrading technology, implementing standards, assuring integrated data sharing, and centralizing MIS functions
7. Providing technical advice
8. Consulting on the budget

-- *The Senior Federal IRM Manager: Major Roles and Responsibilities As We Move Into the 1990s.*

Act calls for government-wide IS planning. While the OMB does in fact create such a plan (the *Five-Year Plan for Meeting the Automatic Data Processing Needs of the Federal Government* issued annually by the OMB), present planning processes are more a matter of form than of real substance. To understand why this is so requires only a brief review of obstacles to federal strategic IS planning.

To take just one obstacle to social control of information technology, there is the fact that a great deal of computer research is defense-related, making oversight by civilian agencies difficult. Beusmans and Wieckert (1989), for instance, raise moral issues about responsibility and control in a variety of contexts: massacre of innocent civilians by runaway military robots, for instance. Do computer professionals have a duty of boycott the research leading to such capabilities? Should Congress legislate to control military IS technology? While there is much room for public policy-making on such matters, American political traditions weigh in favor of leaving military technology largely to the military with Congress focusing only on overall cost and inter-service balance.

Conflict of interest within the Office of Management and Budget is another obstacle to federal IS planning. On the one hand, the OMB is responsible for obtaining annually the five-year IS plans from the departments and assembling them into a government-wide report. On the other hand, the OMB is the executive agency responsible for budgetary management and, in particular, finding areas to cut costs. There is a tension between the managerial planning role and the budgetary cost-cutting role. Given that OMB's budgetary role has always been dominant, agencies submitting IS plans to the OMB are always well aware that the reporting process has a hidden agenda (cost cutting) beyond strategic information management planning. Agencies have strong motives to emphasize projects which reduce actual spending or promise other efficiencies. As Houser (1989a: 78) points out, "The problem with cost avoidance is the tendency to be rather nebulous and prone to optimism. Project managers anticipate savings in the staffs and budgets of other managers in the agencies. But even if these other managers agree (which is not normally the case), the project manager is not really responsible for implementing the savings." Requirements under the Paperwork Reduction Act are seen by IS managers as a "wasteful bureaucratic burden" (Caudle, 1988c: 38). The dual OMB roles of management and budget foster irresponsible planning — irresponsible not in the popular sense but in the sense that those doing the planning are separated from those responsible for implementing their plans' bottom lines. They adopt a cynical attitude toward the planning process. In the end, as Caudle (1988c: 50) notes,

Figure 6: Obstacles to Federal Strategic Planning for Information Technology

* The classified, defense-related nature of the largest federal outlays for information technology.

* The conflict of interest between the OMB role as cost-cutter and the OMB role as information technology planner.

* The public sector's lag behind information technology in the private sector.

* Agency pressure to maintain independence from efforts to control the bureaucracy.

"the oversight and control that characterized the Paperwork Reduction Act may have deadened the innovation needed for IRM development " and for true strategic planning.

Another obstacle to federal strategic IS planning is that the federal government lags so far behind the private sector. Often struggling to catch up to contemporary standards, federal agencies are frequently in no position to plan realistically for state-of-the-art future developments. For instance, studies show the federal government uses less software and employs older systems than companies in the Fortune 1000 (Papciak, 1988). The General Services Administration's study, *Computer Obsolescence: Federal Government and the Private Sector* (1988) found that the government's computers were 90% older than those of the 500 largest corporations, averaging nearly 8 years old. "All measures show that the government significantly lags behind the private sector in terms of age and capacity of equipment", the report concluded (Power, 1988e: 33). When investment does not keep up with planning, planning falters. This is the case in many federal agencies.

Proposals for greater legislative oversight are not always greeted warmly. In 1989, for instance, the General Services Administration, an arm of Congress, proposed increasing its oversight of computer system planning and procurements. This proposal, which arose after allegations of Navy bias in favor of IBM in IS purchases, set forth requirements for additional agency documentation prior to the GSA granting procurement authority. In addition, some 100 specific procurements a year were to be tracked in detail and the number of reviews was to be tripled. A typical reaction came from Edward Hanley, director of IRM for the Environmental Protection Agency. Haley said the GSA was overreacting to unproved charges and that the increased oversight would burden agencies such as the EPA as well as bog down the GSA itself. Having to provide the GSA with copies of proposed solicitations, justifications for sole-source purchases, software conversion studies, written notices of any vendor concerns, and other data would be just the opposite of what the GSA should be doing: enhancing agency capabilities to assure cost-effectiveness in information systems matters (Power, 1989f).

In spite of debate over how much legislative oversight and administrative control is enough, the federal government has taken steps to establish central IRM (Information Resource Management) offices in all major departments. As discussed earlier, legislation regulating information management has been adopted with increasing frequency and now constitutes a sizable body of law and regulation. At state and lower levels of government, however, oversight is much more episodic.[20]

In summary, while IS provides the potential for revolutionizing central legislative oversight of the executive and of the bureaucracy, thus far there is little evidence that it will. On the other hand, it may be that it is normal for organizations to first concentrate on the "housekeeping" aspects of new technology) e.g., office automation, electronic mail, electronic calendars and voting) before developing more innovative applications such as those that would provide legislatures powerful new tools for oversight (Miewald, Mueller, and Sittig, 1987).

Conclusion: Information Technology and Public Policy Accountability

In his book *American Genesis: A Century of Invention and Technological Enthusiasm* (1989), Thomas Hughes argues that technology has transformed American society more profoundly than has politics or business. Hughes is thinking of how industrial assembly-line technology influenced social classes and standards of living, how electric power technology such as the TVA transformed underdeveloped regions of the country, and how nuclear technology helped end WWII and set the framework for nearly half a century of Cold War. When it comes to information technology, however, it is much more difficult to make the argument that IT has had profound political effects, either in the nation or even within organizational power structures. Hughes does not discuss information technology, perhaps for this reason. Nonetheless, even though the political effects of IT are diffuse, weak, and often self-canceling, the rapid growth and sweeping scope of modern computing has generated many concerns about holding information systems accountable to democratic principles.

A General Accounting Office symposium late in 1989 addressed many of the issues discussed in this chapter. This report called for an approach to accountability which emphasized formation of internal and external partnerships through review boards and advisory committees which would feed into detailed long-term planning processes. "Agency leaders," the report argued, "should also involve Congress as an active partner in defining and implementing their vision...agency management needs to evaluate and discuss with the Congress the impact its vision will have on the organizational structure and congressional constituencies. Technological change often entails organizational change; agencies should have a plan for managing both and could communicate these plans to the Congress. With a clearer understanding of the agency's vision and goals, the Congress will be in a better position to make informed oversight decisions and assist in resolving difficult issues" (GAO, 1990a: 7-8).

This vision of how to achieve effective oversight of information systems is one which gained a high degree of consensus. That consensus, however, probably derives from the airy generality of the plan. Its call for voluntary advisory committees ignored the tendency of such committees to be captured by narrow industry interests. It also assumed such committees would motivate more candid interactions of agencies with Congress. Congress in turn was assumed to be attentive. The supposition seemed to be that Congress was prevented from effective IS oversight only by poor articulation of issues by the agencies. From a political science viewpoint, however, this analysis of the situation seems naive.

Those involved in management information systems tend to assume everyone is concerned with the issues raised by IS. Ultimately, accountability in a democracy depends on whether concern about an issue is widespread and so pushes the issue toward the top of policy agendas. In reality IS is like many other administrative reforms -- legislators have difficulty becoming excited about it and there is little if any popular pressure to force IS issues to center stage. As one state-level study showed, this is so in spite of vigorous staff efforts to make legislators more aware. "At the end," the authors wrote, "our conclusions may be somewhat disappointing for anyone who wants to see autonomous legislative policy makers boldly constructing ever more vital political institutions...the next step in legislative reform, we suggest, is for the legislators themselves to put the issue high on their agenda. The staffs have done as much as they can" (Miewald, Mueller, and Sittig, 1987: 101). Legislators, however, are unlikely to be so motivated until there is constituency pressure such as might arise due to common dissatisfactions with existing information systems.

Figure 7: Mini-Case Study: Information Policy at the High School Level

In 1985 the School Board of Montgomery County, Maryland, faced a problem in establishing public policy toward tracking information. Its traditional 4.0 grading scale was challenged by honor students on fairness grounds, arguing that the greater effort in honors courses compared to regular courses was such that honor grades should be weighted more than regular course grades in calculating grade point averages (GPAs).

The student council opposed change, arguing that honor students should not be bribed to take honor courses, that the proposed honors grading was too arbitrary, that students who were outstanding in subject areas where honor courses were unavailable would be disadvantaged as might conscientious students in regular courses.

The School Board's Department of Educational Accountability was able to establish three facts:

1. Over half of American high schools weight grades in advanced courses, but there is much variation in criteria and type of course.
2. Most colleges known for selectivity use weighting, especially for calculating class rank.
3. Student ranks in the top decile seem unaffected by weighting, though students in deciles 2 through 6 may be affected.

Using this information, the school board decided on a compromise to weight honors grades for calculation of class rank but not for calculation of the GPA. It was assumed that colleges could do this weighting themselves if desired.

The Montgomery County School Board decision on weighting student grades illustrates three common characteristics of IS issues:

(1) definition of critical indicators is a controversial, even political matter which cannot be resolved at a technical level;
(2) use of multiple indicators (eg.; student rank as well as GPA) may be helpful in resolving some of the political issues involved;
(3) IS initiatives must be closely tied to the political and policy leadership of the organization which oversees their operation (Shoenberg, 1987).

Thus satisfaction with an information system, in this case one tracking high school performance often has much more to do with the political sensitivity of managers in defining what information is to be entered into the system and what is done with the information in the process of record-keeping and reporting than it does with technical factors alone.

The question of accountability then turns on the related issue, "What makes people satisfied or dissatisfied with IS outcomes?" Some believe that whether IS systems are seen as good depends on where you stand. For instance, a study of social work computing found attitudes toward IS were divided along job lines, with managers being far more favorable (Gandy and Tepperman, 1990). Weiss, Gruber, and Carver (1986) have argued that the benefits associated with new IS systems are "in the eye of the beholder" and have much to do with the beholder's location in the organizational structure. In a study of views on public education data programs, these authors found "the value of information is profoundly and predictably shaped by the patterns of control in which information systems are located" (p. 504).

Federal officials tended not to agree that federal education data policies had negative side effects, whereas local officials felt that they did. Officials with program responsibilities in general education administration tended to see no negative side effects, whereas officials working in civil rights did see such effects. Officials in some geographic locations were more critical than others. However, in spite of strong statements by Weiss, Gruber, and Carver, the correlations in this study, while statistically significant in a technical sense, always accounted for less than 20% of the variance in perceptions of data policy (see Table 1, p. 501). That is, structural location would seem to be only one of many determinants of positive or negative perceptions of outcomes. The nature of implementation may play a more important role (Weiss, Gruber, and Carver, 1986).

In summary, a great deal has been undertaken to make information systems accountable to democratic values, both in government and in the private sector. However, federal legislation and planning initiatives only scratch the surface of the issues involved. Few studies rigorously evaluate the meaningfulness of initiatives such as the Paperwork Reduction Act. In the 1989-1993 period, the Office of Management and Budget's Office of Information Resource Administration (OIRA) remained in political deadlock, without a permanent head. The degree of partisan political influence in OIRA was a major issue, raising questions about the ability of the federal government to regulate information systems effectively. The General Services Administration's Trail Boss training program was based on non-coercive planning mechanisms but in spite of successes was limited in its focus, centering on IS procurement issues. Other planning groups such as the Interagency Committee on Information Resource Management would seem to be relatively ineffective in holding IS accountable but, as in most IS areas, empirical evaluation has not been undertaken.

The General Accounting Office (GAO) has been vigorous in issuing reports and audits on various IS initiatives. Because the GAO is an arm of Congress its reports have a direct input to legislative oversight processes. Thus it may have a greater de facto role in democratic oversight of IS than the OMB, even though that executive agency has been given formal planning authority for federal IS. However, it appears no research has systematically evaluated the effectiveness of GAO reports on information systems as a device for oversight, much less presented a clear picture of the organizational processes by which the GAO comes to its decisions in these matters. In many of the most important areas of federal information planning we simply do not know which of several patterns of control are at work: iron triangles (control by a coalition of users, managers and designers), relatively unconstrained managerial control, technological determinism, partisan political control, or various alternatives and combinations.

Information technologies are of public policy concern because they have broad actual or potential impacts on the privacy of citizens, access by reporters or public interest groups to vital data, freedom of communication, and equal opportunity. Political concern is also aroused because of the linkage of computing with valid governmental interests in promoting national productivity and competitiveness, regulating labor relations and the treatment of employees, and limiting the burden of IS requirements on businesses, organizations, and individuals. From the perspective of IS managers, the political processes which surround planning and implementation often take the largest proportion of their time. Political processes reflect conflict over objectives and interests as different social, market, and organizational forces affect the political process, giving varying emphases on imposed regulations, bargained outcomes, market determinations, and group consensus. The accountability of information systems ultimately rests not on legislation per se but on the web of influences formed by such complex political processes.

ENDNOTES

[1] E.g., Dahl and Lindblom, 1953; Gawthrop, 1971; Wamsley and Zald, 1973; Sharkansky, 1979; Musolf and Seidman, 1980; Bozeman, 1984, 1987; Coursey and Bozeman, 1990; Adams and McCormick, 1993.

[2] Examples of the latter include joint ventures, public corporations, nonprofit agencies, and ventures involving coinvestment, coproduction, and codetermination in the U.S. and abroad.

[3] That is, authors such as Crow and Bozeman focus on the external environment of organizations to derive their definition of publicness, whereas public goods theory focuses on the nature of the good or service provided by the organization. Crow and Bozeman characterize their definition as "dimensional", contrasting it with dichotomous public/private distinctions. However, the definition of publicness in public goods theory is equally dimensional (non-dichotomous) in this sense. Hence I prefer to characterize the approach of Crow, Bozeman, and similar others as "environmental" rather than "dimensional".

[4] Likewise Nitzan and Ostrom (1992) elsewhere have sought to redirect public goods theory toward the assumption that mixed goods, not purely public or purely private goods, take up most of the attribute space in any given policy analysis.

[5] Publicness has also been measured by a variety of criteria such as measures based on demographic scaling (see Hayes and Slottje, 1987).

[6] Scholars in this field are quick to acknowledge the difficulty of measuring publicness and of defining optimal distribution (Coursey and Bozeman, 1990: 526; Perry and Rainey, 1988).

[7] For instance, in the area of condominium ownership as a public good, as noted by Silverman and Barton (1986), the publicness aspect of private ownership forces homeowners to form a private system of government to formally establish and maintain public values and standards of order and to cooperatively manage property without the protection of a formally specialized set of political actors.

[8] As the state increasingly recognizes the publicness of medical services and services in other professional domains, regulation through the private government of self-regulating professions is increasingly challenged. We in the universities are not exempt. Nelson (1989) notes, for instance, that the evolution of technology involves the coevolution of a latent public good which requires preservation and which underlies policy-oriented debates on the need for more control of intellectual property rights, the proprietary capabilities of university scientists, and preservation of the role of universities as vehicles for making technological knowledge public.

[9] Section 1.5 of the ACM code covers the "imperative" to "honor property rights" which Section 1.6 deals further with intellectual property rights.

[10] Lest the author be accused of assuming an inexorable technological determinism in the foregoing discussion of the tendencies of private government in IS and other professions, let it quickly be added that there are other forces defending private government and professional property rights. Prime among these is the weakness of normative theory itself and, in particular, of liberal normative theory. Michael Walzer (1984), a political theorist at Harvard, addressed this best in noting that liberal writers have been sensitive to avoiding tyrannies through separating church and state, civil society and political community, and the public and private realms. However, he noted, liberal theory has tended to focus on the atomistic individual when, in fact, people are inseparable from their institutional ties. This misplaced focus of liberal theory leads to underemphasizing or overlooking radical inequalities in the market which generate forms of private government that can tyrannize civil society. In turn, liberal theory fails to call for a transformation of corporate structure to assure the separation of corporate power from governmental power in the subsidy, taxation, and regulation of

goods imbued with publicness.

[11] The need to control American information systems more tightly has come under increasing Congressional scrutiny in recent years. An example is found in the testimony of Charles Bowsher, U. S. Comptroller General, speaking before the House Government Operations Subcommittee on Legislation and National Security. Bowsher, addressing information systems in the Department of Defense, stated, "Defense is not effectively controlling major (automated information) systems development efforts." Citing a study of eight specific IS systems, Bowsher stated that all involved some degree of uncontrolled spending, "some in the hundreds of millions of dollars." Subcommittee chairperson Rep. John Conyers (D-MI) labelled these accusations "horror stories" and called for investigation and possible Congressional action (Schwartz, 1989a: 6).

[12] The Brooks Act is PL 89-306 and is named after its author, Representative Jack Brooks (D-TX).

[13] On March 26, 1985, the Federal Information Resources Management Regulations (FIRMR) became effective, establishing the Federal Information Resources Management Review program. It was a descendant of the ADP and telecommunications sections of the Federal Property Management Regulations and the Federal Procurement Regulations. FIRMR set forth policies that the General Services Administration, the Office of Management and Budget, and other agencies would follow in acquisition and management of ADP and telecommunications equipment in the course of implementing their IRM responsibilities under the Paperwork Reduction Act of 1980.

The Office of Management and Budget (OMB) Circular A-130 (1985), attempted to implement OMB's responsibilities and objectives under the 1980 Paperwork Reduction Act. It provided for each department to appoint a senior official to develop five-year information plans with triennial reviews and it set forth general guidelines with objectives providing for access, confidentiality, efficiency, and minimization of paperwork burden. For instance, the annual five-year IRM plans must include efforts to assure security and must list information collections planned for the upcoming period. In spite of lingering Congressional opposition and attempts to abolish OIRA altogether, the Paperwork Reduction Act was re-authorized in 1986. In 1990 a new FIRMR was issued to implement it. The new FIRMR centralized procurement authority, clarified accountability for larger computer-related contracts, mandated more procurement planning, but allowed greater flexibility (Petrillo, 1991a, 1991b). Specifically, it required agencies to obtain delegations of procurement authority (DPAs) from the GSA for all computer and telecommunications acquisitions of $2.5 million or more, including hardware, off-the-shelf software, maintenance, and timeshare services. In an attempt to increase accountability, it also required agencies to identify the senior program, technical and contracting officials associated with each acquisition and to report a description of each project's organizational structure, including a listing of job experience and responsibilities for each official (Power, 1991a).

[14] At the state level, studies by Caudle (1990) have found that management trends included increased emphasis on management of information as a resources even though the primary focus of the states was remained on technological aspects of data processing and telecommunications. By 1990 some 13 states had legislation mandating a telecommunications function for state government and 34 states had at least one official council, commission, board, or committee devoted to setting the direction of the state's information resources management policy. Most of these initiatives date only from the mid to late 1980s, paralleling federal developments discussed above. These groups increasingly discussed such IRM concerns as public access, privacy, data integrity, data ownership, security, and other management topics going beyond simple technological solution.

[15] This council was advocated by John Sculley, CEO of Apple Computer, who urged Vice President Al Gore be named its chair.

[16] Feb. 22, 1993, USGPO 1993-347-397/80142.

[17] In contrast to private-sector strategic planning, public organizations are generally characterized by higher levels of interdepartmental interdependence and higher levels of accountability. This in turn accounts for their relying more on formal budget-related planning processes and less on steering committees for information systems planning than is the case for corporations (Bretschneider, 1990). Although the differences between public and private are small there is, nonetheless, a significant difference having to do with what is called "accountability in planning" if you like it and "red tape" if you don't. It is not that public organizations plan more or better but they do go about strategic planning differently. While scholars have emphasized the primacy of managerial decision over environmental constraints (Kraemer, King, Dunkle, and Lane, 1989), greater interdependence in the public sector makes extra-organizational factors more important in IS planning and management. Correspondingly, IS prescriptions emanating from the organization's information processing department are more likely to be modified by planning processes than in the private sector (Bretschneider, 1990).

[18] Writing about hospital settings, for instance, one early observer predicted "The net effect of the microprocessor technology is inherently centrifugal...the problem within single institutions such as hospitals is that, unless they are managed, the effect might be further to compartmentalize and fragment institutional systems" (Lindberg, 1978: 134).

[19] The four agencies were the Federal Aviation Administration, the Forest Service, the Internal Revenue Service, and the Veterans Affairs Department.

[20] At the state level, strategic planning for IS has been extensive but not as much so as at the federal level. In a study of seven states selected to illustrate the diversity found in all states, Kresslein and Marchand (1987: 118-119) found most states (six of the seven studied) had centralized at least planning responsibility for all information technologies in a single agency. Telecommunications planning has been a primary concern in this, but the linkages of communications with data processing and office automation are increasingly recognized. State-level support for integrated approaches to IS is increasing. In Florida, for instance, the Office of Planning and Budgeting (OPB, responsible for central computing) is the central actor in the state planning process mandated in 1984 (Klay and Yu, 1988: 199). The OPB, for example, alerts the governor and key officials to important trends by issuing reports with graphics showing potential developments to be addressed in the strategic planning process (the Issue Detection and Early Alert System, I.D.E.A.S.).

Although most state-level IS managers saw the spread of microcomputers in the 1980s as a development not disrupting IS planning (Garson, 1987a: ch. 6), the rise of end-user computing has been another force against centralized IS planning. End-user computing was contrasted with centralized computing and centralized IS planning. Some studies of computerization have found, at least in local government, that user-centeredness is the key to successful planning. Once computing power is put in the hands of users, numbers of users will develop fruitful applications that could not have been envisioned by any degree of central planning (Kirby, 1986: 11).

Most states put oversight responsibility at a high organizational level where it may be used to enforce statewide policies and standards regarding acquisition, networking, and computer usage. Although originating in concerns for managing technology, states partly following the federal model, are gradually shifting to the broader concerns of managing information. A major study sponsored by NASIS (National Association for State Information Systems, Inc.) surveyed 2,200 program managers and information system directors, finding that in the past decade IRM efforts have led in various degrees to planning processes for statewide information technology architectures (Caudle, Marchand, et al., 1989: xxxix). While over half the states required an information systems planning process (p. xxi), only a few had comprehensive planning processes integrating computing, telecommunications, and office automation. Moreover, the planning processes which exist tended to focus on short-range budget justifications, not strategic issues.

In the end, however, a strict policy of centralization is not feasible even if it were to be desired. As Kresslein and Marchand found, "states are not centralizing all management responsibility in a single state government authority. Instead they are structuring a management framework that permits departments, boards, and commissions as much latitude as possible to tailor information systems according to their unique requirements" (Kresslein and Marchand, 1987: 117). While planning responsibility is centralized in some states (CA, SC, MN, VA, TX, FL, for example) and while many states have procurement guidelines which coordinate IS equipment, no state as of 1990 could be said to have a comprehensive, unified IS policy.

A survey of state legislatures undertaken for the U. S. Office of Technology Assessment in 1984 found "no state closing in rapidly on ... a centralized, comprehensive, regularized process of administrative review based on independently desired information" (Miewald, Mueller, and Sittig, 1987: 97). Although the states exhibit great variation, there is a tendency toward centralization of the technology, if not of the oversight of information. Some states (e.g., Florida) started centralized while others (e.g., Minnesota) have sought to impose centralization after the fact. In large and complex environments (e.g., California, New York) centralization has seemed the only feasible direction. At the same time, the states have not been immune to the decentralizing influences of the "microcomputer revolution". Few states are committed to developing independent databases for policy decision-making. On the contrary, most are satisfied with data from the executive departments.

In fact, the state governments have had to be flexible in the face of the "microcomputer revolution" and end-user computing that marked the 1980s. While there is talk of an integrated approach to data processing, telecommunications, and automated office systems, state governments and other jurisdictions are only at the beginning phases of planning processes -processes which have great difficulty keeping up with the rapidly evolving technological environment. This rapid rate of change together with great diversity of function geographic dispersion, sunk investments in a variety of technologies, and the natural risk-aversion and pluralism of governmental bodies all combine to make centralized planning more a symbolic goal than a reality even in jurisdictions where it is advocated.

Bibliography

ABA (1984)
Report on computer crime. Washington, D.C.: American Bar Association, Task Force on Computer Crime.

Abercrombie, Nicholas and John Urry (1983).
Capital, labor, and the middle classes. London: George Allen and Unwin.

ACM (Association for Computing Machinery) (1992).
ACM proposed code of ethics and professional conduct. *Communications of the ACM*, Vol. 35, No. 5 (May): 94-99.

Adams, Roy D. and Ken McCormick (1993).
The traditional distinction between public and private goods needs to be expanded, not abandoned. *Journal of Theoretical Politics*, Vol. 5, No. 1 (Jan.): 109-116.

Adelman, L. (1982).
Involving users in the development of decision-analytic aids: The principal factor in successful implementation. *Journal of Operation Research Society*, Vol. 33, No. 4: 333-342.

Adler, Jerry (1992).
Typing without keys. *Newsweek*, Vol. 120, No. 23 (Dec. 7): 63-64.

Adler, Sy (1987).
The new information technology and the structure of planning practice. *Journal of Planning Education and Research*, Vol. 6, No. 2: 93-98.

Adler, Sy and Sheldon M. Edner (1988).
Technological change in urban transportation organizations. *Public Productivity Review*, Vol. 12, No. 2 (Winter): 151-163.

Ahituv, Niv, Seev Neumann, and M. Hadass (1984).
A flexible approach to information systems development. *MIS Quarterly*, Vol. 8, No. 2 (June, 1984): 69-78.

Ahituv, Niv and Seev Neumann (1986).
Principles of information systems management, 2nd edition. Dubuque, IA: W. C. Brown, 1986.

Aines, Andrew A. (1988a).
U. S. recognizes information age, but is it too late?. *Government Computer News*, July 22: 103.

Aines, Andrew A. (1988b).
Freedom of information: Too much of a good thing? *Government Computer News*, Oct. 24: 99.

Albert, S. (1984).
A delete design model for successful transitions. In J. R. Kimberly and R. E. Quinn, eds.,*Managing Organizational Transitions* (Homewood, IL: Irwin): 169-191.

Alexander, Cynthia Jacqueline (1987).
The administrative politics of EDP in the three prairie governments. Kingston, Canada: Queen's University, doctoral dissertation.

Alexander, M. (1990).
Complex crimes stall enforcers. *Computerworld*, Vol. 24, No. 12: 1, 4.

Allen, J. (1987).
Natural language understanding. Menlo Park, CA: Benjamin/Cummings Publishing Company.

Allen, Leilani E. (1987a).
Expert systems solve real-life needs. *Government Computer News*, 20 November 1987: 73, 78.

Allen, Leilani E. (1987b).
AI needs advocates within agencies to promote it. *Government Computer News*, 20 Nov. 1987: 79.

Alter, Allan E. (1990a).
Beyond the beans. *CIO*, Vol. 3, No. 9 (June): 51-58.

Alter, Allan E. (1990b).
All the President's computers. *CIO*, Vol. 3, No. 9 (June): 38-47.

Alter, Allan E. (1991).
Sharing the wealth. *CIO*, Vol. 4, No. 8 (May): 39-41.

Alter, Allen E. (1992).
International affairs. *CIO*, Vol. 6, No. 5 (Dec.): 34-42.

Alter, S. (1980).
Decision support systems: Current practice and continuing challenge (Reading, MA: Addison-Wesley).

Anderson, Dean R., Donna Wendt, and Bob Christensen (1987).
CAMS: An integrated system for viewing geographically criminal activity. *URISA 1987*, Vol. 3: 126-136.

Anderson, Ronald (1985).
A classification of the literature on computers and social sciences. *Computers and the Social Sciences*, Vol. 1, No. 2: 67-76.

Anderson, Ronald E., Deborah G. Johnson, Donald Gotterbarn, and Judith Perrolle (1993).
Using the new ACM code of ethics in decision-making. *Communications of the ACM*, Vol. 36, No. 2 (February): 98 - 107.

Anderson, Ronald and Kay A. Knapp (1990).
Structured sentencing simulation systems design. *Conference Proceedings: Advanced Computing for the Social Sciences*, Williamsburg, VA, April 10-12.

Anshen, M. (1960).
The manager and the black box. *Harvard Business Review*, Vol. 38, No. 6 (Nov./Dec.): 85-92.

Anshen, M. and G. L. Bach, eds. (1985).
Management and corporations 1985. NY: McGraw-Hill.

Antonoff, Michael (1989a).
Computing is the medium for the message. *Personal Computing*, Vol. 13, No. 10 (October): 163-168.

Antonoff, Michael (1989b).
Fighting city hall at 2400 baud. *Personal Computing*, Vol. 13, No. 10 (October): 170-172.

Anzovin, Steven (1991).
Online freedom. *Compute!*, Vol. 13, No. 4 (April 1): 46.

Applegate, L. M., J. I. Cash, and D. Q. Mills (1988).
Information technology and tomorrow's manager. *Harvard Business Review*, Vol. 66, No. 6 (Nov.-Dec.): 128-136.

Arbeit, David, James Heald, and James Szkotak (1987).
Development tracking in Austin, Texas: The land development review system. *URISA 1987*, Vol. 3: 169-180.

Arbona, Consuelo and Philip A. Perrone (1989).
The use of the computer in counseling college students. *Computers in Human Services*, Vol. 5, Nos. 3/4: 99-112.

Argyris, Chris (1966).
Interpersonal barriers to decision-making. *Harvard Business Review*, Vol. 44, No. 2 (March/April): 84-97.

Argyris, Chris (1971).
Management information systems: The challenge to rationality and emotionality. *Management Science*, Vol. 17, No. 6: B275-92.

Ariav, G., and M. J. Ginzberg (1982).
DSS design: A systemic view of decision support. *Communications of the ACM*, Vol. 28 (1982): 1045-1052.

Associated Press (1992a).
Experts want U. S. to harness new technology. Reprinted in *News and Observer* (Raleigh, N.C.), Jan 23: 10C.

Associated Press (1992b).
Computer 'kills' Hartford jurors. Reprinted in *News and Observer* (Raleigh, N. C.), Sept. 30: 3A.

Atelsek, Jean (1992).
Software pirates 'fess up. *PC Computing*, Vol. 5, No. 3 (March): 202-206.

Atkinson, Steven D. and Judith Hudson (1990).
Women online. Binghamton, NY: Haworth Press.

Attewell, Paul (1987a).
Big brother and the sweatshop: Computer surveillance in the automated office. *Sociological Theory*, Vol. 5, No. 1: 87-100.

Attewell, Paul (1987b).
The deskilling controversy. *Work and Occupations*, Vol. 14, No. 2: 323-346.

Attewell, Paul and James Rule (1984).
Computing and organizations: What we know and what we don't know. *Communications of the ACM*, Vol. 27, No. 12 (Dec.): 1184-1192.

Aydin, Carolyn E. (1989).
Computer adaptation to computerized medical information systems. *Journal of Health and Social Behavior*, Vol. 30: 163-179.

Ayer, Steve J. and Frank S. Patrinostro (1986).
Software implementation documentation. Software development documentation series, Vol. 5. Sunnyvale, CA: Technical Communications Associates.

Azubuike, Abraham A. (1988).
The computer as mask: A problem of inadequate human interaction examined with particular regard to online public access catalogues. Journal of Information Science, Vol. 14, No. 5: 275-83.

Badagliacco, Joanne M. (1990).
Gender and race differences in computing attitudes and experience. *Social Science Computer Review*, Vol. 8, No. 1 (Spring): 42-62.

Badagliacco, Joanne M. and Robert S. Tannenbaum (1989).
Computing: Gauging gender and race differences in experience and attitudes, and stratification in access. Delivered to the American Sociological Association, 1989 Annual Conference.

Bailey, David and Donna Thompson (1990a).
How to develop neural-network applications. *AI Expert*, Vol. 5, No. 6 (June): 38-47.

Bailey, David and Donna Thompson (1990b).
Developing neural-network applications. *AI Expert*, Vol. 5, No 9 (Sept.): 34-41.

Bailey, F. L. and H. B. Rothblatt (1984).
Defending business and white collar crimes: Federal and state, Second Edition. San Francisco: Bancroft-Whitney Co.

Bailey, J. E. and S. W. Pearson (1983).
Development of a tool for measuring and analyzing computer user satisfaction. *Management Science*, Vol. 29, No. 6: 519-529.

Bailey, Robert W. (1982).
Human performance engineering: Using human factors/ergonomics to achieve computer system usability. Englewood Cliffs, NJ: Prentice-Hall. Rev. ed. 1989.

Baily, Martin Neil (1989).
Great expectations: PCs and productivity. *PC Computing*, Vol. 2, No. 4 (April): 137-144.

Bailyn, Lotte (1989).
Toward the perfect workplace? *Communications of the ACM*, Vol. 32, No. 4 (April): 460-471.

Baker, Juli Ann (1991).
Processes of change: An anthropological inquiry into resistance to technological changes in an organization. Boulder, CO: University of Colorado-Boulder, doctoral dissertation.

Baker, Louis (1989).
Artificial intelligence with Ada. NY: McGraw-Hill.

Baker, Steve (1990).
Owens Corning Fiberglass makes gains with computer power: Productivity case study. *Industrial Computing plus Programmable Controls*, Vol.9, No. 4 (July 1): 24-27.

Baker, T. C. and S. R. Platman (1985).
A decentralized mental health reporting program. *Hospital and Community Psychiatry*, Vol. 36: 19-21.

Balas, Janet (1990).
The People's Electronic Exchange. *Computers in Libraries*, Vol. 10, No. 1 (Jan. 1): 30-32.

Baldry, Christopher (1989).
Computers, jobs, and skills: The industrial relations of technological change. New York, NY: Plenum Publishing Corp.

Banker, Stephen (1988).
Great moments in computing: The best of the worst. *PC/Computing* (August): 156-157.

Banks, J. and F. A. Rossini (1987).
Management science failures in the public sector. *Public Productivity Review*, Vol. 10, No. 4: 293-310.

Banks, Martha E. and Rosalie J. Ackerman (1990).
Ethnic and gender computer employment status. *Social Science Computer Review*, Vol. 8, No. 1 (Spring): 75-82.

Bariff, M. and E. J. Lusk (1977).
Cognitive and personality tests for MIS. *Management Science*, Vol. 23 (1977): 820-829.

Barley, S. R. (1986).
Technology as an occasion for structuring evidence from observations of CT scanners and the social order of radiology departments. *Administrative Science Quarterly*, Vol. 31: 78-108.

Barlow, John Perry (1991).
Private life in cyberspace. *Communications of the ACM*, Vol. 34, No. 8 (August): 23-25.

Barlow, John Berry (1992).
Decrypting the puzzle palace. *Communications of the ACM*, Vol. 35, No. 7 (July): 25-31.

Barnard, Chester (1938).
The functions of the executive. Cambridge, MA: Harvard University Press.

Baroudi, J. J., M. H. Olson, and B. Ives (1986).
An empirical study of the impact of user involvement on system usage and information satisfaction. *Communications of the ACM*, Vol. 29: 232-238.

Bartholomew, Doug (1992a).
The price is wrong. *InformationWeek*, No. 391 (Sept. 14): 26-36.
Bartholomew, Doug (1192b).
RSI. *InformationWeek*, No. 399 (Nov. 9): 33-44.
Baudrillard, Jean (1983).
In the shadow of the silent majorities. NY: Semiotexte.
Baylor, J. (1985).
Assessment of microcomputer attitudes of education students. Mid-South Educational Research Association, annual meeting, Biloxi, MS.
Beardsley, T. M. (1987).
Electronic taskmasters: Does monitoring degrade the quality of working life? *Scientific American*, Vol. 257, No. 6: 32-37.
Beck, Melinda and Nadine Joseph (1992).
Never too old to go on line. *Newsweek*, Vol. 119, No. 24 (June 15): 64.
Becker, H. J. (1987).,
Using computers in instruction. *Byte*, Vol. 12, No. 2: 149-162.
Becker, J. H. (1983).
National survey examines how schools use microcomputers. Baltimore: Center for the Social Organization of Schools, Johns Hopkins University, Reports Nos. 1-6.
Becker, L. G. (1984).
Computer abuse and misuse: Assessment of federal and state legislative initiative, DA Paper p-1798. Alexandria, VA: Institute of Defense Analysis.
Becker, T. and R. Scarce (1984).
Teledemocracy emergent: State of the art and science. American Political Science Association 1984 Annual Meeting, Washington, Aug. 30-Sept. 2.
Begley, Sharon (1993).
The code of the future. *Newsweek*, Vol. 121, No. 23 (June 7): 70.
Behar, Joseph E. (1988).
Course syllabus: The social impact of computer information technology. *Science, Technology & Society*, Vol. 69, No. 4 (Dec.): 7-12.
Behar, Joseph E. (1989).
Profits for people: Information services, authors, and copyrights. *Social Science Computer Review*, Vol. 7, No. 2 (Summer).
Behar, Joseph E. (1993).
Computer ethics: Moral philosophy or professional propaganda? *Computers in Human Services*, Vol. 9, Nos. 3/4: 441-453.
Bell, Daniel (1973).
The coming of post-industrial society. NY: Basic Books.
Bell, Daniel (1980).
The social framework of the information society. In Michael Dertouzos and Joel Moses, eds., *The computer age: A twenty-year view*. Cambridge, MA: MIT Press.
Benbenishty, Rami (1989).
Designing computerized clinical information systems to monitor interventions on the agency level. *Computers in Human Services*, Vol. 5, Nos. 1/2: 69-88.
Beniger, James R. (1986a).

The information society: Technological and economic origins. In Sandra J. Ball-Rokeach and Muriel G. Cantor, eds., *Media, audience, and social structure*. Beverly Hills, CA: Sage Publications: Part I, Ch. 4.

Beniger, James R. (1986b).
The control revolution: Technological and economic origins of the information society. Cambridge, MA: Harvard University Press.

Beniger, James R. (1988).
Information society and global science. *Annals of the American Academy of Political and Social Science*, Vol. 495 (Jan.): 14-28.

Bennett, Colin J. (1988).
Regulating the computer: Comparing policy instruments in Europe and the United States. *European Journal of Political Research*, Vol. 16, No. 5 (Sept.): 437-466.

Bennett, Colin J. (1991).
Computers, personal data, and theories of technology: Comparative approaches to privacy protection in the 1990s. *Science, Technology and Human Values*, Vol. 16 (Winter): 51-69.

Bequai, August (1986).
Technocrimes: The computerization of crime and terrorism. Lexington, MA: Lexington Books (now a division of Macmillan).

Berg, Eric N. (1991).
The latest quest by the idea man of communications. *New York Times*, Vol. 140 (April 218): F10(N).

Berkeley, Edward (1962).
The computer revolution. NY: Doubleday.

Berkwitt, G. J. (1966).
The new executive elite. *Dun's Review*, Vol. 88, No. 5: 40-42 ff.

Berry, Patrick (1991).
The lowdown on viruses. *Shareware Magazine*, Vol. 6, No. 3 (May/June): 32-33.

Berry, Wendell (1991).
Why I am not going to buy a computer. Charles Dunlop and Rob Kling, eds., *Computerization and controversy : Value conflicts and social choices*. NY: Academic Press, 1991: 76-81.

Betts, Mitch (1988).
Keeping big brother out of government expert systems. *Computerworld*, 24 October: 82.

Betts, Mitch (1990).
Consumers fear threat to privacy. *ComputerWorld*, Vol. 24, No. 25: 4.

Betts, Mitch (1991).
VDT monitoring under stress. *Computerworld* (Jan. 21): 1, 14.

Beusmans, Jack and Karen Wieckert (1989).
Computing, research, and war: If knowledge is power, where is responsibility? *Communications of the ACM*, Vol. 32, No. 8 (August): 939-951.

BIFU (1982).
New technology in banking, insurance, and finance. London: Banking, Insurance and Finance Union.

Bikson, T. K. (1987).
Flexible interactive technologies for multiperson tasks: Current problems and future prospects. Paper, Symposium on Technological Support for Work Group Collaboration, Center for Research on Informaiton Systems, New York University, May: 171. Cited in Perin (1991a: 79).

Bjerknes, G., P. Ehn, and M. Kyng, eds. (1987).
Computers and democracy - a Scandinavian challenge. Aldershot, UK: Avebury.

Bjorn-Anderson, Niels and G. B. Davis, eds. (1988).
Information sytems assessment: Issues and challenges. NY: Elsevier Science.

Bjorn-Anderson, Niels, Ken Eason, and Daniel Robey (1986).
Managing computer impact: An international study of management and organization. Norwood, NJ: Ablex.

Blackler, Frank and David Oborne, eds. (1987).
Information technology and people: Designing for the future. Letchworth, U.K.: British Psychological Society.

Blair, D. C. (1984).
The management of information: Basic distinctions. *Sloan Management Review* (Fall): 13-23.

Blank, Grant (1988).
New technology and the nature of sociological work. *The American Sociologist*, Vol. 19, No. 1 (Spring): 3-15.

Blauner, Robert 1964).
Alienation and freedom: The factory worker and his industry. Chicago: University of Chicago Press.

Bloombecker, J. J. Buck (1988).
An open letter on piracy. *Software Magazine* (March): 10-11.

Bloombecker, J. J. Buck (1990).
Spectacular computer crimes. Homewood, IL: Dow Jones-Irwin.

Boal, A. (1987).
Games for actors and nonactors./ London: Routledge.

Boden, Margaret (1977).
Artificial intelligence and natural man. NY: Basic Books.

Boland, R. J., Jr. (1978).
The process and product of system design. *Management Science*, Vol. 24, No. 9: 887-898.

Boland, R. J., Jr. (1985).
Phenomenology: A preferred approach to research on information systems. In Mumford, Hirschheim, Fitzgerald, and Wood-Harper et al., eds. (1985): 193-202.

Boland, R. J., Jr. and W. Day (1981).
The process of system design: A phenomenological approach. In Ginzberg and Ross, eds. (1982): 31-45.

Bomengen, Heidi and Walter Ulrich (1991).
Major study mulls future for e-mail. *Network World*, Vol. 8, No. 44 (Nov. 4): 6-8.

Bonner, Paul (1987).
Study says info systems rarely provide sustainable advantage. Vol. 4, No. 47 *PC Week*, (Nov. 24, Sec. 2): C/1.

Bonner, Paul (1990).
CD-ROM power: Knowledge in hand. *PC/Computing* (February): 64-75.
Booker, Ellis (1989).
Who pays the price of chitchat? *Computerworld*, Vol. 23, No. 43 (Oct. 23): 55-56.
Boone, Linda (1993).
Electronic mail and the right to privacy: Organizational communication issues. *News Computing Journal*, Vol. 8, No. 4: 19-36.
Boroughs, D. L. et al. (1990).
Desktop dilemma. *U. S. News and World Report* (Dec. 24): 46-48.
Borrell, Jerry (1992).
America's shame: How we've abandoned our children's future. *Macworld*, Vol. 9, No. 9 (Sept.): 25-30.
Borsook, Paulina (1993).
Seeking security. *Byte*. Vol. 18, No. 6 (May): 119-128.
Bosch-Font, Francisco (1985).
Retail banking and technology: An analysis of skill mix transformation. Institute for Research on Educational Finance and Governance, Report 85-B3 (Palo Alto, CA: School of Education, Stanford University).
Bovard, M. G. and J. Bouvard (1975).
Computerized information and effective protection of individual rights. *Society*, Vol. 12, No. 6 (Sept.-Oct.): 62-8.
Bowes, Nancie L., John J. Kenney, and Carol L. Pearson (1993).
The impact or automation on atittudes and productivity in a human services agency: An emerging issue for employee assistance program administrators. *Computers and Human Behavior*, Vol. 9, Nos. 1/2: 75 - 95.
Bowers, C. A. (1988).
The cultural dimensions of educational computing: Understanding the non-neutrality of technology. NY: Teachers College Press.
Bowers, J. M. and S. D. Benford, Eds. (1991).
Studies in computer supported cooperative work: Theory, practice and design. Amsterdam: North Holland.
Boynton, A. C. and R. W. Zmud (1984).
An assessment of critical success factors. *Sloan Management Review*, Vol. 26, No. 1 (Summer): 17-27.
Bozeman, Barry (1984).
Dimensions of 'publicness': An approach to public organization theory. In B. Bozeman and J. Straussman, eds., *New directions in public administration.* Belmont, CA: Brooks-Cole.
Bozeman, Barry (1987).
All Organizations Are Public: Bridging Public and Private Organizational Theories. San Francisco, CA: Jossey-Bass Publishers.
Bozeman, Barry and Stuart Bretschneider (1986).
Public management information systems: Theory and prescription. *Public Administration Review*, Special Issue, Vol. 46 (November): 475-487.
Bradley, Gunilla (1988).
Women, work, and computers. *Women and Health*, Vol. 13, No. 3-4: 117-132.

Brandin, David H. and Michael A. Harrison (1987).
The technology war: A case for competitiveness. NY: Wiley-Interscience.

Bratton, John (1991).
Japanization at work: The case of engineering plants in Leeds. *Work, Employment and Society*, Vol. 5, No. 3 (Sept.): 377-395.

Brennan, Jean F. (1971).
The IBM Watson Laboratory at Columbia University: A history. Armonk, NY: IBM Corporation.

Bretschneider, Stuart (1990).
Management information systems in public and private organizations: An empirical test. *Public Administration Review*, Vol. 50, No. 5 (Sept./Oct.): 536-545.

Briefs, U., C. Ciborra, and L. Schneider, eds. (1983).
Systems design for, with, and by the users. Amsterdam: North Holland.

Brod, Craig (1982).
Technostress: The human cost of the computer revolution (Reading, MA: Addison-Wesley).

Brooks, Douglas C. (1987).
Politicization of civil service becomes IRM issue. *Government Computer News*, 20 Nov. 1987: 22-26.

Brower, A. M. and E. Mutschler (1985).
Evaluation systems for practitioners: Computer-assisted information processing. Pp. 223-250 in C. B. Germain, ed., *Advances in clinical social work practice.* Silver Springs, MD: National Association of Social Workers.

Brower, Emily (1988).
Knowledge Navigator draws fire. *MacWEEK*, Dec. 6: 3.

Brown, Carol V. (1990).
Choosing the right approach for end-user computing management. *Information Executive*, Vol. 3, No. 4 (Fall): 30-34.

Brown, Donald E. (1990).
Inference engines for the mainstream. *AI Expert*, Vol. 5, No. 2 (Feb.): 32-37.

Brown, J. Randall and Erwin L. Herman (1978).
Parks maintenance management system: Interim computer program and documentation. Washington, DC: Office of Policy Development and Research, Department of Housing and Urban Development. Report No. HUD-0000421.

Bruce, Margaret and Gill Kirkup (1986)
An analysis of women's roles under the impact of new technology in the home and office. In Gro Bjerknes et al., *Computers and Democracy: A Scandinavian Challenge* (Bucks, England: Institute of Educational Technology, Open University): Ch. 18.

Bruwer, P. J. S. (1984).
A descriptive model of success for computer-based information systems. *Information and Management*, Vol. 7, No. 2: 63-67.

Bryce, Milt (1987).
The IRM idea. *Datamation*, Vol. 33, No. 8: 89-92.

Bryce, Milt and Tim Bryce (1988).
The IRM revolution: Blueprint for the 21st century. Palm Harbor, FL: MBA Press.

Buchanan, Bob (1988).
Administrative error causes most major system failures. *Government Computer News* (Feb. 19): 34.

Buchanan, D. A and D. Boddy (1983).
Advanced technology and the quality of working life: The effects of computerized controls on buiscuit-making operators. *Journal of Occupational Psychology*, Vol. 56: 109-119.

Buchanan, D. A., D. Boddy, et al. (1983).
Organizations in the computer age: Technological imperatives and strategic choice. Brookfield, VT: Gower.

Buchanan, D. A. and D. Boddy (1983).
Advanced technology and the quality of working life: The effects of computerized controls on biscuit-making operators. *Journal of Occupational Psychology*, Vol. 56: 109-119.

Bullen, Christine V. and John F. Rockhart (1981).
A primer on critical success factors. Cambridge, MA: MIT, Center for Systems Research, Working Paper #1220-81.

Bullen, Christine V. and John L. Bennett (1991).
Groupware in practice: An interpretation of work experiences. In Charles Dunlop and Rob Kling, eds., *Computerization and controversy : Value conflicts and social choices*. NY: Academic Press, 1991: 257-287.

Burch, J. G. (1986).
Designing information systems for people. *Journal of Systems Management*, Vol. 37 (Oct.): 30-33.

Burch, J. and G. Grudnitski (1989).
Information systems: Theory and practice, 5th edition. NY: John Wiley and Sons.

Burck, G. (1964).
The age of the computer: Management will never be the same. *Management Review*, Vol. 53, No. 9: 16-20.

Bureau of National Affairs, Inc. (1984).
Document No. 220: A-4 - A-5. Washington, DC.

Burlingame, J. F. (1961).
Information technology and decentralization. *Harvard Business Review*, Vol. 39, No. 6 (Nov./Dec.): 121-126.

Burnham, David (1983).
The rise of the computer state. NY: Pantheon Books.

Bush, Vannevar (1945).
Science: The endless frontier. Washington, DC: U. S. Government Printing Office.

Bush, Vannevar (1988).
As we may think. *The Atlantic Monthly* (1948). Reprinted in Irene Greif, ed., *Computer-supported cooperative work: A book of readings*. San Mateo, CA: Morgan-Kaufman.

Buss, Martin D.J. (1984).
Legislative threat to transborder data flow. *Harvard Business Review*, Vol. 62, No. 3 (May/June): 111.

Butterfield, William H. (1986).
Computers in social work and social welfare: Issues and perspectives. *Journal of Sociology and Social Welfare*, Vol. 13: 5-26.

Butterfield, William H. (1988).
Artificial intelligence: An introduction. *Computers in Human Services*, Vol. 3, Nos. 1/2: 23-35.

Bynum, Peter (1991).
Marketing social service programs using political campaign technology. *Computers in Human Services*, Vol. 8, No. 1: 67-72.

Caldwell, Bruce (1989a).
Shell launches centralization strategy. *InformationWeek* (Oct. 23): 32.

Caldwell, Bruce (1989b).
What is it all worth, anyway? *InformationWeek* (Sept. 18): 128-132.

Caldwell, Bruce (1990a).
Cure or confusion? *InformationWeek*, No. 287 (Sept. 17): 45.

Caldwell, Bruce (1990b).
Whose mail is it anyway? *InformationWeek*, No. 283 (August 20): 53.

Caldwell, Bruce (1990c).
Big brother is watching. *InformationWeek*, No. 279 (June 18): 34-36.

Caldwell, Bruce (1990d).
Whose system is it anyway? *InformationWeek*, No. 299 (Dec. 10): 17.

Caldwell, Bruce (1990e).
And the SIM survey says... *InformationWeek*, No. 257 (Feb. 12): 51.

Caldwell, Bruce (1990f).
Sour on technology. *InformationWeek*, No. 275 (June 18): 20.

Caldwell, Bruce (1990g).
Is NASA out of space? *InformationWeek*, No. 263 (March 26): 48.

Caldwell, Bruce (1990h).
New generation. *InformationWeek*, No. 274 (June 11): 29-34.

Caldwell, Bruce (1990i).
When IS and HR collide. *InformationWeek*, No. 255 (Jan. 29): 48-49.

Caldwell, Bruce (1991a).
More e-mail controversy: Former Nissan employees file invasion of privacy suit. *InformationWeek*, No. 303 (Jan. 14): 51-2.

Caldwell, Bruce (1991b).
New vision through information. *InformationWeek*, No. 351 (Dec. 16): 30-31.

Caldwell, Bruce (1991c),
Black & Decker retools. *InformationWeek*, No. 339 (Sept. 23): 30-33.

Caldwell, Bruce (1991d).
A cure for hospital woes. *InformationWeek*, No. 337 (Sept. 9): 34-40.

Caldwell, Bruce (1992a).
Down and out in Chicago. *InformationWeek*, No. 369 (April 20): 12-13.

Caldwell, Bruce (1992b).
Feds alarmed by bank outsourcing practices. *InformationWeek*, No, 354 (Jan. 6): 13.

Caldwell, Bruce (1992c).
Up in arms over outsourcing. *InformationWeek*, No. 359 (Feb. 10): 10-11.

Caldwell, Bruce (1992d).
Missing persons. *InformationWeek*, No. 402 (Nov. 30): 54-61.

Caldwell, Bruce (1993a).
High hopes for high tech. *InformationWeek*, No. 409 (Jan. 25): 22-24.

Caldwell, Bruce (1993b).
A banner IS shop loses altitude: Turbulence at AMR. *InformationWeek*, No. 434 (July 19): 38-50.

Caldwell, Bruce and Chuck Appleby (1993).
Florida fiasco. *InformationWeek*, No. 422 (April 26): 12-13.

Calhoun, Craig and Martha Copp (1988).
Computerization in legal work: How much does new technology change professional practice? *Research in the Sociology of Work*, Vol. 4: 233-259.

Canning, R. G. (1977).
Getting the requirements right. *EDP Analysis*, Vol. 15, No. 7: 1-4.

Caporael, L. (1984).
Computers, prophecy, and experience: A historical perspective. *Journal of Social Issues*, Vol. 40, No. 3 : 15-29.

Caporael, L. and W. Thorngate (1984).
Introduction: Towards the social psychology of computing. *Journal of Social Issues*, Vol. 40, No. 3: 1-13.

Cardinali, Richard (1990).
User involvement - an assessment of the need for this vital link in the system development process. *Information Executive*, Vol. 3, No. 4 (Fall): 37-40.

Carper, William B. (1992).
Society impacts and consequences of transborder data flows. In S. Palvia, P. Palvia, and R. M. Zigli, eds., *The global issues of information technology management* (Harrisburg, PA: Idea Group Publishing): 427-449.

Carr, Clark (1988).
Spreadsheet sketches for rule-based systems. *AI Expert*, Vol. 4, No. 11 (Nov.): 30-35.

Carr, Frank (1989a).
Executive info systems don't help real executives. *Government Computer News*, 10 July: 90.

Carr, Frank (1989b).
How changes in 1970s paved IRM road for the '90s. *Government Computer News*, 13 Nov.: 102.

Carr, Frank (1989c).
Focus on the right side of the productivity equation. *Government Computer News*, 6 March: 142.

Carr, Frank (1990).
Federal IRM managers should heed predecessors. *Government Computer News*, February 5: 86.

Carr, Marilyn (1990).
AS EUC moves to adulthood, IS is faced with new challenges. *Computing Canada*, Vol. 16, No. 25 (Dec. 6): 41.

Carson, Kerry D. and Rodger W. Griffeth (1990).
Changing a management information system: Managing resistance by attending to the rights and responsibilities of employees. *Employee Responsibilities and Rights Journal*, Vol. 3, no. 1 (March): 47-58.

Carter, N. M. (1984).
Computerization as a predominate technology: Its influence on the structure of newspaper organizations. *Academy of Management Journal*, Vol. 27: 247-270.

Carter, Norman (1988).
The project manager: An emerging professional. *Journal of Information Systems Management*, Vol 5, No. 4 (Fall): 8 - 14.

Cash, James and Roger Woolfe (1992).
IT gets in line. *InformationWeek*, No. 392 (Sept. 21): 38-44.

Cassagne, Jean and Toru Iioshi (1992).
The world view. *Macworld*, Vol. 9, No. 9 (Sept.): 237-239.

Cassedy, Ellen and Karen Nussbaum (1983).
Nine to five: The working woman's guide to office survival. NY: Penguin.

Cassell, Catherine, Mike Fitter, David Fryer, and Leigh Smith (1988).
The development of computer applications by non-employed people in community settings. *Journal of Occupational Psychology*, Vol. 61, No. 1 (March): 89-102.

Cassidy, Peter (1991).
The information border police. *InformationWeek*, No. 336 (Sept. 2): 38-9.

Caudle, Sharon L. (1987).
High tech to better effect. *The Bureaucrat*, Spring 1987: 47 - 51.

Caudle, Sharon L. (1988a).
Federal information resources management after the Paperwork Reduction Act. *Public Administration Review*, Vol. 48, No. 4 (July/August): 790-799.

Caudle, Sharon L. (1988b).
Off the IRM mark at the federal level. *Journal of Systems Management*, Vol. 39, No. 8: 6-10.

Caudle, Sharon L. (1988c).
Study reveals agencies' confusion about IRM role. *Government Computer News*, 4 March: 38, 50.

Caudle, Sharon L. (1990).
Managing information resources in state government. *Public Administration Review*, Vol. 50, No. 5 (Sept./Oct.): 515-535.

Caudle, Sharon L. and Donald A. Marchand, with S. I. Bretschneider, P. T. Fletcher, and K. M. Thurmaier (1989).
Managing information resources: New directions in state government. Syracuse, NY: Center for Science and Technology, School of Information Studies, August 1989.

Celko, Joe (1987).
Faster development means higher maintenance costs. *Software News*, October 1987: 83-84.

Cerullo, M. J. (1979).
MIS: What can go wrong. *Management Accounting*, Vol. 60, No. 10: 43-48.

Chambers, S. M. and V. A. Clarke (1987).
Is inequity cumulative? The relationship between disadvantaged group membership and students' computing experience, knowledge, attitudes and intentions. *Journal of Educational Computing Research*, Vol. 3, No. 4: 495-518.
Chamot, D. (1987).
Electronic work and the white-collar employee. In R. Kraut, ed. (1987): 22-34.
Chen, M. (1986).
Gender and computers: The beneficial effects of experience on attitudes. *Journal of Educational Computing Research*, Vol. 2, No. 3: 265-282.
Cheney, Paul H. and George M. Kasper (1993).
Responding to world competition: Development of the global IS professional. *Journal of Global Information Management*, Vol. 1, No. 1 (Winter).
Chisholm, Rupert F. (1988).
Introducing advanced information technology into public organizations. *Public Productivity Review*, Vol. 11, No. 4 (Summer): 39-56.
Cho, Yong-Kil and Kenneth E. Kendall (1989).
Management of the information center: The relationship of power to end-user performance and satisfaction. *Information Resources Management Journal*, Vol. 2, No. 2 (Spring): 1-11.
Christensen, K. E. (1986).
Ethics of information technology. In R. Geiss and N. Viswanathan, eds., *The Human Edge*. NY: Haworth Press: 72-91.
Chronicle of Higher Education (1993).
On line. *Chronicle of Higher Education*, Vol. 39, No. 37 (May 19): A25.
Cisler, Steve (1993).
Community computer networks: Building electronic greenbelts. Electronic paper on the Internet at ftp.apple.com (June 20).
Clark, I., I. McLaughlin, and H. Rose (1988).
The process of technological change: New technology and social choice in the workplace. Cambridge, UK: Cambridge University Press.
Clark, Thomas D. Jr. (1992).
Corporate systems management: An overview and research perspective. *Communications of the ACM*, Vol. 35, No. 2 (Feb.): 61-75.
Clarke, Roger A. (1988).
Information technology and dataveillance. *Communications of the ACM*, Vol. 31, No. 5 (May): 498-512.
Clement, Andrew (1989).
A Canadian case study report: Towards self-managed automation in small offices. *Information Technology Development*, Vol. 4, No. 2: 185-233.
Cleveland, Harland (1985a).
The knowledge executive. NY: E. P. Dutton.
Cleveland, Harland (1985b).
The twilight of hierarchy: Speculations on the global information society. *Public Administration Review* (Jan./Feb.): 185-195. Reprinted in B. Guile, ed., *Information technologies and social transformation*. Washington, D.C.: National Academy Press.

Clippinger, John H. (1976).
Who gains by communications development? Studies of information technologies in developing countries. Working Paper 76-1. Cambridge, MA: Program on Information Technologies and Public Policy, Harvard University.

Cnaan, Ram A. (1989).
Social work practice and information technology - an unestablished link. *Computers in Human Services*, Vol. 5, Nos. 1/2: 1-15.

Coates, Joseph F. (1987).
Computing in an ethical wasteland. *EPPD Newsletter* (American Society for Engineering Education). November.

Cohen, Alan M. (1991).
A guide to networking. Boston: Boyd and Fraser Publishing Co.

Cohen, Carl (1984).
Electronic democracy. *PC World*, Vol. 2, No. 7 (July): 21-22.

Cohen, Jon D. (1990).
HIV/AIDS confidentiality: Are computerized medical records making confidentiality impossible? *Software Law Journal*, Vol. 4, No. 1 (Oct.): 93-115.

Collins, Randall (1992).
Sociological insight: An introduction to non-obvious sociology, 2nd ed. NY: Oxford University Press.

Collins-Williams, J. and D. Lyn (1987).
Automated indexing of the decisions of administrative boards and tribunals: The Ontario Labour Relations Board, Employment Standards Branch, and Human Rights Commission. *Government Publications Review*, Vol. 14 (1987): 525-539.

Collis, B. (1985).
Psychosocial implications of sex differences in attitudes toward computers: Results of a survey. *International Journal of Women's Studies*, Vol. 8, No. 3: 207-213.

Collis, Betty A. and Lloyd Ollila (1986).
An examination of sex differences in secondary school students' attitudes toward writing and toward computers. *Alberta Journal of Educational Research*, Vol. 32, No. 4 (Dec.): 297-306.

Commission on Freedom of Equality of Access to Information (1986)
Freedom and equality of access to information: A report to the American Library Association. Chicago: ALA.

Commission on Federal Paperwork (1977).
A report of the commission on federal paperwork: Information resources management. Washington, DC: Superintendent of Documents.

Communications of the ACM (1989).
Can robots learn from experience? *Communications of the ACM*, Vol. 32, No. 12 (December): 1499.

Communications of the ACM (1990).
Special section on EC '92. *Communications of the ACM*, Vol. 33, No. 4 (April): 404-438.

Communications of the ACM (1992a).
Too much of a good thing. *Communications of the ACM*, Vol. 35, No. 3 (March): 9-10.

Communications of the ACM (1992b).
NSF grant to fund mentoring project for women and minorities. *Communications of the ACM*, Vol. 35, No. 1 (Jan.): S2.

Comptroller General of the U.S. (1977).
Federal information sources and systems, Congressional Sourcebook Series. Washington: GAO, 1977.

Computer Technology Review (1990).
Security is a people problem. *Computer Technology Review*, Vol. 10, No. 7 (June): 1.

Computing Reviews (1991).
Computer Reviews, Vol. 32, No. 12 (Dec.): front cover.

Conger, James L. (1988).
Using financial tools for non-financial simulations. *Byte* (Jan.): 291-296.

Conger, Sue (1993).
Issues in teaching globalization in information systems. In Mehdi Khosrowpour and Karen D. Loch, eds., *Global information technology education: Issues and trends* (Harrisburg, PA: Idea Group Publishing): 313-353.

Conly, Catherine H. (1989).
Organizing for computer crime investigation and prosecution. Washington, DC: Office of Justice Programs, National Institute of Justice. Series: *Issues and Practices in Criminal Justice*, J 28.23:C 86/3.

Conomikes, G. (1967).
Computers are creating personnel problems. *Personnel Journal*, Vol. 46: 52-53.

Cooper, James A. (1989).
Computer and communications security: strategies for the 1990's. NY: Intertext/ McGraw-Hill.

Cooper, Randolph B. (1988).
Review of management information systems research: A management support emphasis. *Information Processing and Management*, Vol. 24, No. 1: 73-102.

Costikyan, Greg (1991).
Closing the net: Will overzealous investigations of computer crime render freedom ot the press technologically obsolete? *Reason*, Vol. 22 (Jan.): 22-27.

Coursey, David and Barry Bozeman (1990).
Decision making in public and private organizations: A test of alternative concepts of "publicness". *Public Administration Review*, Vol. 50, No. 5 (Sept./ Oct.): 525-535.

Crawford, A. B. (1982),
Corporate electronic mail -- a communication-intensive application of information technology. *MIS Quarterly*, Vol. 6, No. 3 (Sept.): 1-13.

Crawford, Dianne (1991).
CEOs unite to influence U.S. technology policy. *Communications of the ACM*, Vol. 34, No. 6 (June): 15-18.

Crawford, Reg (1988).
Inside classrooms: Word processing and the fourth grade writer. *Canadian Journal of English Language Arts*, Vol. 11, No. 1: 42-46.

Creative Computing (1985).
Choosing and using business forecasting software. *Creative Computing*, Vol. 7 (Jan.): pp. 121 ff.

Crockett, Barton (1990).
Bank-by-phone services fill void left by home banking. *Network World*, Vol. 7 (July 23): 2-3.

Crockett, Barton (1991).
HP centralizes control of networks to rein in costs. *Network World*, Vol. 8, No. 39 (Sept. 30): 1-2.

Cross, Thomas B. and Marjorie Raizman (1986).
Telecommuting: The future technology of work. Homewood, IL.: Dow Jones-Irwin, 1986.

Crow, Michael M. (1985).
The effect of publicness on organizational performance: A comparative study of R&D laboratories. Syracuse, NY: Department of Political Science, Syracuse University, Ph.D. Dissertation.

Cunningham, L. N. (1985).
Computers and educational governance. *Microcomputers and Education. Yearbook. Part 1*. (Chicago: National Society for the Study of Education).

Currid, Cheryl (1990a).
Today's PC support staffs aren't ready for downsizing. *PC Week*, Vol. 7, No. 15 (April 16): 171.

Currid, Cheryl (1990b).
Big corporate changes start with small successes. *PC Week*, Vol. 7, No. 20 (May 22): 103.

Currid, Cheryl (1991a).
Information generation spawns computer junkies. *PC Week*, Vol. 8, No. 19 (May 13): 62.

Currid, Cheryl (1991b).
Eight success factors can help create great IS. *PC Week*, Vol. 8, No. 37 (Sept. 16): 85.

Cwikel, Julie and Menachem Monnickendam (1993).
Factors in acceptance of advanced information technology among social workers: An exploratory study. Pp. 279-291 in Marcos Leiderman, Charles Guzetta, Leny Struminger, and Menachem Monnickendam, eds. (1993). *Technology in people services: Research, theory, and applications*. NY: Haworth Press.

Cyert, R. (1987).
Why I believe there is a revolution underway in higher education. In *Campus of the Future: Conference on Information Resources* (Dublin, Ohio: Online Computer Library Center): 15.

Cyert, Richard M. and David C. Mowery, eds. (1987).
Technology and employment: Innovation and growth in the U. S. economy. Washington, DC: National Academy Press.

Czepiel, J. A. (1974).
Word of mouth processes in the diffusion of a major technological innovation. *Journal of Marketing Research*, Vol. 11: 172-180.

Dahl, Robert and Charles Lindblom (1953).
Politics, economics, and welfare. NY: Harper and Row.

Dahm-Larsen, Merrilee (1989).
Helping your staff adapt to point-of-sale technology. *Computing Canada*, Vol. 15, No. 20 (Oct. 12): 65.

Dambrot, F., M. Watkins-Malek, S. Silling, R. Marshall, and J. Garvey (1985).
Correlates of sex differences in attitudes toward and involvement with computers. *Journal of Vocational Behavior*, Vol. 27: 71-86.

Daniel, Dianne (1989).
Human element is key to an IS transition, seminar told. *Computing Canada*, Vol. 15, No. 24 (Nov. 23): 19.

Danziger, James N. (1977).
Computers, local government, and the litany to EDP. *Public Administration Review*, Vol. 37, No. 1 (Jan./Feb.).

Danziger, James N. (1979).
The "Skill Bureaucracy" and interorganizational control: The case of the data processing unit. *Sociology of Work and Occupations*, Vol. 6, No. 2 (May): 204-226.

Danziger, James N. (1986).
Computing and the political world. *Computers and the Social Sciences*, Vol. 2, No. 4 (Oct.-Dec.): 183-200.

Danziger, James N. (1988).
Waiting for the revolution: The use of microcomputers by social scientists. *The American Sociologist*, Vol. 19, No. 1 (Spring, 1988): 32-53.

Danziger, James N., W. Dutton, R, Kling, and K. Kraemer (1982).
Computers and politics: High technology and American local governments. NY: Columbia University Press.

Danziger, James N. and Kenneth Kraemer (1985).
Computerized data-based systems and productivity among professional workers: The case of detectives. *Public Administration Review*, Vol. 45, No. 1 (January): 196-209.

Danziger, James N. and Kenneth L. Kraemer (1987).
People and computers: The impact of computing on end users in organizations. NY: Columbia University Press.

Danziger, James N., Kenneth L. Kraemer, Debora E. Dunkle, and John Leslie King (1993).
Enhancing the quality of computing service: Technology, structure, and people. *Public Administration Review*, Vol. 53, No. 2 (March/April): 161-169.

Darany, Theodore S. (1984).
Computer applications to personnel (Releasing the genie - harnessing the dragon). *Public Personnel Management*, Vol. 13, No. 4 (1984): 451-474.

Database Searcher (1987).
Dun and Bradstreet Credit Services block labor unions, others from access to financial records. *Database Searcher*, Vol. 3, No. 10 (December): 8, 10.

Database Searcher (1988).
Librarians battle for electronic freedom. *Database Searcher*, Vol. 4, No. 7 (Sept.): 37.

Database Searcher (1990a).
Controversial personal data on HRIN. *Database Searcher*, Vol. 6, No. 7 (Sept.): 10.

Database Searcher (1990b).
News hotline. *Database Searcher*, Vol. 6, No. 10 (Dec.): 7.

Davis, G. B. (1974).
Management Information Systems: Conceptual foundations, structure, and development. NY: McGraw-Hill, 1974.

Davis, G. B. and M. Olson (1985).
Management information systems - Conceptual foundations, methods, and development, second edition. NY: McGraw-Hill.

Davis, Gina (1991).
A public economy approach to education: Choice and co-production. *International Political Science Review*, Vol. 12, No. 4: 313-335.

Davis, Jinnie Y. (1992).
Scholarly communication in peril: Addressing the crisis. *The NCSU Libraries Focus*, Vol. 12, No. 2: 1-5.

Davis, John J. (1989).
Demand up for info execs, *Information Center*, Vol. 5, No. 7 (July): 15.

Davis, L. V. (1985).
Female and male voices in social work. *Social Work*, Vol. 30: 106-113.

Davis, Stan and Bill Davidson (1991).
2020 Vision: Transform Your Business Today to Succeed in Tomorrow's Economy. NY: Simon and Schuster.

Dawson, Gaye C., William C. Cummings, and Lanny J. Ryan (1987).
The human vs. computer conflict in community mental health agencies. *Journal of Mental Health Administration*, Vol. 14, No. 2 (Fall): 30-34.

Dawson, P. and I. McLaughlin (1986).
Computer technology and the redefinition of supervision: A study of the effects of computerization on railway freight supervisors. *Journal of Management Studies*, Vol. 23: 116-132.

Dean, N. J. (1968).
The computer comes of age. *Harvard Business Review*, Vol. 46, No. 1 (Jan./Feb.): 83-91.

DeBenedictis, Don J. (1990).
E-mail snoops: reading others' computer messages may be against the law. *ABA Journal*, Vol. 76, No. 26 (Sept.): 2.

DeBrabander, B. and G. Thiers (1984).
Successful information system development in relation to situational factors which affect effective communication between MIS users and EDP specialists. *Management Science*, Vol. 30, No. 2: 137-155.

Decker, Elizabeth Jane and John Patrick Plumlee (1985).
Microcomputers, manpower, and performance in a public utility. *Public Productivity Review*, Vol. 9, No. 2-3 (Summer/Fall): 213-225.

DeJean, David (1988b).
Gameplan simulates corporate culture, goal is to teach effective management. *PC Week*, Feb. 23: 74, 83.

DeJean, David (1988b).
The electronic workgroup. *PC Computing*. Oct.: 72-80.

DeJean, David (1989).
Making sense of SQL, *PC/Computing*, Vol. 2 No. 7 (July): 142-148.

Dejoie, Roy, George Fowler, and David Paradice, eds. (1991).
Ethical issues in information systems: A book of readings. Cincinnati, OH: South-Western.

DeLoughry, Thomas J. (1993)
Colleges and telephone companies battle over future of the Internet. *Chronicle of Higher Education*, Vol. 39, No. 37 (May 19): A25-A27.

DeMarco, Tom and Timothy Lister (1987).
Peopleware: Productive projects and teams. NY: Dorset House.

Deming, W. Edwards (1982).
Quality, productivity, and competitive position. Cambridge, MA: MIT, Center for Advanced Engineering Study.

Deming, W. Edwards (1986).
Out of the Crisis. Cambridge, MA: MIT, Center for Advanced Engineering Study.

de Neufville, Judy I. (1975).
Social indicators and public policy: Interactive processes of design and application. NY: Elsevier.

Denning, Dorothy P. (1991).
The United States vs. Craig Neidorf: A debate on electronic publishing, constitutional rights, and hacking. *Communications of the ACM*, Vol. 34, No. 3 (March): 24-32.

Denning, Dorothy E. (1993).
To tap or not to tap. *Communications of the ACM*, Vol. 36, No. 3 (March): 24-33. A commentary by eight experts follows this article, then a final defense by Denning (pp. 34-45).

Denning, Peter J. (1986).
The science of computing: Will machines ever think?. *American Scientist*, Vol. 74:344-346.

Denning, Peter J. (1987).
A new paradigm for science. *American Scientist*, Vol. 75 (Nov./Dec.): 572-573.

Denning, Peter J. (1988).
Computer viruses. *American Scientist*, Vol. 76 (June): 236-238.

Denning, Peter J. (1990).
Computers under attack: Intruders, worms, and viruses. NYC, NY: ACM Press.

Depew,C. Henry (1985).
Fla. agency commitment brings smooth PC use. *Government Computer News*, 7 June: 75.

Desky, Joanne (1991).
Telecommuting trends rising: Traditional management practices challenged. *PA Times*, Vol. 14, No. 9 (Sept.): 1, 20.

Dickson, G. W. (1968).
Management information - decision systems. *Business Horizons*, Vol. 11, No. 6: 17-26.

Dickson, G. W., R. I. Leitheiser, J. C. Wetherbe, and M. Nechis (1984).
Key information systems issues for the 1980's. *MIS Quarterly*, Vol. 8, No. 3 (Sept.): 135-159.

Diebold, J. (1969).
Bad decisions on computer use. *Harvard Business Review*, Vol. 47, No. 1 (Jan./Feb.): 13-16 ff.

Donner, F. J. (1981).
The age of surveillance. NY: Random House.

Dooley, Tom (1988).
Computer cross sections unite at law conference. *Management Information Systems Week*, 15 Feb: 4-5.

Dos Santos, B. L. 1986).
A management approach to systems development projects. *Journal of Systems Management*, Vol. 37 (August): 35-41.

Downing, John et al. (1991).
Computers for social change: Introduction. *Computers in Human Services*, Vol. 8, No. 1: 1-8. Reprinted in J. Downing et al., *Computers for Social Change and Community Organizing* (Binghamton, NY: Haworth Press, 1991).

Downing, John D. H. (1989).
Computers for political change: PeaceNet and Public Data Access. *Journal of Communication*, Vol. 39, No. 3 (Summer): 154-162.

Downing, Hazel (1980).
Word processors and the oppression of women. In Tom Forester, ed., *The microelectronics revolution*. Cambridge, MA: MIT Press: 275-287.

Downs, Anthony (1967).
A realistic look at the final payoffs from urban data systems. *Public Administration Review*, Vol. 77, No. 3 (May/June): 204-210.

Dreyfus, Hubert L. (1979).
What computers can't do. NY: Harper and Row.

Dreyfus, Hubert L. and Stuart Dreyfus (1986).
Mind over machine: The power of human intuition and expertise in the era of the computer. NY: Free Press.

Droste, Therese (1987).
High mortality data call for planning. *Hospitals*, 20 Jan.: 17-18.

Drucker, Peter (1988).
The coming of the new organization. *Harvard Business Review*, Vol. 66, No. 1 (Jan./Feb.): 45-53.

Drucker, Peter (1992).
Managing for the future: The 1990s and beyond. NY: Truman Tally Books/ Dutton.

Drummond, Marshall Edward and Peter J. Landsberger (1989).
Defining the target environment: A "shared vision" methodology for information systems planning - a case study. *Information Resources Management Journal*, Vol. 2, No. 4 (Fall): 17-30.

Drury, D. H. (1983).
An empirical assessment of the stages of data processing growth. *MIS Quarterly*, Vol. 7, No. 2 (June): 59-70.

Drury, D. H. (1984).
An evaluation of data processing steering committees. *MIS Quarterly*, Vol. 8, No. 4 (Dec.): 257-266.

Dubinskas, (1986).
Collapsing the user-designer divide: Electronic communication software and the social construction of advanced technology. In Ron Westrum, ed., *Organizations, Designs, and the Future*. Ypsilanti, MI: Eastern Michigan University, conference proceedings.

Dudek, Virginia (1989).
Planning for network disasters: Establishing strategy is the key, *MIS Week*, 12 June: 31, 36.

Duffy, Ann D., D. Glenday, and N. Pupo (1992).
Canadian clerical workers and the introduction of microtechnology: Do unions make a difference? American Sociological Association, Annual Conference, paper.

Duffy, J. C. and J. J. Waterton (1984).
Under-reporting of alcohol consumption in sample surveys: The effects of computer interviewing in field work. *British Journal of Addiction*, Vol. 79: 303-308.

Duncan, Joseph W. and William C. Chelton (1978).
Revolution in United States government statistics: 1926-1976. Washington, DC: Department of Commerce, Office of Federal Statistical Policy and Standards.

Dunkle, John O. (1990).
Working well in a work-group environment. *Computerworld*, Vol. 24, No. 23 (June 4): 31-33.

Dunlop, Charles and Rob Kling (1991).
The dreams of technological utopianism. In Charles Dunlop and Rob Kling, eds., *Computerization and controversy : Value conflicts and social choices*. NY: Academic Press, 1991: 14-30.

Dutton, William H. (1992).
Political science research on teledemocracy. *Social Science Computer Review*, Vol. 10, No. 1 (Winter).

Dutton, William H., Jay G. Blumler, and Kenneth L. Kraemer (1987a).
Continuity and change in conceptions of the wired city. In Dutton, Blumler, and Kraemer, eds. (1987c): ch. 1.

Dutton, William H., Jay G. Blumler, and Kenneth L. Kraemer (1987b).
A comparative analysis. In Dutton, Blumler, and Kraemer (1987c): ch. 28.

Dutton, William H., Jay G. Blumler, and Kenneth L. Kraemer, eds. (1987c).
Wired cities: Shaping the future of communications. Boston: G. K. Hall and Co.

Dutton, William H. and K. Kendall Guthrie (1991).
The political construction of an information utility. *Informatics and the Public Sector*.

Dutton, William H. and Kenneth L. Kraemer (1985).
Modeling as negotiating. Norwood, NJ: Ablex.

Dutton, William H. and Robert G. Meadow (1987).
A tolerance for surveillance. In Levitan, ed. (1987): 147-170.

Dyson, Esther (1988).
Esther Dyson (column). *PC-Computing*, Vol. 1, No. 2 (Sept.): 21.

Eason, Ken (1988).
Information technology and organizational change. Bristol, PA: Taylor and Francis, Inc.

Eastman, Beva (1991).
Women, computers, and social change. *Computers in Human Services*, Vol. 8, No. 1:41-53.

Eastman, Susan and Kathy Krendl (1987).
Computers and gender: Differential effects of electronic search on students' achievement and attitudes. *Journal of Research and Development in Education*, Vol. 20,, No. 3 (Spring): 41-48.

Ebel, K. H. (1987).
Some workplace effects of CAD and CAM. *International Labor Review*, Vol. 127 (May/June): 351-370.

EDUCOM Review (1993).
Special focus on the Bill of Rights and Responsibilities for Electronic Learners. *EDUCOM Review*, Vol. 28, No. 3 (May/June): 24 - 47.

Edwards, Clark (1991).
The Americans with Disabilities Act. *News Computing Journal*, Vol. 7, No. 3: i-ix.

Edwards, John (1988).
Fujitsu obtains IBM's protected source code, *Online Today* (March): 13.

Edwards, Paul N. (1990).
The army and the microworld: Computers and the politics of gender identity. *Signs*, Vol. 16, No. 1 (Autumn): 102-127.

Edwards, Roger and K. G. Englehardt (1989).
Microprocessor based innovations and older Americans: AART survey results and their implications for service robotics. *International Journal of Technology and Aging*, Vol. 2, No. 1: 43-55.

Ehn, Pelle and A. Sandberg (1979)
Systems development: Critique of ideology and the division of labor in computer field, in Sandberg, ed. (1979): 34-46.

Ehn, Pelle, M. Kyng, and Y. Sundblat (1983).
The UTOPIA project: On training, technology, and products viewed from the quality of work perspective. In U. Briefs, C. Ciborra, and L. Schneider, eds., *Systems design for, with and by the users*. Amsterdam: North-Holland: 439-449.

Ehn, Pelle (1989).
The art and science of designing computer artifacts. *Scandinavian Journal of Information Systems* (August): 21-42.

Ein-Dor, Phillip and Eli Segev (1978).
Organizational context and the success of managment information systems, *Management Science*, Vol. 24, No. 1: 1064-1077.

Ein-Dor, Phillip, eli Segev and Moshe Orgad (1993).
The effect of national cultural environments on IS: Implications for global information management. *Journal of Global Information Management*, Vol. 1, No. 1 (Winter).
Elliot, J. D. (1958).
EDP - Its impact on jobs, procedures and people, *Journal of Industrial Engineering*, Vol. 9, No. 5: 407-410.
Elliot, Thomas R. (1988).
Rallying round the standard(s), *Journal of Information Systems Management*, Vol. 5, No. 1 (Winter, 1988): 58-60.
Ellis, C. A., S. J. Gibbs and G. L. Rein (1991).
Groupware: Some issues and experiences. *Communications of the ACM*, Vol. 34, No. 1 (Jan.): 38-58.
Emmert, Mark A. and Michael M. Crow (1988).
Public, private and hybrid organizations: An empirical examination of the role of publicness. *Administration and Society*, Vol. 20, No. 2 (August): 216-244.
Emurian, Henry H. 1989).
Human-computer interactions: Are there adverse health consequences? *Computers in Human Behavior*, Vol. 5: 265-275.
Epstein, Earl F. and Howard Roitman (1987).
Liability for information, in *URISA, 1987*, Vol. IV: 115-25.
Erdman, Harold P. and Sharon W. Foster (1988).
Ethical issues in the use of computer-based assessment, *Computers in Human Services*, Vol. 3, Nos. 1/2: 71-87.
Eriksson, I., B. Kitchenham, and K. Tijdens, eds. (1991).
Women, work and computerization: Understanding and overcoming bias in work and education. Proceedings of the IFIP TC9/WG9.1 Conference (Helsinki). Amsterdam: North-Holland.
Ermann, M. D., Mary B. William, and Claudio Gutierrez, eds. (1990).
Computers, ethics, and society. NY: Oxford University Press.
ERGO (1987).
Vision experts report VDT's not harmful to the eyes, *ERGO: An Ergonomics Digest* (Fall/Winter): 2.
Ess, Charles (1987).
Computers and ideology: Limits of the machine. *Quarterly Journal of Ideology*, Vol. 11, No. 2 (April): 33-39.
Estabrooks, Maurice (1988).
Programmed capitalism: A computer-mediated global society (Armonk, NY: M. M. Sharpe).
Estrin, D. (1986).
The organizational consequences of inter-organizational computer networks, *ACM Transactions on Office Automation Systems* (October): 11-20.
Etkowitz, Henry, Carol Kemelgor, Michael Neuschat, and Brian Uzzi (1990).
The final disadvantage: Barriers to women in academic science and engineering. Paper, International Sociological Association, annual meeting.

Eveland, J. D. and T. K. Bikson (1988).
Work group structures and computer support: A field experiment. *ACM Transactions in Office Information Systems*, Vol. 6, No. 4 (Oct.): 354-379.

Ewing, David W. (1982).
Due process: Will business default?, *Harvard Business Review*, Vol. 60, No. 6 (Nov./Dec.): 114.

Ewusi-Mensah, Kweku and Zbigniew H. Przasnyski (1991).
On information systems project abandonment: An exploratory study of organizational practices. *MIS Quarterly*, Vol. 15, No. 1 (March): 67-87.

Falbowski, E. (1987).
The electronic commute. *Network World*, Vol. 4, No. 23 (June 8): 31-33.

Fanning, T. and B. Raphael (1986).
Computer teleconferencing: Experience at Hewlett Packard. In *Proceedings, MCC Conference on Computer-Supported Cooperative Work*, Austin, TX, Dec.: 291-306.

Farrell, Pamela (1987).
Writer, peer tutor, and computer: A unique relationship. *Writing Center Journal*, Vol. 8, No. 1 (Fall-Winter): 29-33.

Federico, Pat-Anthony (1985).
Management information systems and organizational behavior, second edition. NY: Praeger Special Studies.

Feenberg, Andrew (1991).
Critical theory of technology. NY: Oxford University Press.

Feigenbaum, Edward and Pamela McCorduck (1985).
The fifth generation: Artificial intelligence and Japan's computer challenge to the world. BY: New American Library.

Feinberg, Lotte (1986).
Managing the freedom of information act and federal information policy. *Public Administration Review*, Vol. 46 (Nov.-Dec.): 615-620.

Feinberg, William E. and Norris R. Johnson (1988).
Outside agitators' and crowds: Results from a computer simulation model. *Social Forces*, Vol. 67, No. 2 (Dec.): 398-423.

Feldman, Jerome A,, Mark A. Fanty, and Nigel H. Goddard (1988).
Computing with structured neural networks. *Computer*, Vol. 21, No. 3 (March): 91-103.

Feldman, M. S. (1986).
Constraints on communication and electronic mail. In *Proceedings, MCC Conference on Computer-Supported Cooperative Work*, Austin, TX, Dec.: 73-90.

Feldman, Roger B. (1985).
Micros help put state's financial house in order. *Government Computer News*, 6 December: 18, 20.

Feretic, Eileen (1988).
Desktop disaster. *Today's Office*, (June): 7.

Ferguson, Charles H. (1990).
Computers and the coming of the U.S. Keiretsu. *Harvard Business Review*, Vol. 68, No. 4 (July/August): 55-71.

Ferkiss, Victor (1970).

Technological Man: The Myth and the Reality. NY: New American Library.

Ferriter, Michael (1993).
Computer aided interviewing in psychiatric social work. *Computers and Human Behavior*, Vol. 9, Nos. 1/2: 59-72.

Fidel, Kenneth and Robert Garner (1987).
Computer professionals: Career lines and occupational identity. Society for the Study of Social Problems, Annual Meeting, Chicago.

Field, G. A. (1970).
Behavioral aspects of the computer. *MSU Business Topics*, Vol. 18, No. 3: 27-33.

FIET (1980).
Bank workers and new technology. Geneva: International Federation of Commercial, Clerical, Professional and Technical Employees.

Fillon, Mike (1992).
Back-up' against the wall., *InformationWeek*, No. 356 (Jan. 20): 30-34.

Fishman, Eric (1988).
Recent rulings may give states copyright immunity. *Government Computer News*, 8 January 1988: 77-8.

Flamm, Kenneth (1987).
Targeting the computer: Government support and international competition. Washington, DC: Brookings Institution.

Fletcher, Patricia, Stuart Bretschneider, Donald Marchand, Howard Rosenbaum, and John Carlo Bertot (1992).
Managing information technology: Transforming county governments in the 1990s. Syracuse, NY: Syracuse University, School of Information Studies.

Flood, Merrill M. (1978).
Let's redesign democracy. *Behavioral Science*, Vol. 23, No. 6 (Nov.): 429-440.

Flynn, John P. (1987).
Simulating policy processes through electronic mail. *Computers in Human Services*, Vol. 2, Nos. 1/2 (Spring/Summer): 13-26.

Flynn, Laurie (1990).
Prodigy denies charge it reads private mail. *InfoWorld*, Vol. 12, No. 49 (Dec. 3): 5.

Form, W. and D. B. McMillen (1983).
Women, men, and machines. *Work and Occupations*, Vol. 10 (1983): 147-78.

Foster, L. W. and D. M. Flynn (1986).
Management information technology: Its effects on organizational form and function. *MIS Quarterly*, Vol. 10: 29-42.

Francik, Ellen, Susan Erlich Rudman, Donna Cooper, and Stephen Levine (1991).
Putting innovation to work: Adoption strategies for multimedia communication systems. *Communications of the ACM*, Vol. 34, No. 12 (Dec.): 53-63.

Frank, Michael W., Michael A. Krassa, Alexander C. Pacek, and Benjamin Radcliff (1988).
Computers and the law. *Social Science Computer Review*, Vol. 6, No. 3 (Fall).

Franklin, C. (1988).
An annotated hypertext bibliography, *Online*, Vol. 12, No. 2 (March): 42-46.

Frantz, Douglas (1988).

B of A's plans for computer don't add up. *Los Angeles Times*, Feb. 8. Reprinted in Charles Dunlop and Rob Kling, eds., *Computerization and Controversy: Value Conflicts and Social Choices*. Boston: Academic Press, 1991: 103-110.

Frantzich, Stephen E. (1982).
Computers in Congress. Beverly Hills, CA: Sage Pub.

Frantzich, Stephen E. (1984).
Congressional applications of information technology. Draft report for the office of technology assessment, Proposal US 84-10/16, Congressional Data Associates, 1984; cited in Kraemer and King, 1987: n. 13.

Frantzich, Stephen E. (1987b).
The use and implications of information technologies in Congress. In Levitan, ed., 1987: ch. 2.

Frantzich, Stephen E. (1989).
APSA computer users' group: It is time for the scholars to be heard. *Social Science Computer Review*, Vol. 7, No. 2 (Summer).

Fredell, Eric (1987).
California tries electronic democracy. *Government Computer News*, Vol. 6, No. 22 (Nov. 6): 24-25.

Fredell, Eric (1988a).
California ends experimental legislative bulletin board. *Government Computer News* (22 July): 117.

Fredell, Eric (1988b).
States approach a new age of data automation. *Government Computer News*, June 24: 82.

Frederickson, Lee W. and Anne W. Riley, eds. (1985)).
Computers, people, and productivity. NY: Haworth Press.

Frederickson, Lee, Anne W. Riley, and J. B. Myers (1984).
Matching technology and organizational structure: A case study in white collar productivity improvement. *Journal of Organizational Behavior Management*, Vol. 6, No. 3/4 (Winter): 59- 80.

Freedman, David (1990).
The roi polloi. *CIO*, Vol. 3, No. 7 (April): 30-40.

Freedman, David (1991).
The myth of strategic IS. *CIO*, Vol. 4, No. 10 (July): 42-48.

Frenkel, Karen A. (1988).
Computers and elections. *Communications of the ACM*, Vol. 31, No. 10 (Oct.): 1176-1183.

Frenkel, Karen A. (1989).
Computing as a political force. *Personal Computing*, Vol. 13, No. 10 (October): 99-106.

Frenkel, Karen A. (1990a).
The politics of standards and the EC. *Communications of the ACM*,, Vol. 33, No. 7 (July): 41-51.

Frenkel, Karen A. (1990b).
The European Community and information technology. *Communications of the ACM*, Vol. 33, No. 4 (April): 404-411.

Frenkel, Karen A. (1990c).

Women and computing. *Communications of the ACM*, Vol. 33, No. 11 (Nov.): 34-46.

Frenzel, Carroll W. (1992).
Management of information technology. Boston, MA: Boyd and Fraser.

Frew. D. R. (1985).
How stress affects productivity in materiel management. *Hospital Materiel Management Quarterly*, Vol. 6 (May): 30-36.

Friis, S. 1988).
Action research on systems development: Case study of changing actor roles. *Computational Sociology*, Vol. 18, No. 1.

Fritz, Mark (1991).
A hazard to your health? *Information Center Quarterly*, Vol. 7, o. 4 (Fall): 16-22.

Frosini, Vittorio (1987).
Social implications of the computer revolution: Advantages and disadvantages. *Informatica e Diritto*, Vol. 13, No. 3 (Sept.-Dec.): 7-23.

Fryer, Bronwyn (1992).
Is Windows worth it?*PC World*, Vol. 10, No. 3 (March): 224-227.

Fuchs, Lucy (1986).
Closing the gender gap: Girls and computers. Florida Instructional Computing Conference, Orlando, FL, Jan. 21-24.

Furger, Roberta (1989).
The growth of the home office. *InfoWorld*, Oct. 9: 45-49.

Gabrieli, E.R. (1985).
Ethical-social consequences of computerized health care services. *Journal of Clinical Computing*, Vol. 13, No. 5: 165-171.

Galegher, J., R. Kraut, and C. Egido, eds. (1990).
Intellectual teamwork: Social and technological foundations of cooperative work. Hillsdale, NJ: Lawrence Erlbaum Associates.

Gallie, Duncan (1991).
Patterns of skill change: Upskilling, deskilling or the polarization of skills? *Work, Employment and Society*, Vol. 5, No. 3 (Sept.): 319-351.

Gandy, John M. and Lorne Tepperman (1989)
False alarm: The computerization of eight social welfare organizations. Waterloo, Ontario, Canada: Wilfrid Laurier University Press. Humanities Press edition, 1989.

Ganley, Gladys D. (1991).
Power to the people via personal electronic media. *Washington Quarterly*, Vol. 14, No. 2 (Spring): 5-22.

Gantz, John (1989a).
Standards: What they are. What they aren't. *Networking Management* (May): 23-34.

Gantz, John (1989b).
Networking: MIS's Waterloo. *Networking Management*, Oct.: 33-44.

GAO (General Accounting Office) (1979).
Uses of national economic models by federal agencies. Washington, DC: Superintendent of Documents.

GAO (General Accounting Office) (1986).

Privacy act: Federal agencies' implementation can be improved. Report to the Chairman, Subcommittee on Government Information, Justice, and Agriculture, Committee on Government Operations, House of Representatives. General Accounting Office, Washington, D.C., August, 1986. Report No.: GAO/GGD-86-107.

GAO (General Accounting Office) (1987a).
Financial integrity act: Continuing efforts needed to improve control and accounting systems. Washington, D.C.: Superintendent of Documents.

GAO (General Accounting Office) (1987b).
ADP modernization: IRS' redesign of its tax administration system. Washington, DC: Superintendent of Documents. No. GAO/IMTEC-88-5FS (Nov. 9).

GAO (General Accounting Office) (1988).
New York Stock Exchange: Capability of automated systems to identify program trading. Washington, DC: Superintendent of Documents. No. GAO/IMTECT-88-36 (April 27).

GAO (General Accounting Office) (1989a).
Computer security: Compliance with training requirements of the computer security act of 1987. Washington, DC: Superintendent of Documents.

GAO (General Accounting Office) (1989a).
Compliance with training requirements of the Computer Security Act of 1987. Washington, DC: Superintendent of Documents.

GAO (General Accounting Office) (1989b).
Unauthorized access to a NASA scientific network. Washington, DC: Superintendent of Documents.

GAO (General Accounting Office) (1989b).
EEOC's charge data system contains errors but system satisfies users. Washington, DC: Superintendent of Documents.

GAO (General Accounting Office) (1990a).
Meeting the government's technology challenge: Results of a GAO symposium. Washington, DC: Superintendent of Documents. Feb. GAO/IMTEC-90-23.

GAO (General Accounting Office) (1990b).
Copyright law constraints on the transfer of certain federal computer software with commercial applications. Washington, DC: U.S. Superintendent of Documents. March 7. GAO/T-RCED-90-44.

GAO (General Accounting Office) (1990c).
Justice automation: Tighter computer security needed. Washington, DC: U.S. Superintendent of Documents. July 30. GAO/IMTEC-90-69.

GAO (General Accounting Office) (1990d).
Information resources: Management commitment needed to meet information challenge. GAO/IMTEC-90-27. Washington, DC: Superintendent of Documents.

GAO (General Accounting Office) (1990e).
Information System: National Health Practitioner Data Bank Has Not Been Well Managed. Washington, DC: Superintendent of Documents. Aug, 21. GAO/IMTECT-90-68.

GAO (General Accounting Office) (1990f).

Computer Security: Governmentwise Planning Process Had Limited Impact. Washington, DC: Superintendent of Documents. May 10. GAO/IMTEC-90-48.

GAO (Government Accounting Office) (1990g).
Air Force ADP: Systems funded without adequate cost/benefit analyses. Washington, DC: Superintendent of Documents. Dec. 28. GAO/IMTEC-90-6.

GAO (General Accounting Office) (1991a).
Financial markets: Computer security controls at five stock exchanges need strengthening. Washington, DC: U. S. Superintendent of Documents. Aug. 28. GAO/IMTECT-91-56.

GAO (General Accounting Office) (1991b).
Alternatives to Grand Design for Systems Modernization. Washington, DC: U. S. Superintendent of Documents. Sept. 4.

GAO (General Accounting Office) (1991c).
Computer security: Hackers penetrate DOD computer systems. Washington, DC: U. S. Superintendent of Documents. Nov. 20. GAO/T-IMTEC-92.5.

GAO (General Accounting Office) (1991d).
War on Drugs: Information management poses formidable challenges. Washington, DC: U. S. Superintendent of Documents. May 31. GAO/IMTEC-91-40.

GAO (General Accounting Office) (1992a).
Computer security: DEA is not adequately protecting national security information. Washington, DC: Superintendent of Documents, Feb. 19. GAO/IMTEC-92-31.

GAO (General Accounting Office) (1992b).
Major NIH computer system: Poor management resulted in unmet scientists' needs and wasted millions. Washington, DC: Superintendent of Documents, Nov. 4. GAO/IMTEC-92-5.

GAO (General Accounting Office) (1992c).
Summary of Federal Agencies' Information Resources Management Problems. Washington, DC: Superintendent of Documents, Feb. 13. GAO/IMTEC-92-13FS.

GAO (General Accounting Office) (1992d).
Practitioner Data Bank: Information on small medical malpractice payments. Washington, DC: Superintendent of Documents, July 7. GAO/IMTEC-92-6FS.

GAO (General Accounting Office) (1992e).
High-technology competitiveness: Trends in U. S. and foreign performance. Washington, DC: Superintendent of Documents, Sept. 16. GAO/NSIAD-92-236.

GAO (General Accounting Office) (1992f).
Department of Energy: Better Information Resources Management Needed to Accomplish Missions. Washington, DC: Superintendent of Documents, Sept. 29. GAO/IMTEC-92-53.

Gardiner, J. A. and T. R. Lyman (1984).
The fraud control game. Bloomington, IN: Indiana University Press.

Gardner, James M., Alba Souza, Amedeo Scabbia, and Anne Breuer (1986).
Microcare - Promises and pitfalls in implementing microcomputer programs in human services agencies. *Computers in Human Behavior*, Vol. 2: 147-156.

Gardner, Sidney L. and Robin White (1983).

Privacy, technology, and human services: 1984 minus one. *New England Journal of Human Services*, Vol. 3 (Winter):12-21.

Gardner, William L. III and Joy Van Eck Paluchette (1991).
Computer-mediated communications in organizational settings: A self-presentational perspective. In Szewczak, Edward, Coral Snodgras, and Mehdi Khosrowpour, eds. (1991). *Management impacts of information technology: Perspectives on organizational change and growth.* Harrisburg, PA: Idea Group Publishing: 165-206.

Gardner, William L. and J. R. Schermerhorn, Jr. (1988).
Computer networks and the changing nature of managerial work. *Public Productivity Review*, Vol. 11, No. 4: 85-99.

Garfinkel, Simson L. (1990).
From database to blacklist. *The Christian Science Monitor*, Aug. 1: 12-13.

Garson, Barbara (1988).
The electronic sweatshop: How computers are transforming the office of the future into the factory of the past. NY: Simon and Schuster. Penguin Books edition, 1989.

Garson, G. David (1974).
On democratic administration and socialist self-management: A comparative survey. Beverly Hills, CA: Sage Publications.

Garson, G. David (1977).
Worker self-management in industry: The west european experience. NY: Praeger.

Garson, G. David (1978).
Group theories of politics. Beverly Hills, CA: Sage Publications.

Garson, G. David (1986).
The job skills data bank: A microcomputer simulation in public personnel administration. *Review of Public Personnel Administration*, Vol. 6, No. 2 (Spring): 72-77.

Garson, G. David (1987a).
Computers in public employee relations. Alexandria, VA: International Personnel Management Association.

Garson, G. David (1987b).
Human resource management, computers, and organization theory. American Political Science Association, 1987 Annual Meeting, Chicago.

Garson, G. David (1987c).
Administrative issues and prospects for public sector management information systems. *New Directions in Public Administration Research*, Vol. 1, No. 2 (Jan.): 1-6.

Garson, G. David (1989a)
Creating new resources for social science research instruction. Ch. 14 in Nagel and Garson, eds., 1989.

Garson, G. David (1989b).
Review of *Datawars. Social Science Computer Review*, Vol. 7, No. 1 (Spring).

Garson, G. David (1989c).

Computer assistance of social scientific writing. *The Social Science Journal*, July 1989.

Garson, G. David (1991).
Comparing expert systems and neural network algorithms with common multivariate procedures for analysis of social science data. *Social Science Computer Review*, Vol. 9, No 3 (Fall): 399-434.

Garson, G. David (1992).
Implementing computer modeling in state government: A human resource information systems focus. *State and Local Government Review*, Vol. 24, No. 2 (Spring): 77-83.

Garvey, Martin (1990).
Too much network. *InformationWeek*, No. 274 (June 11): 46.

Gassee, Jean-Louis (1992).
Making ISDN safe for electronic surveillance. *MacWeek*, Vol. 6 (April 13): 33.

Gattiker, Urs E., Barbara A. Gutek, and Dale E. Berger (1988).
Office technology and employee attitudes. *Social Science Computer Review*, Vol. 6, No. 3 (Fall).

Gattiker, Urs E. and L. Larwood (1986).
Resistance to change: Reactions to workplace computerization in offices. Annual Meeting of TIMS/ORSA, Los Angeles.

Gattiker, Urs E. and Todd W. Nelligan (1988).
Computerized offices in Canada and the United States: Investigating dispositional similarities and differences. *Journal of Organizational Behavior*, Vol. 9, No. 1 (Jan.): 77-96.

Gattiker, Urs E. and D. Paulson (1987).
Testing for effective teaching methods: Achieving computer literacy for end-users. *INFOR: Information Systems and Operations Research*, Vol. 25 (9187): 256-276.

Gawthrop, Louis (1971).
Administrative politics and social change. NY: St. Martins.

Geake, Elizabeth (1990).
Interpersonal computing. *Practical computing*, Vol. 13, No. 5 (May 1): 62-64, 66.

Gelder, Lindsy Van (1985).
The strange case of the electronic lover. *Ms. Magazine* (October): 364-375.

Georgas, N. (1984).
How word processing can help your kids. *Personal Computing*, (Oct.): 132-136.

George, Joey F. (1986).
Computers and the centralization of decision-making in U. S. local governments. Irvine, CA: University of California - Irvine, doctoral dissertation.

George, Joey F. and John L. King (1991).
Examining the computing and centralization debate. *Communications of the ACM*, Vol. 34, No. 7 (July): 63-72.

Gerber, Cheryl 1993).
Booming commercial use changes fact of Internet. *Infoworld*, Vol. 15, No. 15 (April 12): 1, 38.

Gilbert, Jerome (1989).

Computer crime: Detection and prevention. *Journal of Property Management*, Vol. 54 (March-April): 64-67.

Gilroy, F. D. and H. B. Desai (1986).
Computer anxiety: Sex, race and age. *International Journal of Man-Machine Studies*, Vol. 25: 711-719.

Ginzberg, M. J. (1978).
Steps towards more effective implementation of MS and MIS. *Interfaces*, Vol. 8, No. 3: 295-300.

Ginzberg, M. J. and G. Ariav (1986).
Methodologies for DSS analysis and design: A contingency approach to their application. *Proceedings of the Seventh International Conference for Information Systems* (1986).

Ginzberg, M. J. and C. Ross, eds. (1982).
Proceedings of the third international conference on information systems. Ann Arbor, MI, Dec. 13-15. The Institute of Management Sciences.

Giuliano, Vincent E. (1982).
The mechanization of office work. *Scientific American*. Vol. 257, No. 2 (Sept.): 148-164.

Gladden, G. R. (1982).
Stop the life-cycle, I want to get off. *ACM SIGSOFT Software Engineering Notes*, Vol. 7, No. 2: 35-39.

Glaize, D. L. and R. D. Myrick (1984).
Interpersonal groups or computers? A study of career maturity and career decidedness. *Vocational Guidance Quarterly*, Vol. 32, No. 3 (March): 168-176.

Glastonbury, Bryan and Walter LaMendola (1992).
The integrity of intelligence: A bill of rights for the information age. NY: St. Martin's Press.

Glenday, Daniel (1990).
The limits to industrial democracy: New management initiatives in worker participation. Paper, International Sociological Association.

Glenn, E. and R. Feldberg (1977).
Degraded and deskilled: The proletarianization of clerical work. *Social Problems*, Vol. 25: 52-64.

Glenn, Evelyn Nakano and Charles M. Tolbert (1987).
Race and gender in high technology employment: Recent trends in computer occupations. Society for the Study of Social Problems, Annual Meeting, Chicago.

Glinert, Ephraim and Bryant W. York (1992).
Computers and people with disabilities. *Communications of the ACM*, Vol. 35, No. 5 (May): 32-35.

Glitman, Russell (1990).
PCs will depend on connections for '90s power. *PC Week*, Vol. 6, No. 1 (Jan. 8): 1-2.

Goff, Leslie (1989).
Lack of definitive VDT info has employers in quandary. *Management Information Systems Week*, 31 July: 28-29.

Goff, Leslie (1990a).

MIS experiences Darwinian evolution. *MIS Week*, Vol. 11, No. 21 (May 21): 1, 37.
Goff, Leslie (1990b).
PCs come full circle. *CIO*, Vol. 4, No. 2 (Nov.): 82-94.
Goldberg, Aaron (1992).
Future software: Made in Japan? *PC Week*, Vol. 9, No. 45 (Nov. 9): 200.
Goldberg, L. R. (1970).
Man versus model of man: A rationale plus some evidence for a method of improving on clinical inferences. *Psychological Bulletin*, Vol. 73: 422-432.
Goldkind, S. (1987).
Machines and intelligence: A critique of arguments against the possibility of artificial intelligence. Westport, CT: Greenwood Press.
Goldman, Benjamin (1991).
The environment and community right to know: Information for participation. *Computers in Human Services*, Vol. 8, No. 1: 19-40.
Goldstein, H. (1972).
The computer from Pascal to von Neumann. Princeton, NJ: Princeton University Press.
Goldstein, Robert C. (1975).
Personal privacy versus the corporate computer. *Harvard Business Review*, Vol. 53, No. 2 (March/April): 62.
Goldstein, Robert C. and I. McCririck (1981).
The stage hypothesis and data administration: Some contradictory evidence. *Proceedings of the Second International Conference on Information Systems*, December, Boston, MA: 309-324.
Goldthorpe, John (1982).
On the service class: Its formation and future. In A. 'Giddens and G. MacKenzie, eds., *Social class and the division of labor*. NY: Cambridge unviersity Press: 162-185.
Goodman, Hannah, Wallace J. Gingerich, and Steve de Shazer (1989).
BRIEFER: An expert system for clinical practice. *Computers in Human Services*, Vol. 5, Nos. 1/2: 53-68.
Goodman, S. E. (1992).
Political activity and international computer networks. *Communications of the ACM*, Vol. 35, No. 2 (Feb.): 174.
Gordon, Steven I. and Richard F. Anderson (1989).
Microcomputer applications in city planning and management. NY: Praeger.
Gore, Albert Jr. (1992).
The Information Infrastructure and Technology Act. *Educom Review*, Vol. 27, No. 5 (Sept./Oct.): 27-29.
Gottfried, Heidi (1982).
Keeping the workers in line. *Science for the People*, Vol. 14, No. 4 (July/Aug.): 19-24.
Government Computer News (1985).
Spotlight on computing. *Government Computer News*, 7 June: 67.
Government Computer News (1986).
Archives tracks down documents with nationwide net. *Government Computer*

News, 28 March: 66-7.
Government Computer News (1987a).
Hanley wants IRM committee to be important voice. *Government Computer News*, 20 Nov. 1987: 31.
Government Computer News (1987b).
Micro network evens scales of justice. *Government Computer News*, 4 Dec.: 74.
Government Computer News (1988a).
It ain't hay. *Government Computer News*, 27 May: 26.
Government Computer News (1988b).
AI-based records analysis saves Customs $300,000. *Government Computer News*, Oct. 10: 43.
Government Computer News (1988c).
Ohio food stamp system becomes a success story. *Government Computer News*, Dec. 5: 69.
Government Computer News (1988d).
E-mail helps Ohio labor specialists stay tuned. *Government Computer News*, Feb. 19: 37.
Government Computer News (1988e).
Federal government tops private sector LAN use. *Government Computer News*, Vol. 7, No. 5 (March 4): 1.
Government Computer News (1990).
Life at the top and how Cray plans to stay there. *Government Computer News*, April 30: 10.
Government Computer News (1990b).
Nurturing a reputation as an IRM standout: An interview with Col. Dennis R. Shaw. *Government Computer News*, Jan. 8: 48, 53.
Government Computer News (1991a).
Forming coalitions and accomodating change: An interview with Cynthia Rand. *Government Computer News*, Vol. 10, No. 24 (Nov. 25): 46-47.
Government Computer News (1992a)
FBI's new systems help keep criminals of the streets: GCN Interview with G. Norman Christensen. *Government Computer News*, April 27: 14.
Government Computer News (1992b).
Have PCs rendered the productivity question moot? *Government Computer News*, Vol. 11, No. 24 (ov. 23): 16.
Grandjean, Etienne (1987).
Ergonomics in computerized offices. Bristol, PA: Taylor and Francis, Inc.
Green, Robert (1989).
Corps can simulate problems with supercomputer. *Government Computer News*, 12 June: 8.
Green, Robert (1990a).
2 systems' mettle tested in Panama. *Government Computer News*, Vol. 9, No. 2 (Jan. 22): 1, 85.
Green, Robert (1990b).
400 companies sign up for AEA ethics program. *Government Computer News*, May

28: 66.

Greene, Richard T. 1989).
Implementing Japanese AI techniques: Turning the tables for a winning strategy. NY: McGraw-Hill.

Greenbaum, Joan M. (1979).
In the name of efficiency: Management theory and shop-floor practice in data processing work. Philadelphia, PA: Temple University Press.

Greenbaum, Joan M. (1992).
A design of one's own. Towards participatory design in the US. In D. Schuler and A. Namioka, eds., *Participatory design, perspectives on systems design.* Hillsdale, NJ: Lawrence Erlbaum Associates.

Greenbaum, Joan and Morten Kyng, eds. (1991).
Design at work: Cooperative design of computer systems. Hillsdale, NJ: Lawrence Erlbaum Associates.

Greenbaum, Joshua and Paul Tate (1992).
Not cheaper by the pound. *InformationWeek*, No. 403 (Dec. 7): 50-60.

Greenberg, D. H. and D. A. Wolf (1985).
Is wage matching worth all the trouble? *Public Welfare* (Winter): 13-20.

Greenberg, D. H. and D. A. Wolf (1986).
Using computers to combat fraud. Westport, CT: Greenwood Press.

Greenberg, S., Ed. (1991).
Computer supported cooperative work and groupware. London: Academic.

Gregory, J. and K. Nussbaum (1982).
Race against time: Automation of the office. Cleveland, OH: Working Women's Education Fund.

Gressard, C. P. and B. H. Loyd (1987).
An investigation of the effects of math anxiety and sex on computer attitudes. *School Science and Mathematics*, Vol. 87, No. 2: 125-135.

Greist, J. H., M. H. Klein, and L. J. VanCura (1973).
A computer interview by psychiatric patient target symptoms. *Archives of General Psychiatry*, Vol. 29: 247-253.

Grenier, Ray and George Metes (1992).
Enterprise networking: Working together apart. Bedford, MA: Digital Press.

Grimm, Vanessa Jo (1988).
ADP, IRM lose feds to greener pastures. *Government Computer News*, 5 Feb. 1988: 1, 14.

Grimm, Vanessa Jo (1988a).
Congress fails to use own technical expertise. *Government Computer News*, 8 Jan. 1988: 25, 81.

Grimm, Vanessa Jo (1988b)
Security legislation slips through Senate. *Government Computer News*, 8 January 1988: 1, 89.

Grimm, Vanessa Jo (1988c).
Bill to regulate data matching moves to floor. *Government Computer News*, 24 June: 4.

Grimm, Vanessa Jo (1988d).
Computer matching bill sent to Reagan. *Government Computer News*, 24

October: 3.

Grimm, Vanessa Jo (1988e).
Security Act overloads NIST staff. *Goverment Computer News*, 10 Oct.L 1, 121.

Grimm, Vanessa Jo (1988f).
HR 145: What's next. *Government Computer News*, 22 Jan.: 1, 6.

Grimm, Vanessa Jo (1988g).
Dummies yield to computer modeling. *Government Computer News*, Sept. 26: 11.

Grimm, Vanessa Jo (1988h).
Union leader assails Customs automation plans. *Government Computer News*, May 13: 12.

Grimm, Vanessa Jo (1989a).
Congress keeps eye on computing in investigations. *Government Computer News*, 12 June: 146.

Grimm, Vanessa Jo (1989b)
House debates FMC's plan for remote retrieval. *Government Computer News*, 3 April: 14.

Grimm, Vanessa Jo (1989c).
ACLU seeks public access to databases. *Government Computer News*, 15 May: 84.

Grimm, Vanessa Jo (1989d).
System blamed for $54m discrepancy at customs. *Government Computer News*, 1 May: 80.

Grimm, Vanessa Jo and Kevin Power (1990).
White House to Hill: Let's abolish OIRA. *Government Computer News*, Vol. 9, No. 10 (May 14): 1, 82.

Griswold, P. A, (1985).
Differences between education and business majors in their attitudes about computers. *AEDS Journal*, Vol. 18, No. 3: 131-138.

Grohowski, Ron, Chris McGoff, Doug Vogel, Ben Martz, and Jay Nunamaker (1990).
Implementing electronic meeting systems at IBM: Lessons learned and success factors. *MIS Quarterly*, Vol. 14, No. 4 (Dec.): 369-384.

Groves, Robert M. and Nancy A. Mathiowetz (1984).
Computer assisted telephone interviewing: Effects on interviewers and respondents. *Public Opinion Quarterly*, Vol. 48, No. 1B (Spring): 356-369.

Grow, Gerald (1988).
Lessons from the computer writing problems of professionals. *College Composition and Communication*, Vol. 39, No. 2 (May): 217-20.

Gruber, Thomas R. (1989).
The acquisition of strategic knowledge. San Diego, CA: Academic Press.

Grudin, Jonathon (1988).
Why CSCW applications fail: Problems in the design and evaluation of organizational interfaces. In *Proceedings of the Second Conference on Computer-Supported Cooperative Work*, Portland, OR, Sept. 26-28. New York: ACM, pp. 85-93.

Grudin, Jonathon (1989).
The case against user interface consistency. *Communications of the ACM*, Vol. 32, No. 10 (Oct.): 1164-1173.

GSA (General Services Administration) and Department of Justice (1991).
Your right to federal records: Questions and answers about the Freedom of Information Act and the Privacy Act. Washington, DC: USGPO. June. Publication no. 1991 0-293-651-QL-3.

GSA (General Services Administration) and Information Resources Management Service (1986).
Personnel issues and recommendations, getting everything ready for the 1990's. Washington, DC: Superintendent of Documents.

GSA (General Services Administration) (1987).
The senior federal IRM manager: Major roles and responsibilities as we move into the 1990's. Washington, DC: Superintendent of Documents.

Guattari, Felix (1984).
Molecular revolution. *NY: Basic Books.*

Gullo, Karen (1989a).
EDI gives banks a competitive edge. *InformationWeek*, 25 Sept.: 20.

Gullo, Karen (1989b).
Stopping runaways in their tracks. *InformationWeek*, 13 Nov.: 63-69.

Gurstein, Penelope Cheryl (1990).
Working at home in the live-in office: Computers, space, and the social life of households. Berkeley, CA: University of California, Berkeley. Doctoral Dissertation.

Gutek, Barbara A. (1983).
Women's work in the office of the future. In J. Zimmerman, ed., *The Technological Woman*. NY: Praeger.

Gutek, Barbara A. and T. K. Bikson (1985).
Differential experience of men and women in computerized offices. *Sex Roles*, Vol. 13: 123-136.

Haase, W. F. (1981).
IRM professionals can win manager's recognition. *Journal of Systems Management*, Vol. 32, No. 5 (May): 19-23.

Habermas, Jurgen (1973).
Theory and practice. Boston: Beacon Press.

Habermas, Jurgen (1979).
Communications and the evolution of society. Boston: Beacon Press.

Habermas, Jurgen (1983).
Modernity--an incomplete project. In Hal Foster, ed., *Postmodern Culture.* London: Pluto Press.

Habermas, Jurgen (1984).
The theory of communicative action. Boston: Beacon Press.

Haefner, Katie and John Markoff (1991).
Cyberpunk: Outlaws and hackers on the computer frontier. NY: Simon and Schuster.

Halachmi, Arie (1992).
The brave new world of information technolocy. *Public Personnel Management*, Vol. 21, No. 4 (Winter): 533-553.

Halbrecht, Herbert Z. (1989).
What's good for the boss...a new breed of chief executive is shaping critical success factors for CIOs. *Computerworld*, Vol. 23, No. 34 (August 21): 78.

Hall, Owen P., Jr. (1986).
Decision support systems and public policy analysis. *Evaluation Review*, Vol. 10, No. 5 (October 1986): 594-608. Theme issue on "Microcomputers and Evaluation Research."

Hamilton, Alex (1989).
Picture this, *Information Center*, Vol. 5, No. 8 (August): 11-16.

Hamilton, C. (1987).
Telecommuting. *Personnel Journal*. Vol. 66, No. 4 (April): 91-101.

Hamilton, Jack (1989).
Decentralization: A balancing act. *InformationWeek*, No. 235 (4 Sept.): 48.

Hamilton, S. and N. L. Chervany (1981).
Evaluation of information system effectiveness: Part I - A comparison of evaluation approaches, *MIS Quarterly*, Vol. 5, No. 3 (Fall): 55-69. An earlier version appeared as Paper No. MISRC-WP-81-03, Minneapolis, MN: MISRC, Graduate School of Business Administration, University of Minnesota.

Hammer, Jeffrey S. (1981).
Life cycle management, *Information Management*, Vol. 4, No. 4: 71-80.

Hammer, Jeffrey S. et al. (1985).
Toward the integration of psychosocial services in the general hospital. *General Hospital Psychiatry*, Vol. 7: 189-194.

Hammer, Jeffrey S., John S. Lyons, and J. J. Strain (1985).
Evaluation of a stand-alone integrated microcomputer system for psychiatric services. *Computers in Psychiatry/Psychology*, Vol. 7: 1-7.

Hammer, Michael and James Champy (1993).
Reengineering the corporation: A manifesto for business revolution. NY: Harper Business Publishers.

Hansen, J. V., L. J. McKell, and L. E. Heitger (1977).
Decision-oriented frameworks for management information systems design. *Information Processing and Management*, Vol. 13, No. 4: 215-225.

Harrington, Susan J. (1989).
Why people copy software and create computer viruses: Individual characteristics or situational factors? *Information Resources Management Journal* Vol. 2, No. 3 (Summer): 28-37.

Harris, Britton (1965).
Urban development models: New tools for planning. *Journal of the American Institute of Planners*, Vol. 31.

Harrison, Ben (1988).
OSI standards: To wait or not to wait? *TPT Magazine*, January, 51-4.

Harrison, Lynda (1992).
Request a human touch. *Computing Canada*, Vol. 18 (April 13): 47-48.

Hart, Anne (1988).
Expert systems: An introduction for managers. East Brunswick, NJ: GP Publishing, Inc.

Hart, Jeffrey A. (1992).
Rival capitalists: International competitiveness in the United States, Japan, and Western Europe. Ithaca, NY: Cornell University Press.

Hart, Jeffrey A., Robert R. Reed, and François Bar (1993).
The building of the Internet: Implications for the future of broadband networks. Unpublished paper distributed on the Internet, Jan. 20. Bloomington, IN: Indiana University.

Hartmanis, Juris (1992).
Computing the future. *Communications of the ACM*, Vol. 35, No. 11 (Nov.): 30-40.

Harty, Paul (1985).
Users cite productivity, access as HRMS assets. *Software News*, February: 51-60.

Harvey, David (1988).
Information and power. *Computer Weekly*, No. 1132 (Sept. 22): 2.

Hattie, John and Donald Fitzgerald (1987).
Sex differences and attitudes, achievement, and use of computers. *Australian Journal of Education*, Vol. 31, No. 1: 3-26.

Haugeland, John (1985).
Artificial intelligence: The very idea. Cambridge, MA: MIT Press.

Hayes, Frank (1992).
The groupware dilemma: Group productivity software gets users to work together - but the trick is getting them to use it. *Unix World*, Vol. 9, No. 2 (Feb.): 46-50.

Hayes, K. J. and D. J. Slottje (1987).
Measures of publicness based on demographic scaling. *Review of Economics and Statistics*, Vol. 69, No. 4: 713-718.

Hayes-Roth, F., D. Waterman, and D. Lenat (1983).
Building expert systems (reading, MA: Addison-Wesley).

Hayes-Roth, Frederick (1984).
Knowledge-based expert systems. *IEEE Computer*, Vol. 17, No. 10: 263-273.

Head, Robert V. (1985).
Information centers are evolving resource. *Government Computer News* (August 30, 1985): 33, 37.

Head, Robert V. (1988a).
New FBI chief shows enthusiasm for computers. *Government Computer News*, 8 January 1988: 29.

Head, Robert V. (1988b).
New security law compels federal agencies to act. *Government Computer News*, 4 March: 33.

Head, Robert V. (1988c).
End users play larger role in designing systems. *Government Computer News*, 22 July: 99.

Head, Robert V. (1988d).
Some Reagan policies on IRM are half-baked. *Government Computer News*, 8 July: 71.

Head, Robert V. (1989).
Agencies without micros don't lack for excuses, *Government Computer News*, 1 May: 88.

Head, Robert V. (1991).
Agencies must adjust their vision of IRM future. *Government Computer News*, Vol. 10, No. 22 (Oct. 28): 63-64.

Head, Robert V. (1992).
Justice and Treasury beefing up fiscal '93 info technology budgets. *Government Computer News*, Vol. 11, No. 11 (May 25): 90.

Heclo, H. and Aaron Wildavsky (1974).
Private government of public money: Community and policy inside British politics. Berkeley, CA: University of California Press.

Hedlund, J. L., R. C. Evenson, I. W. Sletten, and D. W. Cho (1980).
The computer and clinical prediction. Pp. 201-234 in J. D. Sidowski, J. H. Johnson, and T. A. Williams, eds., *Technology in mental health care delivery systems*. Norwood, NJ: Ablex.

Hedlund, J., B. Vieweg, and D. Cho (1985).
Mental health computing in the 1980s: General information systems and clinical documentation. *Computers in Human Services*, Vol. 1, No. 1: 3-33.

Heinssen, R. K. Jr., C. R. Glass, and L. A. Knight (1984).
Assessment of computer anxiety: The dark side of the computer revolution. Paper, Association for Advancement of Behavior Therapy, Philadelphia, Nov.

Heinssen, R. K. Jr., C. R. Glass, and L. A. Knight (1987).
Assessing computer anxiety: Development and validation of the computer anxiety rating scale. *Computers in Human Behavior*, Vol. 3: 49-59.

Helander, M. (1988).
Handbook of human-computer interaction. NY: North-Holland.

Hendry, John (1989).
Innovating for failure: Government policy and the early British computer industry. Cambridge, MA: MIT Press.

Heterick, Robert C. Jr. (1993).
Where is the 'E' in the NII? *EDUCOM Review*, Vo. 28, No. 4 (July/August): 51-52.

Higgins, Steve (1992).
'Electronic democracy' wins votes. *PC Week*, Vol. 9, No. 20 (May 18): 19.

Higgins, Steve (1993).
Clinton's tech policies face hardball politics. *PC Week*, Vo. 9, No. 52 (Jan.): 7.

Highland, Harold J. (1988).
A secure network must be an unfriendly network. *Government Computer News*, 10 Oct.: 91.

Highland, Harold J. (1990).
If the password's 'anything goes', it's your loss. *Government Computer News*, 29 Oct.: 61.

Hildreth, Charles R. (1986).
Communicating with online catalogs and other retrieval systems: The need for a standard command language. *Library Hi Tech*, Vol. 4, No. 1 (Spring): 7-12.

Hill, Stephen 1988).
The tragedy of technology: Human liberation versus domination in the late twentieth century. London: Pluto Press.

Hill, W. A. (1966).
The impact of EDP systems on office employees: Some empirical conclusions. *Academy of Management Journal*, Vol. 9, No. 3: 9-19.

Hilton, Howard J. (1991).
Private sector offers best bet for online info access. *Federal Computer Week*, Vol. 5, No. 30 (Sept. 23): 21.

Hiltz, Starr Roxanne (1988).
Productivity enhancement from computer mediated communication: A systems contingency approach. *Communications of the ACM*, Vol. 31, No. 12 (Dec.): 1438-1454.

Hiltz, Roxanne Starr and Murray Turoff (1978)
The network nation: Human communication via the computer. Reading, MA: Addison Wesley Advanced Books.

Hiltz, Roxanne Starr and Murray Turoff (1985).
Structuring computer-mediated communication systems to avoid information overload. *Communications of the ACM*, Vol. 28, No. 7 (July): 680-689.

Himelstein, Linda (1990).
Public interest group clamors for North's diaries: In search of Iran-Contra history. *Legal Times*, Vol. 12, No. 30 (Jan. 1): 2.

Ho, T. H., K. S. Raman, and R. T. Watson (1989).
Group decision support systems: The cultural factor. In *Information Systems, Proceedings of the tenth international conference*. Boston, MA, Dec. 4-6, edited by J. DeGross, J. Henderson, and B. Konsynski. NY: ACM Press: 119-129.

Hodges, Judith and Deborah Melewski (1993).
Top 100: Market approachs $17B. *Software Magazine*, Vol. 13, No. 10 (July): 75 - 82.

Hoffman, Lance J. (1990).
Rogue programs: Viruses, worms, and Trojan horses. NYC, NY: Van Nostrand Reinhold.

Hoffman, Thomas (1989).
How IT contributes to the greenhouse effect. *InformationWeek* (Oct. 30): 92-98.

Hoffman, Thomas (1990).
Database control. *InformationWeek*, No. 277 (July 9): 26.

Holmes, R. W. (1970).
12 areas to investigate for better MIS. *Financial Executive*, Vol. 38, No. 7: 24-31.

Hong, Dora (1988).
Database management system benefits city (Torrance, CA), *Office*, Vol. 108 (Oct.): 117-120.

Hoos, I. R. (1960).
When the computer takes over the office. *Harvard Business Review*, Vol. 38, No. 4 (July/Aug.): 102-112.

Horton, F. W., Jr. (1974).
The evolution of MIS in government. *Journal of Systems Management*, Vol. 25, No. 3: 14-20.

Horton, F. W. (1985).
Information resources management (Englewood Cliffs, NJ: Prentice-Hall).

Horton, F. W., Jr., and D. A. Marchand (1982).
Information management in public administration. Arlington, Va.: Information Resources Press, 1982.

Horton, Len (1988).
Tools are an alternative to 'playing computer', *Software Magazine*, Jan. 1988: 58-70.

Hosinski, Joan M. (1988).
Intricate network of advisers supports FTS 2000. *Government Computer News*, 8 July: 3.

Hosinski, Joan M. (1989).
Fingerprint ID system not just for spooks, *Government Computer News*, 12 June: 8.

House Committee on House Administration, U. S. Congress (1979).
Information policy: Public laws from the 95th Congress. Washington, DC: USGPO. [27 P. Edrs: ed 168 586; hc (02), mf (01)].

House, W. C., ed. (1971).
The impact of information technology on management operation. NY: Auerbach.

Houser, Walter R. (1989a).
What's behind OMB's annual request for reports? *Government Computer News*, 16 Oct.: 78.

Houser, Walter R. (1989b).
Acquisition team must share the helm to reach goal. *Government Computer News*, Vol. 8, No. 23 (Nov. 13): 23.

Houser, Walter R. (1992).
The ghost of e-mail past could come back to haunt you. *Government Computer News*, Vol. 11, No. 17 (Aug. 17): 25.

Howell, Thomas R. (1986).
International competition in the information technologies: Foreign government interventiona and the U. S. response. *Stanford Journal of International Law*, Vol. 22 (Fall): 215-262.

Hsu, Jeffrey and Joseph Kusnan (1989).
The fifth generation: The future of computer technology. Blue Ridge Summit, PA: Windcrest.

Hudson, Walter W. (1989).
Automated faculty merit reviews. *Computers in Human Services*, Vol. 5, Nos. 3/4: 131-146.

Hudson, Walter W., Paula S. Nurius, and Sorel Reisman (1988).
Computerized assessment instruments: Their promise and problems. *Computers in Human Services*, Vol. 3, Nos. 1/2: 51-70.

Huff, Sid L., Malcolm C. Munro, and Barbara H. Martin (1988).
Growth stages of end user computing. *Communications of the ACM*, Vol. 31, No. 5 (May): 542-550.

Hughes, Thomas P. (1989).
American genesis: A century of invention and technological enthusiasm (NY: Penguin Books).

Hunt, H. Allan and Timothy Hunt (1986)
Clerical employment and technological change. Kalamazoo, MI: W. E. Upjohn Institute for Employment Research.

Hunt, J. G. and P. F. Newell (1971).
Management in the 1980's revisited. *Personnel Journal*, Vol. 50: 35-43.

Iacono, Susan and Rob Kling (1984).
Computerization, office routines, and changes in clerical work. *IEEE Spectrum*, June: 73-76.

IBM (1973).
Organizing the data processing activity (White Plains, NY: Technical Publications Systems Department, Manual #GC20-1622-2, October).

IBM (1984).
Business systems planning: Information systems planning guide. White Plains, NY: IBM.

Ibrahim, F. A. (1985).
Human rights and ethical issues in the use of advanced technology. *Journal of Counseling and Development*, Vol. 64: 134-135.

IIA (1991).
Principles for state and local government information: An analysis. Washington, DC: Information Industry Association.

Information Today (1991).
IIA responds to moves by states to charge fees for access to government info. *Information Today*, Vol. 8, No. 5 (May): 54-55.

Information Today (1992).
IIA advises Congress on enhancing access to public information. *Information Today*, Vol. 9, No. 4 (April): 23.

Information USA (1990).
Federal database finder. Chevy Chase, MD: Information USA.

InformationWeek (1993).
Viruses: How big? How bad? *InformationWeek*, No. 434 (July 19): 25-26.

InformationWeek (1989a).
Business before IS: Companies are seeking fewer 'techno-nerds,' more MBAs in IS recruiting. *InformationWeek*, 19 Sept.: 113-120.

InformationWeek (1989b).
Lending their ears: As MIS wins its seat in the boardroom, its voice is heard company wide. *InformationWeek*, 19 Sept.: 122-126.

InformationWeek (1989c).
Executive digest. *InformationWeek*, June 26: 47.

InformationWeek (1992a).
Cross-industry profile. *InformationWeek*, No. 338 (Sept. 16): 38-104.

InformationWeek (1992b).
Not so black and white. *InformationWeek*, No. 382 (July 13): 40.

InformationWeek (1992c).
Straight talk. *InformationWeek*, No. 387 (Aug. 17): 36-40.

Insight (1988).
Computer 'virus' leads to conviction. *Insight*, 17 Oct.: 61.
International City Management Association (1984).
The surprising revolution: Final report of the 1983-4 ICMA committee on telecommunications, January 1984, *Public Management* (May): 7-13.
International City Management Association (ICMA), (1985).
Computer use in local government. *Baseline Data Report*, Vol. 17, No. 9 (Sept.): i.
Irving, R. H., C. A. Higgins, and F. R. Safayeni (1986).
Computerized performance monitoring systems: Use and abuse. *Communications of the ACM*, Vol. 19, No. 8: 794-801.
Isherwood, G. B. and T. Blacklock (1988).
The politics of computing. *Journal of Research on Computing in Education*, Vol. 20, No. 4 (Summer): 339-346.
Ives, B., S. Hamilton, and G. Davis (1980).
A framework for research in computer-based management information systems. *Management Science*, Vol. 26, No. 9: 910-934.
Ives, B., and G. P. Learmonth (1984).
Information systems as a competitive weapon. *Communications of the ACM*, Vol. 27, No. 12 (Dec.): 1193-1201.
Ives, B. and M. Olson (1984).
User involvement and MIS success: A research review, *Managment Science*, Vol. 30, No. 5: 586-603.
Ives, B., M. H. Olson, and J. J. Baroudi (1983).
The measurement of user information satisfaction, *Communications of the ACM*, Vol. 26, No. 10: 785-793.
Jackson, Lee A., Jr. (1987).
Computers and the social psychology of work. *Computers and Human Behavior*, Vol. 3, No. 3/4: 251-262.
Jackson, R. S. (1970).
Computers and middle management. *Journal of Systems Management*, Vol. 21, No. 4: 22-24.
Jameson, Frederic (1984).
Postmodernism, or the cultural logic of late capitalism. *New Left Review*, Vol. 146: 53-92.
Jander, Mary (1989).
The naked network. *Computer Decisions* (April): 39-42.
Jarvenpaa, Sirkka L. and Blake Ives (1991).
Executive involvement and participation in the management of information technology. *MIS Quarterly*, Vol. 15, No. 2 (June): 205-228.
Jerome, Marty (1989).
Clothes wars. *PC Computing*, Vol. 2, No. 7 (July): 171-172.
Johansen, Robert (1984a).
Teleconferencing and beyond. NY: McGraw-Hill.
Johansen, Robert (1988).
Groupware: Computer support for business teams. NY: Free Press.

Johnson, Carmen A., Mary Adams, Martha Norman, and Linda Kazetsky (1987). A computer simulation of patient flow in a public psychiatric emergency service. *Journal of Mental Health Administration*, Vol. 14, No. 2 (Fall): 52-59.

Johnson, F. E. (1985).
Installing a solution center: Think big, start small. *Infosystems*, Vol. 32, No. 6: 40-44.

Johnson, Glenn O. (1987).
Toward an emergency preparedness planning and operations system, *URISA 1987*, Vol. 2: 171-183.

Johnson, J. P. (1982).
Can computers close the educational equity gap? *Perspectives: The Civil Rights Quarterly*, Vol. 14, No. 3: 20-25.

Johnson, R. A., F. Kast, and J. E. Rosenzweig (1967).
The theory and management of systems. NY: McGraw-Hill, 1967.

Johnson-Lentz, P. and T. Johnson-Lentz (1982).
Groupware: The process and impacts of design choices. In E. B. Kerr and S.R. Hiltz, eds., *Computer-Mediated communication systems: Status and evaluation*. New York: Academic Press.

Jones, Mary and R. Leon Price (1991).
A modified SDLC. *Information Executive*, Vol. 4, No. 3 (Summer): 45-49.

Jones, Robert Snowdon (1988).
PC support systems aid novice users. *InfoWorld*, 8 Feb. 1988: 38.

Jöreskog, K. G. and D. Sörbom (1989).
LISREL 7: A guide to the program and applications. Chicago: SPSS Inc.

Joshi, Kailash (1991).
A model of users' perspective on change: The case of information systems technology implementation. *MIS Quarterly*, Vol. 15, No. 2 (June): 229-243.

Joyce, Edward J. (1987).
Software bugs: A matter of life and liability. *Datamation*, (May 15): 88-92.

Kaltnekar, Zdravko (1991).
Information technology and the humanization of work. In Szewczak, Edward, Coral Snodgras, and Mehdi Khosrowpour, eds. (1991). *Management impacts of information technology: Perspectives on organizational change and growth*. Harrisburg, PA: Idea Group Publishing: 493-532.

Kang, Shin Cheol (1990).
An empirical analysis of causal relationships among quality of work life factors in end user computing. Lincoln, NE: University of Nebraska, Doctoral dissertation.

Kanter, Jerry (1989).
Taking the personal out of personal computing: The big guys are back in charge. *Information Management Journal*, Vol. 2, No. 2 (June):1-2.

Kantor, Jerry (1992).
Electronic democracy? *PC Magazine*, Vol. 11, No. 22 (Dec. 22): 31.

Kaplinsky, Raphel (1987).
Microelectronics and employment revisited: A review. Geneva: International Labour Office.

Karasik, Eve H. (1990).
A normative analysis of disclosure, privacy, and computers: The state cases. *Computer Law Journal*, Vol. 10, No. 4 (Dec.): 603-634.

Karger, Howard Jacob and Larry W. Kreuger (1988).
Technology and the 'not always so human' services. *Computers in Human Services*, Vol. 3, Nos. 1/2: 111-126.

Karon, Paul (1987a).
America's computer gamble: Has it paid off? *PC Week*, Dec. 8: 64-78.

Karon, Paul (1987b).
'Groupware': Putting teamwork on the PC. *PC Week*, Vol. 4, No. 43 (Oct. 27): 65-66.

Kass, Elliot M. (1990).
Playing with fire. *InformationWeek*, April 2: 48-54.

Kay, Robin H. (1989).
Gender differences in computer attitudes, literacy, locus of control and commitment. *Journal of Research on Computing in Education*, Vol. 21, No. 3 (Spring): 307-316.

Kay, Robin H. (1990).
The relation between locus of control and computer literacy. *Journal of Research on Computing in Education*, Vol. 22, No. 4 (Summer): 464-474.

Kay, Sheryl (1990).
MIS on the hiring line. *InformationWeek*, No. 270 (May 19): 26-28.

Keen, Peter G. W. (1981).
Information systems and organizational change. *Communications of the ACM*, Vol. 24, No. 1 (Jan.): 24-33.

Keen, Peter G. W. (1986).
Using telecommunications for competitive advantage. Cambridge, MA: Ballinger Publishing Co. Rev. ed. 1988.

Keen, Peter G. W. (1989).
Strategic information systems planning. In *Information systems planning for competitive advantage*. Wellesley, MA: Q.E.D. Information Sciences.

Keen, Peter G. W. and Michael S. Scott Morton (1978).
Decision support systems: An organizational perspective. Reading, MA: Addison-Wesley.

Keider, Stephen P. (1984).
Managing systems development projects. *Journal of Information Systems Management*, Vol. 1, No. 3 (Summer): 31-36.

Keisling, P. (1984).
The case against privacy. *Washington Monthly* (May): 12-28.

Kelleher, Joanne (1985).
Human factors. *Business Computer Systems* (August 1985): 64-73.

Kelly, Rob (1993).
Borland releases spy case details. *InformationWeek*, March 15: 12.

Kerr, Elaine B. and Starr Roxanne Hiltz (1982).
Computer-mediated communication: Status and evaluation. NY: Academic Press.

Keyes, Jessica (1993).
Infotrends: The competitive use of information. NY: McGraw-Hill.
Kiely, Thomas (1991).
Taking a byte out of crime. *CIO*, Vol. 5, No. 5 (Dec.): 22-27.
Kiely, Thomas (1992a).
Downsizing: Keeping up with the ins and outs. *CIO*, Vol. 5, No. 10 (April): 34-42.
Kiely, Thomas (1992b).
The measure hunt. *CIO*, Vol. 5, No. 14 (June): 60-64.
Kiely, Thomas (1992c).
The wrong goodbye. *CIO*, Vol. 5, No. 17 (Sept. 1): 34-43.
Kiely, Thomas (1992d).
Her Majesty's data guardians. *CIO*, Vol. 6, No. 2 (Oct. 15): 48-49.
Kiesler, Sarah (1984).
Computer mediation of conversation. *American Psychologist* Vol. 39: 1123-1134.
Kiesler, Sarah (1986).
The hidden messages in computer networks. *Harvard Business Review*, Vol. 64, No. 1: 46-60.
Kiesler, Sarah, Jane Siegel, and J. McGuire (1984).
Social-psychological aspects of computer-mediated communication. *American Psychologist*, Vol. 39, No. 4: 1123-1134.
Kiesler, Sara and Lee S. Sproull (1986).
Response effects in the electronic survey. *The Public Opinion Quarterly*, Vol. 50, No. 3 (Fall): 402-413.
Kiesler, Sarah, D. Zubrow, A. Moses, and V. Geller (1985).
Affect in computer-mediated communication: An experiment in synchronous terminal-to-terminal discussion, *Human-Computer Interaction*, Vol. 1 (1985): 77-104.
Kim, Chulho (1990).
An empirical study on system success factors and a system success index. Mississippi State, MS: Mississippi State University, D.B.A. dissertation.
King, John Leslie (1983).
Centralized versus decentralized computing: Organizational considerations and management options. *ACM Computing Surveys*, Vol. 15, No. 4 (Dec.): 319-349.
King, John Leslie, James N. Danziger, Debora E. Dunkle, and Kenneth L. Kraemer (1992).
In search of the knowledge executive: Managers, microcomputers, and information technology. *State and Local Government Review*, Vol. 24, No. 2 (Spring): 48-57.
King, John Leslie and Kenneth L. Kraemer (1983).
Changing data processing organization. *The Bureaucrat* (Summer, 1983): 21-7.
King, John Leslie and Kenneth L. Kraemer (1984a).
Information systems and intergovernmental relations. In T. C. Miller, ed., *Public sector performance: A conceptual turning point.* Baltimore: Johns Hopkins Univ. Press: 102-130.

King, John Leslie and Kenneth L. Kraemer (1984b).
Evolution and organizational information systems: An assessment of Nolan's stage model. *Communications of the ACM*, Vol. 27, No. 5 (May): 466-475.

King, William R. (1978).
Strategic planning for management information systems. *MIS Quarterly*, Vol. 2, No. 1: 27-37.

King, William R., V. Grover, and E. H. Hufnagel (1989).
Using information and infromation technology for sustainable competitive advantage: Some empirical evidence. *Infomration and Management*, Vol. 17: 87-93.

King, William R. and J. L. Rodriguez (1978).
Evaluating management information systems. *MIS Quarterly*, Vol. 2, No. 3: 43-51.

King, William R. and Ananth Srinivasan (1988).
The systems development life cycle and the modern information systems environment. Ch. 10 in Rabin and Jackowski, 1988.

King, William R. and R. Zmud (1981).
Managing information systems: Policy planning, strategic planning, and operational planning. *Proceedings of the Second International Conference on Information Systems*. Boston, MA. December.

Kinnell, S. K. (1988).
Information retrieval in the humanities using hypertext. *Online*, Vol. 12, No. 2 (March): 34-35.

Kirby, Michael P. (1986).
Politics, policy and computers in local government: Is there a role for the political scientist? *Urban and Regional Information Systems Association, Proceedings, 1986, Volume IV* (URISA, 1986): 1-20.

Klapp, Orrin E. (1986).
Overload and boredom: Essays on the quality of life in the information society. Westport, CT: Greenwood Press.

Klay, William Earle and Pyeong J. Yu (1988).
Constitutional and administrative implications of computers. *Public Productivity Review*, Vol. 12, No. 2 (Winter): 193-203.

Klein, H. K. and R. A. Hirschheim (1983).
Issues and approaches in appraising technological change in the office: A consequentialist perspective. *Office Technology & People*, Vol. 2, No. 1 : 15-42.

Klein Robert D. (1984).
Adding international business to the core program via the simulation game. *Journal of International Business Studies* (Spring-Summer): 151.

Kleinschrod, Walter A. (1989).
The pluses and perils of leasing. *Today's Office*, July: 24-30.

Kleinschrod, Walter A. (1990).
Forms software fills in the blanks. *Today's Office*, Feb.: 22-26.

Klemanski, John and Karen Maschke (1992).
Managing freedom of information laws: A survey of state-level departments. Chapter 4 in G. David Garson and Stuart Nagel, eds., *Advances in Social Science*

and Computers, Vol. 3. Greenwich, CT: JAI Press.

Kling, Rob (1978a).
Automated welfare client-tracking and service integration: The political economy of computing. *Communications of the ACM*, Vol. 21, No. 6 (June): 484-93.

Kling, Rob (1978b).
Automated information systems as social resources in policy making. In *Proceedings of the 1978 ACM National Conference*. Washington, DC: 666-674.

Kling, Rob (1980a).
Social analyses of computing: Theoretical perspectives in recent empirical research. *Computing Surveys*, Vol. 12, No. 1 (March): 61-110.

Kling, Rob (1980b).
When organizations are perpetrators: Assumptions about computer abuse and computer crime. *Computer Law Journal*, Vol. 2, No. 2 (Spring): 403-427.

Kling, Rob (1983).
Value conflicts and the design and organization of EFT systems. *Telecommunications Policy* Vol. 7, No. 1 (March): 12-34.

Kling, Rob (1990).
Reading 'all about' computerization: Five common genres of social analysis. In Doug Schuler, ed., *Proceedings of the 1990 Conference on Directions and Implications of Advanced Computing* (Norwood, NJ: Ablex Publishing).

Kling, Rob (1991).
Cooperation, coordination and control in computer-supported work. *Communications of the ACM*, Vol. 34, No. 12 (Dec.): 83-89.

Kling, Rob and Suzanne Iacono (1984a).
Computing as an occasion for social control. *Journal of Social Issues*, Vol. 40, No. 3: 77-96.

Kling, Rob, and Suzanne Iacono (1984b).
The control of information systems development after implementation. *Communications of the ACM*, Vol. 27, No. 12 (Dec.): 1218-1226.

Kling, Rob and Suzanne Iacono (1988).
The mobilization of support for computerization: The role of computerization movements. *Social Problems*, Vol. 35, No. 3: 226-243.

Kling, Rob and Suzanne Iacono (1989).
Desktop computerization and the organization of work. In Tom Forester, ed., *Computers in the Human Context: Information Technology, Productivity, and People*. Cambridge, MA: MIT Press.

Kling, Rob and Suzanne Iacono (1991).
Making a 'computer revolution'. In Charles Dunlop and Rob Kling, eds., *Computerization and Controversy: Value Conflicts and Social Choices*. Boston: Academic Press, 1991: 63-75.

Kling, Rob and W. Scacchi (1982).
The web of computing: Computer technology as social organization, advances in computers, Vol. 21. NY: Academic Press.

Kling, Rob and W. Scacchi (1980).
Computing as social action: The social dynamics of computing in complex organizations. In Yovitts, ed. (1980).

Koester, R. and F. Luthans (1979).
The impact of the computer on the choice activity of decision-makers: A replication with actual users of computerized MIS. *Academy of Managment Journal*, Vol. 22, No. 2: 416-422.

Koh, T. T. B. (1984).
Computer-assisted negotiations: A case history from the Law of the Sea Negotiaitons and speculation regarding future uses. In H. Pagels, ed., *Computer culture: The scientific, intellectual, and social impact of the computer*. NY: New York Cademy of Sciences.

Kohl, J. E. and M. Harman, (1987).
Attitudes of secondary school students toward computer access and usage: Do gender and socioeconomic status make a difference? Paper, American Sociological Association, Chicago, August.

Kolleck, Bernd (1993).
Computer information and human knowledge: New thinking and old critique. Pp. 455-464 in Marcos Leiderman, Charles Guzetta, Leny Struminger, and Menachem Monnickendam, eds. (1993). *Technology in people services: Research, theory, and applications*. NY: Haworth Press.

Komsky, Susan H. (1986).
Acceptance of computer-based models in local governmnet: Infomration adequacy and implementation. *Computers and the Social Sciences*, Vol. 2: 209-220.

Kondos, George S. (1988).
Basic considerations in investigating and proving computer-related federal crimes. Washington, DC: U. S. Government Printing Office.

Konsynski, Benn R. (1984).
Advances in information system design. *Journal of Management Information Systems* (Winter): 5-15.

Konsynski, Benn R. and Arnold Greenfield (1988).
Data administration: Conceptual frameworks and dictionary instruments. In Rabin and Jackowski, eds., 1988: ch. 16.

Koohang, Alex A. (1989).
A study of attitudes toward computers: Anxiety, confidence, liking and perception of usefulness. *Journal of Research on Computing in Education*, Vol. 22, No. 2 (Winter): 137-150.

Kraemer, Kenneth L. (1991).
Strategic computing and administrative reform. Pp. 167-180 in Charles Dunlop and Rob Kling, eds., *Computerization and controversy: Value conflicts and social choices*. NY: Academic Press.

Kraemer, Kenneth et al. (1986).
Curriculum recommendations for public management education in computing. NASPAA Ad Hoc Committee, *Social Science Microcomputer Review*, Vol. 4, No. 1 (Spring): 1-37.

Kraemer, Kenneth L. and James N. Danziger (1984).
Computers and control in the work environment. *Public Administration Review*, Vol. 44 (Jan./Feb., 1984): 32-42.

Kraemer, Kenneth L. and James N. Danziger (1990).
The impacts of computer technology on the worklife of information workers. *Social Science Computer Review*, Vol. 8, No. 4 (Winter): 592-612.

Kraemer, Kenneth L., Siegfried Dickhoven, Susan Fallows Tierney, and John Leslie King (1987).
Datawars: The politics of federal policymaking. NY: Columbia University Press.

Kraemer, Kenneth L. and William Dutton (1979).
The interests served by technological reform. *Administrative Sociology*, Vol. 11, No. 1: 80-106.

Kraemer, Kenneth L. and John Leslie King (1979).
A requiem for USAC. *Policy Analysis*, Vol. 5, No. 3 (Summer): 319-349.

Kraemer, Kenneth L. and John Leslie King (1986).
Computing and public organizations. In *Public Administration Review*, Vol. 46, Special Issue (Nov. 1986): 488-496.

Kraemer, Kenneth L. and John Leslie King (1987).
Computers and the constitution: A helpful, harmful, or harmless relationship? *Public Administration Review*, Vol. 47, No. 1 (Jan./Feb.): 93-105.

Kraemer, Kenneth L., John Leslie King, Debora E. Dunkle, and Joseph P. Lane (1989).
Managing information systems. San Francisco, CA: Jossey-Bass.

Kraemer, Kenneth L. and Rob Kling (1985).
The political character of computerization in service organizations: Citizen interests or bureaucratic control. *Computers and the Social Sciences*, Vol. 1, No. 2 (April-June: 77- 90.

Kraemer, Kenneth L. and Alana Northrop (1984).
Computers in public management education: A curriculum proposal for the next ten years. *Public Administration Quarterly*, Vol. 8, No. 3 (Fall): 343-368.

Kraemer, Kenneth L. and Alana Northrop (1989).
Curriculum recommendations for public management education in computing: An update. *Public Administration Review*, Vol. 49, No. 5 (Sept./OCt.): 447-453.

Kraft, Joan (1987).
Women, computers, and information work. Washington, DC: American University. Doctoral dissertation.

Kraft, Philip (1977).
Programmers and managers. NY: Springer Verlag.

Kraft, Philip (1987).
Computers and the automation of work. In Robert E. Kraut, ed. *Technology and the transformation of white-collar work*. Hillsdale, NJ: Lawrence Erlbaum Associates, 1987.

Krasnoff, Barbara (1989).
Keeping democracy alive in China. *Personal Computing*, Vol. 13, No. 10 (October): 48.

Krass, Peter (1990a).
Capitol investments. *InformationWeek*, No. 286 (Sept. 10): 76-80.

Krass, Peter (1990b).
The MBA influence on MIS. *InformationWeek*, No. 255 (Jan. 20): 56-61.

Krass. Peter (1990c).
Learning from Uncle Sam. *InformationWeek*, No. 263 (March 19): 40 - 43.
Krass, Peter (1990d).
Data problems bug EPA. *InformationWeek*, No. 299 (Dec. 10): 15.
Krass, Peter (1990e).
Focus on outsourcing, *InformationWeek*, No, 277 (July 9): 30-34.
Krass, Peter (1990f).
The dollars and sense of outsourcing. *InformationWeek*, No. 259 (Feb. 26): 26-31.
Krass, Peter (1991a).
War provokes security measures at data centers. *InformationWeek*, Jan. 21: 12-13.
Krass, Peter (1991b).
Managing without managers. *InformationWeek*, No. 346 (Nov. 11): 44-51.
Krass, Peter (1991c).
Lincoln kills imaging project. *InformationWeek*, No. 351 (Dec. 16): 36-37.
Krass, Peter (1992a).
MIS recovering at Blue Cross. *InformationWeek*, No. 366 (March 30): 24-28.
Krass, Peter and Bruce Caldwell (1991).
Wall Street debates the role of IT. *InformationWeek*, No. 325 (June 17): 12.
Krauss, L. I. (1970).
Computer-based managment information systems. NY: American Management Association.
Kraut, A. I. (1962).
How EDP is affecting workers and organizations. *Personnel*, Vol. 39, No. 4: 38-50.
Kraut, Robert E., ed. (1987a).
Technology and the transformation of white-collar work. Hillsdale, NJ: Lawrence Erlbaum Associates.
Kraut, Robert E. (1987b).
Social issues and white-collar technology: An overview. In Kraut, ed. (1987a): 1-22.
Kraut, Robert E. (1987c).
Predicting the use of technology: The case of telework. In R. Kraut, ed. (1987a): 113-134.
Kraut, Robert E., Susan T. Dumais, and Susan Koch (1989).
Computerization, productivity, and the quality of work-life. *Communications of the ACM*, Vol. 32, No. 2 (Feb.): 220-238.
Kresslein, John C. and Donald A. Marchand (1987).
A comparative view of information resources management: practices in state government. In Levitan, 1987: ch. 6.
Kydd, Christine T. and Louise H. Jones (1989).
Corporate productivity and shared information technology. *Information and Management*, Vol. 17: 277-282.
Lacina, L. J. (1983).
Computer equity in public education. *Education*, Vol. 104, No.2: 128-130.
Ladner, Richard E. (1989).
Computer accessibility for federal workers with disabilities: It's the law. *Communications of the ACM*, Vol. 38, No. 8 (August): 952-956.

LaFrance, Marianne (1990).
Stories knowledge engineers tell about expert systems. *Social Science Computer Review*, Vol. 8, No. 1 (Spring): 13-23.

Lambert, Matthew E. (1989).
Using computer simulations in behavior therapy training. *Computers in Human Services*, Vol. 5, Nos. 3/4: 1-12.

Lambert, Matthew E., James L. Hedlund, and Bruce W. Vieweg (1990a).
Computer simulations in mental health education: Current status. *Computers in Human Services*, Vol. 7, Nos. 3/4: 211-229.

Lambert, Matthew E., James L. Hedlund, and Bruce W. Vieweg (1990a).
Computer simulations in mental health education: Two illustrative projects. *Computers in Human Services*, Vol. 7, Nos. 3/4: 231-245.

Lambert, Matthew E. and Gerard Lenthall (1989).
Effects of psychology courseware use on computer anxiety in students. *Computers in Human Behavior*, Vol. 5, No. 3: 207-214.

Langefors, B. (1973).
Theoretical analysis of information systems. Lund, Sweden: Studentlitteratur.

LaPlante, Alice (1988a).
Membership has its privileges: IBM big accounts go first class, *Government Computer News*, 1 Feb. 1988: 1, 73.

LaPlante, Alice (1988b).
Users sticking to programs they know best, study shows. *Info World*, June 13: 8.

LaPlante, Alice (1989).
IBM study: PCs aid in decision process. *InfoWorld*, Vol. 11, No. 49 (December): 1, 8.

LaPlante, Alice (1989).
Is leasing right for you?, *InfoWorld*, 22 May: 39, 42.

LaPlante, Alice (1990a).
Is Big Brother watching? *InfoWorld*, Vol. 12, No. 43 (Oct. 22): 58, 65-66.

LaPlante, Alice (1990b).
Adapt or die: The information center evolves to survive. *InfoWorld*, Vol. 12, No. 45 (Nov. 5): 57-58.

LaPlante, Alice (1990c).
Role of MIS is redefined as PCs edge mainframes. *InfoWorld*, Vol. 12, No. 25 (June 18): 1, 117.

LaPlante, Alice (1991a).
Here come the hybrids. *Computerworld*, Vol. 25, No. 24 (June 17): 57-58.

LaPlante, Alice and Rachel Parker (1989).
PC vendors calm technology fears. *InfoWorld*, May 1 (Vol. 11, No. 18): 1, 117.

Larwood, L. (1984).
Organizational behavior and management. Boston: Kent Publ.

Lasden, M. (1982).
Keeping pace in data entry. *Computer Decisions*, Vol. 14 (April): 90-111.

Laudon, Kenneth C. (1974).
Computers and bureaucratic reform. N.Y.: John Wiley.

Laudon, Kenneth C. (1977).
Communications technology and democratic participation. NY: Praeger.

Lee, Yvonne (1990b).
E-mail's potential largely untapped, readers say. *InfoWorld*, Vol. 12, No. 35 (Aug. 27): 31.

Lehman, Tom (1991).
Information networks and innovation approaches. *Public Productivity Review*, Vol. 15, No. 2 (Winter): 245-251.

Leibs, Scott (1989).
Who's afraid of the dark? *InformationWeek*, No. 232 (Aug. 14): 36-38.

Leibs, Scott (1990a).
Information: Plug in, turn on, tune up. *InformationWeek*, No. 296 (12 Nov.): 76-80.

Leibs, Scott (1990b).
The info faucet: Hot and cold running data. *InformationWeek*, No. 296 (12 Nov.): 80.

Leitschuh, Jan (1989).
Electronic age links students to Chinese protests: Computers now a key tool of revolution. *News and Observer* (Raleigh, NC), 7 June: 1D, 3D.

Leveson, Nancy G, (1991).
Software safety in embedded computer systems. *Communications of the ACM*, Vol. 34, No. 2 (Feb.): 34-46.

Levin, Richard B. 1990).
The computer virus handbook. Berkeley, CA: Osborne/McGraw-Hill.

Levine, Arnold S. (1985).
Bowsher urges complete financial systems overhaul. *Government Computer News*, 7 June: 12.

Levine, Arnold S. (1986).
GSA issues end-user computing sequel. *Government Computer News*, 4 July 1986: 35.

Levine, Arnold S. (1991).
Problems in end-user computing still years away from solutions. *Federal Computer Week*, Vol. 5, No. 5 (Feb. 25): 13-14.

Levinson, Marc (1993).
Cutting edge? *Newsweek*, Vol. 121, No. 10 (March 8): 42 - 43.

Levinson, Marc, William Burger, and Bill Powell (1993).
Can anyone spare a job? *Newsweek*, Vol. 121, No. 24 (June 14): 46-48.

Levy, Steven (1984).
Hackers: Heroes of the computer revolution. NY: Doubleday.

Levy, Steven (1989).
Access for all. *Macworld*, August: 43-52.

Levy, Sydelle B. and Arlene R. Gordon (1988).
Age-related vision loss: Functional implications and assistive technologies. *International Journal of Technology and Aging*, Vol. 1, No. 2: 116-125.

Levy, D., D. Navon, and R. Shapira (1991).
Computers and class - computers and social-inequality in Israeli schools. *Urban Education*, Vol. 25, No. 4: 483-499.

Lie, M. and B. Rasmussen (1987).
Step by step: New systems in an old structure. Trondheim, Norway: Institute for Social Research in Industry.

Lindberg, D. A. B. (1979).
The growth of medical information systems in the United States. Lexington, MA: Lexington Books.

Linn, M. C. (1985).
Gender equity in computer learning environments. *Computers and the Social Sciences*, Vol. 1: 19-27.

Linstrum, Kathy (1991).
The end-user in the age of automation: Deskilled or empowered? *Educational Technology*, Vol. 31 (July): 53-55.

List, Steven P. (1989).
Zeno's paradox ... or the art of rapid prototyping. *DBMS* (Jan.): 64-73.

Livingston, William L. (1987).
Complexity, misapplied concepts doom OA projects. *Government Computer News*, 4 Dec.: 62-63.

Loch, Karen D., Houston H. Carr, and Merrill Warkentin (1991).
Why won't organizations tell you about computer crime? *Information Management Bulletin*, Vol. 4, No. 1 (Feb.): 5-6.

Lockheed, M. E. (1985).
Women, girls, and computers: A first look at the evidence. *Sex Roles*, Vol. 13, Nos. 3/4:229-240.

Lockheed, M. E. and S. B. Frakt (1984).
Sex equity: Increasing girls' use of computers. *The Computing Teacher*, Vol. 11: 16-18.

Lohmann, Roger A. (1990).
Automating the social work office. *Computers in Human Services*, Vol. 7, Nos. 3/4: 19-30.

Long, Larry (1989).
Management information systems. Englewood Cliffs, NJ: Prentice-Hall.

Loyd, Brenda H., Douglas E. Loyd, and Clarice P. Gressard (1987).
Gender and computer experience as factors in the computer attitudes of middle school students. *Journal of Early Adolescence*, Vol. 7, No. 1 : 13-19.

Loyd, Brenda H. and Clarice P. Gressard (1984).
The effects of sex, age, and computer experience on computer attitudes. *AEDS Journal*, Vol. 18, No. 2: 67-77.

Lucas, Henry C., Jr. (1975a).
Performance and the use of a management information system, *Management Science*, Vol. 3, No. 4: 908-919.

Lucas, Henry C., Jr. (1975b).
Why information systems fail. NY: Columbia University Press.

Lucas, Henry C., Jr. (1976).
The analysis, design, and implementation of information systems. NY: McGraw-Hill.

Lucas, Henry C., Jr. (1981).
Implementation: The key to successful information systems. NY: Columbia University Press.

Lucas, Henry C., Jr. (1989).
Managing information services. NY: Macmillan Publishing.

Lucas, Henry C., F. Land, T. Lincoln, and K. Supper, eds. (1980).
The information systems environment. Amsterdam: North Holland.

Lucas, Henry C., Jr. and J. A. Sutton (1977).
The stage hypothesis and the s-curve: Some contradictory evidence. *Communications of the ACM*, Vol. 20, No. 4 (April): 254-259.

Lucas, R. W., P. J. Mullen, C. B. X. Luna, and D. C. McInroy (1977).
Psychiatrist and computer interrogators of patients with alcohol-related illnesses: A comparison. *British Journal of Psychiatry*, Vol. 131: 160-167.

Lulofs, J. G. (1981).
A market theoretical approach to professions. *Mens en Maatschappij*, Vol. 56, No. 4 (Nov,): 349-377.

Lund, R. and J. Hansen (1986).
Keeping America at work: Strategies for employing the new technologies. NY: Wiley.

Lund, John (1991).
Computerized work performance monitoring and production standards: A review of labor law issues. *Labor Law Journal*, Vol. 42 (April): 195-203.

Lunin, Lois F. (1991).
White House Conference on Library and Information Services adopts 100 recommendations. *Information Today*, Vol. 8, No. 8 (Sept.): 1, 15-16.

Luthans, F. and R. Koester (1976).
The impact of computer generated information on the choice activity of decision-makers. *Academy of Management Journal*, Vol. 19, No. 2: 328-32.

Lyman, Peter (1982).
Being reasonable: On anger and order in middle class culture. Society for the Study of Social Problems, 1982 Annual Meeting.

Lyman, Peter (1984).
Reading, writing and word processing: Toward a phenomenology of the computer age. *Qualitative Sociology*, Vol. 7, Nos. 1/2 (Spring/Summer): 75-89.

Lyman, Peter (1988).
Sociological literature in an age of computerized texts. *The American Sociologist*, Vol. 19, No. 1 (Spring): 16-31.

Lynch, A. (1985).
Computerizing the ICU: A question of ethics. *Canadian Information Processing Society Review*, Vol. 9, No. 4 (July): 10-14.

Lynch, R. K. (1984).
Implementing packaged application software: Hidden costs and new challenges, *Systems, Objectives, Solutions*, Vol. 4, No. 4: 227-234.

Lynch, R. K. (1985)
Nine pitfalls in implementing packaged applications software, *Journal of Information Systems Management*, Vol. 2, No. 2: 88-92.

Lyons, Daniel J. (1989).
Modems, technology empower Chinese fighting for reform. *PC Week*, 19 June: 71-2.

Lyons, Daniel J. (1990).
Failing semiconductor industry bodes poorly for U. S. PC makers. *PC Week* (Feb. 19): 127.

Lyons, John S., Jeffrey S. Hammer, and Richard E. White (1987).
Computerization of psychosocial services in the general hospital: Collaborative information management in the human services department. *Computers in Human Services*, Vol. 2, Nos. 1/2 (Spring/Summer): 27-36.

Lyotard, Jean-Francois (1984).
The postmodern condition: A report on knowledge. Minneapolis: University of Minnesota Press.

Lyytinen, Kalle (1987).
Different perspectives on information systems: Problems and solutions, *ACM Computing Survey*, Vol. 19, No. 1 (March): 5-46.

Lyytinen, Kalle (1987a).
Different perspectives on information systems: Problems and solutions. *ACM Computing Surveys*, Vol. 19, No. 1 (March): 5-46.

Lyytinen, Kalle (1987b).
Information system failure: A survey and classification of empirical literature. *Oxford Survey of Information Technology*, Vol. 4.

Mace, Scott (1988).
Supreme Court moves general ledger to PC. *InformationWeek*, July 4: 17.

Mace, Scott and Shawn Willett (1993).
IS managers assail data encryption rule. *InformationWeek*, Vol. 15, No. 23 (June 7): 1, 103.

Machlup, Fritz (1962)
The production and distribution of knowledge in the United States. Princeton, NJ: Princeton University Press.

Machrone, Bill (1992).
Electronic mail: Threat or menace? *PC Magazine*, Vol. 11, No. 19 (Nov. 10): 87-88.

MacIver, Robert (1963).
The web of government. NY: Macmillan. Orig. pub. 1947.

MacKenzie, Donald (1990).
Inventing accuracy: A historical sociology of nuclear missile guidance. Cambridge, MA: MIT Press.

Magal, Simha R., Houston H. Carr, and Hugh R. Watson (1988).
Critical success factors for information center managers. *MIS Quarterly*, Vol. 12, No. 3 (Sept.): 412-425.

Majchrzak, Ann (1988).
The human side of factory automation. San Francisco: Jossey-Bass.

Majchrzak, Ann, Tien-Chien Chang, Woodrow Barfield, Ray Roberts, and Gabriel Salvendy (1987).
Human aspects of computer-aided design. Philadelphia: Taylor and Francis.

Majchrzak, Ann and John Cotton (1988).
A longitudinal study of adjustment to technological change: From mass to computer-automated batch production. *Journal of Occupational Psychology*, Vol. 61, No. 1 (Special Issue: Technological change and innovation) (March): 43-66.

Mallory, Jim (1991).
Public libraries go online. *Link-Up*, Vol. 8, No. 5 (Sept./Oct.): 1, 12.

Management Information Systems Week (1985).
U.S. agency shapes plans for workstation standards. *Management Information Systems Week* (11 Dec.): 54.

Mandell, Steven F. (1989).
Resistance and power: The perceived effect that computerization has on a social agency's power relationships. *Computers in Human Services*, Vol. 4, Nos. 1/2: 29-40.

Mandinach, E. B. and M. C. Linn (1987).
Cognitive consequences of programming: Achievements of experienced and talented programmers. *Journal of Educational Computing Research*, Vol. 3, No. 1: 53-72.

Mann, F. C. and L. K. Williams (1958).
Organizational impact of white collar automation. *Annual Proceedings of Industrial Research Associates*: 59-68.

Mann, F. C. and L. K. Williams (1960).
Observations on the dynamics of a change to electronic data-processing equipment. *Administrative Science Quarterly*, Vol. 5, No. 1: 217-256.

Mantei, Marilyn M. and Toby J. Teorey (1988).
Cost/benefit analysis for incorporating human factors in the software lifecycle. *Communications of the ACM*, Vol. 31, No. 4 (April): 428-439.

Manzolillo, Lisa and Richard Cardinalli (1990).
Ethics and computer crime: A guide for managers. *Datacenter Manager*, Vol. 2, No. 6 (Nov./Dec.): 16-20.

March, Richard (1989).
User faces prison for destroying data. *PC Week*, Vol. 6, No. 47 (27 Nov.): 1, 6.

March, J. G. and Herbert A. Simon (1958).
Organizations. NY: Wiley.

Marchand, Donald A. and John C. Kresslein (1988).
Information resources management and the public sector administrator. In Rabin and Jackowski, eds., 1988: ch. 15.

Margulius, David L. (1989).
Your right to what Uncle Sam knows: Is big business pulling the plug? (October): 78-85.

Markus, M. Lynne (1983).
Power, politics, and MIS implementation. *Communications of the ACM*, Vol. 26, No. 6 (June): 430-444.

Markus, M. Lynne (1984).
Systems in organizations: Bugs and features. Marshfield, MA: Pitman.

Markus, M. Lynne and J. Pfeffer (1983).
Power and the design and implementation of accounting and control systems. *Human Relations*, Vol. 36: 203-226.

Markus, M. Lynne and Daniel Robey (1988)
Information technology and organizational change: Causal structure in theory and research. *Management Science*, Vol. 34, No. 5 (May): 583-598.

Marshall, Jon C. and Susan Bannon (1988).
Race and sex equity in computer advertising. *Journal of Research on Computing and Education*, Vol. 21, No. 1 (Fall): 15-26.

Marshall, Ray and Marc Tucker (1992).
Thinking for a living: Educationa and the wealth of nations. NY: Basic Books.

Martin, E. W. (1985).
Critical success factors of chief MIS/DP executives. *MIS Quarterly*, Vol. 6, No. 2 (June): 1-19.

Martin, James (1981).
Design and strategy for distributed data processing. Englewood Cliffs, NJ: Prentice-Hall.

Martin, James (1982).
Applications development without programmers (Englewood Cliffs, NJ: Prentice-Hall).

Martin, James (1983).
Managing the data-base environment. Englewood Cliffs, NJ: Prentice Hall.

Martin, James, Kathleen K. Chapman, and The Arben Group, Inc. (1987).
SNA: IBM's networking solution (Englewood Cliffs, NJ: Prentice-Hall).

Martin, James and Joe Leben (1989).
Strategic information planning methodologies, 2nd edition. Englewood Cliffs, NJ: Prentice-Hall.

Martin, John (1993).
Reengineering government. *Governing*, Vol. 6, No. 6 (March): 26-30.

Martin, John A. and E. Sam Overman (1988).
Management of cognitive hierarchies: What is the role of management information systems? *Public Productivity Review*, Vol. 11, No. 4 (Summer): 69-84.

Marx, G. T. and N. Reichman (1984).
Routinizing the discovery of secrets. *American Behavioral Scientist*, Vol. 27, No. 4 (March-April): 423-452.

Marx, G. and S. Sherizen (1986).
Monitoring on the job: How to protect privacy as well as property. *Technology Review*, Vol. 89, No. 8: 62-72.

Mason, J. (1983).
VDT alert: Safety under study. *Management World*, Vol. 12 (April): 14-15.

Mason, R. O. and I. I. Mitroff (1973).
A program for research on management information systems. *Management Science*, Vol. 19, No. 5: 475-487.

Mason, R. O. and I. I. Mitroff (1981).
Challenging strategic planning assumptions. NY: Wiley.

Mass, Rita (1982).
Records, words, data ... Whatever you call it, it's still information. *Information and Records Management* (June): 18-20.

Massey, David (1988).
Liability for failed software. *Journal of Information Systems Management*, Vol 5, No. 4 (Fall): 47 - 53.

Masud, S. A. (1988).
FBI system is a 'window on the world'. *Government Computer News*, July 8: 16.

Masud, S. A. (1992).
Study says fed comm spending up 7% yearly, *Government Computer News*, Vol. 11, No. 11 (May 25): 47.

Matheson, A. D. (1993).
Innovative use of computers for planning in human service organizations. Pp. 383-395 in Marcos Leiderman, Charles Guzetta, Leny Struminger, and Menachem Monnickendam, eds. (1993). *Technology in people services: Research, theory, and applications*. NY: Haworth Press.

Matheson, Kimberly and Mark P. Zanna (1990).
Computer-mediated communications: The focus is on me. *Social Science Computer Review*, Vol. 8, No. 1 (Spring): 1-12.

McCarthy, John (1989).
Networks considered harmful for electronic mail, *Communications of the ACM*, Vol. 32, No. 12 (December): 1389-1390.

McCormick, John (1989).
NASA network gets 'WANKed' by worm attack. *Government Computer News*, 30 Oct.: 4.

McCullough, Michael F. (1991).
Democratic questions for the computer age. *Computers in Human Services*, Vol. 8, No. 1: 9-18.

McDougall, Walter A. (1985).
The heavens and the earth: A political history of the space age. NY: Basic Books.

McFarlan, F. Warren (1990).
Privacy and IT use. CIO, Vol. 3, No. 5 (Feb.): 82-85.

McFarlan, Warren (1981).
Portfolio approach to information systems. *Harvard Business Review*, Vol. 59, No. 5 (Sept.-Oct.): 142-150.

McFarlan, Warren and James L. McKenney (1983a).
Corporate information systems management: The issues facing senior executives. Homewood, IL: Irwin, 1983.

McFarlan, Warren and James L. McKenney (1983b).
The information archipelago governing the new world. *Harvard Business Review* (July-Aug.): 91-99.

McFarland, Bruce (1989).
Voice messaging in the IC. *Information Center*, Vol. 5, No. 7 (July): 35-38.

McGee, G. W. (1987).
Social context variables affecting the implementation of microcomputers. *Journal of Educational Computing Research*, Vol. 3: 189-207.

McGee, Howard, James Seroka, and Richard Thomas (1988).
Microcomputer applications in teaching graduate public administration (Carbondale, IL: Illinois Association of Graduate Programs in Public Administration).
McGraw, Tim (1987a).
Union objecting to IRS case management system. *Government Computer News*, Sept. 11: 11.
McGraw, Time (1987b).
HHS organizes to eliminate personnel paperwork. *Government Computer News*, Dec. 4: 88.
McGraw, Tim (1988a).
Computer expert stresses ADP's role in the office. *Government Computer News*, 8 January: 7.
McGraw, Tim (1988b).
Board hashes out proposal for FBI's NCIC system. *Government Computer News*, 1 January: 88.
McGraw, Tim (1988c).
Data centers are changing but aren't disappearing. *Government Computer News*, 8 Jan.: 20.
McGraw, Tim (1988d).
Questions raised about Justice IRM reorganization. *Government Computer News*, 18 March: 2.
McGuire, Timothy W., Sarah Kiesler, and Jane Siegel (1987).
Group and computer-mediated discussion effects in risk decision making. *Journal of Personality and Social Psychology*, Vol. 52: 917-930.
McInerney, William D. (1989).
Social and organizational effects of educational computing. *Journal of Educational Computing Research*, Vol. 5, No. 4: 487-506.
McKeown, Kate (1990).
Everyone can be a leader. *PC-Computing*, Vol. 3, No. 1 (Jan.): 110-116.
McLuhan, Marshall (1964).
Understanding the media. NY: McGraw-Hill.
McPartlin, John P. (1990).
The terrors of technostress. *InformationWeek*, No. 280 (July 30): 30-33.
McPartlin, John P. (1991).
The hidden costs of downsizing. *InformationWeek*, No. 347 (Nov. 18): 35-38.
McPartlin, John P. (1992a).
S&L crisis: Federal bailout agency digs the hole deeper. *InformationWeek*, No. 362 (March 2): 10-11.
McPartlin, John P. (1992b).
"Buy American? Not This Time". *InformationWeek*, No. 368 (April 20): 54.
McPartlin, John P. (1992c).
Is the 'O' word becoming a non-no? *InformationWeek*, No. 375 (May 25): 73.
McPartlin, John P. (1992d).
The smart alternative? Keeping control by outsourcing employees. *InformationWeek*, No. 364 (March 16): 50.

McPartlin, John P. (1992e).
Outsourced employees sue. *InformationWeek*, No. 366 (March 30): 15.
McPartlin, John P. (1992f).
Environmental agency 'held hostage' by outsourcer. *InformationWeek*, No. 363 (March 9): 12-13.
McPartlin, John P. (1992g).
Ethics. *InformationWeek*, No. 382 (July 13): 30-36. (Cover story).
McPartlin, John P. (1992h).
Investing in the future. *InformationWeek*, No. 382 (July 13): 23.
McPartlin, John P. (1992i).
The collapse of CONFIRM. *InformationWeek*, No. 396 (Oct. 19): 12-14.
McPartlin, John P. (1993a).
Ten years of hard labor. *InformationWeek*, No. 418 (March 29): 52.
McPartlin, John P. (1993b).
You built it, we own it. *InformationWeek*, No. 437 (Aug. 9): 58.
McPartlin, John P. and Bruce Caldwell (1992).
Wanna know a secret: Debating what companies should tell IS employees about outsourcing plans. *InformationWeek*, No. 360 (Feb. 17): 52.
McPartlin, John P. and Joseph C. Panettieri (1993).
Towers without power. *InformationWeek*, No. 415 (March 8): 12-13.
Mead, Ron and Bill Trainor (1985).
New users require special attention. *Government Computer News*, 25 October: 65.
Megginson, L. C. (1963).
Automation: Our greatest asset - our greatest problem. *Academy of Management Journal*, Vol. 6, No. 3: 232-244.
Mehler, Mark (1991).
Reining in runaway systems. *InformationWeek*, No. 351 (Dec. 16): 20-24.
Menkus, Belden (1987).
New nature of office work hinders automation efforts. *Government Computer News* (Dec. 4): 49, 56.
Metz, E. (1986).
Managing change towards a leading edge information culture. *Organizational Dynamics*, Vol. 15: 28-40.
Meyer, N. Dean and Mary E. Boone (1987).
The information edge. NY: McGraw-Hill, 1987.
Meyrowitz, J. (1986).
No sense of place: The impact of electronic media on social behavior. NY: Oxford University Press.
Miewald, Robert D., Keith Mueller, and Robert F. Sittig (1987).
State legislative use of information technology is oversight. Ch. 5 in Levitan, ed., 1987: 87-103.
Miewald, Robert D. and Keith Mueller (1987).
The use of information technology is oversight by state legislatures. *State and Local Government Review* Vol. 19: 22-28.
Miles, J. B. (1988a).
Inquiries threaten FTS 2000. *Government Computer News*, 1 Jan. 1988: 1, 89.

Miles, J. B. (1988b).
GSA releases draft amendments to FTS 2000 plan. *Government Computer News*, 8 Jan. 1988: 89.

Miles, J. B. (1988c).
EPA ties diverse systems to nationwide network. *Government Computer News*, April 1: 67.

Miles, R. E. and C. C. Snow (1978).
Organizational strategy, structure, and process. NY: McGraw-Hill.

Miller, A. S. (1976).
The modern corporate state: Private government and the American Constitution. Westport, CT: Greenwood Press.

Miller, Boulton B. (1988).
Managing information as a resource. In J. Rabin and E. M. Jackowski, eds., *Handbook of Information Resource Management.* (NY: Dekker): ch. 1.

Miller, D. and P. H. Friesen (1978).
Archetypes of strategy formulation. *Management Science*, Vol. 24, No. 9: 921-933.

Miller, . W. (1988).
Developing information technology strategies. *Journal of Systems Management.* Vol. 39, NO. 9 (Sept.): 28-35).

Miller, Richard K., Terri C. Walker, and Anne M. Ryan (1990).
Neural net applications and products. Madison, GA: Technical Publications.

Miller, Robert (1990).
Marshal your resources with project management software. *Today's Office* (January): 22-25.

Millman, Zeeva and Jon Hartwick (1987).
The impact of automated office systems on middle managers and their work. *MIS Quarterly*, Vol. 11, No. 4: 479-491.

Mills, Edward R. (1992).
Profiles in management. *CIO*, Vol. 5, No. 10 (April): 24-27.

Mills, Miriam (1984).
Teleconferencing: Managing the 'invisible worker'. *Sloan Management Review*, Vol. 25, No. 4 (Summer).

Mills, William deB. (1990).
Rule-based analysis of Sino-soviet negotiations. *Social Science Computer Review*, Vol. 8, No. 2 (Summer): 181-194.

Minabe, S. (1986).
Japanese competitiveness and Japanese management. *Sciences*, Vol. 233: 301-304.

Minsky, M. (1986).
The society of mind. NY: Simon and Schuster.

Minsky, M. and S. Papert (1988).
Perceptrons. Cambridge, MA: MIT Press.

Mintzberg, H. and McHugh, A. (1985).
Strategy formation in an adhocracy. *Administrative Science Quarterly*, Vol. 30, No. 2: 160-197.

Mintzberg, H. and J. A. Waters (1985).
Of strategies, deliberate and emergent. *Strategic Management Journal*, Vol. 6: 157-273.

Mintzberg, L. (1979).
The structuring of organizations: A synthesis of the research. Englewood Cliffs, NJ: Prentice-Hall.

MIS Week (1989).
June 12: 44.

MIS Week (1990).
The shape of things. *MIS Week* (Feb. 5): 36.

Mitsch, Robert J. (1983).
Ensuring privacy and accuracy of computerized employee record systems. *Personnel Administrator* (September): 37-41.

Mizrahi, Terry, John Downing, Rob Fasano et al., eds. (1991).
Computers for social change and community organizing. Binghamton, NY: Haworth Press.

Moir, Brian R. (1991).
"Safeguards" don't guarantee quality. *Networking Management*, Vol. 9, No. 14 (Dec.): 74.

Mokyr, Joel (1990).
The lever of riches. N.Y.: Oxford University Press.

Molina, Alfonso . (1989).
The social basis of the microelectronics revolution. Edinburgh, UK: Edinburgh University Press.

Molotch, Harvey L. and Deirdre Boden (1985).
Talking social structure: Discourse, domination, and the watergate hearings. *American Sociological Review* (June): 273-288.

Monnickendam, Menachem and A. Solomon Eaglstein (1993).
Computer acceptance by social workers: Some unexpected research findings. *Computers in Human Services*, Vol. 9, Nos. 3/4: 409 - 424.

Montague, Steve (1986).
Government MIS: the pregnant pyramid. *Optimum*, Vol. 17, No. 2: 67-75.

Morahan-Martin, Janet, Alan Olinsky, and Phyllis Schumacher (1992).
Gender differences in computer experience, skills, and attitudes among incoming college students. *Collegiate Microcomputer*, Vol. 10, No. 1 (Feb.): 1-8.

Moran, Paul (1990).
Betting on it. *InformationWeek*, 12 March: 41-42.

Moran, Robert (1991).
FBS, Social Security data stolen. *InformationWeek*, No. 352 (Dec. 23): 14.

Moran, Robert (1992a).
SAS: More things to more users. *InformationWeek*, No. 359 (Feb. 10): 44.

Morgan, Cynthia (1990).
Toting up federal micros: Analysis finds 1.6 Million. *Government Computer News*, Jan. 8: 1.

Morgan, Cynthia (1991a).
Art of Negotiating simply dishes out common sense. *Government Computer News*, April 29: 67.

Morgan, H. and J. Soden (1973).
Understanding MIS failures. *Data Base*, Vol. 5, No. 1.

Morris, David C. (1988).
A survey of age and attitudes toward computers. *Journal of Educational Technology Systems*, Vol. 17, No. 1: 73-78.

Morris-Suzuki, Tessa (1987).
Capitalism in the computer age. *New Left Review*, No. 160: 81-90.

Morris-Suzuki, Tessa (1988).
Beyond computopia: Information, automation and democracy in Japan. NY: Routledge.

Morrison, David (1989).
Software crisis: The Pentagon is trying to cope with the costs and the bugs associated with the computer software that makes its 'smart' weapons smart. *National Journal*, Vol. 21 (January 14): 72-5.

Mosco, Vincent (1988).
Information in the pay-per society. In Mosco and Wasko, eds. (1988).

Mosco, Vincent and Janet Wasko, eds. (1988).
The political economy of information. Madison, WI: University of Wisconsin Press.

Mothe, John R. de la (1987).
Educating for progress? Postmodernist images of the university-industry interface. *Quarterly Journal of Ideology*, Vol. 11, No. 2 (April): 89-95.

Mouritsen, Jan and Niels Bjorn-Anderson (1991).
Understanding third wave information systems. In C. Dunlop and R. Kling, eds., *Computerization and controversy.* NY: Academic Press, 1991: 308-320.

Muir, Donal E. (1983).
An adaptive systems theory: Toward reductionism, *Sociological Inquiry*, Vol. 53, No. 4: 435-448.

Muir, Donal E. (1986).
A mathematical model/computer simulation of adaptive system interaction, *Behavioral Science*, Vol. 31, No. 1: 29-41.

Muir, Donal E. (1987).
Sociological side effects of the computer revolution. *Quarterly Journal of Ideology*, Vol. 11, No. 2: 17-25.

Muir, Donal E. (1988a).
Assessing the psycho-social impact of computers, brain research, and behaviorism: The von Neumann effect. *Sociological Forum*, Vol.' 3, No. 3: 606-612.

Muir, Donal E. (1988b).
The cognitive impact of the information age: A test of the Von Neumann effect. *Journal of Social Behavior and Personality*, Vol. 3, No. 3: 269-274.

Muller, Michael J., S. Kuhn, and J. A. Meskill, eds. (1992).
PDC'92. In *Proceedings of the participatory design conference*. Cambridge, MA: Computer Professionals for Social Responsibility.

Muller, Michael J., Daniel M. Wildman, and Ellen A. White (1993).
Taxonomy of PD practices: A brief practitioners guide. *Communications of the ACM*, Vol. 36, No. 4 (June): 26-27.

Mullins, Carolyn J. (1988).
Teaching technical writing with PCs. *Technical Writing Teacher*, Vol. 15, No. 1 (Winter): 64-72.

Mumford, E. (1981).
Values, technology and work. The Hague, Netherlands: Martinus Nijhoff Publishers.

Mumford, E. (1983).
Designing human systems - The ETHICS method. Cheshire, England: Manchester Business School.

Mumford, E. (1984).
Participation: From Aristotle to today. In Bemelmans, ed. (1984): 95-104.

Mumford, E., R. A. Hirschheim, G. Fitzgerald, and A. T. Wood-Harper, eds. (1985).
Research methods in information systems. Amsterdam: North Holland.

Murphree, M. C. (1984).
Brave new office: The changing world of the legal secretary. In K. Sacks and D. Remy, eds., *My troubles are going to have trouble with me: Everyday trials and triumphs of women workers*, New Brunswick, NJ: Rutgers University Press.

Murphy, John W. (1988).
Computerization, postmodern epistemology, and reading in the postmodern era. *Educational Theory*, Vol. 38, No. 2 (Spring): 175-182.

Murphy, John W. and John T. Pardeck, eds. (1986).
Technology and human productivity. Westport, CT: Greenwood Press.

Murphy, John W. and John T. Pardeck (1988).
The computer micro-world, knowledge, and social planning. *Computers in Human Services*, Vol. 3, Nos. 1/2:127-141.

Murphy, John W. and John T. Pardeck (1989).
Technology, computerization, and the conceptualization of service delivery. *Computers in Human Services*, Vol. 5, Nos. 1/2: 197 - 211.

Murray, J. Michael (1988).
Information systems and data processing organizations: Functions, evolution, structure, and issues. In Rabin and Jackowski, eds., 1988: ch. 7.

Murray, J. P. (1984).
How an information center improved productivity. *Management Accounting*, Vol. 65, No. 9: 38-44.

Murray, William H. (1992).
Who holds the keys? *Communications of the ACM*, Vol. 35, No. 7 (July): 13-15.

Musolf, L. and H. Seidman (1980).
The blurred boundaries of public administration. *Public Administration Review*, Vol. 40: 124-130.

Mutschler, Elizabeth and Richard Hoefer (1990).
Factors affecting the use of computer technology in human service organizations. *Administration in Social Work*, Vol. 14, No. 1: 87-101.

Mutschler, Elizabeth and Y. Hasenfeld (1986).
Integrated information systems for social work practice. *Social Work*, Vol. 31: 345-349.

Myers, C. A. (1966).
Some implicatins of computers for management. *San Francisco Industrial Relations Research Association Proceedings*: 189-201.
Myers, Kara (1990).
Cracking the glass ceiling. *InformationWeek*, No. 284 (August 27): 38-41.
Myktyn, Peter P. Jr. and Kathleen Myktyn (1991).
Legal perspectives on expert systems. *AI Expert*, V. 6, No. 12 (Dec.): 40-45.
Naiman, A. (1985).
Avoiding "compubabble". *Personal Computing* (March): 47.
Nakaseko, M., E. Grandjean, W. Hunting and R. Gierer (1985).
Studies on ergonomically designed alphanumeric keyboards. *Human Factors*, Vol. 27, No. 2: 175-187.
Namm, J. (1986).
The case of the changing technology: Impact of micro-computer technology on a *Fortune 500* company. 95-101 in Murphy and Pardeck, eds. (1986).
Narayanan, Gita (1989).
The social impact of computers on women clerical workers. Pittsburgh, PA: University of Pittsburgh. Doctoral dissertation.
NAS/NRC (National Academy of Sciences/National Research Council) (1984).
The race for the new frontier: International competition in advanced technology - decisions for America. NY: Simon and Schuster.
Nash, Jim (1991).
Lack of standards inhibits groupware. *Computerworld*, Vol. 25, No. 50 (Dec. 16): 68.
Nash, Stephen, ed. (1990).
A history of scientific computing. NY: ACM Press.
National Research Council (1978).
Energy modeling for an uncertain future, Supporting Paper No. 2. Washington, DC: National Academy of Sciences.
National Research Council (1991).
Computers at risk: Safe computing in the information age. Washington, DC: National Academy Press.
National Research Council (1991a).
Computers at risk: Safe computing in the information age. Washington, DC: National Academy Press.
National Research Council (1991b).
Intellectual property issues in software. Washington, DC: National Academy Press.
Nelson, Richard R. 1989).
What Is Private and What Is Public about Technology? *Science, Technology, and Human Values*, Vol. 14, No, 3 (Summer): 229-241.
Nelson, Robin (1989).
CEOs: Computing in high places. *Personal Computing*, April: 70-84.
Nelson, Robin (1990).
Graphics: The wretched excess, *Personal Computing*, Vol. 14, No. 2 (February): 49-50.

Neumann, Peter G. (1992).
Fraud by computer. *Communications of the ACM*, Vol. 35, No. 8 (Aug.): 154.
Neumann, Peter G. (1993).
Modeling and simulation. *Communications of the ACM*, Vol. 36, No. 4 (June): 124.
Neumann, S. and M. Hadass (1980).
DSS and strategic decisions. *California Management Review*, Vol. 22, No. 3: 77-84.
Neumann, S. and E. Seger (1980).
Evaluate your information system. *Journal of Systems Development*, Vol. 32, No. 2: 165-173.
Newcomer, Kathryn E. and Sharon L. Caudle (1991).
Evaluating public sector information systems: More than meets the eye. *Public Administration Review*, Vol. 51, No. 5 (Sept./Oct.): 377-384.
Newkirk, M. Glenn (1990).
Electronic democracy: Equal access of information is needed for all citizens. *InformationWeek*, No. 257 (Feb. 12): 60.
News Media and the Law (1990).
Requesters can't demand computer tape disclosure. *News Media and the Law*, Vol. 14, No. 18 (Winter): 22.
New York Times (1989).
New computers link public to officials. *New York Times*, Vol. 138, No. 47,789 (Feb. 22): A14.
New York Times (1992).
Sophisticated virus-fighters. *New York Times*, March 8: 8 (Business Section).
Nickell, Daniel B. (1983).
Forecasting on your microcomputer. Blue Ridge Summit, PA: TAB Books.
Nickell, Gary S. and J. N. Pinto (1986).
The computer attitude scale. *Computers in human Behavior*, Vol. 2: 301-306.
Nickell, Gary S. et al. (1987).
Gender and sex role differences in computer attitudes and experience. Paper, Southwestern Psychological Association, New Orleans, April 16-18.
Nilles, J. and et al. (1976).
Telecommunications-transportation tradeoffs: Options for tomorrow. NY: John Wiley and Sons, 1976.
Nimmer, Raymond and Patricia A. Krauthaus (1986).
Computer error and user liability risk. *Jurimetrics Journal*, Vol. 26: 121-37.
Nitzan, Shmuel and Elinor Ostrom (1992).
The nature and severity of collective-action problems -- The voluntary, collective provision of mixed goods approach. Bloomington, IN: Indiana University, Workshop in Political Theory and Policy Analysis, Paper D91-19.
Noble, D. F. (1984).
Forces of production: A social history of industrial automation. NY: Knopf.
Nolan, Richard L. (1973).
Managing the computer resource: A stage hypothesis. *Communications of the ACM*, Vol. 16, No. 7 (July): 399-405.

Nolan, Richard L. (1977).
Management accounting and control of data processing. NY: National Association of Accountants.
Nolan, Richard L. (1979).
Managing the crisis in data processing. *Harvard Business Review*, Vol. 57, No. 2 (March/April): 115-127.
Nolan, Richard L. and H. H. Seward (1974).
Measuring user satisfaction to evaluate information systems. In R. L. Nolan, ed., *Managing the data resource function*. St. Paul, MN: West Publ.
Noonan, D. E. (1991).
Information technology: Promises remain unfulfilled. *Computerworld* (Feb. 18): 25.
Norman, Donald A. (1983).
Design rules based on analyses of human error. *Communications of the ACM*, Vol. 26, No. 4 (April): 254-258.l
Norman, Donald A. (1990).
Commentary: Human error and the design of computer systems. *Communications of the ACM*, Vol. 33, No. 1 (January): 4-7.
Norman, Ronald J. and Jay F. Nunamaker, Jr. (1989).
CASE productivity preceptions of software engineering professionals. *Communications of the ACM*, Vol. 32, No. 9 (September): 1102-1108.
Noro, K. and A. S. Imada, eds. (1991).
Participatory ergonomics. London: Taylor and Francis.
Norris, Donald F. (1981).
Academic technical assistance in a period of fiscal retrenchment: The Case for computer technology, *State and Local Government Review*, Vol. 13, No. 3 (September, 1981): 109-114.
Norris, Donald F. (1985).
Small local governments and information management, *Government Publications Review*, Vol. 12 (Sept./Oct. 1985): 403-10.
Norris, Donald F. (1987).
Computing in small local governments: A view from the American Great Plains. *Journal of Rural Studies*, Vol. 3, No. 1: 43-56.
Norris, Donald F. (1988).
Microcomputers in financial management: Case studies of eight American cities. *Public Budgeting and Finance*, Vol. 8, No. 1 (Spring): 69-82.
Norris, Donald F. (1989a).
Microcomputers and local government. Washington, DC: International City Management Association.
Norris, Donald F. (1989b).
High tech in city hall: Uses and effects of microcomputers in United State local governments. *Social Science Computer Review*, Vol. 7, No. 2 (Summer): 137-146.
Norris, Donald F. (1992).
Gender, job and the effects of microcomputers in public organizations. *State and Local Government Review*, Vol. 24, No. 2 (Spring): 65-70.

Norris, Donald F. and Lyke Thompson (1988).
Computing in public administration: Practice and education. *Social Science Computer Review*, Vol. 6, No. 4 (Winter): 548-557.

Northrop, Alana, Kenneth L. Kraemer, Debora Dunkle, and John Leslie King (1990).
Payoffs from computerization: Lessons over time. *Public Administration Review*, Vol. 50, No. 5 (Sept./Oct.): 505-514.

Norton, Henry (1988).
Computing procurement: Guidelines and procedures. NY: Oxford University Press.

Norton, David P. and Ronald L. Evans (1989).
Keeping pace with technology. *PC/Computing* (Jan.): 205-214.

Null, Cynthia H. (1988).
Science, politics, and computers. *Behavior Research Methods, Instruments, and Computers*, Vol. 20, No. 2 (April): 73-80.

Nunamaker, J. F., A. R. Dennis, J. S. Valacich, D. R. Vogel, and J. F. George (1991).
Electronic meeting systems to support group work. *Communications of the ACM*, Vol. 34, No. 7 (July): 40-61.

Nussbaum, Karen (1992).
Workers under surveillance. *Computerworld* (Jan. 6): 21.

Nycum, Susan H. (1986).
Computer crime legislation in the United States. *Israel Law Review*, Vol. 21, No. 1 (Winter): 64-89.

Nycum, Susan H. and William A. Lowell (1981).
Common law and statutory liability for inaccurate computer-based data. *Emory Law Journal*, Vol. 30: 445-70.

Oborne, D. (1985).
Computers at work: A behavioural approach. NY: Wiley.

Ogozalek, Virginia Z. (1991).
The social impacts of computing: Computer technoiogy and the Graying of America. *Social Science Computer Review*, Vol. 9, No. 4 (Winter).

O'Leary, Meghan (1988).
An on-line club for information center pros, *PC Week*, Feb. 9: 50-51.

O'Leary, Meghan (1990).
E pluribus unum. *CIO*, Vol. 3, No. 9 (June): 72-80.

O'Leary, Meghan (1992).
Downsizing: Hearts and minds. *CIO*, Vol. 5, No. 10 (April): 44-46.

O'Leary, Meghan (1993).
A new life for purchasing. *CIO*, Vol. 6, No. 11 (May 1): 32-36.

Olsen, Florence (1989).
PC software lets govt. employees work at home, *Government Computer News*, July 24: 24.

Olsen, Florence (1990).
HUD links more than 100 LANs over mail system. *Government Computer News*, Oct. 15: 31.

Olsen, Florence (1991a).
Government data too costly, groups complain. *Government Computer News*, May 13: 6.

Olsen, Florence (1991b).
End-user forum targets managers. *Government Computer News*, Vol. 10, No. 5 (March 4): 32.

Olsen, Florence (1992a).
Electronic meetings save Army big bucks on travel. *Government Computer News*, Vol. 11, No. 8 April 13): 27, 31.

Olsen, Florence (1992b).
Do computers add to feds' productivity? *Government Computer News*, Vol. 11, No. 17 (Aug. 17): 1, 86.

Olson, Margrethe H. (1982).
New information technology and organizational culture. *MIS Quarterly* Vol. 6 (Dec.): 71-92.

Olson, Margrethe H. (1983).
Remote office work: Changing work patterns in space and time, *Communications of the ACM*, Vol. 26, No. 3 (March): 182-187.

Olson, Margrethe H., Ed. (1989a).
Technological support for work group collaboration. Hillsdale, NJ: Lawrence Erlbaum Associates.

Olson, Margrethe . (1989b).
Work at home for computer professionals: Current Attitudes and future prospects. *ACM Transactions in Information Systems*, Vol. 17, No. 4 (Oct.): 317-338.

Olson, Margrethe H. and H. Lucas (1982).
The impact of office automation on the organization: Some implications for research and practice, *Communications of the ACM*, Vol. 25: 838-847.

Olson, Margrethe H. and S. Primps (1984).
Working at home with computers: Work and nonwork issues, *Journal of Social Issues*, Vol. 40, No. 3: 97-112.

O'Malley, Christopher (1989a).
The power of information access, *Personal Computing*, Vol. 13, No. 10 (October): 71-74.

O'Malley, Christopher (1989b).
A laptop brigade that focuses on the customer, *Personal Computing*, Vol. 13, No. 10 (October): 76-79.

OMB (Office of Management and Budget) (1982).
Computer matching guidelines. Washington, DC: Superintendent of Documents. May.

Oskamp, Stuart and Shirlynn Spacapan, eds. (1990).
People's reactions to technology. Newbury Park, CA: Sage Publications.

Ostrom, Vincent and Elinor Ostrom (1977).
Public goods and public choice. In E. S. Savas, ed., *Alternatives for delivering public services: Toward improved performance*. Boulder, CO: Westview Press, 7-49.

Otsuki, Mikiro (1992).
Surplus from publicness in consumption and its equitable distribution. *Journal of Public Economics*, Vol. 47, No. 1 (Feb.): 107-124.

Overman, E. Sam (1984).
Information resource managers in state government, *Education for the Public*

Service (BY: Maxwell School for Citizenship, Syracuse University).

Overman, E. Sam (1985).
Decentralization and microcomputer policy in state government, *Public Productivity Review*, Vol. 9: 143-153.

Overman, E. Sam (1988).
Using the systems development life cycle for computer applications in human services, *Computers in Human Services*, Vol. 3, No. 3/4: 55-69.

Overman, E. Sam and Don F. Simanton (1986).
Iron triangles and issue networks of information policy, *Public Administration Review*, Vol. 46 (Nov. 1986): 584-589.

Oyserman, Daphna and Rami Benbenishty (1993).
The impact of clinical information systems on human service organizations. *Computers in Human Services*, Vol. 9, Nos. 3/4: 425-438.

Pack, Howard and Janet Pack (1977).
The resurrections of the urban development model. *Policy Analysis*, Volume 3 (Summer, 1977): 407-427.

Packard, Vance (1964).
The naked society. N.Y.: David McKay.

Page, Bruce (1989).
Crossing borders. *PC Computing*, Vol. 2, No. 7 (July): 167-168.

Palmer, Marlene A. (1990).
Expert systems and related topics: Selected bibliography and guide to information sources. Harrisburg, PA: Idea Group Publishing.

Palmer, Paul W. (1987).
A successful approach to implementing PC data security. *Micro User's Guide*, Winter: 42-5.

Palvia, Prashant, Shailendra Palvia, and Ronald Zigli (1990).
Strategic information systems: Extensions and use for national economic development. In Mehdi Khosrowpour and Gayle J. Yaverbaum, eds., *Information technology resources utilization and management: Issues and trends*. Harrisburg, PA: Idea Group Publishing, 1990: 33-55.

Palvia, Shailendra, Prashant Palvia, and Ronald Zigli, eds. (1992).
The global issues of information technology management. Harrisburg, PA: Idea Group Publishing.

Pane, Patricia J. (1990).
Business software is underutilized, ACTS study finds. *InfoWorld*, Vol. 12, No. 40 (Oct. 1): 51.

Panko, R. R. (1984)
Office work. In *Office: Technology and People*, Vol. 2 (1984): 205-238.

Panko, R. R. (1988).
End-user computing: Management, applications, and technology. NY: Wiley.

Papa, M. J. (1990).
Communication network patterns and employee performance with new technology. *Communication Research*, Vol. 17, No. 2 (June): 344-68.

Papciak, Walter (1988).
A conservative profile. *Software Magazine*. (July): 55-56.

Parady, John E. (1991).
Free market at last: But the lack of a technology infrastructure presents an awesome obstacle. *InformationWeek* (July 15): 60.

Parker, Charles S. (1989).
Management information systems. NY: McGraw-Hill.

Parker, Don B. Marilyn M. Swope, and S. Baker (1990).
Ethical conflicts: In information and computer science, technology, and business. Wellesley, MA: Q.E.D. Press.

Parker, Don B., Marilyn M. Swope, H. E. Trainor, and Robert J. Benson (1989).
Information strategy and economics. Englewood Cliffs, NJ: Prentice-Hall.

Parker, John (1991).
A revolution in distribution. *InformationWeek*, No. 339 (Sept. 23): 36, 40.

Parker, Rachel (1990)
Kapor strives to establish rules for living in a computer frontier. *InfoWorld*, Vol. 12, No. 30 (July 23): 39.

Parker, Thomas S,. and Leon O. Chua (1989).
Practical numerical algorithms for chaotic systems. NY: Springer-Verlag New York, Inc.

Parsons, Darrell James (1990).
Information technology and productivity in Canadian banking. Toronto, Canada: University of Toronto, Ph.D. dissertation. *Dissertation Abstracts*, Vol. 51/10-B: 4926.

Parsons, G. L. (1983).
Information technology: A new competitive weapon. *Sloan Management Review*, Vol. 25, No. 1 (Fall): 3-14.

Patel, Virat (1992).
Pan-European high-speed networks: Fact or fiction? *Telecommunications*, Vol. 26, No. 4 (April): S5-S8.

PA Times, (1987).
Computers complicate public records access. *PA Times*, Vol. 10, No. 17 (11 Sept. 1987).

PA Times, (1992).
Innovative state and local programs awarded. *PA Times*, Vol. 15, No. 10 (Oct. 1): 2.

Patrick, Jonathon C. (1990).
Traditionalists and believers: Dealing with computer 'zealots' and 'phobics'. *Computerworld*, Vol. 24, No. 15 (April 9): 81-84.

PC Computing (1989).
PC imaging systems. *PC Computing*, Vol. 2 No. 7 (July): 68-70.

PC Week (1988).
Volume buyers remain unwilling to compromise. *PC Week*, Oct. 31: 82-87.

PC Week (1990a).
Computer virus growth could chill PC industry. *PC Week*, Vol. 7, No. 13 (April 2): 111.

PC Week (1990b).
Project management levels the load. *PC Week*, Jan. 29: 41, 44, 48.

PC Week (1992).
PC Week Special Report: Groupware. *PC Week*, Oct. 26: S1 - S34.

Pearce, Alan (1990).
The taming of telecom: Impending regulatory changes favor users. *Network World*, Vol. 7, No. 26 (June 25): 1-7.

Pearson, Faith and Myron E. Weiner (1981).
Computers without programmers. *Government Finance*, Vol. 10, No. 3.

Pepper, Jon D. (1991).
Getting along with the CEO. *InformationWeek*, No. 319 (May 6): 36-45.

Pepper, Jon D. (1992a).
Decentralize? Centralize? Yes. *InformationWeek*, No. 380 (June 29): 34-42.

Pepper, Jon D. (1992b).
The horizontal organization. *InformationWeek*, No. 387 (Aug. 17): 32-36.

Perin, Constance (1991a).
Electronic social fields in bureaucracies. *Communications of the ACM*, Vol. 34, No. 12 (Dec.): 75-82.

Perin, Constance (1991b).
The moral fabric of the office: Panopticon discourse and schedule flexibility. In *Organizations and Professions*, P. S. Tolbert and S. R. Barley, eds., Vol. 8, *Research in the sociology of organizations*. Greenwich, CT: JAI Press: 243-270.

Perkins, Joan (1987).
Providing access to government data valuable to the policy-making process. In *URISA, 1987*, Vol. IV: 83-91.

Perrolle, Judith A. (1986).
Intellectual assembly lines: The rationalization of managerial, professional, and technical work. *Computers and the Social Sciences*, Vol. 2, No. 3: 111-121.

Perrolle, Judith A. (1987a).
Computers and social change: Information, property, and power. Belmont, CA: Wadsworth.

Perrolle, Judith A. (1987b).
Conversations and trust in computer interfaces. Eastern Sociological Society, Boston.

Perrolle, Judith A. (1988a).
The social impact of computing: Ideological themes and research issues. *Social Science Computer Review*, Vol. 6, No. 4 (Winter): 469-480.

Perrolle, Judith A, (1988b).
Computer modelling and environmental protection. Oak Ridge National Laboratory, Oak Ridge, TN.

Perrolle, Judith A, (1988c).
Risk and responsibility in a computerized environement. American Sociological Association, Annual Meeting, Atlanta, GA.

Perrolle, Judith A. (1991a).
Conversations and trust in electronic interfaces. In C. Dunlop and R. Kling, eds., *Computerization and controversy*. NY: Academic Press: 350-363.

Perrolle, Judith A. (1991b).
Expert enhancement and replacement in computerized mental labor. *Science, Technology, and Human Values*, Vol. 16, No. 2 (Spring): 195-207.

Perrow, Charles (1984).
Normal accidents: Living with high risk technology. NY: Basic Books.

Perry, James L. and Hal G. Rainey (1988).
The public-private distinction in organizational theory. *Academy of Management Review*, Vol. 13, No. 2 (April): 182-201.

Perry, William E. (1988).
Managers need to establish a standard DP product. *Government Computer News*, 2 Feb. 1988: 24.

Perry, William E. (1989).
A new kind of software virus: Analysis paralysis. *Government Computer News*, 16 Oct.: 79.

Perry, William E. (1992).
The only thing to fear is lack of TQM vision. *Government Computer News*, Vol. 11, No. 10 (May 11): 80.

Personal Computing (1989).
Top database management programs. *Personal Computing*, Vol. 13, No. 10 (October): 201.

Personal Workstation (1991).
An information management strategy isn't enough: Are smart machines replacing smart people in business? *Personal Workstation*, Vol. 3, No. 4 (April): 24-25.

Peters, Paul Evan (1993).
Balancing act: Making federal information more accessible. *EDUCOM Review*, Vo. 28, No. 4 (July/August): 6-8.

Petheram, Brian (1989).
An approach to integrating technology in human service applications. *Computers in Human Services*, Vol. 5, Nos. 1/2: 187 - 195.

Petrillo, Joseph J. (1991a).
New regs aim to clarify Brooks Act powers. *Government Computer News*, 7 Jan.: 60.

Petrillo, Joseph J. (1991b).
New FIRMR advocates simpler planning. *Government Computer News*, 27 May: 79.

Petroski, H. (1985).
To engineer is human: The role of failure in successful design. NY: St. Martins.

Pfeffer, J. (1982).
Organizations and organization theory. Boston: Pitman.

Pfeffer, J. and H. Leblebici (1977).
Information technology and organizational structure. *Pacific Sociological Review*, Vol. 20, No. 2 (April): 241-161.

Pfleeger, Charles P. (1989).
Security in computing. Englewood Cliffs, NJ: Prentice-Hall.

Phillips, David (1993).
New technology and the human services: Implications for social justice. *Computers in Human Services*, Vol. 9, Nos. 3/4: 465-477.

Piller, Charles (1992).
Separate realities: The creation of the technological underclass in America's public schools. *Macworld*, Vol. 9, No. 9 (Sept.): 218-230.

Pitta, Julie (1990).
Electronic democracy. *Forbes*, Vol. 146, No. 7 (Oct. 1): 132.
Piturro, Marlene (1989a).
Redefining old jobs, creating new ones. *Personal Computing*, Vol. 13, No. 10 (October): 141-144.
Piturro, Marlene (1989b).
Telecommuting comes of age, again. *Information Center*, Nov,: 35-36.
Piturro, Marlene (1990).
Electronic monitoring. *Information Center*, Vol. 6, No. 7 (July): 26-31.
Platter, Adele (1988).
Computer experiences of young adults: An empirical analysis. *Social Indicators Research*, Vol. 8, No. 3 (June): 291-302.
Police Chief (1989).
Special focus: Computer applications. Symposium issue of *Police Chief*, Vol. 56 (June): 20 ff.
Porat, Marc U. (1978).
Communication policy in an information society. In Robinson, ed. (1978).
Porter, Michael E. (1980).
Competitive strategy: Techniques for analyzing industries and competitors. NY: Free Press.
Porter, Michael E. (1985).
Competitive advantage: Creating and sustaining critical performance. NY: Free Press.
Porter, Michael E. and V. E. Millar (1985).
How information gives you competitive advantage. *Harvard Business Review*, Vol. 63, No. 4 (July-August): 149-160.
Portner, Leslie R. and Janis L. Gogan (1988).
Coming to terms with end-user systems integration. *Journal of Information Systems Management*, Vol. 5, No. 1 (Winter): 8-16.
Powell, Bill and John Schwartz (1992).
Good-bye, Mr. Chips: Why high-tech deals with Japan could backfire. *Newsweek*, Vol. 120, No. 5 (August 3): 60.
Powell, Dave (1989).
Videoconferencing: A wise strategy. *Networking Management* (December): 29-38.
Powell, Dave (1991).
Is ANI an invasion of privacy? *Networking Management* (February): 21-26.
Power, Kevin (1987).
IRM budgets still rising. *Government Computer News*, 20 Nov.: 1, 8.
Power, Kevin (1988a).
Guidelines stress computer access for disabled feds. *Government Computer News*, 8 Jan.: 6.
Power, Kevin (1988b).
GSA sets forth its IRM ideals. *Government Computer News*, 5 Feb.: 15.
Power, Kevin (1988c).
Half million micros dot fed desks. *Government Computer News*, 27 May: 1, 89.

Power, Kevin (1988d).
Trail boss appointments will further GSAs reform plan. *Government Computer News*, 29 April: 4.

Power, Kevin (1988e).
Government computing capability still lagging. *Government Computer News*. 8 July: 33.

Power, Kevin (1989a).
Bush likely to maintain IT spending. *Government Computer News*, 17 April: 1, 100.

Power, Kevin (1989b).
Vendors slacking on modifications for disabled users. *Government Computer News*, 12 June: 139.

Power, Kevin (1989c).
ADP equipment spending down $785.7M from 1987. *Government Computer News*, 3 April: 87.

Power, Kevin (1989d).
GSA tells agencies to clarify IRM responsibilities. *Government Computer News*, 3 April: 91.

Power, Kevin (1989e).
Government needs fewer managers, better technical skills. *Government Computer News*, 1 May: 78.

Power, Kevin (1989f).
GSA plans more ADP supervision. *Government Computer News*, 3 April: 1, 93.

Power, Kevin (1989g).
Analysts prepare to review agency security plans. *Government Computer News*, 9 Jan.: 81.

Power, Kevin (1989h).
Financial systems require reforms, GAO says. *Government Computer News*, Jan. 9: 83.

Power, Kevin (1989i).
Agencies depending on paper despite automation. *Government Computer News*, March 20: 8.

Power, Kevin (1990a).
DOD course might be used for Trail Boss training. *Government Computer News*, 2 April: 57.

Power, Kevin (1990b).
IRMS reports says govt. owns 1 million micros. *Government Computer News*, 1 Oct.: 3.

Power, Kevin (1990c).
Trail Boss II seeking to build on success. *Government Computer News*, 30 April: 1, 83.

Power, Kevin (1991a)
Agencies embrace new FIRMR and spending cap. *Government Computer News*, 29 April: 77.

Power, Kevin (1991b).
NIST official aims to pin down ADP security jobs. *Government Computer News*, 2 Sept.: 10, 93.

Power, Kevin (1991c).
OMB delays release of proposed changes in A-130. *Government Computer News*, Vol. 10, No. 23 (Nov. 11): 121.
Power, Kevin (1991d).
IT spending up 11% despite budget cuts. *Government Computer News*, Vol. 10, No. 26 (Dec. 23): 1, 56.
Power, Kevin (1992a).
Bush seeks big boost for priority systems. *Government Computer News*, Vol. 11, No. 3 (Feb. 3): 1, 60.
Power, Kevin (1992b).
DSS security weak, GAO official testifies. *Government Computer News*, Vol. 11, No. 10 (May 11): 1, 80.
Power, Kevin (1992c).
OMB releases draft of revised federal IRM policy. *Government Computer News*, Vol. 11, No. 10 (May 11): 81.
Power, Kevin (1992d).
Guidelines will not affect ADP out-sourcing. *Government Computer News*, Vol. 11, No. 3 (Feb. 3): 59.
Power, Kevin (1992e).
Online fees for tariff info are debated. *Government Computer News*, Vol. 11, No. 11 (May 25): 1, 88.
Power, Kevin (1992f).
GSA launches program to groom future IRM chiefs. *Government Computer News*, Vol. 11, No. 15 (July 20): 76.
Power, Kevin (1992g).
NIST plan for technology center includes help from private sector. *Government Computer News*, Vol. 11, No. 17 (Aug. 17): 83.
Power, Kevin (1992h).
You want data protected? Give us money, feds say. *Government Computer News*, Vol. 11, No. 21 (Oct. 12):1, 80.
Power, Kevin (1992i).
Nation's prosperity depends upon fed IT policy, OMB official says. *Government Computer News*, Vol. 11, No. 24 (Nov. 23): 8.
Power, Kevin (1993a).
GAO to Clinton: Beware of deficiencies in systems. *Government Computer News*, Vol. 12, No. 2 (Jan. 18): 1, 63.
Power, Kevin (1993b).
OMB tells agencies to train users in computer security. *Government Computer Review*, Vol. 12, No. 6 (March 15): 65.
Power, Kevin and Robert Green (1990).
Most of procurement ethics law back in force. *Government Computer Review*, 12 Nov.: 8.
Power, Kevin and Margaret M. Seaborn (1991).
White House ignores OIRA reauthorization proposal. *Government Computer News*, April 29: 81.

Power, Kevin and James M. Smith (1989).
IRM chiefs want defined ethics rules. *Government Computer News*, 29 May: 1, 80.
Powers, Michael J., Paul H. Cheney, and Galen Crow (1990).
Structured system development, 2nd ed. Boston, MA: Boyd and Fraser.
Powers, R. F. and G. S. Dickson (1973).
MIS project management: Myths, opinions, and reality. *California Management Review*, Vol. 15, No. 3: 147-156.
Price, C. J., ed. (1990).
Knowledge engineering toolkits. Englewood Cliffs, NJ: Prentice-Hall.
Price, Don K. (1965).
The scientific estate. NY: Oxford University Press.
Price, Douglas S. (1988).
Battles over Paperwork Act recalled. *Government Computer News*, 4 Dec.: 25-26.
Privacy Protection Study Commission (1977).
Personal privacy in an information society. Washington, DC: USGPO.
Public Administration Review, (1986).
Symposium on public management information systems. November 1986.
Public Management (1989).
The electronic democracy. *Public Management*, Vol. 71 (Nov.): 2 - 13.
Puttre, Michael (1990).
MIS must play a bigger role in facilities management. *MIS Week*, Vol. 11, No. 25 (June 18): 34.
Quarterman, J. S. (1990).
The matrix. Digital Press.
Quindlen, Terrey Hatcher (1991).
OTA spots system weakness. *Government Computer News*, Vol. 10, No. 25 (Dec. 9): 6.
Quindlen, Terrey Hatcher (1992a).
NCIC marks a new milestone with upgraded system. *Government Computer News*, Vol. 11, No. 3 (Feb. 3): 62.40
Quindlen, Terrey Hatcher (1992b).
NREN success hinges on NSF technical leadership. *Government Computer News*, Vol. 11, No. 10 (May 12): 77.
Quindlen, Terrey Hatcher (1992c).
New House bill offers boost to federal telecommuting. *Government Computer News*, Vol. 11, No. 13 (June 22): 100.
Quindlen, Terrey Hatcher (1992d).
Gore's new bill promotes federal technology sharing. *Government Computer News*, Vol. 11, No. 15 (July 20): 86.
Quindlen, Terrey Hatcher (1993a).
Judge to decide if presidential e-mail is federal record. *Government Computer News*, Vol. 12, No. 1 (Jan. 4): 58.
Quindlen, Terrey Hatcher (1993b).
Harris will overhaul FBI's NCIC. *Government Computer News*, Vol. 12, No. 7 (March 29): 1, 93.

Quindlen, Terrey Hatcher (1993c).
When is e-mail a record? Answers continue to elude feds. *Government Computer News*, Vol. 12, No. 12 (June 7): 1, 8.

Quindlen, Terrey Hatcher (1993d).
HUD plans contractor-operated BBS for its policies. *Government Computer News*, Vol. 12, No. 5 (March 1): 75.

Quindlen, Terrey Hatcher and Shawn P. McCarthy (1993).
Ruling says most federal e-mail records must be preserved. *Government Computer News*, Vol. 12, No. 3 (Feb. 1): 77.

Race, Tim (1990).
Private eyes stalk computer criminals. *InformationWeek* (Jan. 8): 36-38.

Radding, Alan (1991a).
Security often complex in distributed computing. *Bank Management*, Vol. 67 (March): 50-53.

Radding, Alan (1991b).
Improve it or lose it: Rising money and user pressures mean data centers must shape up or ... *Computerworld*, Vol. 25, No. 19 (May 13): 71-74.

Rafaeli, A. (1986).
Employee attitudes towards working with computers. *Journal of Occupational Behavior*, Vol. 7: 89-106.

Raitt, D.I. (1986).
Mini debate: Small is not necessarily beautiful: Advantages and disadvantages of microcomputer use in libraries. *Electronic Library*, Vol. 4, No. 5 (Oct.): 248-257.

Ratcliffe, Mitch (1991).
Groupware may bring legal tussles: Copyright laws may be inadequate. *MacWEEK*, Vol. 5, No. 40 (Nov. 19): 23.

Raths, David (1989).
The politics of executive information systems: What happens when CEO's use computers to peer into their companies operations? *InfoWorld*, Vol. 11, No. 20 (May 15): 50-52.

Raymond, L. (1985).
Organizational characteristics and MIS success factors in the context of small business. *MIS Quarterly*, Vol. 9, No. 1 (March): 37-52.

Reder, Stephen and Robert G. Schwab (1989).
The communicative economy of the workgroup: Multichannel genres of communication. *Office: Technology and People*, Vol. 4, No. 3 (June): 177-195.

Reddit, Kay and Tom Lodahl (1989).
The human side. *Management Information Systems Week*, 24 July: 25.

Reece III, Laurence H. (1990).
Legal theories in actions against software developers. *Programmer's Update*, Vol. 8, No. 5 (June): 60-67.

Reed, Chris, ed. (1990)
Computer law. London: Blackstone Press.

Reid, A. A. L. (1977).
Comparing telephone with face-to-face contact. In Pool, ed. (1977).

Rein, Gail L. and Clarence A. Ellis (1989).
The Nick experiment reinterpreted: Implications for developers and evaluators of groupware. *Office: Technology and People*. Vol. 5, No. 1 (August): 47-75.
Reinecke, Ian (1984).
Electronic illusions: A skeptic's view of our high tech future. NY: Penguin.
Reines, Herbert G. (1985).
The PCs are here; Who should be in charge? *Government Computer News*, 7 June: 40.
Reisman, Jane (1990).
Gender inequality in computing. *Computers in Human Services*, Vol. 7, Nos. 1/2: 45-63.
Rens, Jean-Guy (1984).
Revolutions in communications: From writing to telematics/revolutions dans la communication: de l'ecriture a la telematique. *Sociologie et Societés*, Vol. 16, No. 1 (April): 13-22.
Reynolds, Cort Van (1977).
Issues in centralization. *Datamation*, Vol. 23, No. 3: 91-100.
Reynolds, W. H. (1969).
The executive synecdoche. *MSU Business Topics*, Vol. 17, No. 4: 21-29.
Rezmierski, Virginia E. (1992).
Ethical dilemmas in information technology use: Opportunity bumps on the road to civilization. *EDUCOM Review*, Vol. 27, No. 4 (July/Aug.): 22-26.
Rheingold, Howard (1991a).
Getting what you see? Global vision for creating tomorrow's technological reality. *Publish!*, Vol. 6, No. 2 (Feb.): 46-47.
Rheingold, Howard (1991b).
Electronic democracy: The great equalizer. *Whole Earth Review*, No. 71 (Summer): 4-12.
Richardson, William (1990).
Earth day 1990 online. *Database Searcher*, Vol. 6, No. 4 (May 1): 14-19.
Richter, M. J. (1992a).
Turning a technological innovation into an empty promise. *Governing*, Vol. 5, No. 4 (Jan.): 65.
Richter, M. J. (1992b).
The economic benefits of first-class telecommunications. *Governing*, Vol. 5, No. 5 (Feb.): 64.
Richter, M. J. (1992c).
Managing information: The county study. *Governing*, Vol.5, No. 11 (August): 31-46.
Richter, M. J. (1992d).
An interstate highway for information. *Governing*, Vol. 6, No. 1 (Oct,): 77.
Richter, M. J. (1993a).
The high cost of not paying the high cost of training. *Governing*, Vol. 6, No. 7 (April): 78.
Richter, M. J. (1993b).
Kentucky's TWIST on 'user-friendly' technology. *Governing*, Vo. 6, No. 11 (August): 84.

Riley, Glenn M. and Steven J. Ickes (1989).
Empowering human services staff. *Computers in Human Services*, Vol. 4, Nos. 3/4:277-286.

Rittner, Don (1992).
Ecolinking: Everyone's guide to online environmental information. Berkeley, CA: Peachpit Press.

Rivard, E. and K. Kaiser (1989).
The benefit of quality IS. *Datamation*, Vol. 35, No. 2 (Jan. 15): 53-58.

Rivard, Suzanne and Sid L. Huff (1988).
Factors of success for end-user computing. *Communications of the ACM*, Vol. 31, No. 5 (May): 552-561.

Robb, David W. (1989).
Instructor-led training is worth the cost, INS finds. *Government Computer News* (Nov. 13): 15.

Robb, David W. (1990a).
Netting crooks easier with micro center guidance. *Government Computer News* (Feb. 5): 15.

Robb, David W. (1990b).
Computer center tracks criminals by their finances. *Government Computer News*, April 30: 66, 67.

Robb, David W. (1990c).
NCIC takes over where Dick Tracy falls short. *Government Computer News*, Oct. 15:75.

Roberts, M. (1990).
Computer waves. *U. S. News and World Report* (Sept. 10): 83-87.

Robey, Daniel (1977).
Computers and management structure: Some empirical findings re-examined. *Human Relations*, Vol. 30: 963-976.

Robey, Daniel (1979).
User attitudes and management information system use. *Academy of Management Journal*, Vol. 22: 527-538.

Robey, Daniel (1981).
Computer information systems and organization structure. *Communications of the ACM*, Vol. 24: 679-687.

Robey, Daniel (1984).
Conflict models for implementation research. In Schultz, ed. (1984).

Robins, Kevin and Frank Webster (1989).
Computer literacy: The employment myths. *Social Science Computer Review*, Vol. 7, No. 1 (Spring): 7-26.

Robinson, Brian (1992).
TIA calls for relaxing telecom export rules. *Electronic Engineering Times*, No. 683 (March 9): 78.

Robinson, Glen O., ed. (1978).
Communications for tomorrow. NY: Praeger.

Robinson, Mark (1990).
Executive support systems. *Information Executive*, Vol. 3, No. 4 (Fall): 34-37.

Robinson, Michelle L. (1988).
Mortality rate study elicits strong reactions. *Hospitals*, 5 June.

Roche, Edward Mozley (1987).
The computer communications lobby, the U.S. Department of State Working Group on Transborder Data Flows, and adoption of the OECD guidelines on the protection of privacy and transborder data flows of personal data. NY: Columbia University, doctoral dissertation.

Rocheleau, Bruce (1985).
Microcomputers and information management: Some emerging issues. *Public Productivity Review*, Vol. 9, Nos. 2-3: 260-270.

Rocheleau, Bruce (1988).
New information technology and organizational context: Nine lessons. *Public Productivity Review*, Vol. 12, No. 2 (Winter): 165-192.

Rocheleau, Bruce (1989).
Human services and the ethics of computer matching. Paper, American Society for Public Administration, Miami, FL, April 11.

Rocheleau, Bruce (1991).
Human services and the ethics of computer matching. *Computers in Human Services*, Vol. 8, No. 2: 37-56.

Rockart, John F. (1979).
Critical success factors. *Harvard Business Review*, Vol. 57, No. 2 (March/April): 81-91.

Rockart, John F. and A. D. Crescenzi (1984).
Engaging top management in information technology. *Sloan Management Review*, Vol. 26, No. 1: 3-16.

Rockart, John F. and David W. DeLong (1988).
Executive support systems: The emergence of top management computer use. Homewood, IL: Dow-Jones Irwin.

Rockart, John F. and L. S. Flannery (1983).
The management of end user computing. *Communications of the ACM*, Vol. 26, No. 10 (Oct.): 776-784.

Rockwell, Mark (1988).
CompuServe asks Greene to review RBOC rules. *Management Information Systems Week*, March 28: 30.

Rockwell, Richard C. (1992).
Rockwell testifies at hearing on user fees. *ICPSR Bulletin*, Vol. XIII, No. 1 (September): 6-7.

Roitman, Howard (1987).
Legal issues in providing public access to an AMS: Case studies and variances. *URISA 1987*, Vol. 2: 13-24.

Romano, C. A. (1987).
Privacy, confidentiality, and security of computerized systems: The nursing responsibility. *Computers in Nursing*, Vol. 5, No. 3 (May): 99-104.

Rosch, Winn L. (1989).
The big question: Is the PC environment a safe place to work? *PC Magazine*, Vol. 8, No. 21 (Dec 12): 275-297.

Rose, Frederick (1988).
Thinking machine: An electronic clone of a skilled engineer is hard to clone". *Wall Street Journal*. (Aug. 12): 1, 14.

Rosen, L. D., D. C. Sears, and M. M. Weil (1987).
Computerphobia. *Behavior Research Methods , Instruments, and Computers*, Vol. 19, No. 2: 167-179.

Rosen, Saul (1990).
The origins of modern computing. *Computing Reviews*, Vol. 31, No. 9 (Sept.): 450-462.

Rosenberg, Laurence C. (1991).
Update on National Science Foundation funding of the "collaboratory". *Communicatins of the ACM*, Vol. 34, No. 12 (Dec.): 83.

Rosenberg, Richard S. (1992).
The social impact of computers, second ed. San Diego, CA: Academic Press. Orig. pub. 1986.

Rosenblatt, Kenneth (1990).
Deterring computer crime. *Technology Review*, Vol. 93 (Feb./Mr.): 34-40.

Rosenbrock, H. H. (1977).
The future of control. *Automation*. Vol. 13.

Rosenbrock, H. H. (1981).
Engineers and work that people do. *IEEE Control Systems Magazine*, Vol. 1, No. 3.

Roszak, Theodore (1986).
The cult of information: The folklore of computers and the true art of thinking. NY: Pantheon Books.

Roth, Al (1991).
The ESPRIT initiative: AI research in Europe. *AI Expert*, Vol. 6, No. 9 (Sept.): 48-51.

Rothfeder, Jeffrey (1988).
When it all goes wrong. *PC Week*, (Jan. 26): 45-49.

Rothfeder, Jeffrey (1990a).
CIO is starting to stand for 'career is over'. *Business Week*, Feb 26: 78.

Rothfeder, Jeffrey (1990b).
Looking for a job? You may be out before you go in. *Business Week*, Sept. 24: 128-129.

Rothfeder, Jeffrey (1992).
E-mail snooping. *Corporate Computing*, Vol. 1, No. 3 (Sept.): 168-174.

Rothschild, Michael (1993).
The coming productivity surge. *Forbes ASAP: A Technology Supplement to Forbes Magazine*, March 29: 17-18.

Rotter, J. (1966).
Generalized expectancies for internal versus external control of reinforcement. *Psychological Monographs*, Vol. 80, No. 609.

Rowlands, Ian and Sandra Vogel (1991).
Information policies: A sourcebook. London: Taylor Graham Publishers.

Rozovsky, L. E. (1985).
Computerized health care: Ethics and politics. *Journal of Clinical Computing*, Vol. 13, No. 5: 162-164.

Rubens, Jim (1983).
Retooling American democracy. *Futurist*, Vol. 17, No. 1 (Feb.): 59-64.

Ruberg, Laurie F. (1989).
Human services on cable: A case study of a data retrieval system designed for public access. *Computers in Human Services*, Vol. 4, Nos. 3/4: 233-241.

Rubin, Barry M. (1986).
Information systems for public management: Design and implementation. In *Public Administration Review*, Vol. 46 (Nov. 1986) 540-552.

Rubin, Charles (1988).
Moving up to micro-based accounting from a mini. *Business Software*, Vol. 6, No. 1 (January): 36-44.

Rubin, Michael Rogers (1987).
The computer and personal privacy, Part I: The individual under assault. *Library Hi Tech*, Vol. 5, No. 1 (Spring): 23-31.

Rubin, Michael Rogers and Brenda Dervin, Eds. (1989).
Private rights, public wrongs: The computer and personal privacy. Norwood, NJ: Ablex.

Rule, James B. (1983).
1984 - the ingredients of totalitarianism. In *1984 revisited: Totalitarianism in our century*. NY: Harper and Row: 166-179.

Rule, James D. and Paul Attewell (1989).
What do computers do? *Social Problems*, Vol. 36, No. 3 (June): 225-241.

Rule, James B., Douglas McAdam, Linda Stearns, and David Uglow (1980).
Preserving individual autonomy in an information-oriented society. Pp. 65-87 in L. Hoffman et al., eds., *Computer privacy in the next decade*. NY: Academic Press.

Rurak, Marilyn (1976).
The American computer industry in its international competitive environment. Washington, DC: Bureauc of Domestic Commerce.

Russell, Denorah (1991).
Computer security basics. Sebastopol, CA: O'Reilly and Associates.

Sackman, Hal (1991).
A prototype IFIP code of ethicks based on participative international consensus. Pp. 698-703 in Charles Dunlop and Rob Kling, eds., *Computerization and Controversy: Value Conflicts and Social Choices*. NY: Academic Press.

Sackman, H. and N. Nie, eds. (1970).
The information utility and social choice. Montvale, NJ: AFIPS Press.

Safayeni, Frank R., R. Lyn Purdy, and Christopher A. Higgins (1989).
Social meaning of personal computers for managers and professionals: Methodology and results. *Behaviour & Information Technology*, Vol. 8, No. 2 (March-April): 99-107.

Saffo, Paul (1991).
Will computer use result in the 'deskilling' of professions? *InfoWorld*, Vol. 12 (April 1): 44.

Salaman, Graeme (1982).
Managing the frontier of control. In Anthony Giddens and Gavin MacKKenzie, eds., *Social class and the division of labor*. Cambridge, UK: Cambridge University Press.
Salerno, Lynn M. (1985).
What happened to the computer revolution? *Harvard Business Review*, Vol. 63, No. 6 (Nov./Dec.): 129-138.
Salzman, Harold (1987).
Computer technology and the automation of skill: The case of computer-aided design. American Sociological Association, Annual Meeting, Chicago.
Samuelson, Pamela (1992).
Copyright law and electronic compilations of data. *Communications of the ACM*, Vol. 35, No. 2 (Feb.): 27-32.
Sanders, Lawrence and James Courtney (1985).
A field study of organizational factors influencing DSS success. *MIS Quarterly*, Vol. 9, No. 1 (March): 77-93.
Sanders, J. S. (1984).
The computer: Male, female, or androgynous? *The Computing Teacher*, Vol. 11: 31-34.
Sanders, Lester (1989).
NSA project cultivates encryption products. *Government Computer News*, 24 July: 74.
Sandler, Gerald (1988).
Computers: Lost without them and sometimes losing with them. *Computerworld*, Vol. 22, No. 25 (June 20): 30-31.
Santosus, Megan (1992a).
Computer-aided crime prevention. *CIO*, Vol. 5, No. 8 (March): 96.
Santosus, Megan (1992b).
Taking care of patient data. *CIO*, Vol. 5, No. 9 (April): 64.
Santosus, Megan (1993a).
Liberation technology. *CIO*, Vol. 6, No. 11 (May): 42-46.
Sapolsky, Harvey 1972).
The Polaris system development. Cambridge, MA: Harvard University Press.
Saunders, C. and R. Scamell (1986).
Organizational power and the information services department: A reexamination. *Communications of the ACM*, Vol. 29: 142-147.
Savage, Charles M. (1990).
5th generation management: Integrating enterprises through human networking. Bedford, MA: Digital Press/Digital Equipment Corporation.
Savage, J. A. (1988).
California smog fuels telecommuting plans. *Computerworld*. Vol. 22, No. 18 (May 2): 65-66.
Savage, J. A. (1990).
Women losing ground in IS. *Computerworld*, Vol. 24 (Nov. 19): 117.
Scheier, Robert L. (1989a).
PC Buyers get word: The party's over, these days top brass insist on strict cost justification. *PC Week*, Feb. 13: 39, 42.

Scheier, Robert L. (1989b).
Global changes force upheaval in IS planning. *PC Week* (Sept. 16): 71.
Scheier, Robert L. (1990a).
City finds fault with outdated PC strategy. *PC Week* (June 11): 115.
Scheier, Robert L. (1990b).
Lockheed learns costly lesson in system design. *PC Week* (Jan. 29): 1, 6.
Scheier, Robert L. (1990c).
Firms trip over the human factor in 'quantum leap' to 3-D CAD. *PC Week*, Vol. 7, No. 21 (May 28): 1-2.
Schellhardt, T.D. (1990).
Middle Managers Get Mired in the Mundane. *Wall Street Journal*, (Nov. 28): B1
Scherrer, Patrick E. (1991).
Review of 'The electronic sweatshop'. *Computing reviews*, Vol. 32, No. 3 (March): 137.
Schleich, John F., William J. Comey, and Warren J. Boe (1990).
Microcomputer implementation in small business: Current status and success factors. *Journal of Microcomputer Systems Management*, Vol. 2, No. 4 (October): 2-10.
Schmerken, Ivy (1990).
Wall Street stretches to step the tide. *Wall Street Computer Review*, Vol. 8, No. 2 (Nov. 1): 20-30.
Schmitt, Rolf R. and R. Rosetti (1987).
SIC pursuits: The consequences and problems of classifying establishments for government statistics. In *URISA, 1987*, Vol. IV: 15-24.
Schrage, Linus (1991).
Lindo: An optimization modeling system, fourth edition. San Francisco, CA: The Scientific Press.
Schrage, Michael (1985).
How you can profit from the coming federal infowar. *Washington Post* (Sept. 29): B-1, 4.
Schrage, Michael (1991).
European high-tech policy a poor model. *Los Angeles Times*, Vol. 110 (April 4): D1.
Schrage, Michael (1992).
Communications future belongs at the state level. *San Jose Mercury News* (Feb. 17): 9E.
Schubert, J. G. (1986).
Ideas about inequality in computer learning. *The Monitor*, Vol. 24, Nos. 7-8: 11-13, 26.
Schubert, J. G. and T. W. Bakke (1984).
Practical solutions to overcoming equity in computer use. *The Computing Teacher*, Vol. 11: 28-30.
Schuler, Douglas and Aki Namioka, eds. (1992).
Participatory design: Principles and practices. Hillsdale, NJ: Lawrence Erlbaum Associates.
Schwartz, John (1991).
The whistle-blower who set TRW straight. *Newsweek*, Oct. 28: 47.

Schwartz, John (1992).
The highway to the future. *Newsweek* (Jan. 13): 56-57.

Schwartz, Karen D. (1989a).
Bowsher relates DOD 'horror stories'. *Government Computer News*, 29 May: 6.

Schwartz, Karen D. (1989b).
Big iron scuttled in Navy PC plan. *Government Computer News*, 23 Jan.: 1, 96.

Schwartz, Karen D. (1990a).
Artificial intelligence system tracks pension plans. *Government Computer News*, Vol. 9, No. 11 (May 28): 57.

Schwartz, Karen D. (1990b).
House examines govt. efforts to promote EDI use. *Government Computer News*, Vol. 9, No. 15 (July 23): 59.

Schwartz, Karen D. (1991a).
Desert Storm war-gaming tools simulate targets. *Government Computer News*, April 29: 48.

Schwartz, Karen D. (1991b).
Stoned' PC virus infects HUD systems. *Government Computer News*, April 29: 6.

Schwartz, Karen D. (1991c).
Statistical software helps TVA control its resources. *Government Computer News*, June 10, 1991: 53.

Schwartz, Karen D. (1992a).
Expert systems speed processing of Census surveys. *Government Computer News*, Vol. 11, No. 5 (March 2): 41.

Schwartz, Melvin (1990).
Computer security: Planning to protect corporate assets. *Journal of Business Strategy*, Vol. 11 (Jan.-Feb.): 38-42.

Sculley, John (1989).
The relationship between business and higher education: A perspective on the 21st century. *Communications of the ACM*, Vol. 32, No. 9 (Sept.): 1056-1061.

Seaborn, Margaret M. (1991a).
IRS head wants to hold off on corporate matching. *Government Computer News*, Vol. 10, No. 1 (July 8): 88.

Seaborn, Margaret M. (1991b).
Union head blames automation for USPS injuries. *Government Computer News*, Vol. 10, No. 17 (August 19): 112.

Segev, Eli and Paul Gray (1989).
Integrating an expert system and DSS for strategic decision support: A case study. *Information Resources Management Journal*, Vol. 2, No. 1 (Winter): 1-12.

Selig, G. J. (1984).
Critical success factors for multinational informaiton resource management planning and administration. *Managerial Planning*, Vol. 32, No. 5 (March-April): 23-27.

Selnow, Gary W. (1988).
Using interactive computer to communicate scientific information. *American Behavioral Scientist*, Vol. 32, No. 2 (Nov./Dec.): 124-135.

Senn, J. A. (1980).
Management's assessment of computer information systems. *Journal of Systems Management*, Vol. 11, No. 9: 6-11.
Servan-Schreiber, Jean-Jacques (1985).
On the computer revolution. *World Policy Journal*, Vol. 2: 569-586.
Sethi, Vijay and Albert J. Lederer (1989).
Pitfalls in planning. *Datamation*, Vol. 35, No. 11 (June 1): 59-62.
Sexton, Tara (1989).
FCC to decide on BBS blocking. *PC Week*, Jan. 16: 33, 37.
Seymour, Jim (1989).
SecretDisk II can solve some of your security problems. *PC Week*, 11 Sept. 1989: 10.
Shaiken, Harley (1984).
Work transformed: Automation and labor in the computer age. NY: Holt, Rinehart, and Winston.
Shallis, M. (1984).
The silicon idol: The microrevolution and its social implications. NY: Schocken.
Shapiro, Allen D. (1987).
Structured induction in expert systems. Reading, MA: Addison-Wesley.
Shapiro, Ehud and David H. D. Warren, eds. (1993).
The 5th generation: Personal perspectives. *Communications of the ACM*, Vol. 36, No. 3 (March): 46-49.
Shapiro, Stuart, ed. (1992).
Encyclopedia of Artificial Intelligence, Second Edition. Y: John Wiley and Sons.
Shapiro, S. I. and Colin G. R. Macdonald (1987).
Computers and the human spirit. *Weaver* (Technology Studies Resource Center, Lehigh University, PA), Vol. 5, No. 2 (Spring): 8-9.
Sharkansky, I. (1979).
Whither the state? Chatham, NJ: Chatham House.
Sharp, I. P. amd F. Perkins (1981).
The impact of effective person-to-person telecommunications on established management structures. *Proceedings of the Conference on Business Telecommunications* (September, 1981): 127-133.
Shattuck, John (1984).
Computer matching is a serious threat to individual rights. *Communications of the ACM*, Vol. 27, No. 6 (June): 538-541.
Shaul, D. R. (1964).
What's really ahead for middle management. *Personnel*, Vol. 41, No. 6: 8-16.
Shields, Jim (1990).
Agencies make progress in quest for compatibility. *Government Computer News*, Feb. 19: 57-59.
Shields, Mark (1985).
Gender, computing experience, and attitudes toward computing: A survey of Brown University undergraduates. Paper, IBM University Advanced Education Projects Conference, June 23-26.
Shneiderman, B. (1980).
Software psychology: Human factors in computer and information systems.

Boston: Little, Brown.

Shuman, Todd M. (1988).
Hospital computerization and the politics of medical decision-making. Pp. 261-87 in *Research in the Sociology of Work, 1988* (Greenwich, CT: JAI Press).

Siegel, Jane, Vitaly Dubrovsky, Sara Kiesler, and Timothy W. McGuire (1986).
Group processes in computer-mediated communication. *Organizational Behavior and Human Decision Processes*, Vol. 37: 157-187.

Siegel, Lenny (1986).
Microcomputers: From movement to industry. *Monthly Review*, Vol. 38, No. 3 (July-August): 110-117.

SIGCAT RECAP (1991).
Minutes of the Sept. 17 and Oct. 17, 1991, meetings. *SIGCAT RECAP*, Oct. 17: 1-4.

SIGCAT RECAP (1992).
Notes from SIGCAT meetings on March 9 and April 27, 1992. *SIGCAT RECAP*, April 27: 1-4.

Silver, Judith (1989).
Lainhart unearths system weaknesses. *Government Computer News*, 24 July: 74.

Silver, Mark S. (1991).
Systems that support decision makers: Description and analysis. NY: John Wiley and Sons.

Silverman, Carol J. and Stephen Barton (1986).
Private property and private government: The tension between individualism and community in condominiums. Conference paper, American Sociological Association, annual meeting.

Simon, Alan R. (1992).
Enterprise computing. NY: Bantam Books.

Simon, Herbert A. (1960a).
The corporation - Will it be managed by machines? In Anshen and Bach, eds. (1985).

Simon, Herbert A. (1960b).
Science of management decision. NY: Harper and Row.

Simon, Herbert A. (1969).
The sciences of the artificial. Cambridge, MA: MIT Press.

Simon, Herbert A. (1977).
The new science of management decision, revised edition. Englewood Cliffs, NJ: Prentice-Hall.

Simons, Peter M. (1988).
Computer composition and works of music: Variation on a theme of ingarden. *Journal of British Sociological Phenomenology*, Vol. 19 (May): 141-154.

Singleton, W. T. (1989).
The mind at work: Psychological ergonomics. NY: Cambridge University Press.

Skinner, B. F. (1971).
Beyond freedom and dignity. NY: Bantam Books.

Skinner, W. (1979).
The impact of changing technology on the working environment. In C. Kerr and J. M. Rosow, eds., p*Work in America: The Decade Ahead.* NY: Van Nostrand.

Smith, Allen N. (1986).
Impact of office systems on information management. *The Office* (Feb.): 86-8.
Smith, Brian Cantwell (1991).
Limits of correctness in computers. Pp. 632-646 in Charles Dunlop and Rob Kling, eds., *Computerization and controversy : Value conflicts and social choices.* NY: Academic Press.
Smith, James M. (1989).
Databases locate $30B for child support. *Government Computer News*, 29 May: 78.
Smith, James M. (1990)
Energy emphasizes IRM, not technology. *Government Computer News*, 12 Nov.: 102.
Smith, James M. (1991a).
GAO blasts EPA on monitoring systems. *Government Computer News*, Vol. 10, No. 24 (Nov. 25): 58.
Smith, James M. (1991b).
How virus plague hits one agency. *Government Computer News*, Vol. 10, No. 24 (Nov. 25): 1, 61.
Smith, James M. 1991c).
Maritime modeling system tracks iceberg threat. *Government Computer News*, Vol. 10, No. 12 (Sept. 2): 90.
Smith, James M. (1992a).
Embassies to exchange their minis for micros. *Government Computer News*, Vol. 11, No. 2 (Jan. 20): 1, 6.
Smith, James M. (1992b).
Forest Service trims $1 billion from cost of GIS buy. *Government Computer News*, Vol. 11, No. 10 (May 11): 5, 80.
Smith, James M. (1992c).
Candidates' records hold clues to who would be 'IT president'. *Government Computer News*, Vol. 11, No. 22 (Oct. 26): 1, 75.
Smith, James M. (1993a).
Need government information fast? It's a phone call away. *Government Computer News*, Vol. 12, No. 4 (Feb. 15): 57.
Smith, James M. and Kevin Power (1990).
OMB revises procedures for agency security plans. *Government Computer News*, 23 July: 93.
Smith, Jennifer (1989).
Computer crime. *Lotus* (June): 18.
Smith, K. E. (1988).
Hypertext—linking to the future. *Online*, Vol. 12, No. 2 (March): 32-40.
Smith, K. F. and P. Hernon (1988).
Pointer - the microcomputer reference program for federal documents. *Government Information Quarterly*, Vol. 5, No. 1: 88.
Smith, Linda A. (1986).
Harried budget office staff welcomes arrival of PCs. *Government Computer News*, 28 March: 32.

Smith, Norman J. and Floyd H. Bolitho (1989).
Information: The hydra-headed concept in the human services. *Computers in Human Services*, Vol. 5, Nos. 3/4: 83 - 98.

Smith, Ralph Lee (1972).
The wired nation: Cable TV: The electronic communications highway. NY: Harper and Row.

Smith, Sara D. (1986).
Relationships of computer attitudes to sex, grade-level, and teacher influence. *Education*, Vol. 106, No. 3 (Spring): 338-344.

Smith, Sara D. (1987).
Computer attitudes of teachers and students in relationship to gender and grade level. *Journal of Educational Computing Research*, Vol. 3, No. 4: 479-494.

Smith, William E. (1993).
Journalism students' attitudes toward and experience with computers: A longitudinal study. *New Computing Journal*, Vol. 8, No. 4: 9-18.

Smith-Gratto, Karen (1989).
Computer literacy and citizenship in a democracy. *Louisiana Social Studies Journal*, Vol. 16, No. 1 (Fall): 30-33.

Snizek, William E, (1987).
Some observations on the effects of microcomputers on the productivity of university scientists. *Knowledge: Creation, Diffusion, Utilization*, Vol. 8, No. 4 (June): 612-624.

Snoddy, William (1989).
Unions allege employers ignore repetitive-motion injuries. *MIS Week* (June 19): 36.

Snyder, Charles A. and Lucretia A. Zienert (1990).
Telecommunications for competitive advantage: The enterprise network. In Mehdi Khosrowpour and Gayle J. Yaverbaum, eds., *Information technology resources utilization and management: Issues and trends*. Harrisburg, PA: Idea Group Publishing, 1990: 119-155.

Snyder, Thomas D. (1988).
Digest of educational statistics, 1988. Washington, DC: National Center for Education Statistics.

Soat, John and Martin Garvey (1991).
The long arm of the software industry. *InformationWeek*, No. 325 (June 17): 40-41.

Soat, John and Rob Kelly (1992).
Whose software is it? *InformationWeek*, No. 365 (March 23): 32-36.

Soat, John and Rob Kelly (1993).
Microsoft pursues price war. *InformationWeek*, (Jan. 18): 12.

Software Magazine, (1988a).
MIS warning: Watch out for your jobs. *Software Magazine* (Jan.): 31.

Software Magazine, (1988b)
Ashton-Tate regroups: Standards group plans to lobby IEEE. *Software Magazine*, January 1988: 26.

Sommer, Daniel (1988a).
Information centers debate billing for services. *InfoWorld* (11 Jan.): 38.

Sommer, Daniel (1988b).
PC managers advised to think like executives. *InfoWorld* (29 Feb.): 40.

Sommer, Mary (1989).
A second look at the changing IS. *Information Center*, Vol. 5, No. 7 (July): 24-33).

Sorokin, Leo T. (1991).
The computerization of government information: Does it circumvent public access under the Freedom of Information Act? *Columbia Journal of Law and Social Problems*, Vol. 24, No. 2 (Spring): 267-298.

Spafford, E. H. (1989).
Crisis and aftermath. *Communications of the ACM*, Vol. 32, No. 6 (June): 678-687.

Speer, Tibbett L. (1992).
Talking tech with your lawyers. *Corporate Computing*, Vol. 1, No. 5 (Nov.): 21-22.

Spencer, Robert W. (1991).
"After" the registration revolution. *College and University*, Vol. 66, No. 4 (Summer): 209-212.

Sprehe, J. Timothy (1987a).
Developing federal information resources management policy: Issues and impact for information managers. *Information Management Review*, Vol. 2 (Winter): 33-41.

Sprehe, J. Timothy (1987b).
Policy on management of federal information resources. *Journal of the American Society for Information Science*, Vol. 38, No. 1: 30-33.

Spinrad, R. J. (1982).
Office automation. *Science*, Vol. 215: 808-813.

Sproull, Lee and Sarah Kiesler (1986).
Reducing social context clues: Electronic mail in organizational communication. *Management Science* (Nov.).

Sproull, Lee, David Zubrow, and Sara Kiesler (1985).
Socialization to computing in college. Pittsburgh: Carnegie-Mellon University, Committee on Social Science Research in Computing.

Stager, Susan F. (1992).
Computer ethics violations: More questions than answers. *EDUCOM Review*, Vol. 27, No. 4 (July/Aug.): 27-30.

Ståhl, Ingolf (1990).
Introduction to simulation with GPSS: On PC, Mac, and VAX. Englewood Cliffs, NJ: Prentice-Hall.

Steinmetz, Ann (1988).
The role of the microcomputer in the social and psychological world of an adolescent male: A naturalistic inquiry. NY: New York University, doctoral dissertation.

Stephens, Mark (1992).
Clinton team to review computer security policy. *InfoWorld*, Vol. 14, No. 49 (Dec. 7): 1, 135.

Sterling, Bruce (1992).
The hacker crackdown. NY: Bantam Books.

Sterling, Theodore D. (1986).
Democracy in an information society. *Information Society* Vol. 4, Nos. 1/2 (1986): 1-143.

Stevens, John M., Anthony G. Cahill, and E. Sam Overman (1992).
The impacts of IST on state-level public sector organizations: An empirical analysis. *State and Local Government Review*, Vol. 24, No. 2 (Spring): 71-76.

Stevens, John M. and Josephine M. LaPlante (1986).
Factors associated with financial decision support systems in state government: An empirical exploration. In *Public Administration Review*, Vol. 46 (Nov.): 522-531.

Stevens, John M. and Robert P. McGowan (1985).
Information systems and public management. NY: Praeger.

Stevens, Larry (1992).
PCs: Agents of culture change. *InformationWeek*, No. 380 (June 29): 28-31.

Stevenson, John (1988).
Eavesdropping on the privacy issue: Computerized databases and personal privacy. *Direct Marketing*, Vol. 51 (July): 112-115.

Stoll, Clifford (1989).
The cuckoo's egg: Tracking a spy through the maze of computer espionage. NY: Doubleday and Co.

Stone, Paula S. (1987).
Security and role of PCs top managers' concerns. *InfoWorld*, July 13: 35.

Stone, Paula S. (1988a).
Managers plan strategies for information distribution. *Government Computer News*, Feb. 1: 33.

Stone, Paula S. (1988b).
Computer instruction for novices still a priority. *InfoWorld*, Feb. 8: 38.

Stone, Paula S. (1988c).
Research report outlines PC managerial models. *InfoWorld*, July 4: 34.

Stone, Philip J. (1985).
Your office is where you are. *Harvard Business Review*, Vol. 63, No. 2 (March/April): 102.

Stonier, Tom (1983).
The wealth of information: A profile of the post-industrial economy. (London: Methuen London Ltd.).

Strassmann, Paul A. (1985).
Information payoff: Transformation of work in the electronic age. NY: Free Press, 1985.

Strassmann, Paul A. (1990).
The business value of computers. New Canaan, CT: Informations Economics Press.

Straub, Detmar W. and W. D. Nance (1989).
Discovering and disciplining computer abuse in organizations: A field study. *MIS Quarterly.*

Straub, Detmar W. and James C. Wetherbe (1989).
Information technologies for the 1990s: An organizational impact perspective. *Communications of the ACM*, Vol 32, No. 11 (November): 1329-1339.

Straw, Ronnie and Lorel Foged (1983).
Technology and employment in telecommunications. *Annals of the American Adademy of Political Scinece*. No. 470 (Nov.): 163-170.

Sullivan, Cornelius H. (1985).
Systems planning in the information age. *Sloan Management Review*, Vol. 27, No. 1 (Winter): 3-11.

Sullivan, Cornelius H. (1988).
The changing approach to systems planning. *Journal of Information Systems Management*, Vol. 5, N 3 (Summer): 8 - 13.

Sullivan, J., et al. (1989).
Development of an expert system for student advisement. In O. T. Hargrave, ed., *Academic advising: Transition and continuity. Proceedings of the National Academic Advising Association Annual Region VII Conference* (Dallas, Texas: May 21-23, 1989). National Academic Advising Association, Pomona, NJ, 23 May 1989.

Sullivan, Judith A. (1985).
Federal IC directory. *Government Computer Expo News*, November: 5.

Sullivan, Judith A. (1986).
Justice's lawyers linked up in upgraded network. *Government Computer News*, 28 March: 50.

Sullivan, Kristina B. (1989).
Road to electronic democracy begins in conferencing system. *PC Week*, Vol. 6, No. 11 (March 20): 29-30.

Susman, Gerald I. (1978).
Autonomy at work: A sociotechnical analysis of participative management. NY: Praeger.

Sussman, Leonard R. (1989).
Power, the press and the technology of freedom: The coming age of ISDN. NY: Freedom House.

Sutton, R. I. and A. Rafaeli 1987).
Characteristics of work stations as potential occupational stressors. *Academy of Management Journal*, Vol. 30 (June): 260-276.

Swain, John W. and Jay D. White (1992).
Information technology for productivity: Maybe, maybe not--an assessement. In Marc Holzer, ed., *Public productivity handbook*. NY: Marcel Dekker: 643-663.

Swart, J. C. and R. A. Baldwin (1971).
EDP effects on clerical workers. *Academy of Management Journal*, Vol. 14, No. 4:497-512.

Swider, Gaile (1988).
Ten pitfalls of information center management. *Journal of Information Systems Management*, Vol. 5, No. 1 (Winter): 22-28.

Talley, Sally A. (1989).
A study of resistance to technological change: Principals and the use of microcomputers as a management tool. La Verne, CA: University of La Verne, doctoral dissertation.

Tannenbaum, Arnold S., ed. (1968).
Control in organizations. NY: McGraw-Hill.

Tapper, Colin (1989)
Computer law, fourth edition. White Plains, NY: Longman.
Tapscott, Don and Art Caston (1992).
Paradigm shift. NY: McGraw-Hill.
Taylor, J. C. and R. A. Asadorian (1985).
The implementation of excellence: STS management. *Industrial Management*, Vol. 24: 5-15.
Taylor, Ron (1991).
ideoconferencing - building ubiquity, cutting costs, and communicating easily. *Telecommunications*, Vol. 25, No. 8 (August): 46-49.
Technology and Learning (1992).
Groupware goes to school: New tools to promote group activity and learning. *Technology and Learning*, Vol. 12, No. 5 (Feb.): 80-84.
Telecommuting Review (1988).
Telecommuting Review: The Gordon Report, Vol. 5, No. 2 (Feb. 1): 12-17.
Telecommuting Review (1991).
Late news: IBM and Lotus groupware deal expected. *Telecommuting Review: The Gordon Report*, Vol. 8, No. 7 (July 1): 8.
Telephony (1991).
Ameritech: Weiss pulls no punches. *Telephony*, Vol. 221, No. 3 (July 15): 36-41.
Tembeck, Shoshanna and Lynn Meisch (1987).
Women in computing: Caught in the middle. *PC World*, Vol. 5, No. 10: 270-276.
Temin, Thomas R. (1992).
Telecommuting: Many would, few actually can. *Government Computer News*, Vol. 11, No. 17 (Aug. 17): 1, 90.
Temple, Linda and Hilary M. Lips (1989).
Gender differences and similarities in attitudes toward computers. *Computers in Human Behavior*, Vol. 5, No. 4: 215-226.
Tenner, Edward (1988).
The paradoxical proliferation of paper. *Harvard Magazine*, (March-April): 23-26.
Tenorio, Jose Orozco (1988).
Information crisis in Latin America. *Database Searcher*, Vol. 4, No. 7 (July/August): 23.
Tepas, Donald I. (1972).
Introductory remarks. *Behavior research methods and instrumentation*, Vol. 4: 42-43.
Tepas, Donald I. (1991).
Computers, psychology, and work: Does the past predict a troubled future for this union? *Behavior Research Methods, Instruments, and Computers*, Vol. 23, No. 2: 101-105.
Thomas, Arthur Peach (1990).
A study of cognitive factors affecting the successful implementation of end-user information technology. Buffalo, NY: State University of New York at Buffalo, Ph.D. dissertation.

Thompson, Dennis, Ed. (1983).
Policy toward public-private relations: A symposium. *Policy Studies Journal*, Vol. 11, No. 3 (March): 419-525.

Thompson, Lyke (1992).
Microcomputers in public organizations: The contingencies of impact. *State and Local Government Review*, Vol. 24, No. 2 (Spring): 58-64.

Thompson, Lyke, Marjorie Sarbaugh-McCall, and Donald F. Norris (1989).
The social impacts of computing: Control in organizations. *Social Science Computer Review*, Vol. 7, No. 4 (Winter): 407-417.

Thompson, Paul (1983).
The nature of work: An introduction to debates about the labour process. London: Macmillan.

Thyfault, Mary E. (1990).
Phone gall. *InformationWeek*, No. 335 (Aug. 26): 12-13.

Thyfault, Mary E. (1991).
Phone fraud: Somebody's got to pay. *InformationWeek*, No. 319 (May 6): 12-13.

Thyfault, Mary E. (1992a).
Feds tap into major hacker ring. *InformationWeek*, No. 382 (July 13): 15.

Thyfault, Mary E. (1992b).
Setting out on a high-speed chase. *InformationWeek*, No. 395 (Oct. 12): 54-56.

Tjoumas, Renee (1987).
Trends in international informational issues. *Communication Quartery*, Vol. 35, No. 3 (Summer): 238-253.

Tobin, William J. (1987).
Desktop videoconferencing: The technology falls into place. *Microcomputer Users' Guide* (Winter): 46-47.

Toffler, Alvin (1980).
The third wave. NY: William Morrow/Bantam Books.

Tolich, Martin Bernard (1990).
Are new workers also deskilled? Deskilling, reskilling and generational reskilling. Paper, American Sociological Association, annual meeting.

Tolich, Martin Bernard (1992).
Check it out, life in the grocery lane: An empirical study of alienation among supermarket clerks. Davis, CA: University of California - Davis, doctoral dissertation.

Tom, Henry (1988).
Standards: A cardinal direction for geographic information systems. *URISA 1988*, Vol. 2 (1988): 142-152.

Tom, Paul (1987).
Managing information as a corporate resource. Glenview, IL: Scott-Foresman.

Tribe, Lawrence L. (1991).
The Constitution in cyberspace: Law and liberty beyond the electronic frontier. In J. Warren, J. Thorwaldson, and B. Koball, eds., *Computers, freedom, and privacy* (Los Alamitos, CA: IEEE Computer Society Press).

Trist, Emery L. (1973).
Organizations and technical change. London: Tavistock Institute of Human Relations.

Trist, E. L. (1981).
The sociotechnical perspective. In van de Ven and Joyce, eds. (1981): 19-75.

Trist, E. L., G. W. Higgins, H. Murray, and A. B. Pollack (1963).
Organizational choice. London: Tavistock Publications.

Turnage, Janet J. (1990).
The challenge of new workplace technology for psychology. *American Psychologist*, Vol. 45, N0. 2 (Feb.): 171-178.

Tuohy, Carolyn . (1976).
Private government, property, and professionalism. *Canadian Journal of Political Science*, Vol. 9, No. 4 (Dec.): 668-681.

Tuerkheimer, Frank M. (1993).
The underpinnings of privacy protection. *Communications of the ACM*, Vol. 36, No. 8 (August): 69-74.

Turkle, Sherry (1984).
The second self: Computers and the human spirit. New York: Simon and Schuster.

Turner, Judith (1982).
Observations on the use of behavioral models in information systems research and practice. *Information Management*, Vol. 5, No. 3: 207-213.

Turner, Judith Axler (1987).
White House rescinds part of policy aimed at limiting access to computer data bases. *Chronicle of Higher Education*, Vol. 33, No. 28 (25 March 1987): 1,10.

Turner, Mary Johnston (1992).
The new players: Common carriers. *Network World*, Vol. 9, No. 6 (Feb. 17): 34.

Turoff, Murray (1985).
Information, value, and the internal marketplace. *Technological Forecasting and Social Change*, Vol. 27 (1985): 357-373.

Turoff, Murray, Roxanne Starr Hiltz, and Miriam Mills (1989).
Telecomputing: Organizational impacts. Ch. 9 in *Research Annual on Social Sciences and Computers, Vol. 2* (Greenwich, CT: JAI Press).

Tuthill, G. Steven (1991).
Legal liabilities and expert systems. *AI Expert*, Vol. 6, No. 3 (March): 45-51.

Unger, J. Marshall (1987).
The fifth generation fallacy: Why Japan is betting its future on artificial intelligence. NY: Ocford University Press.

Uris, A. (1963).
Middle management and technological change, *Management Review*, Vol. 52, No. 10: 55-58.

U. S. Department of Health, Education, and Welfare (1973).
Report of the secretary's advisory committee on automated personal data systems: Records, computers, and the rights of citizens. Washington, DC: HEW.

U. S. House of Representatives (1968).
Privacy and the National Data Bank concept. Committee on Governmental Operations. Aug. 1. Washington, DC: Superintendent of Documents.

U. S. House of Representatives (1986a).
Electronic collection and dissemination of information by federal agencies. Hearings April 29, June 26, October 18, 1985, Subcommittee of the Committee

on Government Operations, House of Representatives, Ninety-Ninth Congress, First Session. Published 1986.

U. S. House of Representatives (1986b).
Technologies in the health care system. Hearings, April 21, 1986, 99th Congress, Second Session, before the Subcommittee on Investigations and Oversight of the Committee on Science and Technology. Washington, DC: Superintendent of Documents.

U. S. House of Representatives (1986c).
Federal government computer security: Hearings, October 29-30, 1985, before the Subcommittee on Transportation, Aviation, and Materials and the Subcommittee on Science, Research, and Technology, House Committee on Science and Technology, 99th Congress, 1st session, Pub. No. 58: 99-58. Washington, DC: Superintendent of Documents.

U. S. House of Representatives (1988).
Implementation of the computer security act: Hearings, September 22, 1988, before the Subcommittee on Transportation, Aviation, and Materials of the House Committee on Science, Space, and Technology, 100th Congress, 2nd Session, Pub. No. 146. Washington, DC: Superintendent of Documents.

U. S. House of Representatives (1990).
Data protection, computers, and changing information practices: Hearings, May 16, 1990, before the Subcommittee on Government Information, Justice, and Agriculture or the House Committee on Government Operations, 101st congress, 1st Session, SD catalog no. Y 4.G 74/7:C 73/31. Washington, DC: Superintendent of Documents.

U. S. National Institute on Disability and Rehabilitation Research (1987).
Access to information technology by users with disabilities: Initial guidelines. Washington: Federal Information Resources Management, General Services Administration.

U. S. Office of Science and Technology Policy (1992).
The federal high performcance computing program. Washington, DC: OSTP.

U. S. Office of Technology Assessment (1985).
Automation of America's offices. Washington, DC: Superintendent of Documents.

U. S. Office of Technology Assessment (1986a).
Intellectual property rights in an age of electronics and information. Congress of the U.S., Washington, D.C. Office of Technology Assessment. April 1986. Report No.: OTA-CIT-302.

U. S. Office of Technology Assessment (1986b).
Federal government information technology: Electronic record systems and individual privacy. OTA CIT-296 (June). Washington, DC: Superintendent of Documents.

U. S. Office of Technology Assessment (1987)
The electronic supervisor: New technology, new tensions. Washington: Superintendent of Documents.

U. S. Office of Technology Assessment (1988a).
Technology and the American economic transition. Washington, DC: Superintendent of Documents.

U. S. Office of Technology Assessment (1988b).
Informing the nation: Federal information dissemination in an electronic age. Washington, DC: Superintendent of Documents, Stock #052-003-01130-1.

U. S. Senate (1986).
Computer Matching and Privacy Protection Act of 1986: Hearing before the Subcommittee on Oversight of Government Management, Committee on Governmental Affairs, 99th Congress, Second Session. Washington, DC: Superintendent of Documents.

Vallas, Steven Peter (1990).
The concept of skill: A critical review. *Work and Occupations*, Vol. 17, No. 4 (Nov.): 379-398.

Vallee, Jacques (1982).
The network revolution. Berkeley, CA: And/Or Press.

Vance, Faith (1991).
HandsNet links advocates. *Link-Up*, Vol. 8, No. 6 (Nov./Dec.): 28.

Varley, Pamela (1991).
Electronic democracy. *Technology Review*, Vol. 94, No. 8 (Nov./Dec.): 42-52.

Venner, Gary S. (1988).
Managing applications as a software portfolio, *Journal of Information Systems Management*, V5., No. 3 (Summer): 14-18.

Vig, Norman J. (1988).
Technology, philosophy, and the state. In Michael E. Kraft and Norman J. Vig, eds., *Technology and politics*. Durham, NC: Duke University Press: ch. 1.

Violino, Bob (1992a).
Networks: No immunity. *InformationWeek*, No. 354 (Jan. 6): 18.

Violino, Bob (1992b).
From big iron to scrap metal. *InformationWeek*, No. 359 (Feb. 10): 20-28.

Violino, Bob (1992c).
Nurses in a league of their own. *InformationWeek*, No. 381 (July 6): 22.

Violino, Bob (1993a).
Are your networks secure? *InformationWeek*, No. 420 (April 12): 30-35.

Violino, Bob (1993b).
Hackers. *InformationWeek*, No. 430 (June 21): 49-56.

Violino, Bob, and Stephanie Stahl (1993).
No place like home. *InformationWeek*, No. 411 (Feb. 8): 22 - 29.

Vrendenburg, K. (1984).
Sex differences in attitudes, feelings, and behaviors toward computers, American Psychological Association, annual meeting, Toronto, Canada.

Waldrop, M. M. (1989).
Phobos at Mars: A dramatic view - and then failure. *Science*, Vol. 245: 1044-1045.

Wall Street Journal (1990).
Baxter to take charge totaling $566 million. April 5: A4.

Walton, R. E. and W. Vittori (1983).
New information technology: Organizational problem or organizational opportunity? *Office: Technology and People*, Vol. 1: 249-273.

Wamsley, G. and M. Zald (1973).
The political economy of public organizations. Lexington, MA: D. C. Heath.

Wang, Zhong-ming (1989).
The human-computer interface hierarchy model and strategies in system development. *Ergonomics*, Vol. 32, No. 11 (Special Issue: Current methods in cognitive ergonomics) (Nov.): 1391-1400.

Walton, R. and G. Susman (1987).
People policies for the new machines. *Harvard Business Review*, Vol. 65: 98-106.

Walton, Richard E. (1989).
Up and running: Integrating information technology and the organization. Cambridge, MA: Harvard Business School Press.

Walzer, Michael (1984).
Liberalism and the art of separation. *Political Theory*, Vol. 12, no. 3 (August): 315-330.

Ware, Mary C. and Mary F. Stuck (1985).
Sex-role messages vis-a-vis microcomputer use: A look at the pictures. *Sex Roles*. Vol. 13, Nos. 3-4 (August): 205-214.

Ware, Robb (1990).
MIS managers are often responsible for training horror stories. *MIS Week*, Vol. 11, No. 21 (May 21): 36.

Wark, David, Joseph Kalkman, Dixie Grace, and Elizabeth Wales (1991).
An evaluation of the Therapeutic Learning Program: Presentation with and without a computer. *Computers in Human Services*, Vol. 8, No. 2: 119-132.

Warshofsky, Fred (1989).
The chip war: The battle for the world of tommorrow. NY: Charles Scribner's Sons.

Wasik, Martin (1991).
Crime and the computer. NY: Oxford University Press.

Wasson, Roger E. (1990).
Organizing for future technologies. *Datamation*, Vol. 36, No. 7 (April 1): 93-96.

Watt, Peggy (1989).
Study shows workers underuse software. *InfoWorld*, 27 March: 17.

Watson, David (1989).
Computers, confidentiality, and privation. *Computers in Human Services*, Vol. 5, Nos. 1/2: 153 - 168.

Watson, Hugh J. and Robert I. Mann (1988).
Expert systems: Past, present, and future. *Journal of Information Systems Management*, Vol. 5, No. 4 (Fall): 39-46.

Watson, R. W., G. DeSantics, and M. S. Poole (1988).
Using a GDSS to facilitate group consensus: Some intended and unintended consequences. *MIS Quarterly*, Vol. 12, No. 3.

Wayner, Peter (1993).
Should encryption be regulated? *Byte*. Vol. 18, No. 6 (May): 129-134.

Webb, Joseph A. (1991).
Judge Greene rescinds RBOC decree. *Link-Up*, Vol. 8, No. 5 (Sept./Oct.): 1, 34.

Webb, Joseph A. (1992).
RBOCs allowed to become information providers. *Link-Up*, Vol. 9, No. 1 (Jan./Feb.): 20.

Webb, N. M. (1985).
The role of gender in computer progrramming learning processes. *Journal of Educational Computing Research*, Vol. 1, No. 4: 441-458.

Weber, Ron (1988).
Computer technology and jobs: An impact assessment and model. *Communications of the ACM*, Vol. 31, No. 1 (Jan.): 68.

Webster, Sally (1992).
Dispatches from the front line: Computer ethics war stories. *EDUCOM Review*, Vol. 27, No. 4 (July/August): 18-21.

Weick, K. E. (1987).
Organizational culture and high reliability. *California Management Review*, Vol. 29, No. 2: 112-127.

Weil, Ulric (1988).
Does government get fair return on ADP dollars? *Government Computer News*, 27 May: 28, 30.

Weil, Y. (1988).
How information technology will change the world. *Government Computer News*, Nov. 21: 86.

Weill, Peter and Margrethe H. Olson (1989).
Managing investment in information technology: Mini case examples and implications. *MIS Quarterly*, Vol. 13, No. 1 (March): 3-17.

Weinberg, G. (1971).
The psychology of computer programming. NY: Van Nostrand.

Weingarten, Fred W. and D. Linda Garcia ((1988).
Public policy concerning the exchange and distribution of scientific information. *Annals of the American Academy of Political and Social Science*, No. 495 (Jan.): 61-72.

Weisman, Shulamith (1983).
Computer games for the frail elderly. *The Gerontologist*, Vol. 23, No. 4: 361-363.

Weiss, Janet A., Judith E. Gruber, and Robert H. Carver (1986).
Reflections on value: Policy makers evaluate federal information systems. In *Public Administration Review*, Vol. 46 (Nov. 1986).

Weiss, S. and A. Casimir (1984).
A practical guide to designing expert systems. Totawa, NJ: Rowman and Allanheld.

Weizenbaum, Joseph (1976).
Computer power and human reason: From judgment to calculation. San Francisco: W. H. Freeman.

Weizenbaum, Joseph (1983).
The computer in your future. *New York Review* (Oct. 27): 58-62.

Weizenbaum, Joseph (1991).
Against the imperialism of instrumental reason. In Charles Dunlop and Rob Kling, eds., *Computerization and controversy : Value conflicts and social choices*. NY: Academic Press: 728-742.

Wessell, Milton R. (1980).
Science and conscience. NY: Columbia University Press.

Wessells, Michael (1990).
Computer, self, and society. Englewood Cliffs, NJ: Prentice-Hall.

Westin, Alan F. (1979).
Computer science and technology: Computers, personnel administration, and citizen rights. Washington, DC: Institute for Computer Sciences and Technology, National Bureau of Standards, July).

Westrum, Ron (1991).
Technologies and society: The shaping of people and things. Belmont, CA: Wadsworth Publishing Co.

Wetmore, Tim (1992).
The multimedia challenge. *InformationWeek*, No. 355 (Jan. 13): 22-30.

Whisler, T. L. (1965).
The manager and the computer. *Journal of Accountancy*. Vol. 122: 27-32.

Whisler, T. L. (1970a).
Information technology and organizational change. Belmont, CA: Wadsworth.

Whisler, T. L. (1970b).
The impact of computers on organizations. NY: Praeger.

White, Halbert (1981).
Consequences and detection of mis-specified nonlinear regression models. *Journal of the American Statistical Association*, Vol. 76: 419-433.

White, Halbert (1989).
Neural-network learning and statistics. *AI Expert*, Vol. 4, No. 12 (Dec.): 48-52.

White House (1993).
Press release on 'Clipper Chip' encryption initiative. April 16. E-mail from Clinton-Info@campaign92.org.

White, John (1991).
ACM speaks out. *Communications of the ACM*, Vol. 34, No. 5 (May): 15.

Whitmore, Sam (1990).
R and D dollars key to U. S. tech leadership. *PC Week*, 8 Jan. 1990: 85.

Whitmore, Sam (1992).
Drop a dime and stop some spooky legislation. *PC Week*, Vol. 9, No. 20 (May 18): 100.

Wicklein, J. (1979).
Electronic nightmare. NY: Viking.

Wigand, Rolf T. (1988).
Integrated telecommunications networking and distributed data processing, in Jack Rabin and Edward M. Jackowski, eds., *Handbook of information resource management*. NY: Dekker, 1988. :ch. 9.

Wilder, G., D. Mackie and J. Cooper (1985).
Gender and computers: Two surveys of computer-related attitudes. *Sex Roles*, Vol. 13, Nos. 3/4: 215-228.

Wilkinson, Barry (1983).
The shopfloor politics of new technology. London: Heineman Educational Books.

Wilkinson, Joseph W. (1989).
Accounting information systems: Essential concepts and applications. NY: Wiley.

Wilkinson, Stephanie (1988).
The politics of managing LANs. *PC Week*, April 12: S11-S13, S37.

Wilkinson, Stephanie (1989).
Centralized systems for decentralized units. *InformationWeek* (Oct. 2): 30, 34.
Wilkinson, Tracy (1989).
Plug in, sign on, find out. *Los Angeles Times*, March 11: 1, 10.
Willett, Shawn (1989).
Image processing reduces cost, adds value for users. *Computer Technology Review*, Vol. 9, No. 8 (July): 1, 11, 14.
Williams, David L. (1993).
A computer program that can censor electronic messages sets off a furor. *The Chronicle of Higher Education*, Vol. 39, No. 36 (May 12): A21-A25.
Williams, Joseph (1991).
Negative consequences of information technology. In Szewczak, Edward, Coral Snodgras, and Mehdi Khosrowpour, eds. (1991). *Management impacts of information technology: Perspectives on organizational change and growth.* Harrisburg, PA: Idea Group Publishing: 48-74.
Williams, Robert E. (1987).
Selling a geographical information system to government policy makers. *URISA 1987*, Vol. 3: 150-156.
Wilson, David L. (1991a).
Reports of pornography on campus networks prompt special audits in Washington State. *Chronicle of Higher Education*, Vol. 38, No. 12 (Nov. 13): A22, A29.
Wilson, David L. (1991b).
High cost could bring big computer advance to some colleges. *Chronicle of Higher Education* (Dec. 4): 1, A32.
Wilson, David L. (1992).
New federal regulations on rights of handicapped may force colleges to provide better access to technology. *The Chronicle of Higher Education*, Vol. 38, N0. 21 (Jan. 29): A1, A21-A22.
Wilson, Laura (1992).
The devil in your data. *InformationWeek*, No. 389 (Aug. 31): 48-54.
Wohl, Amy D. (1992).
Groupware: Collaborative computing comes of age. *Office Technology Management*, Vol. 26, No. 7 (Jan.): 10-12.
Wolman, Rebekah (1990).
Technology and the basic skills crisis. *Information Center*, January: 16-24.
Women's Bureau (1985).
Women and office automation: Issues for the decade ahead. Washington, DC: Women's Bureau, Department of Labor.
Wood, James R. (1985).
Forest service makes financial decisions with aid of micros. *Government Computer News*, 7 June: 60.
Wood, Robert Chapman (1988).
On the biological frontier: Japanese companies explore living computers. *High Technology Business* August): 12.
Working Women (1980).
Race against time: Automation of the office. Cleveland, OH: Working Women.

Wright, Barbara Drygulski (1987).
Women, work, and technology: Transformations. Ann Arbor, MI: University of Michigan Press.

Wright, Erik Olin and Joachim Singleman (1982).
Proletarianization in the changing American class structure. *American Journal of Sociology*, Vol. 88, Supplement: S177-S209.

Wright, Karen (1990).
The road to the global village. *Scientific American*, Vol. 262, No. 3 (Mar.): 83-94.

Wright, P. and A. Monk 1992).
A cost-effective evaluation method for use by designers. *International Journal of Man-Machine Studies*, Vol. 35, No. 6: 891-912.

Wu, Yi-Kuo and Michael Morgan (1989).
Computer use, computer attitudes, and gender: Differential implications of micro and mainframe usage among college students. *Journal of Research on Computing in Education*, Vol. 22, No. 2 (Winter): 214-228.

Wuthnow, Robert (1982).
The moral crisis in American capitalism. *Harvard Business Review*, Vol. 60, No. 2 (March/April): 76.

Wybo, Michael D. and Detmar W. Straub, Jr. (1989)
Protecting organizational information resources. *Information Resources Management Journal*, Vol. 2, No. 4 (Fall): 1-15.

Wyckoff, James Humphrey (1982).
The publicness of public sector activities: An application to public and primary secondary education. Chapel Hill, NC: University of North Carolina at Chapel Hill, Ph.D. dissertation.

Yankelovich, D. and J. Immerwahr 1983).
Putting the work ethic to work. NY: The Public Agenda Foundation.

Yarnall, Louise (1989).
The new, improved government input device. *CIO*, Vol. 3, No. 3 (Nov.): 26-35.

Young, Marilyn (1989).
Locating missing children. *Personal Computing*, Vol. 13, No. 10 (October): 54.

Young, Leo (1989).
Electronics and computing. *Annals of the American Academy of Political and Social Science*, Vol. 502 (March): 82-93.

Zarley, Craig (1988a).
Air-traffic model aims to get you there on time. *PC Week*, March 10: 57, 71.

Zarley, Craig (1988b).
The sky's the limit: Simmod untangles air traffic. *PC Week*, July 11: 47-48.

Zarley, Craig (1988c).
The crisis in managing corporate PC assets. *PC Week*, 26 April 1988: 41, 46.

Zawrotny, Stanley B. (1989).
Key to IS success: Alignment with corporate goals. *Information Resources Management Journal*, Vol. 2, No. 4 (Fall): 32-38.

Zetka, James R. (1991).
Automated technologies, institutional environments, and skilled labor processes: Toward an institutional theory of automation outcomes. *The Sociological Quarterly*, Vol. 32, No. 4 (Winter): 557-574.

Zimmerman, Michael R. (1991).
Drug dealers find haven in on-line services. *PC Week*, March 4: 43, 49.

Zmud, R. (1984).
Design alternatives for organizing information system activities. *MIS Quarterly*, Vol. 8, No. 2 (June 1984): 79-93.

Zmud, R. W. (1979).
Individual differences and MIS success: A review of empirical literature. *Management Science*, Vol. 25 (1979): 966-979.

Zmud, R. W. and L. E. Apple (1988).
Measuring the infusion of a multi-business unit innovation. Working Paper, Florida State University. Cited in Markus and Robey, 1988: 591.

Zuboff, Shoshana (1982).
New worlds of computer mediated work. *Harvard Business Review*, Vol. 60: 142-152.

Zuboff, Shoshana (1985).
Automate/informate: The two faces of intelligent technology. *Organizational Dynamics*, Vol. 14, No. 2: 5-18.

Zuboff, Shoshana (1988a).
In the age of the smart machine: The future of work and power. NY: Basic Books.

Zuboff, Shoshana (1988b).
Into the future shackled to the past. *CommunicationsWeek*, o. 227 (Dec. 19): S99.

APPENDIX

ACM Code of Ethics and Professional Conduct*

Preamble. Commitment to ethical professional conduct is expected of every member (voting members, associate members, and student members) of the Association for Computing Machinery (ACM).

This Code, consisting of 24 imperatives formulated as statements of personal responsibility, identifies the elements of such a commitment. It contains many, but not all, issues professionals are likely to face. Section 1 outlines fundamental ethical considerations, while Section 2 addresses additional, more specific considerations of professional conduct. Statements in Section 3 pertain more specifically to individuals who have a leadership role, whether in the workplace or in a volunteer capacity such as with organizations like ACM. Principles involving compliance with this Code are given in Section 4.

The Code shall be supplemented by a set of Guidelines, which provide explanation to assist members in dealing with the various issues contained in the Code. It is expected that the Guidelines will be changed more frequently than the Code.

The Code and its supplemented Guidelines are intended to serve as a basis for ethical decision making in the conduct of professional work. Secondarily, they may serve as a basis for judging the merit of a formal complaint pertaining to violation of professional ethical standards.

It should be noted that although computing is not mentioned in the imperatives of section 1.0, the Code is concerned with how these fundamental imperatives apply to one's conduct as a computing professional. These imperatives are expressed in a general form to emphasize that ethical principles which apply to computer ethics are derived from more general ethical principles.

It is understood that some words and phrases in a code of ethics are subject to varying interpretations, and that any ethical principle may conflict with other ethical principles in specific situations. Questions related to ethical conflicts can best be answered by thoughtful consideration of fundamental principles, rather than reliance on detailed regulations.

1. GENERAL MORAL IMPERATIVES. *As an ACM member I will . . .*

1.1 Contribute to society and human well-being.
1.2 Avoid harm to others.
1.3 Be honest and trustworthy.
1.4 Be fair and take action not to discriminate.
1.5 Honor property rights including copyrights and patents.
1.6 Give proper credit for intellectual property.
1.7 Respect the privacy of others.
1.8 Honor confidentiality.

2. MORE SPECIFIC PROFESSIONAL RESPONSIBILITIES. *As an ACM computing professional I will . . .*

2.1 Strive to achieve the highest quality in both the process and products of professional work.
2.2 Acquire and maintain professional competence.
2.3 Know and respect existing laws pertaining to professional work.
2.4 Accept and provide appropriate professional review.
2.5 Give comprehensive and thorough evaluations of computer systems and their impacts, including analysis of possible risks.
2.6 Honor contracts, agreements, and assigned responsibilities.

2.7 Improve public understanding of computing and its consequences
2.8 Access computing and communication resources only when authorized to do so.

3. ORGANIZATIONAL LEADERSHIP IMPERATIVES. *As an ACM member and an organizational leader, I will . . . . .*

3.1 Articulate social responsibilities of members of an organizational unit and encourage full acceptance of those responsibilities.
3.2 Manage personnel and resources to design and build information systems that enhance the quality, effectiveness and dignity of working life.
3.3 Acknowledge and support proper and authorized uses of an organization's computing and communication resources.
3.4 Ensure that users and those who will be affected by a computing system have their needs clearly articulated during the assessment and design of requirements; later the system must be validated to meet requirements.
3.5 Articulate and support policies that protect the dignity of users and others affected by a computing system.
3.6 Create opportunities for members of the organization to learn the principles and limitations of computer systems.

4. COMPLIANCE WITH THE CODE. *As an ACM member, I will . . . .*

4.1 Uphold and promote the principles of this Code.
4.2 Treat violations of this code as inconsistent with membership in the ACM.

GUIDELINES

1. GENERAL MORAL IMPERATIVES. *As an ACM member I will ....*

1.1 Contribute to society and human well-being.

This principle concerning the quality of life of all people affirms an obligation to protect fundamental human rights and to respect the diversityof all cultures. An essential aim of computing professionals is to minimize negative consequences of computing systems, including threats to health and safety. When designing or implementing systems, computing professionals must attempt to ensure that the products of their efforts will be used in socially responsible ways, will meet social needs, and will avoid harmful effects to health and welfare.

In addition to a safe social environment, human well-being includes a safe natural environment. Therefore, computing professionals who design and develop systems must be alert to, and make others aware of, any potential damage to the local or global environment.

1.2 Avoid harm to others.

"Harm" means injury or negative consequences, such as undesirable loss of information, loss of property, property damage, or unwanted environmental impacts. This principle prohibits use of computing technology in ways that result in harm to any of the following: users, the general public, employees, employers. Harmful actions include intentional destruction or modification of files and programs leading to serious loss of resources or unnecessary expenditure of human resources such as the time and effort required to purge systems of "computer viruses."

Well-intended actions, including those that accomplish assigned duties, may lead to harm unexpectedly. In such an event the responsible person or persons are obligated to undo or mitigate the negative consequences as much as possible. One way to avoid unintentional harm is to carefully consider potential impacts on all those affected by decisions made during design and implementation.

To minimize the possibility of indirectly harming others, computing professionals must minimize malfunctions by following generally accepted standards for system design and testing. Furthermore, it is often necessary to assess the social consequences of systems to project the likelihood of any serious harm to others. If system features are misrepresented to users, co-workers, or supervisors, the individual computing professional is responsible for any resulting injury.

In the work environment the computing professional has the additional obligation to report any signs of system dangers that might result in serious personal or social damage. If one's superiors do not act to curtail or mitigate such dangers, it may be necessary to "blow the whistle" to help correct the problem or reduce the risk. However, capricious or misguided reporting of violations can, itself, be harmful. Before reporting violations, all relevant aspects of the incident must be thoroughly assessed. In particular, the assessment of risk and responsibility must be credible. It is suggested that advice be sought from other computing professionals. See principle 2.5 regarding thorough evaluations.

1.3 Be honest and trustworthy.

Honesty is an essential component of trust. Without trust an organization cannot function effectively. The honest computing professional will not make deliberately false or deceptive claims about a system or system design, but will instead provide full disclosure of all pertinent system limitations and problems.

A computer professional has a duty to be honest about his or her own qualifications, and about any circumstances that might lead to conflicts of interest.

Membership in volunteer organizations such as ACM may at times place individuals in situations where their statements or actions could be interpreted as carrying the "weight" of a larger group of professionals. An ACM member will exercise care to not misrepresent ACM or positions and policies of ACM or any ACM units.

1.4 Be fair and take action not to discriminate.

The values of equality, tolerance, respect for others, and the principles of equal justice govern this imperative. Discrimination on the basis of race, sex, religion, age, disability, national origin, or other such factors is an explicit violation of of ACM policy and will not be tolerated.

Inequities between different groups of people may result from the use or misuse of information and technology. In a fair society,all individuals would have equal opportunity to participate in, or benefit from, the use of computer resources regardless of race, sex, religion, age, disability, national origin or other such similar factors. However, these ideals do not justify unauthorized use of computer resources nor do they provide an adequate basis for violation of any other ethical imperatives of this code.

1.5 Honor property rights including copyrights and patents.

Violation of copyrights, patents, trade secrets and the terms of license agreements is prohibited by law in most circumstances. Even when software is not so protected, such violations are contrary to professional behavior. Copies of software should be made only with proper authorization. Unauthorized duplication of materials must not be condoned.

1.6 Give proper credit for intellectual property.

Computing professionals are obligated to protect the integrity of intellectual property. Specifically, one must not take credit for other's ideas or work, even in cases where the work has not been explicitly protected by copyright, patent, etc.

1.7 Respect the privacy of others.

Computing and communication technology enables the collection and exchange of personal information on a scale unprecedented in the history of civilization. Thus, there is increased potential for violating the privacy of individuals and groups. It is the responsibility of professionals to maintain the privacy and integrity of data describing individuals. This includes taking precautions to ensure the accuracy of data, as well as protecting it from unauthorized access or accidental disclosure to inappropriate individuals. Furthermore, procedures must be established to allow individuals to review their records and correct inaccuracies.

This imperative implies that only the necessary amount of personal information be collected in a system, that retention and disposal periods for that information be clearly defined and enforced, and that personal information gathered for a specific purpose not be used for other purposes without consent of the individual(s). These principles apply to electronic communications, including electronic mail, and prohibit procedures that capture or monitor electronic user data, including messages,without the permission of users or bona fide authorization related to system operation and maintenance. User data observed during the normal duties of system operation and maintenance must be treated with strictest confidentiality, except in cases where it is evidence for the violation of law, organizational regulations, or this Code. In these cases, the nature or contents of that information must be disclosed only to proper authorities. (See 1.9)

1.8 Honor confidentiality.

The principle of honesty extends to issues of confidentiality of information whenever one has made an explicit promise to honor confidentiality or, implicitly, when private information not directly related to the performance of one's duties becomes available. The ethical concern is to respect all obligations of confidentiality to employers, clients, and users unless discharged from such obligations by requirements of the law or other principles of this Code.

2. MORE SPECIFIC PROFESSIONAL RESPONSIBILITIES.
As an ACM computing professional I will . . .

2.1 Strive to achieve the highest quality, effectiveness and dignity in both the process and products of professional work.

Excellence is perhaps the most important obligation of a professional. The computing professional must strive to achieve quality and to be cognizant of the serious negative consequences that may result from poor quality in a system.

2.2 Acquire and maintain professional competence.

Excellence depends on individuals who take responsibility for acquiring and maintaining professional competence. A professional must participate in setting standards for appropriate levels of competence, and strive to achieve those standards. Upgrading technical knowledge and competence can be achieved in several ways:doing independent study; attending seminars, conferences, or courses; and being involved in professional organizations.

2.3 Know and respect existing laws pertaining to professional work.

ACM members must obey existing local, state,province, national, and international laws unless there is a compelling ethical basis not to do so. Policies and procedures of the organizations in which one participates must also be obeyed. But compliance must be balanced with the recognition that sometimes existing laws and rules may be immoral or inappropriate and,therefore, must be challenged. Violation of a law or regulation may be ethical when that law or rule has inadequate moral basis or when it conflicts with another law judged to be more important. If one decides to violate a law or rule because it is viewed as unethical, or for any other reason, one must fully accept responsibility for one's actions and for the consequences.

2.4 Accept and provide appropriate professional review.

Quality professional work, especially in the computing profession, depends on professional reviewing and critiquing. Whenever appropriate,individual members should seek and utilize peer review as well as provide critical review of the work of others.

2.5 Give comprehensive and thorough evaluations of computer systems and their impacts, including analysis of possible risks.

Computer professionals must strive to be perceptive, thorough, and objective when evaluating, recommending, and presenting system descriptions and alternatives. Computer professionals are in a position of special trust, and therefore have a special responsibility to provide objective, credible evaluations to employers, clients, users, and the public. When providing evaluations the professional must also identify any relevant conflicts of interest, as stated in imperative 1.3.

As noted in the discussion of principle 1.2 on avoiding harm, any signs of danger from systems must be reported to those who have opportunity and/or responsibility to resolve them. See the guidelines for imperative 1.2 for more details concerning harm,including the reporting of professional violations.

2.6 Honor contracts, agreements, and assigned responsibilities.

Honoring one's commitments is a matter of integrity and honesty. For the computer professional this includes ensuring that system elements perform as intended. Also, when one contracts for work with another party, one has an obligation to keep that party properly informed about progress toward completing that work.

A computing professional has a responsibility to request a change in any assignment that he or she feels cannot be completed as defined. Only after serious consideration and with full disclosure of risks and concerns to the employer or client, should one accept the assignment. The major underlying principle here is the obligation to accept personal accountability for professional work. On some occasions other ethical principles may take greater priority.

A judgment that a specific assignment should not be performed may not be accepted. Having clearly identified one's concerns and reasons for that judgment, but failing to procure a change in that assignment, one may yet be obligated, by contract or by law, to proceed as directed. The computing professional's ethical judgment should be the final guide in deciding whether or not to proceed. Regardless of the decision, one must accept the responsibility for the consequences.

However, performing assignments "against one's own judgment" does not relieve the professional of responsibility for any negative consequences.

2.7 Improve public understanding of computing and its consequences.

Computing professionals have a responsibility to share technical knowledge with the public by encouraging understanding of computing, including the impacts of computer systems and their limitations. This imperative implies an obligation to counter any false views related to computing.

2.8 Access computing and communication resources only when authorized to do so.

Theft or destruction of tangible and electronic property is prohibited by imperative 1.2 - "Avoid harm to others." Trespassing and unauthorized use of a computer or communication system is addressed by this imperative. Trespassing includes accessing communication networks and computer systems, or accounts and/or files associated with those systems, without explicit authorization to do so. Individuals and organizations have the right to restrict access to their systems so long as they do not violate the discrimination principle (see 1.4). No one should enter or use another's computer system, software, or data files without permission. One must always have appropriate approval before using system resources, including .rm57 communication ports, file space, other system peripherals, and computer time.

3. ORGANIZATIONAL LEADERSHIP IMPERATIVES. *As an ACM member and an organizational leader, I will . . . . .*

BACKGROUND NOTE:This section draws extensively from the draft IFIP Code of Ethics,especially its sections on organizational ethics and international concerns. The ethical obligations of organizations tend to be neglected in most codes of professional conduct, perhaps because these codes are written from the perspective of the individual member. This dilemma is addressed by stating these imperatives from the perspective of the organizational leader. In this context"leader" is viewed as any organizational member who has leadership or educational responsibilities. These imperatives generally may apply to organizations as well as their leaders. In this context"organizations" are corporations, government agencies,and other "employers," as well as volunteer professional organizations.

3.1 Articulate social responsibilities of members of an organizational unit and encourage full acceptance of those responsibilities.

Because organizations of all kinds have impacts on the public, they must accept responsibilities to society. Organizational procedures and attitudes oriented toward quality and the welfare of society will reduce harm to members of the public, thereby serving public interest and fulfilling social responsibility. Therefore,organizational leaders must encourage full participation in meeting social responsibilities as well as quality performance.

3.2 Manage personnel and resources to design and build information systems that enhance the quality of working life.

Organizational leaders are responsible for ensuring that computer systems enhance, not degrade, the quality of working life. When implementing a computer system, organizations must consider the personal and professional development, physical safety, and human dignity of all workers. Appropriate human-computer ergonomic standards should be considered in system design and in the workplace.

3.3 Acknowledge and support proper and authorized uses of an organization's computing and communication resources.

Because computer systems can become tools to harm as well as to benefit an organization, the leadership has the responsibility to clearly define appropriate and inappropriate uses of organizational computing resources. While the number and scope of such rules should be minimal, they should be fully enforced when established.

3.4 Ensure that users and those who will be affected by a system have their needs clearly articulated during the assessment and design of requirements; later the system must be validated to meet requirements.

Current system users, potential users and other persons whose lives may be affected by a system must have their needs assessed and incorporated in the statement of requirements. System validation should ensure compliance with those requirements.

3.5 Articulate and support policies that protect the dignity of users and others effected by a computing system.

Designing or implementing systems that deliberately or inadvertently demean individuals or groups is ethically unacceptable. Computer professionals who are in decision making positions should verify that systems are designed and implemented to protect personal privacy and enhance personal dignity.

3.6 Create opportunities for members of the organization to learn the principles and limitations of computer systems.

This complements the imperative on public understanding (2.7). Educational opportunities are essential to facilitate optimal participation of all organizational members. Opportunities must be available to all members to help them improve their knowledge and skills in computing, including courses that familiarize them with the consequences and limitations of particular types of systems. In particular, professionals must be made aware of the dangers of building systems around oversimplified models, the improbability of anticipating and designing for every possible operating condition, and other issues related to the complexity of this profession.

4. COMPLIANCE WITH THE CODE. *As an ACM member I will ...*

4.1 Uphold and promote the principles of this Code.

The future of the computing profession depends on both technical and ethical excellence. Not only is it important for ACM computing professionals to adhere to the principles expressed in this Code, each member should encourage and support adherence by other members.

4.2 Treat violations of this code as inconsistent with membership in the ACM.

Adherence of professionals to a code of ethics is largely a voluntary matter. However, if a member does not follow this code by engaging in gross misconduct, membership in ACM may be terminated.

---

* This Code and the supplemental Guidelines were developed by the Task Force for the Revision of the ACM Code of Ethics and Professional Conduct: Ronald E. Anderson, Chair, Gerald Engel, Donald Gotterbarn, Grace C. Hertlein, Alex Hoffman, Bruce Jawer, Deborah G. Johnson, Doris K. Lidtke, Joyce Currie Little, Dianne Martin, Donn B. Parker, Judith A. Perrolle, and Richard S. Rosenberg. The Task Force was organized by ACM/SIGCAS and funding was provided by the ACM SIG Discretionary Fund. This Code and the supplemental Guidelines were adopted by the ACM Council on October 16, 1992.

Index

O

P

Q

R

S

T

U

V

W

About the Author

G. David Garson is professor of political science and public administration at North Carolina State University. He is editor of the *Social Science Computer Review*, published by Duke University Press, and is author or editor of a dozen books and monographs on research methods, public administration, and American politics. His most recent works are *Analytic Mapping and Geographic Databases*, Sage Publications, 1992, and the software package, *Presidential Campaign!*, St. Martin's Press, 1993. His forthcoming work is a set of six political science simulations to be published by Prentice-Hall. Dr. Garson is a graduate of Princeton and Harvard Universities and presently serves as Full Professor of Political Science and Associate Dean of the College of Humanities and Social Sciences at North Carolina State University. As Associate Dean, he supervises three computer laboratories in social science and the humanities.